Global Entertainment Media

CONTENT, AUDIENCES, ISSUES

Edited by

Anne Cooper-Chen
Ohio University

LEA

LAWRENCE ERLBAUM ASSOCIATES, PUBLISHERS
2005   Mahwah, New Jersey   London

Lawrence Erlbaum Associates, Inc., Publishers
10 Industrial Avenue
Mahwah, New Jersey 07430

Cover design by Sean Trane Scarrione.
Interior maps by Shereen Hall.

Library of Congress Cataloging-in-Publication Data

Global entertainment media : content, audiences, issues / edited by
Anne Cooper-Chen.
p. cm.
ISBN 0–8058–5168–2 — ISBN 0–8058–5169–0 (pbk.)
1. Television programs. 2. Television broadcasting. I. Title.
PN1992.5.C64 2005
791.45'09—dc22   2004053297

Books published by Lawrence Erlbaum Associates are printed on acid-free paper,
and their bindings are chosen for strength and durability.

Printed in the United States of America
10 9 8 7 6 5 4 3 2

Global Entertainment Media

CONTENT, AUDIENCES, ISSUES

LEA's Communication Series
Jennings Bryant/Dolf Zillmann, General Editors

Selected titles in Mass Communication (Alan Rubin, Advisory Editor) include:

Alexander/Owers/Carveth/Hollifield/Greco • *Media Economics: Theory and Research, Third Edition*

Bunker • *Critiquing Free Speech: First Amendment Theory and the Challenge of Interdisciplinarity*

Galician • *Sex, Love, and Romance in the Mass Media: Analysis and Criticism of Unrealistic Portrayals and Their Influence*

Harris • *A Cognitive Psychology of Mass Communication, Fourth Edition*

Perse • *Media Effects and Society*

Wicks • *Understanding Audiences: Learning to Use the Media Constructively*

Van Evra • *Television and Child Development, Third Edition*

Zillmann/Vorderer • *Media Entertainment: The Psychology of Its Appeal*

For a complete listing of titles in LEA's Communication Series, contact Lawrence Erlbaum Associates, Inc., at www.erlbaum.com

FOR
Adam, Amy, Allison
Derek
Meg, Mac, Bonnie
Dylan and Tara

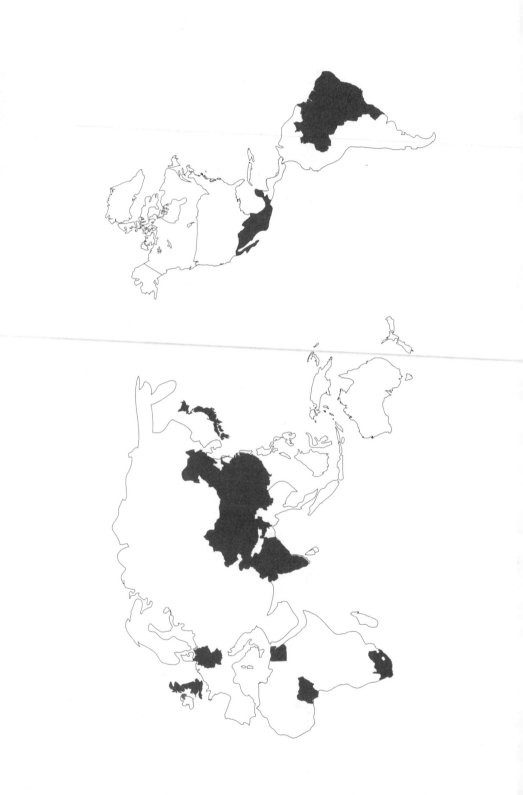

Contents

Preface

Aristotle deliberated about what we should do with our leisure time. The Declaration of Independence refers to the "pursuit of happiness." Mass media entertainment, if defined to include newspapers, stretches back to the 15th century in Europe and the 8th century in China. Yet as Zillmann and Vorderer (2000, p. viii) observe, "It is astounding, in fact, how little genuine scholarship and basic research have addressed questions as fundamental as . . . comedy . . . and tragedy."

Entertainment television is a key part—even the key part—of modern mass culture, but scholars tend instead to study news and information, both domestically and internationally. Stephenson (1967, p. 206) stated, "Enough has been said to ask for far more serious regard of play, and not of information, as the primary concern of any communication theory." Ten years later, Katz (1977, p. 113) challenged us "to take entertainment seriously."

The elevation of news over entertainment in the study of international media carries through to textbooks, most of which concentrate on journalism (e.g., deBeer & Merrill, 2003) or news (Hachten & Scotton, 2002). This book is unique in shifting the emphasis to entertainment. In Ecuador, for example, nearly 90% of prime time programming is entertainment rather than information (Davis, 2003).

Thus this volume does not include analysis of news reporting per se, but the prime time program grids in chapters 3–12 will give readers a sense of news versus entertainment emphasis. The grids are also useful for noting the presence of imported TV programs, many of which—about one third worldwide (Banerjee, 2002)—come from the United States. Likewise, the program grids reveal the extent of sports programming in prime time. The country chapters do not attempt to discuss sports, but the psychology of watching TV sports is treated in chapter 1, while the meaning of sports as a global phenomenon is treated in chapter 13, "The Olympics."

Observers of mass mediated culture seem to fall into two groups: critics and "celebrators" (Real, 1989, p. 31). Pessimistic critics "wring their hands over the deplorable state of the popular arts" (Real, 1989, p. 30). Social philosophers such as Jacques Ellul (1986) lament mass media's depersonalized technology. In *Amusing Ourselves to Death*, Neil Postman (1985,

p. 8), presents a "lamentation about the most significant American cultural fact of the second half of the twentieth century: the decline of the Age of Typography and the ascendancy of the Age of Television." A student critic (Gayzik, 2003, p. 2) bemoans the "deleterious effect that television is having on our society."

The celebrators of mass mediated culture include those who praise the access and vast marketplace that television has created (Real, 1989, p. 32). Humanist Daniel Boorstin (1980, p. 153) sees an aversion to television on the part of academics, who "are troubled by the way television trespasses on the book. Of course, TV is 'vulgar'—because it's not in their control."

Rather than engage in a new form of the old debate about high and low culture, this text takes its inspiration from McLuhan (1964, p. 20), who declared that "electrically contracted, the world is no more than a village." Forty years ago, McLuhan's idea of a global village was prediction more than fact. Even by the end of the 1960s, only half the world's nations had joined the TV age. The expansion of television in China and India, the most populous nations on the planet, came relatively late. Now the medium is a worldwide phenomenon as well as a global industry. And McLuhan's prediction has only partially come true; the world sometimes gathers as a village to watch the same fare, but much more often, separate "villages" (countries or regions) watch themselves reflected on the small screen.

The 10 countries profiled here represent major domestic markets and, in many cases, are major TV exporters. Japanese animation, for example, crops up on screens from Asia to Germany to the U.S.'s Cartoon Network. Brazil's exports, in an ironic twist, now "dominate the prime time programming of its former colonial power, Portugal" (Straubhaar, 2003, p. 79). For a wider comparative media study, the reader could research other countries, given this broad base. Each country chapter author is a native or resident (for at least part of each year) of the nation about which he or she is writing. In the focus countries, the value of $1 U.S. (as of late 2004) is .54 U.K. pounds, .76 Euros, 6.2 Egyptian pounds, 6.01 South African rand, 45 Indian rupees, 103.2 Japanese yen, 8.28 Chinese yuan, 2.79 Brazilian reais, and 11.37 Mexican pesos. A kilometer equals .6 miles.

The chapter authors have my sincere gratitude for their generosity and hard work. I also thank my husband, Charles Chen, for his support in this 3-year project; my sister, Connie Messerly Kehoe, who sat with me in front of various TV sets in various places as we grew up; and my colleagues and students at Ohio University. Finally, this book would not be in your hands without the patience of Linda Bathgate, Debbie Ruel, and Karin Wittig Bates of Lawrence Erlbaum Associates.

REFERENCES

Banerjee, I. (2002) The locals strike back? Media globalization and localization in the new Asian television landscape. *Gazette*, 64(6), 517–535.

Boorstin, D. (1980, March 17). Americans are "haunted by a fear of technology." *U.S. News and World Report*, p. 70.

Davis, L. (2003). Cultural proximity on the air in Ecuador. In M. Elasmar (Ed.), *The impact of international television* (pp. 111–132). Mahwah, NJ: Lawrence Erlbaum Associates.

DeBeer, A., & Merrill, J. (2003). *Global journalism* (4th ed.). New York: Longman.

Ellul, J. (1986) *The formation of modern culture.* New York: Knopf.

Gayzik, S. (2003, November 3). *Wasting our lives in front of TV.* Ohio University *Post*, p. 2.

Hachten, W., & Scotton, J. (2002). *The world news prism* (6th ed.). Ames, IA: Iowa State Press.

Katz, E. (1977). Can authentic culture survive the media? *Journal of Communication, 27,* 113–121.

McLuhan, M. (1964). *Understanding media.* New York: Signet.

Postman, N. (1985). *Amusing ourselves to death.* New York: Viking.

Real, M. (1989). *Supermedia.* Newbury Park, CA: Sage.

Stephenson, W. (1967). *The play theory of mass communication.* Chicago: University of Chicago Press.

Straubhaar, J. (2003). Choosing national TV: Cultural capital, language and cultural proximity in Brazil. In M. Elasmar (Ed.), *The impact of international television* (pp. 77–110). Mahwah, NJ: Lawrence Erlbaum Associates.

Zillmann, D., & Vorderer, P. (Eds). *Media entertainment: The psychology of its appeal.* Mahwah, NJ: Lawrence Erlbaum Associates.

I

INTRODUCTION

Chapter 1

The World of Television

Anne Cooper-Chen
Ohio University

We climbed and rested, climbed and rested. The mountain path was hard-packed in some places, crumbly and slippery in others. After 35 minutes, we reached Danilo's tin-roofed shack, behind his host family's home. With neither running water nor electricity, his Peace Corps "mama" made a fire-cooked meal that restored our energies. After lunch, the family fell back into its normal routine. On a black-and-white TV set, powered by a solar battery on the roof, the tallest antenna I've ever seen brought to the family, dubbed in Spanish, "The Simpsons."

For the Benitez family in the Dominican Republic, whom the author visited in December 2002—as for most global families—television takes its place as "the centerpiece of our entertainment lives" (Merrill Brown, personal communication, July 10, 1989). Entertainment constitutes the largest category of TV content almost everywhere in the world. Now that television is accessible to people in China and India, the two most populous nations on the planet, as well as smaller countries like the Dominican Republic, the medium is a worldwide phenomenon.

The three most TV-saturated countries in the world are China (370 million TV sets), the United States (233 million sets), and Japan (91 million sets; Banerjee, 2002). Now that television truly entertains the world, research about it takes on new importance.

Zillmann and Vorderer (2000) state:

Commercial prerogatives limit research to staking out consumer interest in particular formats without concern for the more fundamental issues of entertainment. These issues must be addressed if media entertainment is to serve the global population better and more successfully in the forthcoming millennium and beyond. (p. viii)

The Latin *tenere*, root of the word "entertain," means "to hold or keep." *The Random House Dictionary* (Stein & Su, 1980, p. 290) gives this definition as the word's first meaning: "to hold the attention of so as to bring about pleasure." Barnouw and Kirkland (1989, p. 102) define the term in its modern mass sense as an "experience that can be sold to and enjoyed by large and heterogeneous groups of people." Browne (1983, p. 188) defines an entertainment mass medium as "that which appears to have as its *primary* purpose the amusement, distraction and/or relaxation of its audience."

THE PSYCHOLOGY OF ENTERTAINMENT

Zillmann and Vorderer (2000, p. viii) believe that "more attention, in terms of both theory and research, must be directed at understanding the basic mechanisms of enlightenment from, and emotional involvement with, the various forms of entertainment." Thus their book *Media Entertainment: The Psychology of Its Appeal* treats many of the dimensions of this complex subfield of media studies: humor/comedy, drama, violence/horror, sex, sports, talk, music, music videos, and video games. Contributing authors discuss how age and gender can affect choices of and responses to forms of entertainment.

TV ratings indicate a gender difference, for example, in the popularity of various Olympic sports (see chapter 13), but do not explain why these differences exist. In the watching and enjoying of TV sports, researchers who study the psychology of sport spectators consistently find a male bias. When females do watch, they enjoy action and artistic movements, as in gymnastics or ice skating; violence and roughness significantly increase enjoyment for male, but not female, viewers (Bryant & Raney, 2000). Moreover, male viewers truly enjoy the suspense of watching athletic competitions, but females enjoy suspense only "up to a 'substantial' level (point spread 5–9)"; extreme suspense decreases their enjoyment, possibly due to distress (Bryant & Raney, 2000, p. 167).

Mood-management theory posits that people know what works for them—what mode of media entertainment cheers them up or relaxes them; the genre of choice is often comedy. Thus comedy is "a winning formula for media entertainment. More often than not, people do look for merriment by picking comedy with all its foolishness over serious, problem-laden program alternatives" (Zillmann, 2000, p. 51).

Many TV shows labeled as entertainment can also successfully satisfy an individual's cognitive (information-seeking) needs. Chapter 14 describes how one particular show—"Who Wants to Be a Millionaire?"—can satisfy all five of the needs that Katz, Gurevitch, and Haas (1973) identified: cognitive, affective (pleasure-seeking), personal integrative (confidence-building), social integrative, and tension release.

Viewers may initially turn to television for tension release or pleasure, but secondarily gain information—and vice versa; "*All* media have properties of entertainment," state Fischer and Melnik (1979, p. xiii). "The myth that 'pure entertainment' exists is slowly but surely being dismantled" (Fischer & Melnik, 1979, p. xix).

INFORMATION VERSUS ENTERTAINMENT

The entertainment–education approach to social change rests on this notion of fluid boundaries between learning and enjoying (Singhal, Cody, Rogers, & Sabado, 2004; Singhal & Rogers, 1999). However, the information–entertainment distinction persists. Even the Universal Declaration of Human Rights, Article 19, emphasizes information: "Everyone has the right to freedom of opinion and expression; this right includes freedom to hold opinions without interference and to seek, receive, and impart information and ideas through any media regardless of frontiers" (quoted in Freedom House, 2003).

Freedom House has, since 1979, assessed "information freedom" and "news flow" for all the world's countries (Freedom House, 2003). The organization uses a multitude of data to rate a nation's media (broadcast and print combined) as free, partly free, or not free. Relevant to entertainment content is its score, 0–30, for economic influences on content, such as bias in granting licenses, withholding government advertising, and negative impact of market competition.

The following scores for the countries in chapters 3–12 represent the degree of freedom from economic pressures, from most to least free: Germany, 7; United Kingdom, 7; Japan, 8; Mexico, 9; Brazil, 9; South Africa, 10; India, 12; Nigeria, 16; China, 20; and Egypt, 24. The United States is freer than all of these nations, with a score of 6.

Several factors have worked to create the somewhat artificial distinction between entertainment and informational TV programs. First, an institutional division within TV networks divides news divisions from entertainment divisions; the program grids in chapters 3–12 show the distinct labeling of news shows. Second, an industry-wide division exists between commercial and noncommercial ("educational") television, such as in the dual systems of the United States, the United Kingdom (see chapter 3), and Japan (see chapter 9). Third, entire networks consider themselves as providing either news/information (e.g., CNN, BBC) or entertainment (STAR TV), as the program grid of a multination satellite service shows (pp. 6–7).

THE EVOLUTION OF TELEVISION

Multination TV viewing provided by transnational companies is relatively recent (see chapter 2)—as is television itself, compared to the history of print media. TV experiments started in industrialized countries during the 1930s and 1940s, but World War II halted the medium's expansion. In the

PRIME TIME, SATELLITE SERVICE, ASIA, JULY 2003

MONDAY							
Channel	7 p.m.	7:30 p.m.	8 p.m.	8:30 p.m.	9 p.m	9:30 p.m.	10 p.m.
English							
Star World	Dharma & Greg	Friends	The King of Queens		Ground for Life	Frasier	Boston Public
CNN International	Talk Asia	Asia Tonight	Business Intl	World News	World Sports	Your World Today	
BBC	Tomorrow's World	News	Asia Today	News	Hard Talk	9:45: World Bus. Report	Click Online

TUESDAY							
Channel	7 p.m.	7:30 p.m.	8 p.m.	8:30 p.m.	9 p.m	9:30 p.m.	10 p.m.
English							
Star World	Dharma & Greg	Friends	The Drew Carey Show	Whose Line Is It Anyway	JAG		Law and Order
CNN International	World Report	Asia Tonight	Business Intl	World News	World Sports	Your World Today	
BBC	Fast Track		Asia Today	News	Hard Talk	News	Science Shack

WEDNESDAY							
Channel	7 p.m.	7:30 p.m.	8 p.m.	8:30 p.m.	9 p.m	9:30 p.m.	10 p.m.
English							
Star World	Dharma & Greg	Friends	Charmed		Ally McBeal		The Practice
CNN International	World Report	Asia Tonight	Business Intl	World News	World Sport	Your World Today	
BBC	Click Online		Asia Today	News	Hard Talk	News	Fast Track

THURSDAY							
Channel	7 p.m.	7:30 p.m.	8 p.m.	8:30 p.m.	9 p.m	9:30 p.m.	10 p.m.
English							
Star World	Dharma & Greg	Friends	Buffy the Vampire Slayer		Angel		NYPD Blues
CNN International	World Report	Asia Tonight	Business Intl	World News	World Sport	Your World Today	
BBC	The Talk Show		Asia Today	News	Hard Talk	News	Mastermind India

FRIDAY							
Channel	7 p.m.	7:30 p.m.	8 p.m.	8:30 p.m.	9 p.m	9:30 p.m.	10 p.m.
English							
Star World	Dharma & Greg	Friends	TNA Wrestling		World's Wildest Police Videos		Nash Bridges
CNN International	The Music Room	Asia Tonight	Business Intl	World News	World Sport	Your World Today	
BBC	Talking Movies	News	Asia Today	News	Hard Talk	News	Question Time

SATURDAY							
Channel	7 p.m.	7:30 p.m.	8 p.m.	8:30 p.m.	9 p.m	9:30 p.m.	10 p.m.
English							
Star World	Xena—Warrior Princess		TNA Wrestling		Mutant		Cameras Cross the Line
CNN International	Business Unusual	World News	Talk Asia	World News	World Sport	World News	Global Edition
BBC	This Week	News 7:40: Great Britons		8:40: Correspondent	Hard Talk	News	Face to Face
SUNDAY							
Channel	7 p.m.	7:30 p.m.	8 p.m.	8:30 p.m.	9 p.m	9:30 p.m.	10 p.m.
English							
Star World	Futurama	Malcolm in the Middle	Kumars at 42	Rendezvous with Simi Garewal	Goodness Gracious Me	Top Drive	X-Files
CNN International	Inside Asia	World News	The Music Room	Global Challenges	World Sport	World News	The Daily Show
BBC	Reporters	Reporters 7:40: Dateline London	News	News 8:40: Holidays in the Axis of Evil News		News	Business Bizarre

United States, television came of age after World War II, in 1948—the first season offering four full network schedules. For half a century, the United States had the most TV sets in the world, but China has since catapulted to first place. Chinese TV viewers can now number as many as 1 billion people, the largest audience on the planet (Chang, 2002).

The period since the late 1980s is often considered the beginning of the "information age," but "entertainment offerings obtrusively dominate media content" so thoroughly that we can say we live in an "entertainment age," as never have human beings had so much entertainment "so readily accessible, to so many, for so much of their leisure time" (Zillmann & Vorderer, 2000, p. viii).

Zillmann (2000, p. 17) refers to the "democratization of entertainment," thanks to television: We have all become nobility—with front row seats that bring to us the "world's greatest actors, singers, athletes, magicians, scholars, cooks, and assorted others." The right to be entertained exists not only in the developed world, but "as more societies become prosperous, this call is likely to be heard around the world" (Zillmann & Vorderer, 2000, p. vii).

CULTURE AND TELEVISION

"The technology of communication is, generally speaking, universal; but the contents and functions of communication are culture-bound," says Kato, a media scholar from Japan (1975, p. 6). "A nation's culture," writes

Hoggart (1990, p. A-10) of the *London Observer*, "is always more interesting than its politics."

Within a nation's culture, TV content is one of its most accessible aspects—aside from its cuisine. A tourist need only turn on the TV set in a hotel room, as many cable systems offer abundant overseas fare. In rural southeast Ohio, for example, the Time Warner nonpremium lineup included, in a recent week, kung fu movies on the Action Channel, foreign-language movies on the Independent and Sundance channels, and Japanese animation on the Cartoon Channel.

Definitions of culture vary widely. Servaes (1988, p. 843), also a mass media scholar, defines culture as "a phenomenon whose content differs from community to community. Therefore, as each culture operates out of its own logic, each culture has to be analyzed on the basis of its own 'logical' structure." According to Martin (1976, p. 430), "Culture, like communication, may be thought of in terms of a continuum. Culture ranges from an individual's unique patterned ways of behaving, feeling and reacting to certain universal norms that are rooted in common biological needs of mankind." To Real (1989, p. 36), author of *Supermedia*, culture is "the systematic way of construing reality that a people acquires as a consequence of living in a group."

Cultural Anthropology

The deepest understanding of culture, however, comes from the field of cultural anthropology (Bernard, 1988), one of four approaches to studying non-Western cultures, along with linguistics, physical anthropology, and archaeology (Ulin, 1984). According to Geertz (1973, p. 4), culture is the concept "around which the whole discipline of anthropology arose." Clifford Geertz ranks as one of 21 "late 20th century theorists" that Beniger (1990, p. 710) isolated in the 1,800-page *International Encyclopedia of Communication*. Geertz (1973, p. 5) defines culture as "the webs of significance [man] himself has spun."

"All anthropological approaches to culture center, however, on regularities within cultural patterns, explicit or implicit," writes Briggs (1989, p. 437). "Culture is seen as being transmitted from one generation to the next through symbols and through artifacts, through records and through living traditions." Taylor, in *Primitive Culture*, published in 1871, defined culture as that "complex whole which includes knowledge, belief, art, morals, customs and many other capabilities and habits acquired by man as a member of society" (quoted in Briggs, 1989, p. 437).

Similarly, Kottak (1989, p. 5) defines culture as "knowledge, beliefs, perceptions, attitudes, expectations, values, and patterns of behavior that people learn by growing up in a given society." To an anthropologist, "not just university graduates, but all people are cultured" (Kottak, 1989, p. 8). Enculturation is "the process whereby one grows up in a particular society and absorbs its culture" (Kottak, 1989, p. 8).

Kottak (1989), for example, studied television in Brazil, using content analysis, interviews with experts and TV personnel, archival and statistical research, and field study at six rural communities. Anthropologists pursue this central question regarding culture (Kottak, 1989, p. 14): How is cultural diversity both influencing and being affected by larger forces?

Kottak's inspiration came from Clifford Geertz, who studied premedia society in Bali. Geertz (1973, p. 23) refers to anthropology's "deepest theoretical dilemma: how is [cultural] variation to be squared with the biological unity of the human species?"

Global Diversity

Hofstede, a social scientist from the Netherlands, can shed light on Geertz's dilemma. Hofstede (2001, p. 9) defines culture as "the collective programming of the mind that distinguishes the members of one group or category of people from another." Hofstede originally developed four dimensions of cultural variability through analysis of a survey of 116,000 IBM employees in 40 countries, in 1968 and 1972. He later added a fifth dimension, new data, and an additional 10 nations (plus three regions). The dimensions—on which each nation is scored—show patterns of cultural distances in any given group of nations (see Table 1.1).

The newest dimension, *long-term orientation*, refers to "the fostering of virtues oriented towards future rewards, in particular, perseverance and thrift" versus "virtues related to the past and present" (Hofstede, 2001, p. 359). *Power distance* refers to societies' responses to inequalities of prestige, wealth, or power, as "different societies put different weights on status consistency" (Hofstede, 2001, p. 79); subordinates' efforts to

TABLE 1.1
U.S. and 10 Countries' Scores on Hofstede's
Dimensions of Cultural Variability

	Uncertainty Avoidance	Power Distance	Individualism/ Collectivism	Masculinity/ Femininity	Long-Term Orientation
United States	46	40	91	62	29
Japan	92	54	46	95	80
Mexico	82	81	30	69	—
Brazil	76	69	38	49	65
China (Taiwan)	69	58	17	45	118*
Egypt (Arab world)	68	80	38	53	—
Germany	65	35	67	66	31
Nigeria (W. Africa)	54	77	20	46	16**
So. Africa	49	49	65	66	—
India	40	77	48	56	61
UK	35	35	89	66	25
Mean (50 countries, 3 regions)	65	57	43	49	—
SD (50 countries, 3 regions)	24	22	25	18	—

*Mainland China, not Taiwan (scores calculated after 0 → 100 scores established)
**Nigeria, not W. Africa.

reduce distance from superiors balance with superiors' efforts to increase that distance. *Uncertainty avoidance* refers to the laws, religions, rituals, and technologies that societies develop to cope with "uncertainty about the future"; the score relates to anxiety and the need for security (Hofstede, 2001, p. 145). *Individualism/collectivism* refers to "the relationship between the individual and the collectivity," whereby "individualism is seen as a blessing [or] . . . as alienating" (Hofstede, 2001, p. 209). *Masculinity* versus *femininity* refers to societies' decisions about "what implications the biological differences between the sexes should have for the emotional and social roles of the genders " (Hofstede, 2001, p. 279).

Like Geertz, Hofstede (2001, p. 171) does not focus on mass media, but he does make some references about the dimensions that shed light on cross-cultural understanding of media; for example, cultures with a low Uncertainty Avoidance Index (i.e., that can tolerate ambiguity) have a "more open-minded mentality, in searching for information and in accessibility to innovation" (in other words, such cultures will likely adopt the Internet and read books and newspapers).

People in highly individualistic nations read more books and had more home PCs, whereas people in collectivist nations enjoyed television more, because individualists "rely more on media and less on, for example, their social networks for information" (Hofstede, 2001, p. 242).

Hofstede's work has three key implications for international media studies. First, he demonstrates the multidimensional nature of culture, which is much more complex than language. Second, he shows indubitably that cultures differ in discernible, measurable ways. Third, he defines culture as "nation."

Despite the potential insights of Hofstede's work, media scholars (e.g., Cooper-Chen, 2003) have only begun to relate his ideas to media content and consumer behavior. Similar to Elasmar's (2003) work, De Mooj (2001) refuted the truism that markets would grow ever more globalized and homogeneous; on the contrary, affluence permits cultural differences to come to the fore, such that "buying and consumption patterns in affluent countries in the 1980s and 1990s diverged as much as they converged" (quoted in Hofstede, 2001, p. 242). The Uncertainty Avoidance and Masculinity dimensions resist convergence most strongly and persist independent of increases in wealth.

The Hofstede scores of the nations in chapters 3–12 must, in three cases, be somewhat inexact: China, Egypt, and Nigeria were not included individually as nations for all the dimensions. Table 1.1 shows the scores as best as they can be rendered from Hofstede's work. Arranged in descending order in terms of Uncertainty Avoidance, Table 1.1 shows that the Japanese people value and court certainty (score, 92), whereas, by contrast, United States (46), Indian (40), and United Kingdom (35) citizens can manage to live with uncertainty.

For Power Distance, Mexico (81) and the Arab world (80) have the highest tolerance for inequality, whereas the United Kingdom and Germany (both 40) value equality. The most Individualistic societies are the United States

(91) and the United Kingdom (89), whereas by far the most Collectivist is China/Taiwan (17). By far, the most Masculine society is Japan (95)—indeed, it is the highest of all 50 countries that Hofstede studied. No nation stands out as Feminine; all of the 10 profiled in this book cluster in the middle ranges, with scores in the 40s, 50s, and 60s. For Long-term Orientation, Mainland China stands out with its score of 118, whereas Nigeria (16) has the strongest need for immediate gratification; unfortunately, Mexico, Egypt, and South Africa do not have scores for this dimension.

TELEVISION AND EFFECTS

A society's culture affects television (Kottak, 1989), as the chapters in this book show; even the casual tourist notices marked country-by-country content differences. Conversely, how does television affect society and the individuals in a society? For example, Putnam (quoted in Severin & Tankard, 2001, p. 266) found that TV viewing is associated with lower civic engagement; "newspaper readers are likely to be joiners, while heavy TV viewers are likely to be loners." But is social isolation an effect of TV viewing? After all, association is not causation. As Elasmar (2003, p. 187) explains, people who watch imported U.S. TV programs might indeed eat more fast food than those who watch domestic shows, but perhaps "those who watch a lot of [U.S.] TV also tend to travel a lot and those who travel a lot tend to eat American fast food."

Severin and Tankard (2001) provide an overview of mass media effects. They observe that the pendulum swings back and forth between powerful effects, such as "the power that propaganda appeared to have in World War I" (Severin & Tankard, 2001, p. 263) and limited effects, a view that prevailed after World War II. In between are moderate effects theories such as agenda setting (McCombs & Shaw, 1972); this theory, as do many others, applies most specifically to news rather than entertainment.

Two types of content specifically related to TV entertainment arouse passionate public and research debate about large versus limited TV effects: sex and violence. The former is beginning to get research attention (Brown, Steele, & Walsh-Childers, 2002), whereas the latter is already well studied.

Violence

It is easy to "point an accusing finger at the entertainment media as the primary reason for mayhem in our midst" (Heins, 2001, p. v). Granted that poverty and availability of guns are likely "proximate causes of crime" and media are "probably a peripheral cause" (Heins, 2001, p. 31), social science research over the last 40 years has accumulated evidence that TV violence "can contribute to aggressive behavior in viewers" (Smith, Nathanson, & Wilson, 2002, p. 84). Learned aggression, along with fear and desensitization, are the main discernible effects.

Learned Aggression.   Bandura's (1986) social cognitive theory "has been widely used to explain the process by which viewers might learn aggression from media violence" (Smith, Nathanson, & Wilson, 2002, p. 87). Four subprocesses govern observational learning: attention, retention, behavioral reproduction, and motivation. Contextual features shown to be associated with learned aggression include attractive perpetrator, justified violence, conventional weapons, extensive/graphic violence, realistic violence, rewards, and humor. Factors shown to decrease the learning of aggression include unjustified violence, punishments, and pain/harm cues.

Fear.   The Cultural Indicators Project initiated by Gerbner (1994) emphasized the fear-inducing aspect of TV violence—its invoking (its "cultivation") in viewers of a skewed view of the real world as a more violent place than it really is. The "Lessons of Violence," according to the video "The Killing Screens," do not induce people to solve their problems with violence, but increase insecurity and the public's willingness to accept an overbearing police force (Gerbner, 1994).

Desensitization.   Graphic violence and humor are further associated with desensitization. Humor can dampen a potential aggressor's empathy, decreasing his or her inhibitions (Bandura, 1990). Violence must escalate to retain its power. Movies, which make their way to U.S. television, have a strong tendency to escalate violence. For example, "Robo Cop" had 32 corpses, but its sequel had 81 corpses; "Death Wish" pictured 9 corpses, but "Death Wish II" pictured 62 corpses (Gerbner, 1994).

Cooper-Chen (2003), who followed the methods of the National Television Violence Study (1997), in researching prime time content, found that about 15% of Chinese and Japanese prime time entertainment TV programs contain some violence, compared to 67% on U.S. broadcast networks. A large share of this Asian violence comes from imported U.S. movies. Beginning in the 1960s U.S. exports accounted for "the lead position" in international TV trade, but now have competition from Japan, Mexico, Brazil, and other producers (Jin, 2002, p. 223).

Chapter 2 explains the dynamics of the TV/film trade. An accounting of import–export volumes takes on added importance because of possible effects that imported TV entertainment has on indigenous cultures. Granting that some nations are net importers of content, do effects in fact occur? The view of presumed effects was so strong that it occupied the United Nations Educational, Scientific, and Cultural Organization (UNESCO) for many years in the form of the New World Information and Communication Order debates 1970–1990. One of the charges was cultural domination by the center (rich) nations of the poorer (peripheral) nations of the world.

Cultural Imperialism?

Beginning with *Electronic Colonialism* (1981) and continuing to the present, McPhail has taken a clear center–periphery view of world communication systems. Another proponent of powerful effects, Schiller (1971, 1989) best articulates the concept of U.S. cultural imperialism (CI). Schiller first blamed the U.S. government and later multinational corporations for imposing "colonial servitude" (Schiller, 1971, p. 2) in their control of other nations' media choices. "Messages 'made in America,'" wrote Schiller (1971, pp. 147–148) "radiate across the globe and serve as the ganglia of national power and expansion."

Schiller died January 29, 2000, at the age of 81, but his paradigm of cultural imperialism (CI) remains as "the roots of all international legislation to protect indigenous culture" (Elasmar, 2003, p. 13). For example, CI proponent Goonaskera (1987, p. 11) warned that "in the face of this media invasion, the indigenous cultures of the Third World would disintegrate consistently and without resistance."

Theories on global media flows, as with general theories, swing between an emphasis on powerful versus limited effects. CI has been challenged by new approaches such as cultural proximity (Straubhaar, 2003), examined in chapter 2. Olson (1999) argues that narratives of U.S. film and TV exports can be read as indigenous because they allow overseas viewers to project their own values onto these "transparent" products that easily cross cultures.

Elasmar (2003) proposes a limited effects approach. He argues that overseas audiences have stubbornly asserted their likes and dislikes. Audiences that like Brazil's or Mexico's telenovelas generally do not like U.S. TV soap operas, which can go on for years and years. Yet even though audiences prefer proximate content, the "powerful appeal of exotic, non-local programming" (Elasmar, 2003, p. 80)—including the action, violence, and sex of U.S. movies—has its place on the world's TV schedules.

As you read chapters 3–12, notice that the size of the audience and placement in a TV schedule are crucial. Are the U.S. shows in prime time? What are their ratings? A meta-analysis of works published from 1960 to 1995 on cross-border TV effects showed that television accounts for only 2% of the variance in persons' holding of values similar to the exporting nation. In sum, "At most, foreign TV exposure may have a weak impact upon audience members" (Elasmar, 2003, p. 152). The "simplistic" (Elasmar, 2003, p. 162) assumptions of CI overlook the building blocks that make media influence such a complex process. As the old saying goes, there are simple answers to complex questions—but they are wrong.

REFERENCES

Bandura, A. (1986). *Social foundations of thought and action: A social cognitive theory.* Englewood Cliffs, NJ: Prentice Hall.

Bandura, A. (1990). Selective activation and disengagement of moral control. *Journal of Social Issues, 46,* 27–46.

Banerjee, I. (2002). The locals strike back? Media globalization and localization in the new Asian television landscape. *Gazette, 64*(6), 517–535.

Barnouw, E., & Kirkland, C. (1989) Entertainment. In E. Barnouw (Ed.), *International Encyclopedia of communications* (pp. 101–104). New York: Oxford University Press.

Beniger, J. (1990). Who are the most important theorists of communication? *Communication Research, 17*(5), 698–715.

Bernard, R. (1988). *Research methods in cultural anthropology.* Newbury Park, CA: Sage.

Briggs, A. (1989). Culture. In E. Barnouw (Ed.), *International encyclopedia of communications* (pp. 437–438). New York: Oxford University Press.

Brown, J., Steele, J., & Walsh-Childers, K. (2002). *Sexual teens, sexual media.* Mahwah, NJ: Lawrence Erlbaum Associates.

Browne, D. (1983). Media entertainment in the western world. In J. Martin & A. Chaudhary (Eds.), *Comparative mass media systems* (pp. 187–208). New York: Longman.

Bryant, J., & Raney, A. (2000). Sports on the screen. In D. Zillmann & P. Vorderer (Eds.), *Media entertainment: The psychology of its appeal* (pp. 153–174). Mahwah, NJ: Lawrence Erlbaum Associates.

Chang, T. K. (2002). *China's window on the world.* Cresskill, NJ: Hampton.

Cooper-Chen, A. (2003). *Entertainment East and West.* Paper presented to the Association for Education in Journalism and Mass Communication annual convention, Kansas City, MO.

DeMooj, M. (2001). *Convergence–divergence.* Unpublished doctoral dissertation. Universidad de Navarra, Spain.

Elasmar, M. (Ed.). (2003). *The impact of international television.* Mahwah, NJ: Lawrence Erlbaum Associates.

Fischer, H., & Melnik, S. (1979). *Entertainment: A cross-cultural examination.* New York: Hastings House.

Freedom House. (2003). *Press freedom rankings.* Available: www.freedomhouse.org

Gerbner, G. (1994). *The killing screens* (video). Northampton, MA: Media Education Foundation.

Geertz, C. (1973). *The interpretation of cultures.* New York: Basic Books.

Goonaskera, A. (1987). The influence of television on cultural values with special reference to third world countries. *Media Asia, 14,* 7–12.

Heins, M. (2001). *Violence and the media: An exploration of cause, effect and the First Amendment.* Nashville, TN: The First Amendment Center.

Hofstede, G. (2001). *Culture's consequences* (2nd ed.). Thousand Oaks, CA: Sage.

Hoggart, S. (1990). A nation's culture is always more interesting than its politics. *Athens* (OH) *Messenger* (April 22), p. A-10.

Jin, D. (2002). Regionalization of East Asia in the 1990s. *Media Asia, 29*(4), 215–217, 223–228.

Kato, H. (1975). Essays in comparative popular culture. *Papers of the East-West Communication Institute, 13.*

Katz, E., Gurevitch, M., & Haas, H. (1973). On the uses of mass media for important things. *American Sociological Review, 38,* 164–181.

Kottak, C. (1989). *Prime time society: Anthropological analysis of television and culture.* Belmont, CA: Wadsworth.

Martin, L. (1976). The contradiction of cross-cultural communication. In H. Fischer & J. Merrill (Eds.), *International and intercultural communication* (pp. 424–434). New York: Hastings House.

McCombs, M., & Shaw, D. (1972). The agenda-setting function of mass media. *Public Opinion Quarterly, 36,* 176–187.

McPhail, D. (1981). *Electronic colonialism.* Beverly Hills, CA: Sage.

National Television Violence Study, vol. 1. (1997). Thousand Oaks, CA: Sage.

Olson, S. (1999). *Hollywood planet.* Mahwah, NJ: Lawrence Erlbaum Associates.

Real, M. (1989). *Supermedia.* Newbury Park, CA: Sage.

Schiller, H. (1971). *Mass communication and American empire.* Boston: Beacon Press.

Schiller, H. (1989). *Culture, Inc.* New York: Oxford University Press.

Servaes, J. (1988). *Cultural identity in East and West.* Paper presented to the 16th Conference, International Association for Mass Communication Research, Barcelona.

Severin, W., & Tankard, J. (2001). *Communication theories: Origins, methods and uses in the mass media.* New York: Longman.

Singhal, A., Cody, M., Rogers, E., & Sabado, M. (2004). *Entertainment–education and social change*. Mahwah, NJ: Lawrence Erlbaum Associates.

Singhal, A., & Rogers, E. (1999). *Entertainment–education*. Mahwah, NJ: Lawrence Erlbaum Associates.

Smith, S., Nathanson, A., & Wilson, B. (2002). Prime-time television: Assessing violence during the most popular viewing hours. *Journal of Communication, 52*(1), 84–111.

Stein, J., & Su, P. (Eds.). (1980). *The Random House dictionary*. New York: Ballantine Books.

Straubhaar, J. (2003). Choosing national TV: Cultural capital, language and cultural proximity in Brazil. In M. Elasmar (Ed.), *The impact of international television* (pp. 77–110). Mahwah, NJ: Lawrence Erlbaum Associates.

Ulin, R. (1984). *Understanding cultures*. Austin: University of Texas Press.

Zillmann, D. (2000). The coming of media entertainment In D. Zillmann & P. Vorderer (Eds). *Media entertainment: The psychology of its appeal* (pp. 1–20). Mahwah, NJ: Lawrence Erlbaum Associates.

Zillmann, D., & Vorderer, P. (Eds.). (2000). *Media entertainment: The psychology of its appeal*. Mahwah, NJ: Lawrence Erlbaum Associates.

Chapter 2

The Transnationals: Media Corporations, International TV Trade and Entertainment Flows

Richard A. Gershon
Western Michigan University

INTRODUCTION

A transnational corporation is defined as a nationally based company with overseas operations in two or more countries. One distinctive feature of the transnational corporation (TNC) is that strategic decision making and the allocation of resources are predicated on economic goals and efficiencies with little regard to national boundaries. What distinguishes the transnational media corporation (TNMC) from other types of TNCs is that the principal commodity being sold is information and entertainment. It has become a salient feature of today's global economic landscape (Albarran & Chan Olmsted, 1998; Demers, 1999; Gershon, 1997, 2002; Herman & McChesney, 1999). The TNMC actively promotes the use of media and telecommunications software and hardware technology, including broadcast and cable television, the Internet, music and film exports, direct broadcast satellite, video games, and VCR and DVD recording technology on a worldwide basis.

The 1990s witnessed an unprecedented number of international mergers and acquisitions that brought about a major realignment of business players. Concerns for antitrust violations seem to be overshadowed by a general acceptance that such changes are inevitable in a global economy. The result has been a consolidation of players in all aspects of business,

17

TABLE 2.1
The Transnational Media Corporation

Companies	World Hdq.	Principal Business Operations
Bertelsmann AG	Germany	Book and record clubs, book publishing, magazines, music, and film entertainment
NBC Universal	USA	Television and film entertainment, cable programming, theme parks
News Corp. Ltd.	Australia/USA	Newspapers, magazines, television and film entertainment, Direct Broadcast Satellite
Sony	Japan	Consumer electronics, videogame consoles and software, music and film entertainment
Time-Warner	USA	Cable, magazines, publishing, music and film entertainment, Internet service provision
Viacom	USA	TV and film entertainment, cable programming, broadcast television, publishing, videocassette and DVD rental/sale
Walt Disney	USA	Theme parks, film entertainment, broadcasting, cable programming, consumer merchandise

including banking, aviation, pharmaceuticals, media, and telecommunications. Table 2.1 identifies, in alphabetical order, the six leading TNMCs, including information pertaining to their country of origin and principal business operations.

The TNMC: Assumptions and Misconceptions

During the past two decades, scholars and media critics alike have become increasingly suspicious of the better known, high-profile media mergers. Such suspicions have given way to a number of misconceptions concerning the intentions of TNMCs and the people who run them. The first misconception is that such companies are monolithic in their approach to business. In fact, just the opposite is true. Researchers like Schein (1984), Morley and Shockley-Zalabak (1991), and Gershon (1997, 2002) argue that the business strategies and corporate culture of a company often directly reflect the person (or persons) who were responsible for developing the organization and its business mission.

The Sony Corp., for example, is a company that was largely shaped and developed by its founders, Masaru Ibuka and Akio Morita. Together, they formed a unique partnership that left an indelible imprint on Sony's worldwide business operations. As a company, Sony is decidedly Japanese in its business values. Senior managers operating in the company's Tokyo headquarters identify themselves as Japanese first and entrepreneurs second (Sony, 1996). By contrast, Bertelsmann AG is a TNMC that reflects the business philosophy of its founder, Reinhard Mohn, who believed in the importance of decentralization. Bertelsmann's success can be attributed to long-range strategic planning and decentralization, a legacy that Mohn instilled in the company before his retirement in 1981 (Gershon, 1997).

A second misconception is that the TNMC operates in most or all markets of the world. Although today's TNMCs are highly global in their approach to business, few companies operate in all markets of the world. Instead, the TNMC tends to operate in preferred markets with an obvious preference (and familiarity) toward one's home market (Gershon, 1997, 2000). News Corp., for example, generates 76% of its total revenues inside the United States and Canada, followed by Europe with 16% and Australasia with 8% (News Corp., 2003). Similarly, a company like Viacom generates an estimated 84% of its revenues inside the United States and Canada. The remaining 16% of Viacom's global revenues are generated largely from Paramount Pictures and the company's Music TV (MTV) international subsidiaries and joint partnerships (Viacom, 2002).

Understanding Core Competency

The principle of core competency suggests that a highly successful company is one that possesses a specialized production process, brand recognition, or ownership of talent that enables it to achieve higher revenues and market dominance when compared to its competitors (Daft, 1997). Core competency can be measured in many ways, including brand identity (Disney, ESPN, CNN), technological leadership (Cisco, Intel, Microsoft), superior research and development (Sony, Philips) and customer service (Dell, Gateway, Amazon.com). A good example of core competency can be seen with Sony Corp., which specializes in consumer electronics (60% of Sony's worldwide business operations).

Historically, the TNMC begins as a company that is especially strong in one or two areas. At the start of the 1980s, for example, Time Inc. (prior to its merger with Warner Communication) was principally in the business of magazine publishing and pay cable television, whereas News Corp. (parent company to Fox Broadcasting) was primarily a newspaper publisher. Today, both companies are transnational in scope, boasting a highly diverse set of media products and services. Over time, the TNMC develops additional sets of core competencies. News Corp., for example, has become the world's preeminent company in the business of direct broadcast satellite communication.

THE GLOBALIZATION OF MARKETS

The globalization of markets involves the full integration of transnational business, nation-states, and technologies operating at high speed. Globalization is being driven by a broad and powerful set of forces, including worldwide deregulation and privatization trends, advancements in new technology, the fall of Communism, and market integration such as the European Community, NAFTA (USA, Canada, and Mexico), and MERCOSUR

(Argentina, Brazil, Paraguay, and Uruguay). The basic requirements for all would-be players is free trade and a willingness to compete on an international basis.

Free Market Trade

A basic tenet of free market competition is that the private sector is the primary engine for growth. Free market competition means opening one's banking and telecommunication systems to private ownership and competition and providing a nation and its citizens with access to a wide variety of choices (Friedman, 1999). The rules of free market economies, when extended internationally, presuppose a willingness to open up one's domestic market to foreign direct investment and elimination—or at least reduction—of tariffs and quotas on imported goods. Not all countries adhere to the principles of free market competition in the same way. Some countries tailor the rules to protect certain industries and/or facets of domestic culture. According to Bauer (1999), disagreement exists concerning the best ways to achieve effective competition:

> Worldwide telecommunications policy has been guided by a belief in the superiority of competition as an economic organizing principle for the industry. Paradoxically, while the idea of competition is widely embraced as a blueprint for practical policy decisions, there exist widely divergent views as to what constitutes competition and how it impacts efficiency. Moreover, policy prescriptions differ dependent on the conceptual lens chosen. (p.1)

Privatization and Economic Change

The changing telecommunications structures of Great Britain, Japan, Chile, and Poland aptly illustrate privatization trends worldwide. Likewise, European Community efforts to eliminate nonessential regulation and trade barriers represent a large-scale effort to promote the cause of competition. Even *perestroika*, the one-time Soviet answer to privatization, was an attempt to reform a failed economic policy. The common motivation behind such regulatory and economic reforms is the perceived inefficiency of central planning and government-protected monopolies. Government-protected monopolies are characterized by:

- poor financial performance
- overstaffing and dependency on government subsidies
- highly centralized and politicized organizations
- exclusionary dealings with competitive imports
- strong adherence to rules and regulations
- poor export performance
- inefficiency (technically noncompetitive)

Privatization is a highly political process that involves the conversion (or selling off) of state-owned enterprises (SOEs) into the private sector. The primary objective is to allow a market economy to flourish and thereby create opportunities and incentives for economic development. The successful privatization of SOEs is intended to improve the quality of goods and services while simultaneously reducing the role of the state in the economy (Lieberman, 1993). The selling off of SOEs, in particular, represents a way for a nation to raise cash that can be applied toward the reduction of a government's operating deficit. Moreover, the same money can be used to support other government services. Another goal of privatization is to promote the development of new technologies and services through Foreign Direct Investment. In principle, FDI promotes job growth and infuses new technology into the host nation's economy.

Foreign Direct Investment

Foreign Direct Investment (FDI) refers to the ownership of a company in a foreign country. This includes the control of assets. As part of its commitment, the investing company transfers some of its managerial, financial, and technical expertise to the foreign-owned company (Grosse & Kujawa, 1988). The decision to engage in FDI is based on the profitability of the market and future growth potential (Behrman & Grosse, 1990; Grosse & Kujawa, 1988). Five reasons help to explain why a company engages in FDI.

1. Proprietary Assets and Natural Resources.   The ownership of talent or specialized expertise can be considered a type of proprietary asset. Sony Corp.'s purchase of CBS records in 1988 and Columbia Pictures in 1989 enabled the company to become a formidable player in the field of music and entertainment. Rather than trying to create an altogether new company, Sony purchased proprietary assets in the form of exclusive contracts with some of the world's leading musicians and entertainers. The company also holds the copyright to various music recordings and films (Gershon, 2000).

2. Foreign Market Penetration.   The market to be served "on location" may exist or may have to be developed. News Corp. employed the latter strategy when it entered the United States in 1985 and purchased 7 TV stations from Metromedia Inc. for $2 billion. These acquired TV stations were all highly ranked stations in 7 of the top 11 U.S. markets. A year later, News Corp. bought 20th Century Fox for $1.55 billion. In 2 short years, the News Corp. CEO, Rupert Murdoch had ensured himself a steady source of programming with ready-made distribution outlets. From the very beginning, Murdoch understood the importance of vertical integration as the basis for launching what would become the future Fox TV network (Gershon, 1997; Litman, 1998).

3. Research, Production, and Distribution Efficiencies.   The cost of research, production, and labor are important factors in the selection of foreign locations. Some countries offer significant advantages such as a well-trained work force, lower labor costs, tax relief, and technology infrastructure. Depending on the country and/or technical facility, such products and services can be produced for less cost and greater efficiency. India, for example, is fast becoming an important engineering and manufacturing facility for many U.S. computer and telecommunications companies. Companies like Texas Instruments and Intel use India as a research and development hub for microprocessors and multimedia chips. Similarly, companies like IBM and Oracle use Indian engineers to develop new kinds of software applications. By some estimates, there are more Information Technology (IT) engineers in Bangalore, India (150,000), than in U.S. high tech Silicon Valley, California (120,000). Research studies performed by Deloitte Research and the Gartner Group report that outsourcing (and work performed in India) have reduced costs to U.S. companies by an estimated 40%–60% ("The Rise of India," 2003, p. 69).

4. Overcoming Regulatory Barriers to Entry.   Nations often engage in various policies designed to protect local industry, usually in the form of tariffs or import quotas. On October 3, 1989, the European Community (EC), in a meeting of the 12 nations' foreign ministers, adopted by a 10 to 2 vote the Television Without Frontiers directive. Specifically, EC Directive 89/552 was intended to promote European TV and film production. The plan called for an open market for TV broadcasting by reducing barriers and restrictions placed on cross-border transmissions. The EC was concerned that the majority of broadcast airtime be filled with European programming. EC directive 89/552 required member states to ensure, where practical and by appropriate means, that broadcasters reserve the majority of airtime for European works, excluding time allocated for news and sports (Cate, 1990; Kevin, 2003).

The EC directive was initially viewed by U.S. TV and film distributors as a form of trade protectionism. In order to offset the potential effects of program quotas, the TNMC and second-tier TV and film distributors began to form international partnerships, including coproduction ventures. This approach had the double benefit of sharing the cost of production while simultaneously overcoming perceived regulatory barriers to entry (Litman, 1998). By becoming a European company (or having a European affiliate), the TNMC was able to circumvent the EC's program quotas.

5. Empire Building.   As Gershon (1997) notes, FDI can sometimes be prompted for reasons that go beyond simple business considerations. News Corp.'s Rupert Murdoch and Viacom's Sumner Redstone have sometimes been characterized as empire builders in the tradition of the press barons of the 19th century (Shawcross, 1997). For CEOs like Murdoch, Redstone, and John Malone (Liberty Media), a certain amount of personal competitiveness and business gamesmanship goes along with managing a major company. Success is measured in ways that go beyond straight profitability. A high premium is placed on successful deal making. Today's generation of transnational media owners and CEOs are risk takers at the highest level, willing and able to spend billions of dollars in order to advance the cause of a new project venture.

TRANSNATIONAL MEDIA AND BUSINESS STRATEGY

As today's media and telecommunication companies continue to grow and expand, staying globally competitive becomes increasingly more difficult. The main role of strategy is to plan for the future as well as to react to changes in the marketplace. Strategic planning is the set of managerial decisions and actions that determine the long-term performance of a company or organization.

The Purpose of a Global Business Strategy

Most companies do not set out with an established plan for becoming a major international company. Rather, as a company's exports steadily increase, it establishes a foreign office to handle the sales and services of its products. In the beginning stages, the foreign office tends to be flexible and highly independent. As the firm gains experience, it may get involved in other facets of international business, such as licensing and manufacturing abroad. Later, as pressures arise from various international operations, the company begins to recognize the need for a more comprehensive global strategy (Gershon, 1997; Robock & Simmonds, 1989). In sum, most companies develop a global business strategy through a process of gradual evolution rather than by deliberate choice.

Cross-Media Ownership

One common strategy for future growth is vertical integration, whereby a company controls most or all of its operational phases. In principle, the TNMC can control a narrative idea from its appearance in a book or magazine, to its debut in domestic and foreign movie theaters, to its later distribution via cable, satellite, or videocassette/DVD. The rationale is that vertical integration allows a large-sized company to be more efficient and creative by promoting combined synergies between (and among) its various operating divisions. One important substrategy for many of today's TNMCs is to engage in cross-media ownership; that is, owning a combination of news, entertainment, and enhanced information services. Cross-media ownership allows for a variety of efficiencies, such as cross licensing and marketing opportunities between company-owned media properties; sharing of newsgathering, printing, and distribution facilities between company-owned media properties; negotiating licensing, rental, and sales agreements across different media platforms; and offering clients

TABLE 2.2
Viacom Media Holdings (2003)

Broadcast Television	Radio & Outdoor
• CBS Television Network	• Infinity Broadcasting
• United Paramount Network	• Viacom Outdoor/Infinity Outdoor
• Viacom Television Stations Group	
(39 stations)	*Motion Pictures & Theatrical Exhibition*
16 CBS owned & operated stations	• Paramount Pictures
4 CBS satellite stations	• Paramount Home Entertainment
18 UPN affiliated stations	• United International Pictures
1 Independent station	(33% stake)
• Paramount Television	
• CBS Enterprises	*Retail & Recreation*
King World Productions	• Blockbuster Video
CBS Broadcast International	• Paramount Parks
	• Famous Players Theaters (Canada).
Cable Television	• United Cinemas International (UCI)
• MTV Networks	
MTV, MTV 2	*Internet & Interactive Media*
Nickelodeon	• MTV.com
Nick at Night	• CBS.com
VH1	• CBSNews.com
CMT	• Nickelodeon.com
The New TNN	• VH1.com.
TV Land	
• Showtime Networks	*Publishing*
Showtime	• Simon & Schuster
The Movie Channel	• Pocket Books
FLIX	• Scribner
Sundance Channel (co-owned)	• The Free Press
• Black Entertainment Television	
• Comedy Central	

Note. Data are from Viacom Inc., Viacom 2002, 10K Report.

package discounts in advertising that cut across different media platforms. TNMCs like Time Warner, Viacom, and News Corp. routinely offer clients package discounts.

For example, Table 2.2 provides an overview of Viacom's media holdings. What is interesting to note is the diversity of media holdings with a particularly strong presence in both broadcast and cable television.

INTERNATIONAL TV/FILM DISTRIBUTION

The study of international media trade cannot be considered without fully appreciating the larger dimensions of the economic system in which they operate. The business of international media trade is affected by many of the same economic forces that apply to other types of commercial enterprises. The sale and distribution of television and film products is first and foremost a business. According to Picard (1989):

Media in the United States are for the most part capitalist ventures operated by private parties for the purpose of generating profit, and are thus subject to the operational principles of the market system. Even not-for-profit media—such as public broadcasting or organizational operated media—are influenced by the principles of the market system and are thus affected by its operations. (p. 14)

Two economic assumptions characterize the foreign sale and distribution of TV and film products. The first is that TV and film products are examples of a "public good." The cost of production is independent of the number of people who consume it. If a foreign viewer watches television, this action does not prevent others from watching (Picard, 1989). A second important assumption is that the costs of TV and film production are fixed. Once the cost of production has been realized, the cost per viewer declines as the size of the audience increases. It costs much less to produce a single program for worldwide distribution than it does to produce separate programs for individual markets (Owen & Wildman, 1992). The objective is, therefore, to maximize audience reach and to favor those distribution media that can accomplish this.

Program producers try to maximize the sale of TV and film products by planning the selection of distribution windows and release times. Owen and Wildman (1992, pp. 26–27) refer to this as *windowing*; that is, the method by which TV and film products are sold and distributed using "different distribution channels at different times." The practice of windowing shapes the many competitive interactions between program producers and the various systems of delivery. Beyond broadcast and theatrical exhibition, the number of distribution windows has significantly increased since the 1980s and now includes basic and pay cable television, DVDs and videocassettes, and Direct Broadcast Satellite (DBS) communication to both domestic and foreign market audiences. Table 2.3 considers some of the more typical release windows for TNMC films and their initial release time.

The practice of windowing allows TV and film producers to price discriminate—that is, to sell their products to individual buyers at different

TABLE 2.3
Release Windows for TNMC Theatrical Films

Theaters	Months From Initial Release
U.S./Canadian theaters	0–4 +
International theaters	4–18+
U.S./Canadian home video (DVD)	4–18+
International home video	8–24+
First U.S./Canadian cable/DBS run	8–24+
U.S./Canadian broadcast television	24–48+
International broadcast television	24–48+

Note. Adapted from the original Owen and Wildman (1992) model.

prices. This ability is especially important when it comes to the sale and distribution of international TV and film products. In principle, the producer can sell television/film products at a price that best reflects their value and affordability within individual markets rather than trying to sell at a uniform price. The producer sells programs at a price that the importing nation (or broadcast service) can afford to pay. Sepstrup's (1990) research indicates that the supply of TV hours and purchase price is determined by a number of related factors, including:

- the size of the home market
- total economic resources available
- language
- per capita income
- the level of commercialization

International TV/Film Trade

Although privatization has led to an increase in numbers of channels, few countries have the production capability to fill the enormous demand for programming. As a result, many domestic TV broadcasters and cable networks continue to rely on imported programming. Historically, the United States has led the way in providing much of the world's TV and film entertainment. The Motion Picture Association of America (MPAA) estimates that in 2002, foreign countries spent an estimated $9.64 billion on U.S. film exports as measured in box office receipts. This represents a 20% increase from the $8.03 billion spent in 2001 (MPAA, 2003).

Throughout the 1970s and 1980s, U.S. TV and film industries designed programs for the U.S. market with the expectation that good programming could be sold abroad. TV programs were produced for the U.S. market regardless of the suitability for a foreign market audience. The export of TV and film products proved highly profitable because no additional production costs were involved. The only real costs associated with the export of U.S. programming were related to distribution and language dubbing. For many nations, the purchase of U.S. made-for-TV programs and films represented a less costly alternative than producing one's own programs.

This is no longer the case. In Europe alone, U.S. made-for-TV programs account for less than 3% of prime time programming (Chernin, 2003). Although the United States is still a major player in the export of such TV programs, several research studies have noted the continued increase in regional production capability in both Latin America (Anatola & Rogers, 1984) and Asia (Waterman & Rogers, 1994).

If given the choice, most TV consumers prefer programs that are nationally and/or locally produced. Straubhaar (1991, 2003) refers to this as the *principle of cultural proximity*; that is, a desire for seeing TV programs that reflect a person's own language, culture, history, and values. Language is often the most important criterion in a host nation's decision to import foreign-made TV programming (Wildman & Siwek, 1988). In Austria, for example, almost 12% of the country's TV show imports come from neighboring Germany. Similarly, Belgium and Switzerland are both major importers of French programming (Kevin, 2003). The principle of cultural proximity holds equally true in Latin America. The Dominican Republic imports a large percentage of its television (Spanish) from Mexico-based Televisa, a major producer for the Latin American market (see chapter 4).

Besides language, there are other aspects of culture that are important in attracting potential TV audiences. Politics, social values, and humor are also important to the fabric of culture (Elasmar, 2003). In past years, Latin American countries used to import a significant number of U.S. TV programs, but this North-to-South flow is no longer as true today. More and more, Latin American countries are simply importing TV programs from each other, given cultural proximity factors that cut across much of Latin America. To that end, part of the TV void is being filled by several Latin American TV and/or film producers, including Televisa, Mexico (see chapter 12); TV Globo, Brazil (see chapter 11); Cisneros, Venezuela; and the Clarin Group, Argentina.

Similarly, the Asian market is filled with a number of regional producers, including NHK and Fuji TV, Japan (see chapter 9); and Chinese Central TV, China (see chapter 10). Europe also hosts a number of regional TV producers, including, to name only a few, Canal Plus, France; ZDF and the Kirch Group, Germany (see chapter 4); and the BBC, United Kingdom (see chapter 3). India (see chapter 8), through its numerous production houses, is arguably one of the largest regional exporters of TV and film products throughout Asia and the Middle East. Collectively, these TV companies represent a second tier of global TV producers and will continue to become ever more important to the business of international TV and film trade.

Global TV Brands

Through the years, branding has emerged as a specialized field of marketing and advertising, reflected by the burgeoning field of business literature. Aaker's (1991) seminal work, *Managing Brand Equity*, suggests that a highly successful brand is one that creates a strong resonance connection in the consumer's mind and leaves a lasting impression. According to Aakers, brands can be divided into five key elements: brand loyalty, brand awareness, perceived quality, brand associations, and proprietary brand assets. Global brands like Coca Cola, IBM, Shell, and McDonald's, for example, traverse nationalities and cultures and represent products used by consumers worldwide. Such products are localized to the extent that they are made to fit in to the local requirements (i.e., language, manufacturing, marketing style) of the host nation and culture.

Over the years, the TNMC has been responsible for creating a number of highly successful TV programs that have become global brands. Cable TV and DBS services like HBO and MTV, for example, are recognized TV

brands that display a high degree of similarity that cuts across countries with respect to content, format, and approach. At the same time, national cultures and institutions tend to absorb and localize such influences in a process that Straubhaar and Duarte (2003, p. 6) call *hybridization:* "Most global firms to tend to gradually recognize a need to localize their global offerings to the culture of that market. However, firms do vary considerably in their willingness to make such change." Straubhaar and Duarte (2003, p. 2) note, "Numerous marketing studies demonstrate the tendency of successful multinationals to adapt their strategies to the specific challenges of new local markets."

Home Box Office.   The real move to modern cable television began on November 8, 1972, when a fledgling company named Home Box Office (HBO) began supplying movies to 365 subscribers on the Service Electric Cable TV system in Wilkes Barre, Pennsylvania. That night, Jerry Levin, then vice-president for programming, introduced viewers to the debut of HBO. The feature programming for that inaugural night was a hockey game between New York and Vancouver and a film prophetically entitled "Sometimes a Great Notion."

In September 1973, Time Inc. demonstrated its confidence in the young company by acquiring HBO as a wholly owned subsidiary. A year later, HBO quickly established itself as the largest pay cable program supplier in the United States. By the early 1980s, HBO had become one of Time Inc.'s most successful business operations. From the beginning, HBO developed a number of strategies that helped promote its rapid growth, including the use of a monthly per-channel fee and the use of microwave and later satellite communications for the transmission of programming, rather than distribution by videotape. Prior to HBO, there was no precedent for the extensive use of satellite-delivered programming in the United States.

HBO's 1975 decision to use satellite communications was significant in two ways. First, it demonstrated the feasibility of using satellite communication for long-haul TV distribution. As a consequence, HBO was able to create an efficient distribution network for the delivery of its programming to cable operators. Second, the development of the satellite/cable interface would usher in a whole new era of cable programmers that were equally capable of leasing satellite time and delivering their programs directly to cable operating systems, including WTBS, 1976; ESPN, 1979; CNN, 1980; and MTV, 1981. Thus was born the principle of cable networking; that is, TV programming designed exclusively for cable operating systems (and later direct broadcast satellite systems). As cable analyst Paul Kagan (1984) once remarked, "Rarely does a simple business decision by one company affect so many. In deciding to gamble on the leasing of satellite TV channels, Time Inc. took the one catalytic step needed for the creation of a new television network designed to provide pay TV programs." Today, HBO has extended its brand worldwide and reaches an estimated 18 million subscribers in more than 50 countries in Latin America, Asia, and Central Europe. (See Table 2.4.)

TABLE 2.4
HBO International Joint Ventures

HBO Asia	HBO Ole
HBO Brasil	HBO Poland
HBO Bulgaria	HBO Romania
HBO Czech	A & E Mundo
HBO Hungary	E Latin America
HBO India	SET Latin America

Note. Data are from Time Warner, Inc. (2003).

Music Television Channel (MTV). The Music Television channel (MTV) is an advertiser supported video/music entertainment cable channel that began as a joint venture between American Express and Warner Amex Communications, then a subsidiary of Warner Communications. In March 1986, MTV, VH1, and Nickelodeon were sold to Viacom for $513 million. Shortly after MTV was acquired, Viacom CEO Sumner Redstone appointed Tom Freston as president of MTV. The company's global success is, in part, due to the innovative management and programming strategies that Freston implemented early in his tenure.

In 1987, MTV launched its first overseas channel in Europe, a single feed consisting of American music programming hosted by English-speaking artists. MTV soon realized that although American music was popular in Europe, it could not offset the obvious differences in language, culture, and preference for local artists. European broadcasters, for their part, understood the importance of MTV as a new programming concept. They soon adapted MTV-style programming and began broadcasting music videos in various languages throughout the whole of Europe. This, in turn, severely affected MTV's financial performance in Europe

In 1995, MTV was able to harness the power of digital satellites in order to create regional and localized programming. MTV's international programming drew on the talent, cultural themes, and languages from select parts of the world, which were then satellite-fed into that geographical location. Approximately 70% of MTV's content is generated locally. This, in turn, makes it easier and more profitable for MTV to sell advertising airtime overseas, given that most advertising needs and budgets of companies tend to be more local than international. MTV airs more than 22 different feeds around the world, all tailored to their respective markets. They comprise a mixture of licensing agreements, joint ventures, and wholly owned operations, with MTV International holding creative control over these programs. MTV's programming is primarily targeted to the 10–34 age group. This age group represents a highly sought-after demographic, making MTV a favorite choice among advertisers in those countries where MTV can be seen.

Presently MTV has a huge market share in Asia, Europe, China, Japan, and Russia in the eastern part of Europe. MTV International is organized into six major divisions: MTV Asia (Hindi, Mandarin), MTV Australia, MTV Brazil (Portuguese), MTV Europe, MTV Latin America (Spanish), and MTV Russia ("Sumner's Gemstone," 2000). The management of MTV's international operations are highly decentralized, giving local managers the ability to develop programming and marketing strategies to fit the needs of each individual market.

Direct Broadcast Satellites (DBS)

The communication satellite has long captivated the imagination of development planners and business entrepreneurs. For many countries, the communication satellite has become an integral part of the development process. Today's generation of satellites, larger and more sophisticated in design, have an amplifying capability that is 200 times more powerful than their predecessors in the 1970s. Direct Broadcast Satellites (DBS) represent the ability to deliver high-powered TV signals to small, inexpensive earth stations. Japan (see chapter 9) can be rightfully credited with being the first country to provide DBS capability to its citizens.

DBS in Japan. The development of DBS was first conceived as an integral part of Japan's overall space development program. Discussions concerning a future DBS program first began in 1968 with the formation of the Space Activities Commission (SAC). Since then, several generations of satellites have been successfully launched under the auspices of SAC and Japan's Ministry of Posts Telecommunications (MPT). Japan's formal entry into DBS began in 1989 despite strong opposition from the country's leading commercial broadcasters.

The decision to launch a DBS system demonstrated a national commitment to advance the cause of a highly sophisticated technology. For Japan's MPT, DBS was clearly a high profile project that would establish Japan as a world leader in satellite communications and high-definition television. What Japan's MPT could not foresee were the difficulties in trying to implement a new system of direct-to-home satellite services involving pay TV satellite services (CS) and the nation's terrestrial broadcasters (BS). In a report issued by the Council on Broadcasting, a private advisory board to Japan's MPT, the deadline for introducing DBS and cable satellite services would be 1996. Japan's traditional broadcasters would have until 2004 in order to make the conversion to digital satellite communications (NHK, 2002).

The year 1996 marked the beginning of DBS in Japan. On October 1, PerfecTV was unveiled using a JCSAT-3 communication satellite. PerfecTV offered a highly diverse package of services, including 53 channels of television and four channels of radio. Starting in January 1997, PerfecTV became a pay TV service. Viewers had to pay a one-time sign-up charge and a monthly subscription fee, as well as the cost of a satellite dish and receiver. In December 1997, a second DBS service was launched called

DirecTV, a joint venture between DirecTV of the United States and the Cultural Convenience Club (CCC), a Japanese video rental company. DirecTV offered a pay TV service using the Superbird communication satellite. PerfecTV and DirecTV were incompatible systems, which meant that subscribers to one pay TV service would have to buy a separate tuner in order to receive the other (NHK, 2002).

Sky PerfecTV. In the meantime, News Corp.'s Rupert Murdoch announced plans in June 1996 to build a 150-channel DBS service called JSkyB, but all parties saw clearly that Japan could not support three DBS services. Murdoch soon made overtures to PerfecTV to form a merger, which occurred in March 1998. By June 2000, Sky PerfecTV, the new entity, had attracted 2 million subscribers. DirecTV, for its part, continued to struggle with declining viewership. The company's assets were acquired by Sky PerfecTV in September 2000. In a matter of 3 years, Japan's CS system of digital broadcasting that began with three players had been pared down to a single company (NHK, 2002). Today, Sky PerfecTV offers DBS pay TV services to more than 3.5 million subscribers ("Total Registrations," 2003).

News Corp.

News Corp. is parent company to the world's largest set of DBS services. News Corp. either fully owns or is a partial investor in seven DBS services located on five continents. According to Peter Chernin, News Corp.'s chief operating officer:

> About 75% of the world's population is covered by satellite and television platforms we control. . . . Mostly in Asia—there are something like 2.5 billion people under that footprint. We believe that in this period of global expansion, there are some important strategic bets to make. And we've been making them. ("There's No Business," 1998, p. 92)

British Sky Broadcasting. News Corp. holds a 35% interest in British Sky Broadcasting plc (BSkyB), which operates the leading pay TV service in the United Kingdom (U.K.) and the Republic of Ireland. BSkyB first began operating in 1983 as the Sky Channel. The company used satellite communications as way to circumvent the U.K. four-channel system (see chapter 6) by delivering alternative programming to subscribers equipped with earth stations. The Sky Channel venture was an abysmal failure during its early years of development, sustaining $1.6 billion in losses ("Murdoch's British Satellite TV," 1994). By 1990, the combined losses of Sky Channel and Fox television appeared out of control, leaving many analysts to speculate whether both projects would eventually imperil the entire News Corp. operation.

Murdoch's solution to the Sky Channel dilemma was to merge his operation with rival DBS player British Satellite Broadcasting to form British

TABLE 2.5
News Corp. International DBS Services

DBS Service	Target Markets	Equity Stake
BSkyB	United Kingdom	100%
Sky Italia	Italy	80%
FOXTEL	Australia	25%
Phoenix Television	China, SE Asia, Australasia	45%
STAR TV	Asia (53 countries)	100%
SkyPerfectTV	Japan	11%
DirecTV (pending)	USA	34%

Sky Broadcasting. The merger enabled both companies to reduce costs and expand programming. By March 1992, BSkyB showed the first signs of profitability. In 1998, BSkyB began offering a fully digital service to its subscribers, including near video-on-demand service. Today, BSkyB services an estimated 7 million U.K. subscribers.

STAR Television.   In July 1993, News Corp. acquired a 63.6% interest in STAR Television Ltd. Murdoch paid $525 million for the Pan Asian satellite network. The original STAR TV network was launched in 1991 by Hong Kong business magnate Li Ka-Shing and his company, Hutchison Whampoa. At the time of the purchase agreement, STAR TV claimed an estimated viewership of 65 million people in 15 million homes ("Murdoch's Star Deal," 1993). Today, STAR TV broadcasts over 40 program services in seven languages to an estimated 300 million viewers in 53 countries across Asia. STAR TV is seen by more than 173 million people weekly. The STAR TV footprint can be seen from Israel to Japan and from Turkey to Indonesia.

DirecTV.   In April 2002, News Corp. announced its intention to acquire 34% of Hughes Electronic, including its DirecTV platform, the leading satellite television service in the United States. This move came after a 2-year-long effort to purchase DirecTV and is awaiting U.S. regulatory approval. Today, News Corp's DBS investments span five continents and include seven DBS services (see Table 2.5).

DISCUSSION

Government-supported broadcasting is now giving way to the private sector. The high cost of TV production has caused many of the world's leading PT&Ts (post, telephone, and telegraph) to reassess the amount of money they are willing to spend on TV production. For government policymakers, the continued privatization of television is not only attractive, but inevitable. The result has been an explosive growth in new commercial ventures, including new broadcast TV services, cable television, and DBS communication.

Privatization has affected the international TV/film market in two important ways. The first is the large-scale increase in the volume of programs being purchased from commercial sources. In Europe, Asia, and Latin America, the demand for new sources of programming has increased dramatically, given the rapid expansion in TV channels due to new media technologies. The TNMC will continue to supply a good proportion of the world's programming software, particularly in the area of film entertainment. In addition to the TNMCs, there is a whole host of second-tier TV/film program suppliers that have emerged in Europe, Latin America, and Asia. Both the TNMCs and second-tier TV/film producers are well positioned to take on the demands of international financing, resource allocation, production capability, and distribution. In order to offset the high cost of production, the number of coproduction ventures will continue unabated.

The second effect of privatization has been the increased competition for software products among potential program buyers. State-controlled broadcasters have traditionally been able to behave as monopolies in their purchase of programming. Today, the number of commercial broadcast, cable, and DBS services far surpasses the number of channels that are government supported. The resulting increased competition between (and among) state and commercial broadcasters for many of the same programs. is one of the reasons that second-tier TV/ film producers have proven so successful. Regional production centers that service a multi-country TV market have emerged (Straubhaar & Duarte, 2003).

The TNMC and the concept of global television (and global brands) are fast becoming realities in terms of news, sports, and music entertainment. The geopolitical and cultural walls that once separated the nations of the earth are becoming increasingly difficult to maintain. The world of global television, whether CNN, Olympic sports coverage (see chapter 15), MTV, or Disney feature films, is quickly eroding the barriers. At the same time, a single, unified market for TV entertainment is not likely to emerge. Differences in culture, including language, shared common experience, and social values, will preclude that possibility.

Tomorrow's TV programmers are likely to target several countries at once. More and more, programs will be produced for regions of the world where there is a commonality of language and experience (i.e., cultural proximity). The importance of the TNMC and coproduction ventures are going to foster a programming philosophy based on the assumption that the world can be broken down according to cultural continents (Cooper-Chen, 1994). With an increase in channel capacity (and expanded windows of distribution), the next generation of global TV viewers are likely to be people who can simultaneously appreciate world MTV and still have a decided preference for locally originated dramatic series or sporting events.

REFERENCES

Aaker, D. (1991). *Managing brand equity: Capitalizing on the value of a brand name*. New York: The Free Press.

Albarran, A., & Chan-Olmsted, S. (Eds.) (1998). *Global media economics*. Ames, IA: Iowa State Press.

Anatola, L., & Rogers, E. (1984). Television flows in Latin America. *Communication Research, 11*(2), 183–202.

Bauer, J. (1999, September 25–27). *Competition as a turbulent process*. Paper presented at the 27th Telecommunications Policy Research Conference. Alexandria, VA.

Behrman, J., & Grosse, R. E. (1990). *International business and governments: Issues and institutions*. Columbia, SC: University of South Carolina Press.

Cate, F. (1990). The European broadcasting directive. *Communications Committee Monograph Series*. Washington, DC: American Bar Association.

Chernin, P. (2003, October 11). *MIPCOM Award Acceptance Speech*. A presentation given at the 2003 MIPCOM conference, Cannes, France.

Cooper-Chen, A. (1994). *Games in the global village: A 50-nation study of entertainment television*. Bowling Green, OH: Popular Press.

Daft, R. (1997). *Management* (4th ed.). New York, NY: Harcourt Brace.

Demers, D. (1999). *Global media: Menace or messiah*. Cresskill, NJ: Hampton Press.

Elasmar, M. (Ed.). (2003). *The impact of international television: A paradigm shift*. Mahwah, NJ: Lawrence Erlbaum Associates.

Friedman, T. (1999). *The Lexus and the olive tree*. New York, NY: Farrar, Straus and Giroux.

Gershon, R. (1997). *The transnational media corporation: Global messages and free market competition*. Mahwah, NJ: Lawrence Erlbaum Associates.

Gershon, R. (2000). The transnational media corporation: Environmental scanning and strategy formulation. *Journal of Media Economics, 13*(2), 81–101.

Gershon, R. (2002). The transnational media corporation and the economics of global competition. In Y. R. Kamalipour (Ed.), *Global communication* (pp. 51–73). Belmont, CA: Wadsworth.

Grosse, R., & Kujawa, D. (1988). *International business: Theory and application*. Homewood, IL: Irwin.

Herman, E., & McChesney, R. (1999). *The global media: The new missionaries of corporate capitalism*. London, UK: Cassell.

Kagan, P. (1984). Remarks. In the *Pay TV Guide: Editor's pay TV handbook*. New York: HBO, Inc.

Kevin, D. (2003). *Europe in the media*. Mahwah, NJ: Lawrence Erlbaum Associates.

Lieberman, I. (1993). Privatization: The theme of the 1990's. *Columbia Journal of World Business, (28)*1, 8–17.

Litman, B. (1998). *The motion picture industry*. Boston, MA: Allyn & Bacon.

Morley, D., & Shockley-Zalabak, P. (1991). Setting the rules: An examination of the influence of organizational founders values. *Management Communication Quarterly, 4*(4), 422–449.

Motion Picture Association of America. (2003). *Snapshot report*. Available: www.mhttp://www.mpaa.org/

Murdoch's British satellite–TV venture. (1994, February 4). *Wall Street Journal*, p. A4.

Murdoch's Star deal transforms Asia. (1993, August 2). *Broadcasting & Cable*, pp. 34–35.

News Corporation, Inc. (2003). *Annual Report*. New York: News Corporation.

NHK (2002). *Broadcasting in Japan*. Tokyo, Japan: NHK.

Owen, B., & Wildman, S. (1992). *Video economics*. Cambridge, MA: Harvard University Press.

Picard, R. (1989). *Media economics*. Newbury Park, CA: Sage.

Robock, S., & Simmonds, K. (1989). *International business and multinational enterprises* (4th ed.) Homewood, IL: Irwin.

Schein, E. (1984, Winter). Coming to a new awareness of organizational culture. *Sloan Management Review*, pp. 3–16.

Sepstrup, P. (1990). *Transnationalization of television in Western Europe.* Monograph #5. London, UK: John Libbey & Co.

Straubhaar, J. (1991). Beyond media imperialism: Asymmetrical interdependence and cultural proximity. *Critical Studies in Mass Communication, 8,* 39–59.

Straubhaar, J. (2003). Choosing national TV: Cultural capital, language and cultural proximity. In M. Elasmar (Ed.), *The impact of international television: A paradigm shift* (pp. 77–110). Mahwah, NJ: Lawrence Erlbaum Associates.

Straubhaar, J., & Duarte, L. (2003, October 24). *Adapting US transnational channels to a complex world: From imperialism to localization.* Paper presented at the 2003 Global Fusion Conference, Austin, TX.

Shawcross, W. (1997). *Murdoch.* New York, NY: Touchstone.

Sony Corporation, Inc. (1996). *Genryu* (2nd ed.). Tokyo, Japan: Sony Corp.

Sumner's gemstone. (2000, February 21). *Forbes,* pp. 105–111.

There's No Business Like Show Business. (1998, June 22). *Fortune,* p. 92.

The rise of India. (2003, December 8). *Business Week,* pp. 66–76.

Time Warner, Inc. (2003). *Time Warner Annual Report.* New York: Author.

Total Registrations and DTH Subscribers (2003). Available: www.skyperfectv.co.jp/skycom/e/frame/fr_new_49.html

Viacom Inc. (2002). *10-K Report.* New York: Author.

Waterman, D., & Rogers, E. (1994). The economics of television program trade in Far East Asia. *Journal of Communication, 44*(3), 89–111.

Wildman, S., & Siwek, S. (1988). *International trade in films and television programs.* Cambridge, MA: Ballinger.

II

REGIONS

Chapter 3

The United Kingdom

Jeffrey Griffin
University of Dayton

ABOUT THE UNITED KINGDOM

The United Kingdom of Great Britain and Northern Ireland consists of England, Wales, Scotland, and Northern Ireland. The country has a population of 59.8 million (CIA, 2002). The islands that make up the United Kingdom are located between the north Atlantic Ocean and the North Sea. English is the predominant language of the country. Welsh, Scottish Gaelic, and Irish Gaelic are the most widely spoken indigenous minority languages.

The United Kingdom is a constitutional monarchy, with the monarch as head of state and the prime minister serving as head of government. The House of Lords and the House of Commons make up the U.K. Parliament. The country is a member of the European Union. One of the world's leading economic powers, the United Kingdom had a gross domestic product estimated at $1.52 trillion in 2002 (CIA, 2002). The economy is largely services-based.

BROADCAST BACKGROUND

History

The United Kingdom figures prominently in the early history of television. The first transmission of a moving image was made by a Scotsman, John Logie Baird, in October 1925. Baird also made the first public demonstration of television in January 1926 in London (Goldstein, 1991). Another milestone came in November 1936, when the British Broadcasting Corp., the country's public broadcaster, began the world's first regular broadcast of an electronic TV service. The signal was transmitted from Alexandra Palace in North London. However, television suffered a setback when the service was suspended in September 1939, just before the start of World War II. BBC Television resumed its service in June 1946 ("History . . .," 2003).

Despite the country's early entry into television, viewer choice developed slowly. The first commercial TV service, ITV, launched in 1955. Nine years later, a second BBC channel, BBC2, launched. Another commercial network, Channel 4, began broadcasting in 1982. Cable and satellite television started in 1989. The fifth terrestrial network, Channel 5, joined the fray in 1997. The slow growth of channels, as well as intrinsic cultural factors, helps explain why the British watch much less TV than Americans: British viewers watch an average of 25 hours a week ("Channel . . .," 2002).

BBC1 and ITV1, as ITV was renamed in 2002, are, far and away, the most-watched channels. They command the largest viewership because they gear their programming much more toward mainstream audiences and mass entertainment than do BBC2 and Channel 4. Channel 5, like BBC1 and ITV1, also caters to a mainstream audience, but it is a relative newcomer that has slowly built its audience base since its 1997 launch.

The analog signal of these terrestrial broadcasters uses the PAL transmission standard, unlike the United States, which uses the NTSC standard. The image produced by a PAL signal consists of 625 lines per screen, compared to 525 for NTSC, and thus has noticeably sharper resolution.

The United Kingdom has 24.7 million TV homes. As of March 31, 2003, nearly 49% of U.K. TV homes had some sort of multichannel TV service, meaning something other than standard analog broadcast television. In other words, those homes have either satellite or cable or digital terrestrial TV. Digital services are growing rapidly. About 44% of U.K. TV homes have digital TV service ("Digital . . .," 2003).

The Terrestrial Networks

The public broadcaster, the BBC, operates under a royal charter that must be renewed periodically. The BBC is accountable to the public through Parliament. Both BBC1 and BBC2 are commercial free. They are funded through the proceeds of an annual license fee that Brits pay for the privilege of having a TV set. The license fee is essentially a TV tax. The license fee increased to £121 per household for a color TV in 2004. For a black-and-white TV, the license fee is £40.50.

BBC1 has a diverse slate of entertaining and informative programming that caters to a mainstream audience. Comedies are a particular strength. BBC2 also airs a wide variety of programming, ranging from documentaries to cutting-edge comedy to lifestyle programming. In a move that would be unthinkable in the U.S. TV market, BBC2 repositioned itself in 2001 as a network appealing to middle-aged viewers! The change in focus paid off—BBC2's ratings went up. Because of the BBC's remit as a public broadcaster, both BBC channels show a good deal of educational and informational programming.

There has been considerable debate over the past 15 years about the role of the BBC and whether it is reasonable for British people to pay a license fee to support it when the number of channels available has steadily increased through satellite, cable, and digital platforms, giving viewers many alternatives.

Leading commercial network ITV1, often referred to simply as Channel 3, has an odd structure. The network is split into 15 regional franchises and one national breakfast TV provider. This structure was intended to ensure regional diversity in TV programming, and the programming slates of the ITV1 franchises reflect some regional variation, although mostly outside of peak time (the British term for prime time).

Regulation previously forbade one company from owning more than one ITV franchise, but the demise of those restrictions led to two companies, Granada and Carlton, becoming the powerhouses of ITV, between them owning 11 of the 15 regional franchises. In late 2002, these two heavyweights proposed a merger, which received government approval in October 2003. The newly combined company began trading shares under the name ITV plc in March 2004. Like BBC1, ITV1 has a diverse programming slate aimed at a mainstream audience. The network is, relatively speaking, best known for its slate of drama series.

Channel 4, unlike ITV1, is not privately owned. It is set up as a non-profit-making independent corporation that, for all intents and purposes, is publicly owned. The network is advertising supported. Channel 4 originally was programmed to complement ITV rather than compete with it. The network's mandate was to provide programming that appealed to tastes and interests that ITV did not cater to and to provide programming that was distinctive and innovative. Channel 4 targets tastes or specific groups out of the mainstream such as ethnic minorities, women, gays, and the disabled. For example, Channel 4 airs a gay drama called "Queer as Folk" (a U.S. version of this series began airing on Showtime in 2000). A great deal of Channel 4 programming is aimed at young adults. For example, Channel 4 screens the British version of the reality show "Big Brother." Much of the network's programming is risqué.

Risqué content also draws an audience. One of the most notorious Channel 4 series, "Eurotrash," lightheartedly celebrates all sorts of odd human behaviors, including shocking perversions and strange fetishes.

Channel 4's programming lineup is dotted with sex-themed programs. For example, a controversial series called "Hidden Love" looks at lesser known aspects of human sexuality. A 1999 episode called "Animal Passions" focused on people who have sex with animals. A more recent episode, "A Man's Best Friend," dealt with "'the anxieties, fears, pleasures, and embarrassing moments' associated with 'having a penis'" ("Love . . .," 2001). The network's penchant for sexcapades even extends to game shows. An episode of "Boys and Girls," which debuted in 2003, included a segment called "Parents on Parade," in which a horrified daughter looked on as her mother simulated fellatio with a banana (Sutcliffe, 2003). Channel 4's line-up does extend beyond sexual shenanigans—its mainstream programming includes one of the nation's more popular soap operas and quite a few U.S. imports.

Channel 4 is provided throughout the United Kingdom, except in Wales, where there is a counterpart service called S4C. Although for the most part it parallels the Channel 4 program schedule, S4C carries about 30 hours a week of Welsh-language programming.

Channel 5 is privately owned, with RTL holding a controlling stake and United Business Media a minority stake. Channel 5 is supported through advertising. Its programming includes lots of movies and an evening soap. Light entertainment, such as stand-up and sketch comedy and wacky game shows, plays a big part in the schedule, as do sports. One controversial aspect of Channel 5 from the outset was its airing of late-night erotic films and sex-themed programming. For example, in 2000, it aired a game show called "The Naked Jungle" in which the host and all the contestants were nude. Channel 5 has signaled a move away from sleazy programming. An example of its upmarket push would be a 12-part series in 2002 on the history of the British monarchs called "Kings and Queens." However, Channel 5 still offers some racy fare. For example, in 2002 it aired a series called "Sex & Shopping," which was purportedly a documentary series focusing on attitudes toward sex.

Multichannel Television

As already noted, nearly half of British households have some other platform than just basic terrestrial television: they may have a digital TV service, which can be satellite, cable or terrestrial, or they may have analog cable TV. Things have changed extraordinarily in the past decade and a half. Until the end of the 1980s, viewers had no options other than basic terrestrial TV.

Satellite broadcasting began in 1989 when Sky Television, owned by Australian-born media mogul Rupert Murdoch, launched a direct-to-home analog service. A rival service, British Satellite Broadcasting, started the next year. Later in 1990 the two services merged, adopting the name British Sky Broadcasting. Murdoch's News Corp. has a controlling interest in British Sky Broadcasting, known as BSkyB. Minority shareholders include Vivendi, Pearson, and Granada.

BSkyB was able to attract far more customers than cable because from the outset it offered satellite-exclusive channels and the number of channels grew steadily. BSkyB began offering a digital satellite service in 1998. In September 2001, it shut down its analog service entirely, so the service is now all digital. By Spring 2003, BSkyB was feeding its 200 channels to 10 million households—6.6 million through its satellite service and 3.4 million through cable (Cowell, 2003).

Cable enjoyed strong growth in recent years by marketing bundled telephone and TV services, but cable penetration remains relatively low. Although cable franchises began being awarded in 1983, cable developed slowly in the United Kingdom. The lack of cable-exclusive channels was a major impediment. The first national cable-exclusive channel in Britain, Wire TV, started up in 1993. Wire TV, which was backed by a consortium of large U.K. cable companies, was an odd hybrid aimed at women in the daytime and males at night. In 1995, Mirror Television, a sister company of the Mirror Group newspapers, bought Wire TV and relaunched it under the name Live TV. Live TV became renowned for some wacky things it did to lure viewers. The network's take on the news was decidedly different— it featured the news bunny, a person dressed in a bunny suit who stood near the desk of the news reader during news broadcasts and made faces or gestures in response to items. Even more infamous was its "Topless Darts" show, which added a risqué twist to the British pastime. Such heavily hyped stunt programming was not enough to sustain the network; Live TV shut down in late 1999. Two former executives announced plans in spring 2003 to revive the network, bringing back its gimmicky programming, including doing the weather in Norwegian.

Another pioneering cable-exclusive network, Channel One, started in 1994. Channel One, which specialized in city news, struggled financially from the outset and was shut down in 1999 by its owners, Daily Mail & General Trust.

The struggles and ultimate failure of pioneering cable networks Live TV and Channel One reflect the programming challenges that helped relegate cable to a back seat in the United Kingdom. Telewest and NTL have emerged as the dominant cable system operators after a great deal of consolidation.

As already noted, digital satellite TV service is available through British Sky Broadcasting, which launched a digital service in 1998. A competing digital terrestrial service, ONdigital, launched that same year. This terrestrial service, which was backed by major ITV franchise holders Granada and Carlton, was later rebranded ITV Digital. By early April 2002, ITV Digital had lost an estimated £800 million, and its owners decided to pull the plug, shutting the service down May 1, 2002. At the time, there were around 1.2 million subscribers.

ITV Digital suffered various technological problems. For one thing, the signal was unreliable, so there was a quality issue. Another problem was reach. Viewers needed a special rooftop aerial. The cost was no cheaper than that of BSkyB's digital satellite service. David Elstein, the former chief executive of Channel 5, sized up the problem: "Consumers were being offered a Trabant when an Audi or BMW was available at the same price" (Elstein, 2002, p. 19). There were customer service inadequacies as well.

A successor digital terrestrial service, Freeview, launched in October 2002, with a compelling strategy. Viewers pay about £75 to £100 for a digital decoder, but receive the service, operated by a consortium consisting of the BBC, Sky, and Crown Castle, for free. By February 2003, Freeview was offering 30 channels. Viewers embraced Freeview. More than 1.5 million homes were connected to Freeview by July 2003—nearly double the number from 9 months earlier, with many new users being cable defectors. By July 2003, digital viewing accounted for 40% of all TV viewing in the United Kingdom (Tryhorn, 2003). The British government has said it will switch off analog terrestrial TV sometime between 2006 and 2010, but has not pinned the date down.

Digital cable services have also been launched and are rapidly growing. The digital revolution also includes some ambitious experiments in advanced television, including one called Yes Television, an experimental broadband service in West London, and a video-on-demand service called HomeChoice, started in London in fall 2000, which transmits its service via the phone line. Through HomeChoice, viewers can have video on demand of films, BBC programming, Channel 4, and some U.S. TV shows, among other programming.

Satellite, Cable, and Digital Networks

The BBC also has a strong presence among the nonterrestrial networks. The BBC operates BBC3, a service aimed at 25- to 34-year-olds that began broadcasting in 2003. BBC3 replaced BBC Choice, which launched in 1998. The public broadcaster's raft of channels also includes BBC4, a culture channel that launched in 2002; News 24, a 24-hour news channel that launched in 1997; BBC Parliament, a government channel, which relaunched in 1998; and BBC Learning, an educational channel that launched in 1999.

Many satellite and cable networks are European or U.K. versions of U.S.-branded channels. An example would be MTV UK, which launched in 1997, providing viewers with a U.K.-dedicated network that replaced the previously available MTV Europe.

The digital era has sparked a boom in the launching of new networks that are mostly only available in digital service lineups. One of the first networks of the digital era was Channel 4's Filmfour, a film-channel spin-off of Channel 4, which launched in 1998. Later in 1998, ITV spun off ITV2, which targets younger viewers than the parent network through its programming slate of ITV repeats as well as originals. Another digital offspring of Channel 4, entertainment network E4, launched in 2001. Even Welsh broadcaster S4C launched S4C Digital. Countless others have been launched, thanks to expanded capacity, and are jockeying for viewers in a new environment.

BROADCAST REGULATION

British broadcasting has been fundamentally altered as a result of the sweeping 1990 Broadcasting Act, which to a large extent deregulated British TV and laid the groundwork for a more competitive environment.

The 1990 Broadcasting Act was pushed through by the Conservative Party government of then Prime Minister Margaret Thatcher. Thatcher's government argued that a competitive environment was needed and that the carefully regulated British TV world should move toward a more free-market system like that of the United States, which was a model because of diversity of choice. The 1990 Broadcasting Act truly revolutionized British television.

One of the most profound forces shaping the British TV landscape over the past 10 to 15 years has been consolidation. Deregulation has paved the way for this steady trend of mergers that have fundamentally reshaped British broadcasting. In 1993, the government ended a restriction that no ITV company could hold two large franchise licenses. This made it possible to create more powerful media companies and thus offered some protection against foreign raiders. Some of the franchise holders merged with others to form more powerful media companies. As already noted, two companies, Granada and Carlton, emerged as the big powers in ITV, with each holding a handful of franchises.

Another potentially far-reaching piece of broadcasting legislation became law in July 2003. The legislation, which further deregulates the broadcasting industry, was introduced in May 2002 by Media Secretary Tessa Jowell. The law makes it possible for non-European companies to own British TV networks. It also paves the way for one company to own ITV. The law also permits a dominant newspaper group to purchase Channel 5, but it stipulates that no newspaper group with more than 20% of the national market can own a stake in ITV. Under the law, one company could potentially own both ITV and Channel 5. The law also greatly eases restrictions on radio station ownership. In addition to its media ownership provisions, the law streamlined the regulation of the broadcasting industry by creating a new regulator, Ofcom, which replaces five existing regulatory agencies with responsibilities for television, radio, and telecommunication.

In the wake of its passage, a massive wave of takeovers is expected. The public, of course, is less concerned with who owns what than with what is on the screens. British television is criticized in much the same way that U.S. television is for excessive violence, sex, and bad language. A survey released in 2003 by the Broadcasting Standards Commission and the Independent Television Commission found that 40% of viewers had been offended by material that aired on television during the previous year. Sounding none too happy, the country's minister for broadcasting, Kim Howells, expressed alarm: "I think people are growing increasingly worried about the levels of violence in television. . . . I think a lot of the content has a corroding effect on the soul" (Hastings, 2003).

BROADCAST CONTENT AND RATINGS

One of the remarkable things about British television, at least from an American mindset, is the extent to which the terrestrial broadcasters continue to dominate viewing. In 2003, BBC1 had a 25.6% audience share, followed by ITV1 at 23.6%, BBC2 at 11%, Channel 4 at 9.7%, and Channel 5 at 6.5%. Satellite, cable, and digital networks accounted for 23.6% of viewing (Wells, 2003). Just as impressive as the overall share accounted for by the terrestrial networks is the extent to which BBC1 and ITV1, in particular, rule the roost. Between them, they account for half of all viewing. In a typical week, all of the top 50 programs are on one of those two networks.

Their obvious dominance notwithstanding, these two networks have faced increasingly stiff competition in recent years and suffered a steady erosion of their audience share. The proliferation of cable, satellite, and digital alternatives, as well as the start-up of Channel 5, has led to a much more competitive environment for the terrestrial networks. Each year since 1991, the share of viewing accounted for by other channels, meaning cable, satellite, and eventually digital, has increased, rising from 4% in 1991 to 23.6% in 2003. And the big four terrestrial networks have not just lost audience share to networks in the "other" category—Channel 5, whose audience share hit 6.5% in 2003, accounts for a small but significant chunk of viewing.

So what do the British watch? British television is remarkably diverse. Peak-time schedules consist of quality dramas, bold sitcoms, addictive soap operas, thoughtfully produced current-affairs programming, fun and informative home-and-garden series, and offbeat game shows, not to mention an array of sports and films. Within that broad mix, certain conclusions are unavoidable. Above all else, British viewers have a passion for crime series and soap operas.

Dramas

The British love a good mystery. Crime series, particularly standard police detective shows, are prevalent on British television.

Two ITV1 series that are veritable institutions are "Taggart," which debuted in 1983, and "The Bill," which premiered the following year. "Taggart," a police series set in Glasgow, managed to keep going strong even after the 1994 death of the actor who played the title character. The curious title of "The Bill" comes from "the old bill," a nickname for police.

Two police series that began long runs in 1992 are "Heartbeat" and "A Touch of Frost." "Heartbeat" is an ITV1 police series set in the 1960s in Yorkshire. "A Touch of Frost" is an enormously popular ITV1 series revolving around a stubborn middle-aged chief inspector of detectives with the unlikely name of Jack Frost.

Another workaholic chief inspector of detectives is "Prime Suspect's" Jane Tennison, played by acclaimed actress Helen Mirren. Tennison is a shrewd and tough police detective who not only has to cope with the stress of solving violent, sordid crimes but also faces additional challenges because of being a woman in a male-dominated police force. "Prime Suspect" originally aired on ITV from 1991 to 1996, and after a 7-year absence the program returned to the network in fall 2003, winning critical acclaim and drawing huge audiences.

One of the most beloved and successful programs in this genre was the ITV1 series "Inspector Morse" (1987–2000), which followed the adventures of a gruff, relentless Oxford police inspector. A fondness for real ale and a passion for opera helped define this atypical detective. In the final episode, "A Remorseful Day," the main character, played by John Thaw, died of a massive heart attack, an unusual way for a show to end. Thirteen million Brits watched the final episode of "Inspector Morse," giving it an impressive 50% audience share. "Inspector Morse" was based on a series of novels by Colin Dexter. Dexter said he decided to kill off Morse while the show was a success. He did not want it to become repetitive. Amazingly, even though the series started in 1987, just 33 "Inspector Morse" mysteries aired in all.

Another British police series that sprang from the pages of a book was the short-lived but memorable "Hamish Macbeth" (1995–1997). "Hamish Macbeth" was a BBC series about a rather unconventional police constable in a village stunningly situated in the Scottish highlands. The series, based on novels by M. C. Beaton, starred Robert Carlyle.

In addition to police procedurals, British viewers are fond of other sorts of mystery series. An example would be "Jonathan Creek," a popular BBC1 series that debuted in 1997 about a shaggy-haired genius who somewhat reluctantly solves crimes.

Although crime series are unusually prevalent on British screens, other forms of drama also air. Medical dramas are popular. Among the most successful have been "Casualty," a BBC1 series that is set in the emergency room, known in Britain as the casualty ward, and "Peak Practice," an ITV1 series about rural doctors. "Casualty" debuted in 1986 and, in the words of the BBC is "now officially the world's longest running and most successful medical drama series on television" ("Maxwell . . .," 2003). "Peak Practice," set in the fictitious Derbyshire village of Cardale, ran from 1993 to 2002.

People in other countries tend to associate British television with historical dramas because so many lavishly done British period dramas have aired around the globe. These costume dramas, as they are called, are often adaptations of literary classics. Both BBC and ITV1 produce a few meticulously made, historically evocative costume dramas each year. For example, in 2002, ITV1 offered "The Forsyte Saga," an adaptation of the John Galsworthy book, and "Doctor Zhivago," based on the novel by Boris Pasternak. ITV1's 2003 slate included an adaptation of the D. H. Lawrence novel "Sons and Lovers."

Soap Operas

In the United Kingdom, soap operas are a prime time staple, airing on every terrestrial network and dominating the ratings. The most-watched and best-loved of the genre are "Coronation Street" and "Eastenders," perennial favorites that draw huge peak-time audiences and typically finish at or near the top of the ratings. Both air four times a week. "Coronation Street" is an ITV1 soap that first was telecast in 1960. BBC1's "Eastenders," which premiered in 1985, is a blue-collar soap set in London.

In addition to "Coronation Street," ITV1 also carries the immensely popular soap "Emmerdale," which has been airing since 1972. "Emmerdale" is set in northern England in a village in the Yorkshire Dales. Queen Elizabeth even paid a visit to the set in 2002 in the run-up to the show's 30th anniversary ("Emmerdale . . .," 2002)!

A key series for Channel 4 since the network's 1982 launch, the soap "Brookside" got demoted to a Saturday afternoon slot in fall 2002 because of waning ratings and was axed in November 2003 after 21 years on the air. Channel 4 carries a teen soap, "Hollyoaks," which began broadcasting in 1995. "Hollyoaks" expanded to five episodes a week in fall 2003. Even S4C, the Welsh version of Channel 4, has its own soap opera, "Pobol y Cwm," which is made in Welsh Gaelic. "Pobol y Cwm," which means "people of the valley," has been on the air since 1974. The setting of the show, which airs five times weekly, is the fictitious village of Cwmderi.

A key part of Channel 5's strategy of building an audience, going back to the network's 1997 launch, has been the soap "Family Affairs," which is aired weekdays at 6:30 p.m.

British soaps differ from their American cousins in several key ways. For one thing, they are considered to be more realistic. One dimension of that is that the cast of characters includes a lot more working-class people, whereas U.S. soaps portray a world of doctors, lawyers, and businessmen. Also, most British soaps have a strong sense of place, reflecting the area in which they are set, unlike so many American soaps, which are set in fictional towns in unidentified states at ambiguous times. BBC1's "Eastenders" derives its name from its setting in the working-class East End of London. The setting of the ITV1 soap "Emmerdale" is the Yorkshire region. Channel 4's "Brookside" was set in Liverpool. "Hollyoaks" takes place in Chester.

Comedy and Light Entertainment

There is a strong tradition of situation comedy in Britain, which cannot be said of most European countries. One of the best-known "Britcoms" of the past two decades is the farcical "Absolutely Fabulous," starring Jennifer Saunders and Joanna Lumley as self-absorbed, boozy, middle-aged friends. Despite the show's enormous success both in Britain and abroad, no new episodes aired from 1996 until 2001, when a batch of six new episodes appeared on BBC1.

In Britain, unlike in the United States, series do not air year in and year out with 22 to 26 new episodes a season until the ratings begin to tail off. Many British series, particularly comedies, have runs as limited as 6 weeks. Sometimes quite a few years elapse between runs. In Britain, a run of a show is called a "series," so the British say something is, for example, "in its fifth series."

British viewers were abuzz in 2002 about a BBC revival of "Auf Wiedersehen, Pet," which ran on ITV from 1983 to 1986. The original premise centered on unemployed British construction workers who moved to Berlin to get a job. For the revival, all but one of the principal actors from the original series participated, which was amazing given how successful some of them had become, including Timothy Spall, whose credits include the film "Secrets and Lies," and Kevin Whately, who costarred in "Inspector Morse."

"My Family," which revolves around a dentist, his wife, and their three children, is one of BBC1's current comedy hits. A traditional family sitcom in most respects, "My Family," which began in 2000, is a departure for British television in that a team writing approach is used. Most British comedy series tend to be written by a single writer. This singularity of vision also plays into the norm of short-run series. The team writing approach employed by American series lends itself to long runs of 22 to 26 episodes, whereas the traditional British approach dictates shorter runs.

One of BBC2's more successful sitcoms in recent years has been "Coupling," a ribald series revolving around the friendships and sexual entanglements of three men and three women. "Coupling" began airing in 2000 on BBC2.

One of the most successful comedies of the past two decades is "Only Fools and Horses," a BBC1 series about two London brothers that began in 1981. A Christmas-day 2001 episode drew more than 21 million viewers and had a remarkable 74% audience share, making it that year's most-watched program. Although the Christmas-day 2002 episode drew a much smaller audience, with 17.4 million viewers, it was still the most watched program of the year.

Another of the bigger comedy hits in recent years was "The Vicar of Dibley," a fish-out-of-water BBC1 sitcom about a traditional English village whose new vicar was not only a woman, but who had an unorthodox style. The series, which ran from 1994 to 2000, starred one of Britain's best-known comedy stars, Dawn French, and was written by Richard Curtis, who also wrote or cowrote the screenplays for three of the most successful British films of all times—"Four Weddings and a Funeral," "Notting Hill," and "Bridget Jones's Diary." Just 16 original episodes of "The Vicar of Dibley" were produced, which is completely foreign to what American TV viewers think of as a series run.

Another top sitcom in recent years was "One Foot in the Grave," a BBC1 comedy about a retired couple that aired from 1990 to 2000. The series ended on a strongly dramatic note with the death of the husband character, Victor Meldrew.

One of the most acclaimed and more offbeat BBC comedy hits in recent years was "The Royle Family" (1998–2000), which debuted on BBC2 and was eventually promoted to BBC1. This unusual sitcom revolved around the home life of a working-class family, the Royles. Episodes typically focused on family members sitting around, watching television, snacking, and talking. A unique aspect of the show was that episodes unfolded in real time.

The all-time favorite British comedy, according to a 2000 poll, is "Fawlty Towers," starring former Monty Python member John Cleese as the owner of a small hotel ("Britain . . .," 2001). Twelve episodes were made, with six airing in 1975 and six in 1979. Nearly three decades after "Fawlty Towers" debuted, the show's reruns still attract a big audience when they are occasionally trotted out by the BBC.

Comedy–Drama

One genre in which the British excel is the blended comedy-drama. A great example is the recent ITV1 series "Cold Feet," which focused on the relationships and friendships of three couples in Manchester. "Cold Feet" (1998–2003) won numerous awards in Britain and Europe, including the Golden Rose of Montreaux.

Another classic comedy-drama is the recent BBC1 series "Ballykissangel" (1996–2001), named after the picture-perfect Irish village in which the series was set. Originally a fish-out-of-water series revolving around the village's new English priest, "Ballykissangel" altered its focus over time as actors came and went, but village life in a changing Ireland always remained at the show's core.

Game Shows and Reality Shows

British television is a veritable breeding ground for game shows, which the British seem to have a knack for creating. The global phenomenon "Who Wants To Be a Millionaire?" (see chapter 15) airs on ITV1. Also popular is "The Weakest Link," a BBC2 quiz show in which sarcastically snippy host Anne Robinson takes verbal jabs at poorly performing contestants.

Just like the United States, Britain has seen a spurt of interest in reality programming in recent years. One reality series that captured the public's imagination was the survival series "Castaway," which aired on BBC1 in 2000. "Castaway" placed 36 people on a remote island off the coast of Scotland. A formatted British version of the reality series "Survivor" aired on ITV1 in 2001 but was a major ratings disappointment. "Big Brother," a reality series about housemates, has been a ratings phenomenon for Channel 4 since the first incarnation ran in 2000. "Big Brother" is based on a Dutch format. The talent contest "Pop Idol" generated a great deal of buzz and huge audiences for ITV1 when it first aired in 2002 and when a second series aired in 2003.

Other

Social and human-interest documentaries are also more popular than in the United States, and science and nature programming is common. In fall 1999, a BBC natural history documentary called "Walking with Dinosaurs" drew remarkable audiences. Over a 4-week run it commanded a 50% share, making it the highest-rated science program in British TV history. So in fall 2001, the BBC followed up with the two-part "Walking With Beasts," which was also a ratings success. Another acclaimed 2001 science program was "Blue Planet," an eight-part BBC1 series about the seas and oceans made by acclaimed documentary filmmaker David Attenborough.

BROADCAST IMPORTS AND EXPORTS

Imports

Even though the United Kingdom has highly developed, vibrant TV and film industries, the producers and distributors of U.S. TV series and films do a brisk business with British TV networks, just as they do everywhere else in the world. For the most part, the Hollywood product, particularly the TV series, serves as filler, fleshing out the schedules. American fare is much more common on the less-viewed networks—BBC2, Channel 4, and Channel 5, as well as on satellite and cable networks.

Rarely does an imported U.S. series appear among the Top 50 programs in any given week. In general, American series tend to attract fairly small audiences. The reason is simple—the British prefer to watch British shows. U.S. films, on the other hand, are popular and are shown on all the networks.

So, what U.S. series do you find on British TV? In 2004, BBC2's slate included comedies ("Malcolm in the Middle" and "My Wife and Kids") and drama ("Kingdom Hospital"). American fare dots the Channel 4 schedule. Among the U.S. comedies carried by Channel 4 in 2004 were "Friends", "Will & Grace," and "Sex and the City," while the network also aired such imported American dramas as "ER," "The O.C.," and "Without a Trace." Channel 5's American imports in 2004 included the dramas "CSI," "CSI: Miami," "Law and Order," and "Charmed," as well as major league baseball.

Although the overwhelming majority of imports are American, a number of Australian soaps have had successful runs on British television. The most successful have been "Neighbors," which airs on BBC1, and "Home and Away," on Channel 5 since 2001. "Home and Away" was a staple on ITV1 for many years before it was canceled by that network and picked up by Channel 5.

Exports

Britain can boast of healthy TV exports, trailing only the United States in annual sales. In 2002, sales of British programming amounted to $666 million, up 6.6% over sales in 2001, according to the British Television Distributors Association ("Better . . .," 2003). The wildlife documentary "Bug World," which sold to 72 countries, was the biggest seller in 2002. Big-selling dramas included "A Touch of Frost," "Taggart," and "Rebus." Three children's programs that sold well internationally were "Bob the Builder," "Teletubbies," and "Worst Witch." One market where British program sales soared was the United States; sales were up 16.4% in 2002.

The United States imports a minuscule percentage of its programming compared to most countries, but nearly all of what American networks import is British. British programming is ubiquitous on PBS and plays a prominent role in the schedules of other networks, including A&E, Comedy Central, and Discovery. American fans of British programming can get round-the-clock British fare on BBC America, a satellite-cable network with relatively small distribution.

Although American viewers have had access to a wide range of British programming in its original form, a much broader avenue of influence in recent years has been through the reformatting of nonfictional British series and the reversioning of British fictional programs.

The early years of the 21st century have seen a flood of British shows being reformatted for American audiences, ranging from TLC's enormously popular home makeover series "Trading Spaces," based on the British "Changing Rooms," to Fox's smash hit "American Idol," based on the British format "Pop Idol." The range of reformatted programs is vast, comprising game shows such as "Who Wants To Be a Millionaire?" (ABC, 1999–2002), "The Weakest Link" (NBC, 2001–2002) and "Don't Forget Your Toothbrush" (Comedy Central, 2000), light entertainment programs such as "Whose Line Is It Anyway?" (ABC, 1998–2004), and lifestyle programs such as "What Not to Wear" (TLC, 2003–present).

The reversioning of British series is hardly a new concept. In fact, three comedy classics were reversioned. The CBS series "All in the Family" (1971–1983) was based on BBC's "Till Death Do Us Part." NBC's "Sanford and Son" (1972–1977) was a reversioning of the BBC series "Steptoe and Son." The ABC series "Three's Company" (1977–1984) was derived from ITV's "Man About the House."

What was a rare phenomenon picked up pace in the mid- to late-1990s and has become increasingly common. The Bill Cosby sitcom "Cosby," which aired on CBS for four seasons beginning in fall 1996, was a reversioning of the British series "One Foot in the Grave." NBC's "Men Behaving Badly," based on the British sitcom of the same name, also debuted in fall 1996 and lasted for a season and a half. In fall 1997, ITV police series "Cracker" was reversioned for U.S. television, airing on ABC for just one season. In spring 1999, CBS aired "Payne," a remake of the British comedy classic "Fawlty Towers." Eight episodes aired. A reversioning of the ITV comedy drama "Cold Feet" debuted in fall 1999 on NBC, but was canceled after just four episodes.

In the new millennium, reversionings of British comedies and dramas are becoming more frequent on U.S. television, although most have been short-lived. "Dotcomedy" was a midseason replacement on ABC in the

2000–2001 season, but the remake of a Channel 4 series was quickly canceled. Another flop reversioning was an NBC lawyer drama called "First Years," a 2001 midseason replacement that lasted just three episodes. "First Years" was a remake of "This Life," a popular BBC2 series. UPN carried a reversioning of a Channel 4 comedy called "As If" in March 2002. "As If" was canceled after just two episodes.

The reversioning trend shows no signs of letting up. A remake of the racy BBC2 sitcom "Coupling" aired on NBC in 2003–2004 but was canceled after just four episodes. In spring 2004, USA Network launched "Touching Evil," a police drama based on an ITV1 series of the same name. NBC scheduled a remake of the offbeat comedy "The Office" for 2004–2005.

British series occasionally get remade for other markets. For example, a Chinese version of the ITV1 soap "Coronation Street" called "Joy Luck Street" began airing in 2000.

RADIO

Radio remains a vibrant medium in the United Kingdom, attracting 43.6 million listeners a week ("BBC Radio 1 . . .," 2003). The BBC operates five national radio services; each has a different personality. BBC Radio 1 is a youth-oriented music service. BBC Radio 2, the nation's most widely listened-to station, with an audience of 13 million weekly, is a talk-based network targeting adults 35 and older; Radio 2's "Today" is a highly influential current affairs program that is something of a national institution. BBC Radio 3 is a classical music service. BBC Radio 4 offers a diverse slate of programming that ranges from news and current affairs to comedy and drama. BBC Radio 5 Live is a news and sports talk network. Since 2002, the BBC has launched a raft of digital networks, starting with the music network 6 Music. Digital network BBC 7 focuses on comedy and drama, whereas BBC Asian Networks caters to listeners who are ethnic Asians, and 1Xtra focuses on Black music. In addition to the national radio services, the BBC operates 12 local radio stations.

Private radio began in 1973. Classic FM, Virgin Radio, TalkSport, and Teamtalk operate national commercial services. There are also regional and local commercial stations. By 2002, the United Kingdom had 257 analog commercial radio stations and 35 digital commercial stations. A unique dimension of British radio is that the most listened-to commercial station is a classical service—Classic FM.

The BBC enjoys a key advantage over its commercial competitors through its preeminence on the FM band: 59% of the FM spectrum is allocated to the BBC ("Listening . . .," 2002). Just as in British radio, the public broadcaster plays a prominent role in the country's television.

REFERENCES

BBC Radio 1 loses listeners. (2003, July 31). BBC News. Available: www.news.bbc.co.uk/1/
    hi/entertainment/tv_and_radio/3110667.stm

Better year for overseas TV sales in 2002. (2003, March 19). British Television Distributors Association. http://www.btda.org/

Britain a nation of TV addicts. (2001, November 22). *The Guardian.* Retrieved from http://www.guardian.co.uk/Archive/Article/0,4273,4304569,00.html

Channel overview. (2002, December 20). *Broadcast,* p. 26.

Central Intelligence Agency. (2002). *The world factbook 2002.* Retrieved from http://www.cia.gov/cia/publications/factbook/print/uk.html

Cowell, A. (2003, April 11). BSkyB: Big gains on big gambles. *The New York Times.* Retrieved from http://www.nytimes.com/2003/04/11/business/11SKY.html

Digital TV marches on. (2003, June 24). BBC News. http://news.bbc.co.uk/1/hi/entertainment/tv_and_radio/3016630.stm

Elstein, D. (2002, May 10). Where did it go wrong for DTT? *Broadcast,* p. 19.

"Emmerdale" celebrates 30 Years. (2002, October 16). BBC News. http://news.bbc.co.uk/1/hi/entertainment/tv_and_radio/2333233.stm

Goldstein, N. (1991). *The history of television.* Godalming, Surrey, England: Colour Library Books.

Hastings, C. (2003, March 9). TV taste and decency in decline, say viewers: New report reveals that more than half the public believe there is too much sex, violence and bad language on screens. *Sunday Telegraph.* http://web.lexis-nexis.com/universe/document?_m=ee723b3440a2ba7d9070024cebc24...

History of the BBC—1930s. (2003). British Broadcasting Corporation. http://www.bbc.co.uk/cgi-bin/education/betsie/parser.pl

Listening for signs of life. (2002, March 22). *Broadcast,* p. 19.

Love conquers all on C4. (2001, September 7). *Broadcast,* p. 10.

Maxwell Caulfield, James Redmond and Suzanne Packer boost regular cast of Casualty as it comes of age. (2003, July 1). BBC press release. http://www.bbc.co.uk/pressoffice/pressreleases/stories/2003/07_july/01/casualty_series18.shtml

Sutcliffe, T. (2003, March 3). First night: It shrieked, whooped and jived, but can boys and girls pull an audience? *The Independent.* Retrieved from http://web.lexis-nexis/universe/document?_m=cb699740e231b6f1aadbc75cbccd23...

Tryhorn, C. (2003, July 31). Freeview connections soar. *MediaGuardian.* Retrieved from http://media.guardian.co.uk/bradcast/story/0,7493,1009215,00.html

Wells, M. (2003, December 31). Channel 4 audience dips below 10%. *Media Guardian.* Retrieved from http://media.guardian.co.uk/bradcast/story/0,7493,1114181,co.html

UNITED KINGDOM, PRIME TIME, AUGUST 4–10, 2003

MONDAY						
Channel	7 p.m.	7:30 p.m.	8 p.m.	8:30 p.m.	9 p.m.	9:30 p.m.
BBC1	The Human Senses: Balance (science)	Real Story With Fiona Bruce (current affairs)	EastEnders (soap)	Ground Force America (garden)	Spooks (drama)	
ITV1	Emmerdale (soap)	Coronation Street (soap)	Tonight With Trevor McDonald (current affairs)	**You Only Live Twice** (U.S. film)		
BBC2	6:30 p.m.: **The New Adventures of Superman** (U.S. drama)	Design Rules (home)	Mastermind (game)	University Challenge (game)	Dead Ringers (sketch comedy)	Two Pints of Lager and a Packet of Crisps (comedy)

Channel 4	Channel 4 News	Today at the Test (sports)	The Oldest Mummies in the World (documentary)		Machines That Time Forgot (history)	
Channel 5	five News	Angel (drama)		Three to Tango (film)		

TUESDAY

Channel	7 p.m.	7:30 p.m.	8 p.m.	8:30 p.m.	9 p.m.	9:30 p.m.
BBC1	Airport (documentary)	EastEnders (soap)	Holby City (drama)		The Eustace Bros. (drama)	
ITV1	Emmerdale (soap)	Carol Vorderman's Better Homes (home)	Package Holiday Undercover (travel)	Don't Drop the Coffin (documentary)	Hotels from Hell (documentary)	
BBC2	6:45 p.m.: Star Trek: The Next Generation (drama)	Your Money or Your Life (business)	Fred Dibhah's Age of Steam (history)	Every Home Should Have One (history)	Journeys to the Bottom of the Sea (documentary)	
Channel 4	Channel 4 News		House Trapped (documentary)		That'll Teach 'Em (documentary)	
Channel 5	five news	The Naked Pilgrim: The Road to Santiago (travel)	Stonehenge: The True Story (history)		CSI: Miami (drama)	

WEDNESDAY

Channel	7 p.m.	7:30 p.m.	8 p.m.	8:30 p.m.	9 p.m.	9:30 p.m.
BBC1	Wildlife on One (nature)	Changing Rooms (home)	Fame Academy II (reality)		Holby City (drama)	
ITV1	Emmerdale (soap)	Coronation Street (soap)	The Bill (drama)		Die Hard (film)	
BBC2	6:45 p.m.: Star Trek: The Next Generation (drama)	Homeground (documentary)	The Joy of Home (home)	How I Made My Property Fortune (documentary)	What Are You Staring At? (documentary)	
Channel 4	Channel 4 News		Other People's Houses (home)		ER (drama)	
Channel 5	five news	Weapons of World War II (history)	Ark Royal (documentary)		World War I in Colour (history)	

THURSDAY

Channel	7 p.m.	7:30 p.m.	8 p.m.	8:30 p.m.	9 p.m.	9:30 p.m.
BBC1	Bargain Hunt (game)	EastEnders (soap)	DIY SOS (home)	U.K.'s Worst: Taxis (documentary)	Traffic Cops (documentary)	
ITV1	Emmerdale (soap)	Flying Through Time (history)	The Bill (drama)		Bad Girls (drama)	
BBC2	Malcolm in the Middle	Science Shack (science)	Ray Mears's Extreme Survival (travel)		Horizon (nature)	
Channel 4	Channel 4 News		No. 57: The History of a House (home)		Arnold Schwarzenegger: Made in Britain (biography)	

Channel 5	five news	Life Doctor (lifestyle)	House Doctor (home)	What Women Want (relationship)	A Mind To Kill (drama)	

FRIDAY

Channel	7 p.m.	7:30 p.m.	8 p.m.	8:30 p.m.	9 p.m.	9:30 p.m.
BBC1	This Is Your Life (light entertainment)	Top of the Pops (music)	EastEnders (soap)	My Hero (sitcom)	Athletics (sports)	
ITV1	Emmerdale (soap)	Coronation Street (soap)	Tonight With Trevor McDonald (current affairs)	A Touch of Frost (drama)		
BBC2	Athletics (sports)				Restoration (home)	
Channel 4	Channel 4 News		World Rally: Finland (sports)	Grand Slam (game)	**Will & Grace** (comedy)	**Scrubs** (comedy)
Channel 5	five news	The History of British Sculpture With Loyd Grossman (fine arts)	Seven Wonders of the Ancient World (documentary)		Getaway (film)	

SATURDAY

Channel	7 p.m.	7:30 p.m.	8 p.m.	8:30 p.m.	9 p.m.	9:30 p.m.
BBC1	6:25 p.m.: Fame Academy II (reality)	The National Lottery: Winning Lines (game)	8:15 p.m.: Fame Academy II (reality)	8:40 p.m.: BBC News	The Beach (film)	
ITV1	6:15 p.m.: Pop Idol: One Year On (reality)	7:15 p.m.: Pop Idol (reality)	8:15 p.m.: The Vault (game)		9:15 p.m.: Being Simon Cowell (biography)	
BBC2	The BBC Proms 2003 (music)				9:15 p.m.: The Tenant of Wildfell Hall (drama miniseries)	
Channel 4	Channel 4 News	7:15 p.m.: World Rally: Finland (sports)	7:45 p.m.: 4Dance (fine arts)	8:15 p.m.: Witness: God Bless Ibiza (documentary)	Ed TV (film)	
Channel 5	6:55 p.m.: five news	7:15 p.m.: **Charmed** (drama)		8:10 p.m.: **High School Reunion** (reality)	CSI (drama)	

SUNDAY

Channel	7 p.m.	7:30 p.m.	8 p.m.	8:30 p.m.	9 p.m.	9:30 p.m.
BBC1	7:10 p.m.: In Search of the Brontes (biography)		Earthride (nature)		Roger Roger (comedy-drama)	

ITV1	6:30 p.m.: Survival Special (nature)	Coronation Street (soap)	Where the Heart Is (drama)	Midsomer Murders (drama)
BBC2		7:10 p.m.: America: Beyond the Colour Line (documentary)	The Best of Top Gear (sports)	Crowded Skies (documentary)
Channel 4	Channel 4 News	Some of My Best Friends Are... Catholic (religion)	Gods in the Sky (science)	Dispatches (current affairs)
Channel 5	6:05 p.m.: **Angels in the Outfield** (U.S. film)		Science of Shark Attacks (nature)	**Any Given Sunday** (U.S. film) (to 12)

Note. **Bold** denotes imported program.

Germany

Klaus Forster
Thomas Knieper
University of Munich

ABOUT GERMANY

The Federal Republic of Germany consists of 16 *Bundesländer* (federal states). Among them are larger states like Bavaria and North Rhine-Westphalia; smaller states like Saxony and Saarland; the city states of Berlin, Bremen, and Hamburg; and nine others: Baden-Wuerttemberg, Brandenburg, Hesse, Lower Saxony, Mecklenburg-Western Pomerania, Rhineland-Palatinate, Saxony-Anhalt, Schleswig-Holstein, and Thuringia. The country has a population of 82.5 million. Germany, located between the North Sea and the Baltic Sea in the north and the Alps in the south, borders on nine neighboring states.

Germany is a democratic federal republic, with the federal president as head of state and the federal chancellor as head of government. The federal president is elected by the Federal Convention, which consists of all members of the *Bundestag* (parliament) and an equal number of members elected by the parliaments of the federal states. The Bundestag, as the parliament of the federal republic, elects the chancellor. Elections to the Bundestag are held every 4 years. The country is a member state of the European Union and the European Monetary Union. Germany had a gross domestic product of Euro 1,989.70 billion in 2002. The economy consists of a wide variety of production industries, agriculture, and services (Federal Statistical Office Germany, 2003).

BROADCAST BACKGROUND

For a long time German television was organized solely in public corporations, which resemble in some ways the British BBC (see chapter 3), but differ in at least two important aspects: decentralized structure and corporate model (Diller, 1999; Humphreys, 1994; Kutsch, 1999; Stuiber, 1998). To explain these differences, we have to take a closer look at the history of German television.

History

In the post-World War I Weimar Republic (1919–1933), what looked like a multitude of regional radio broadcasters under private law was, in fact, in many ways a centralized and state-dominated system (Humphreys, 1994; Stuiber, 1998). State domination and centralization of broadcasting was made almost complete in two subsequent broadcasting reforms in 1926 and 1932 (Stuiber, 1998). Thus when the Nazis seized power, the whole broadcasting system could easily be brought under the central control of Goebbels' ministry of propaganda (Humphreys, 1994).

After Germany's defeat in World War II, the United States and Great Britain would not permit state-controlled broadcasting (Tonnemacher, 2003). However, private (commercial) broadcasting requires a developed advertising industry and a certain degree of spending power by the consumers, which did not exist in the aftermath of World War II (Tonnemacher, 2003). Moreover, industry's close ties to the government and army of Hitler's Third Reich largely disqualified it as a source of capital for broadcasting in the public interest. Furthermore, the "public's distaste for powerful media owners" (Nerone, 1995, p. 80) was a factor in the United States. For these reasons and a scarcity of frequencies, no commercial radio and television existed in the Federal Republic of Germany until 1984.

Instead, the British BBC served in many aspects as a blueprint for the German broadcasting corporations, at first of course in the British occupation zone. The underlying principles of this organizational form departed completely from the Weimar broadcasting tradition (Kutsch, 1999). The new broadcasters were established as "non-profitmaking, self-administered 'corporations governed under public law'" (Humphreys, 1994, p. 139). But whereas the British military government established a single centralized broadcasting corporation, the North West German Broadcasting

Service (NWDR), the American Office of Military Government in Germany, U.S. (OMGUS) followed a federalist approach with one broadcasting corporation for each of the four German states in the U.S.-occupied zone (Bavaria, Bremen, Hesse, Wuerttemberg-Baden); the "Americans considered federalism to be self-evidently a superior system, while the British and French were in many respects unrepentant centralizers" (Humphreys, 1994, p. 129).

After the end of the Allied military government, the decentralized federal model was applied in West Germany. In East Germany, controlled by the Communist Union of Soviet Socialist Republics, a Communist state-owned broadcasting system was institutionalized—which vanished with the 1990 German reunification. Until 1984 broadcasting corporations under public law and public control were the only providers of TV and radio programs in Western Germany (Stuiber, 1998). In this system, control of broadcasting is in the hands of delegates from "socially significant groups" (Humphreys, 1994, p. 6) such as trade unions, industry, political parties, churches, and environmental groups.

The First TV Ruling of the German Federal Constitutional Court (Humphreys, 1994) did not outlaw privately owned commercial broadcasting, but a shortage of frequencies and means of financing kept German broadcasting as a public system (Herrmann, 1994; Stuiber, 1998). From 1984, with commercial support and more frequencies available through broadband cable networks, Germany developed the dual broadcasting system that it has today (Humphreys, 1994; Stuiber, 1998).

Technical Aspects

The analog signal of the terrestrial broadcasters uses the PAL transmission standard. In 2002 Germany had more than 33 million TV homes. As of January 1, 2002, only 8.8% of German TV homes received the traditional analog terrestrial signal, while 36.1% of the TV homes had satellite reception and a majority (55.1%) received television via cable (Media Perspektiven, 2002). Digital services are growing slowly. In 2001, only about 7% of German cable TV homes had digital television service (Media Perspektiven, 2002). With ARD-digital, ZDF.vision, and BR-alpha (the digital service of the Bavarian Broadcasting Corporation), the public broadcasters are getting ready for the digital age (ALM, 2001).

BROADCAST REGULATION

The German public broadcasting system and its federal structure is a heritage of the Allied military government (Humphreys, 1994; Stuiber, 1998) and a result of the interpretation of the constitution of the Federal Republic of Germany, the Basic Law, through the Federal Constitutional Court. As broadcasting is seen as part of culture, it is subject to "the cultural jurisdiction of the states" (Humphreys, 1994, p. 53), not the federal government

(Herrmann, 1994). Broadcasting in more than one German state has to be regulated through "inter-state treaties" (Humphreys, 1994, p. 139). In the case of nationwide broadcasters, all German states have to sign such a treaty.

After reunification, as of August 31, 1991, the State Treaty Concerning Broadcasting in the United Germany (Humphreys, 1994), which replaced the numerous interstate treaties, contained all regulations on broadcasting (Stuiber, 1998). Since then, this legal basis for broadcasting in Germany had been modified six times (Tonnemacher, 2003), with a seventh alteration in progress (Stuiber, 2002).

The German public broadcasting corporations are accountable to the public through broadcasting councils, as previously noted, "composed of representatives autonomously chosen by the so-called 'socially significant groups'" (Humphreys, 1994, p. 130). Despite differences between the various state broadcasting corporations and the other public service broadcasters, in view of parliamentary and political influence on the supervisory boards, similarities prevail (Stuiber, 1998). The broadcasting council elects the head of the broadcasting corporation, a director general, who is "responsible for program arrangements and the entire operation of the corporation" (Humphreys, 1994, p. 143).

The public broadcasting corporations are funded mainly through an annual license fee that Germans pay and to a lesser extent through commercials (Stuiber, 1998). In 2002, the fee consisted of a radio or basic fee of 5.32 Euro per month and an additional TV fee of 10.83 Euro per month (Media Perspektiven, 2002).

As of 1984, as noted earlier, numerous licenses have been given to privately owned commercial broadcasters. The licenses are issued by the state media authorities, which are "the regulatory bodies of the private sector" (Humphreys, 1994). These authorities have, in many ways, a structure similar to the public broadcasting corporations (Stuiber, 1998). Instead of the Broadcasting Councils we find, for example, Media Councils, which are constituted along the same lines as the supervisory bodies of the public corporations.

According to the German constitution every person is allowed to express his or her personal opinion freely. This freedom of expression applies to the mass media as well. There is no governmental "pre-censorship" (Herrmann, 1994, p. 126) in Germany. However, some restrictions on content in broadcasting exist. These restrictions are normally enforced by the regulatory bodies mentioned above and in some cases by legal action before a court. The limits of the freedom of broadcasting are defined by general laws, laws for the protection of youth, and laws against libel. Therefore it is not allowed to broadcast content which violates someone's personal rights, spurs on racial hatred, glorifies violence, or shows pornography. Furthermore, it is prohibited to broadcast content which is considered to have a negative influence on the moral development of young people, does not respect moral or religious beliefs of others, or is aimed against the constitution (Herrmann, 1994).

Interestingly, German regulatory boards are far more concerned with violence than with sex. Sam Raimi's *Evil Dead* and Tobe Hooper's *Texas Chainsaw Massacre* had been banned for years, but no longer are. By contrast, no regulatory board in Germany said anything against *Basic Instinct.*

BROADCAST CONTENT AND RATINGS

The public service broadcasters, the only TV and radio program providers in the Federal Republic of Germany for more than 30 years, still play an important and vital role in the German TV and radio market. ARD and ZDF have been in existence for more than 50 years.

"The First" German Television (ARD)

The *Arbeitsgemeinschaft der öffentlich-rechtlichen Rundfunkanstalten der Bundesrepublik Deutschland* (ARD) or the Association of Public Broadcasting Corporations in West Germany, was founded in 1950 and consisted initially of the six public broadcasting corporations established during the Allied occupation. From 1950 on, the *Nordwestdeutscher Rundfunk* (NWDR) experimented with TV signals (Diller, 1999; Stuiber, 1998). In 1952, the date seen as the official beginning of West German television, the NWDR started the first TV service on a regular basis.

To take advantage of economies of scale, ARD in 1954 started the first nationwide TV programming as "a common television channel on a cooperative basis" (Humphreys, 1994, p. 151) called *Erstes Deutsches Fernsehen* (First German Television). Today the ARD has 10 public broadcasters as members and still produces one of the major nationwide TV programs now called *"Das Erste"* ("The First"; ARD, 2003, p. 203), which is aimed at a mainstream audience. (See program grid.)

In some aspects, "The First's" programming reflects the initial political assumption in Germany that the three major tasks of television are education, information, and entertainment. However, this idealistic conception is, of course, not sufficient to describe the actual program content (Ludes, 1999). Nevertheless, this thinking exemplifies the concept of public broadcasting as a *Vollprogramm* ("whole program"; Stuiber, 1998), which still influences the programming strategies in Germany not only in the public broadcasting sector (Anschütz, 1999).

In the case of "The First" (ARD), a significant departure of the initial concept can be seen in the area of education. The closest category is "culture and science," which had a total share of only 5.5% in 2001 (Media Perspektiven, 2002). The lack of educational programs in the main public channels was originally counterbalanced by the Third Programs, but since the early 1970s the proportion of educational programs has been reduced there as well (Stuiber, 1998). Informational programs, which include all kinds of broadcast journalism, had only slightly less than a 50% share of the total program time in 2002 in ARD (Weiss & Trebbe, 2003, p. T92).

The entertainment section in ARD had a share of about 37% of the total program time in 2002 (Weiss & Trebbe, 2003). For whatever reasons, the most popular entertainment shows on ARD are so-called *Volksmusik* concerts, which have only little in common with traditional German music, but attracted up to 6.3 million viewers in 2002 with a audience share of over 22% (Darschin & Gerhard, 2003). One explanation might be the audience structure according to age groups. Over 19% of the viewers of ARD were older than 50 in 2002 (ARD, 2003).

In fictional entertainment, the front runner in the main ARD program is a crime series named *"Tatort"* (Crime Scene). The series is a coproduction of the ARD, the Austrian public broadcaster ORF, and the Swiss broadcasting corporation SF (until 2001). It is filmed on different German, Austrian, and Swiss locations with changing but regularly reappearing teams of police investigators. With its origins in 1970, the series still got top ratings in 2002, with more than 7.8 million viewers and an audience share of over 23% (Darschin & Gerhard, 2003). Despite lower ratings, the first weekly German soap opera, called *"Lindenstrasse"* (Linden Street), is noteworthy as well. In 1985 this new type of drama series was established with the deliberate decision that the protagonists had to resemble the look and appearance of ordinary people (Ludes, 1999).

A variety of national and international movies are shown as well on the ARD channel. They are mostly placed after prime time and they are seldom blockbusters. Their share of total airtime was about 12% in 2002. TV movies had an additional share of about 8% (Weiss & Trebbe, 2003). Recapitulating, ARD is still an influential programmer with a total audience share in prime time of slightly less than 15% in 2002 (Media Perspektiven, 2002).

The Second German Television (ZDF)

Shortly after ARD had been established in 1954, a debate about a second TV channel began (Stuiber, 1998). When the federal government under Chancellor Konrad Adenauer tried to create a new broadcasting corporation at the federal level, the German states brought suit against the so-called "Adenauer TV" (Humphreys, 1994, p. 159). In its judgment, the Federal Constitutional Court ruled against the federal government; broadcasting remained the responsibility of the German states (Herrmann, 1994). This First TV Ruling of the Federal Constitutional Court is seen as the Magna Carta of the German broadcasting system (Herrmann, 1994; Humphreys, 1994). The prime ministers of the German states cooperated to create *Zweites Deutsches Fernsehen* (ZDF) or the Second German Television through a state treaty (Stuiber, 1998). Similar to the broadcasting corporations in the German states, ZDF is a public corporation, but has more political party influence in the supervisory board (Humphreys, 1994).

The ZDF was the second most prominent German TV channel until 1984; after 1984, despite private competition, it still garnered an audience share of 14% to 17% in prime time 2002 (Media Perspektiven, 2002). Conceived to have general appeal, like ARD (ALM, 2001), the share of genuine educational programming (culture and science and children and youth) was up to 18% of the total program output in 2001 (Media Perspektiven, 2002).The information sector in general had a share of over 55% of hours in 2002 (Weiss & Trebbe, 2003), whereas entertainment had about 30% in 2002 (Weiss & Trebbe, 2003).

The most popular game show in German television is "*Wetten, dass . . .?*" (Would You Bet on It?) with over 13 million viewers and a total audience share of over 45% in 2002. In this program, national and international celebrities like Naomi Campbell or Ozzy Osbourne bet on whether or not ordinary people can succeed at amazing tasks like balancing an automobile on top of wine glasses. The host of the show is Thomas Gottschalk, a former teacher and radio DJ and today one of the most successful German TV personalities. The ZDF version of the inevitable sentimental music show is "*Melodien für Millionen*" (Melodies for Millions) with an audience share of over 16% in 2002 and more than 5.7 million viewers.

The most popular fictional entertainment on the ZDF in 2002 was the romantic drama series "Rosamunde Pilcher," named after the popular author, with more than a 21% audience share and over 6.8 million viewers, followed by two crime series with audience shares of nearly 20%, and a romantic drama series "*Das Traumschiff*" (The Dreamship) with an audience share of over 18% (Darschin & Gerhard, 2003). Movies and TV movies account for about 14% (Weiss & Trebbe, 2003).

The Third Programs

In addition to "The First" television program, the members of the ARD produce seven so-called "Third Programs," which are mainly aimed at the audiences in the original transmission areas of each public broadcaster (e.g., the Third Program of the Bavarian Broadcasting Corp. is aimed at Bavarian viewers), but through cable and satellite, the transmission areas have been largely extended (Tonnemacher, 2003). Originally conceived as educational programs, they now air nearly the same mix of shows, series, newscasts, and movies as the two main public service programs, with a little more weight on regional topics and characteristics (Stuiber, 1998; Tonnemacher, 2003).

Joint Offerings of ARD, ZDF and Third Parties

In addition to the two main nationwide schedules of public broadcasters ARD and ZDF, Germans can view cooperative productions. Since 1984 the channel 3sat (terrestrial, cable, and satellite) has aired productions of four German-language broadcasters: ARD and ZDF, as well as the Swiss and Austrian broadcasting corporations. The offerings are a general-appeal typical mix of information and entertainment, but the audience share is quite low (Stuiber, 1998; ARD, 2003).

A peculiarity is the European culture channel ARTE, on air since 1992 (via satellite and cable). A joint venture of ARD, ZDF, and the French ARTE Corp., it offers four theme-night programs that focus on one issue the whole evening. Due to its intellectual style, the audience share is minimal (Stuiber, 1998; ARD, 2003).

The children's channel KI.KA had a respectable audience share of more than 10% in 2002 in the age group from 3 to 13 years (ARD, 2003) despite the fact that it only can be received via cable and satellite. A joint venture of ARD and ZDF, it airs fictional series, cartoons, some informational magazines, and a children's newscast (Stuiber, 1998; ARD, 2003).

The fourth common provider, likewise an ARD/ZDF (cable and satellite) venture, is the event and documentary channel Phoenix, which had a low audience share of only a half percent in 2002 (Stuiber, 1998; ARD, 2003). The newest ARD/ZDF joint venture is international German TV.

Commercial Broadcasting

Although the beginning of commercial broadcasting in Germany was in 1984 (Stuiber, 1998), in 1986 the Federal Constitutional Court provided for the first time a "legal basis for a deregulated private commercial sector" (Humphreys, 1994, p. 257). In its Fourth TV Judgment, also known as the Lower Saxony Judgment, the court proposed a dual broadcasting system in which commercial and public broadcasters could operate side by side (Stuiber, 1998). The public broadcasting corporations "would remain responsible for providing the basic broadcasting services to the whole of the population and fulfilling their classical public service duties" (Humphreys, 1994, pp. 255), while commercial broadcasters could operate their stations with lower requirements with regard to diversity of program content demanded by the Basic Law (Herrmann, 1994). Given this legal basis to produce mainly entertainment-oriented programs, the commercial stations did just that.

Only a couple of years after the Fourth TV Judgment of the Federal Constitutional Court, the new broadcasting landscape took shape. The most influential players in the newly established broadcasting market could be easily identified by their sales figures. The two main competitors in the commercial marketplace are the RTL-Group and the Pro7-SAT.1 Media Joint Stock Company.

The RTL-Group. The main shareholder of the Radio TV Luxembourg (RTL) Group is the Bertelsmann Joint Stock Co. The most successful station of the group is RTL, which had an audience share in prime time of about 15% in 2002 (Media Perspektiven, 2002). Its information programs took about 33% of the total programming time in 2002 (Weiss & Trebbe, 2003), but it has to be noted that in this category fall not only newscasts, but also infotainment shows (with a clear emphasis on the "tainment" and not on the "info"). For instance, talk shows in the Oprah style, which formerly accounted for a large share in the information category, are being replaced by "informative" court programs in which real judges, state attorneys, and lawyers wrestle with somewhat implausible cases and often tongue-tied laymen in the name of TV justice (Brunst, 2002).

True information, the RTL prime time newscast, had an audience share of nearly 19% in 2002. The magazine *"Explosiv,"* with mostly soft news and human interest stories, had an even bigger share of more than 21%. Furthermore, two renowned political print magazines present their TV versions on RTL. Human interest stories on *"Stern TV,"* with the second most popular TV host Günther Jauch (interestingly, a former colleague of Thomas Gottschalk) garnered an audience share of 15%. The political magazine *"Spiegel TV"* had a share of nearly 10% in 2002 (Darschin & Gerhard, 2003).

Entertainment took about 38% of the airtime of RTL in 2002 (Weiss & Trebbe, 2003). The viewers' favorite game shows are both hosted by Günther Jauch: The German edition of "Who Wants to Be a Millionaire?" (see chapter 15) with the second largest total audience share in 2002 of 30% and over 9 million viewers, and the "SKL-Show" in sixth place with a nearly 19% share and nearly 6 million viewers.

Very popular on RTL, with an audience share of over 21% in 2002, was "The 80s Show" in which a somehow ironic look back at a divided Germany in the 1980s is presented. German comedy series such as *"Die Camper"* and *"Ritas Welt"* score high with an audience share of up to 21%. German crime series are also quite successful on RTL with up to nearly a 19% market share (Darschin & Gerhard, 2003). It is interesting that the share of movies in the total airtime of RTL is quite low. In 2002 most fictional entertainment consisted of TV series, where the amount of German productions dominates (Weiss & Trebbe, 2003).

Successful imports, with mostly U.S. origins, include "Beverly Hills, 90210" and "South Park," but overall RTL has a distinctly German program structure. An exception is the Hollywood movies frequently aired on RTL like *The Green Mile*, with over 7.3 million viewers in 2002 (Gerhards & Klingler, 2003).

The second most popular channel of the RTL Group is RTL II. It had an audience share of 3.9% in 2002 (Media Perpektiven, 2002). No top rated programs are on this channel, but it was the broadcaster that premiered the notorious "Big Brother" show in 2000; since then it aired, in part in cooperation with its sister broadcaster RTL, in subsequent seasons with originally impressive but then steadily dropping ratings (Gustedt, 2002). Basically conceived of as an entertainment channel, the share of informational programs is quite low and the number of international productions as well as movies is relatively high (Weiss & Trebbe, 2003). Among the more successful programs are the sci/fi series "Stargate" and "Andromeda" and the 2003 premier of "24" in Germany, but also a variety of international movies. Because of animated cartoons of mostly Japanese origin, RTL II is quite popular among children.

VOX had an audience share of 3.3% in 2002 (Media Perspektiven, 2002). It got a boost by airing "Ally McBeal," which was at first a flop, but after a better programmed rerun of the first season, the series finally succeeded in Germany. The information section of the channel is twice as large as the informational programming on RTL II with nearly 20% of the total airtime in 2002 (Weiss & Trebbe, 2003). This percent may be due to the original concept of the broadcaster as a kind of commercial culture channel, but not much of this concept is left. Series and movies make the most of the fictional entertainment with a fair number of international productions like "C.S.I." (Weiss & Trebbe, 2003).

Every Thursday night, the last remains of the somewhat anarchistic early days of German commercial broadcasting can be observed. After 1984, the young commercial stations tried to provoke attention by any and all means, so they used sex to attract audiences. Disguised as a game show, in which not even the host could explain the rules, "Tutti Frutti" mainly exposed bare breasts and paved the way for a variety of program formats with more or less sexually explicit content and various grades of quality. Like "Tutti Frutti," which was cancelled after only a short time (Brunst, 2002), all of these shows and magazines have long ago disappeared—even those appreciated by some media critics, like *"Liebe Sünde"* (Love Sin). The only exception is *"Wa(h)re Liebe"* (a pun meaning "True Love," as well as "Love for Sale" when the bracketed "h" is omitted), an erotic magazine/talk show on VOX. In the show, various topics related to sexuality and erotica are presented, hosted by cross-dresser Lilo Wanders. After 20 years of commercial broadcasting in Germany, it is quite obvious that, despite the common saying, sex does not sell so well in a competitive TV market in which the broadcasters have to aim at mass audiences and to provide optimal advertising environments.

Together with the family channel Super RTL, the RTL-Group had an audience share of nearly 25% in 2002, making it the commercial broadcaster with the biggest market share in German television (Media Persepektiven, 2002).

The Pro7-SAT.1 Media-Joint Stock Company.

The Pro7-SAT.1 Media-Joint Stock Company. The broadcasting group around the two channels Pro7 and SAT 1 originally belonged to the KirchMedia Co. which went insolvent in 2002 under the weight of a giant debt of more than 9 billion Euro (Gustedt, 2002). KirchMedia was founded by Leo Kirch, one of the most prominent personalities in German commercial broadcasting. After the retreat of Leo Kirch from all business operations, the new chairman of Pro7-SAT.1 Media is the U.S. entrepreneur Haim Saban. He took over not only two of the most successful commercial stations but inherited as well the role of the main competitor of the RTL-Group and Bertelsmann.

SAT.1 is, after RTL, the second commercial channel with an audience share of 10% in 2002. No shows and only one informational magazine of SAT.1 were among the top-rated programs in 2002. SAT.1 still has a share of over 10% with its prime time newscast (Darschin & Gerhard, 2003).

The share of both its entertainment and informational programs is about 30% each. The dominant fictional entertainment genre is the TV series; only a small number of movies are shown. As with RTL, in 2002 SAT.1 has a distinct German program profile; over 45% of all productions are German. Most other programs were produced in the United States (Weiss & Trebbe, 2003). As the self-designated "Star Trek" channel, it airs the spin-offs "Deep Space Nine," "Voyager," and "Enterprise," and regularly the "Star Trek" movies; the original series and the "Next Generation" now show on sister broadcaster Cable 1. Distinct characteristics of SAT.1 are its court shows and its real-life "Doku Series" in the afternoon as well as the "Harald Schmidt Show," a Jay Leno/David Letterman style late-night talk show. This show is often applauded as the most intelligent contemporary TV entertainment in Germany. At the end of 2003, Harald Schmidt announced he would take a creative sabbatical in 2004, and it is uncertain if he will return to SAT.1 at a later date.

Pro7 is the German movie and TV series channel. It had a total audience share of 7% in 2002. Its prime time newscast had a share of under 5% in 2001, which indicates that Pro7 is not a channel for an information-oriented audience (Media Perspektiven, 2002). The informational programs had a share of nearly 30% in 2002, but magazines with soft news and talk shows dominate in this category. In entertainment, fictional programs are clearly in the lead, with movies and sitcoms dominating this sector. A majority of the programs shown on Pro7 in 2002 were produced in the United States (Weiss & Trebbe, 2003). Current productions like the "Buffy" spin-off "Angel," "Alias," "Sex and the City," or "Charmed" are shown regularly on Pro7, which was the channel on which "The X-Files" and "Buffy, the Vampire Slayer" premiered.

Cable 1 (Kabel 1) is the channel for reruns of series like "Star Trek," "The X-Files," or "Twin Peaks" and older movies. However, quite recently Cable 1 started airing some up-to-date shows like "Cold Case." It had an audience share of under 5% in 2002. Along with the newscaster N24, these are the four channels of Pro7-SAT.1 Media, with a total audience share of over 21% in 2002 (Media Perspektiven, 2002).

Others. The digital pay-TV broadcaster Premiere, which belonged to the Kirch Group, was in part responsible for the insolvency of its parent company, KirchMedia. It is now no longer a part of the Pro7-SAT.1 broadcasting family, in which it was counted until the demise of KirchMedia. The broadcaster is burdened with heavy financial losses and airs a wide variety of mostly international movies, TV series, and sports events on 28 digital channels, among them the German versions of SciFi and the Disney Channel.

There are numerous other programs available in German TV households, like the music channels MTV and VIVA, the sports channels DSF, which belonged originally to the Kirch Group, and Eurosport or the CNN affiliate and newscaster n-tv (Media Perspektiven, 2002), but they all have only a very limited audience share. Among these smaller stations is one interesting exception to the dominant TV business model of advertising: 9LIVE, financed mainly through telephone fees that are due when viewers participate in game shows via telephone, is surprisingly profitable (Gustedt, 2002).

BROADCAST IMPORTS AND EXPORTS

This chapter outlined the mainly U.S. imports that run on commercial television. Public broadcasters also import programming. On ZDF there are, for example, shows of national and international origin, including some blockbuster movies like *Notting Hill*, with over 7.8 million viewers in 2002 (Gerhards & Klingler, 2003). There is a fixed program window for mostly international movie productions on Monday nights after prime time, "*Montagskino*" (Monday's Cinema).

In the realm of exports, the newest joint venture of ARD and ZDF is German TV, airing since April 2002 and aimed at an international audience with the motto "Viewing What Germany Views." The programming consists of a variety of the contents of ARD, ZDF and DW-tv, the TV arm of Deutsche Welle (ARD, 2003).

The foreign channel DW-tv is aimed at an international audience to give a comprehensive picture of contemporary Germany. Deutsche Welle, Germany's external broadcaster, is a member of the ARD group (ARD, 2003; Tonnemacher, 2003).

REFERENCES

ALM, Arbeitsgemeinschaft der Landesmedienanstalten. (2001). *Programmbericht zur Lage und Entwicklung des Fernsehens in Deutschland 2000/01* [Program report on the state and the development of television in Germany 2000/01]. Konstanz: UVK.

Anschütz, U. (1999). Vollprogramme werden wichtiger [Whole programs are gaining in importance]. In H. Paukens & A. Schümchen. (Eds.), *Programmplanung—Konzepte und Strategien der Programmierung im deutschen Fernsehen* [Program planning: Concepts and strategies of programming in German television] (pp. 46–52). München: Fischer.

ARD, Arbeitsgemeinschaft der öffentlich-rechtlichen Rundfunkanstalten der Bundesrepublik Deutschland (2003). *ARD-Jahrbuch 03* [ARD-Yearbook 03]. Hamburg: Hans-Bredow-Institut.

Brunst, K. (2002). Von der Krönungsmesse bis zum TV-Duell. Ein Streifzug durch 50 Jahre deutsches Fernsehprogramm [From the coronation mass to the TV debate: Wanderings through 50 years of German television]. *tendenz. Magazin für Funk und Fernsehen der Bayerischen Landeszentrale für neue Medien, 4*, 20–23.

Darschin, W., & Gerhard, H. (2003). Tendenzen im Zuschauerverhalten. Fernsehgewohnheiten und Fernsehreichweiten im Jahr 2002 [Tendencies in people's viewing behavior: Viewing habits and audience shares in the year 2002]. *Media Perspektiven, 4,* 158–166.

Diller, A. (1999). Öffentlich-rechtlicher Rundfunk [Broadcasting under public law]. In J. Wilke (Ed.), *Mediengeschichte der Bundesrepublik Deutschland* [Media history of the Federal Republic of Germany] (pp. 146–166). Bonn: Bundeszentrale für politische Bildung.

Federal Statistical Office Germany. (2003). Available: www.destatis.de

Gerhards, M., & Kingler, W. (2003). Programmangebote und Spartennutzung im Fernsehen 2002. Analyse auf Basis der AGF/GfK Programmcodierung [Program offerings and viewing of program categories in television 2002: Analysis based on the AGF/GfK program coding]. *Media Perspektiven, 11*, 500–509.

Gustedt, V. (2002). 50 Jahre deutsches Fernsehen. Einmal Privatfernsehen . . . und zurück? [50 years of German television: One-way to commercial television . . . and back?]. *tendenz. Magazin für Funk und Fernsehen der Bayerischen Landeszentrale für neue Medien, 4,* 4–11.

Herrmann, G. (1994). *Rundfunkrecht. Fernsehen und Hörfunk mit Neuen Medien. Juristisches Kurzlehrbuch für Studium und Praxis* [Broadcasting law. Television and radio including new media. Brief legal textbook for studies and practice]. München: Beck.

Humphreys, P. J. (1994). *Media and media policy in Germany: The press and broadcasting since 1945* (2nd ed.). Oxford: Berg.

Kutsch, A. (1999). Rundfunk unter alliierter Besatzung [Broadcasting under allied occupation]. In J. Wilke (Ed.), *Mediengeschichte der Bundesrepublik Deutschland* [Media history of the Federal Republic of Germany] (pp. 59–90). Bonn: Bundeszentrale für politische Bildung.

Ludes, P. (1999). Programmgeschichte des Fernsehens [Program history of television]. In J. Wilke (Ed.), *Mediengeschichte der Bundesrepublik Deutschland* [Media history of the Federal Republic of Germany] (pp. 255–276). Bonn: Bundeszentrale für politische Bildung.

Media Perspektiven. (2002). *Basisdaten. Daten zur Mediensituation in Deutschland 2002* [Basic data: Facts about the situation of the media in Germany]. Frankfurt a.M.: Arbeitsgemeinschaft der ARD-Werbegesellschaften.

Nerone, J. C. (Ed.). (1995). *Last rights: Revisiting four theories of the press.* Urbana: University of Illinois Press.

Stuiber, H.-W. (1998). *Medien in Deutschland, Band 2. Rundfunk* [Media in Germany, Vol. 2. Broadcasting]. Konstanz: UVK.

Stuiber, H.-W. (2002). 50 Jahre Rundfunkpolitik [50 years of broadcasting policy]. *tendenz. Magazin für Funk und Fernsehen der Bayerischen Landeszentrale für neue Medien, 4,* 32–35.

Tonnemacher, J. (2003). *Kommunikationspolitik in Deutschland. Eine Einführung* [Communication policy in Germany: An introduction] (2nd ed.). Konstanz: UVK.

Weiss, H-J., & Trebbe, J. (2003). *ALM-Fernsehprogrammanalyse. Senderbericht Herbst 2002* [ALM television program analysis. Broadcast station report, Fall 2002]. Potsdam: GöfaK.

GERMANY, PRIME TIME, NOVEMBER 24–30, 2003

MONDAY							
Channel	**7 p.m.**	**7:30 p.m.**	**8 p.m.**	**8:30 p.m.**	**9 p.m.**	**9:30 p.m.**	**10 p.m.**
ARD The First	6:50–7:50 p.m.: Metropolitan Police Precinct (crime series)	7:50 p.m.: Weather	Daily News-reel (news)	8:15–9:05 p.m.: The Female Inspector (crime series)	9:05–9:45 p.m.: Fact (news magazine)	9:45–10:30: Dimension PSI (science series)	
ZDF Second German Television	7:00–7:25 p.m.: Today (news)	7:25–8:15 p.m.: WISO (economic magazine)		8:15–9:45 p.m.: Till Death Us Do Part (TV-movie/comedy)		9:45–10:13 p.m.: Today's Journal (news magazine)	

Channel	7 p.m.	7:30 p.m.	8 p.m.	8:30 p.m.	9 p.m.	9:30 p.m.	10 p.m.
BR Third Program Bavarian Television	7:00–7:30 p.m.: Garden Guide (service magazine)	7:30–8:15 p.m.: Life Lines (documentary)	8:15–9:00 p.m.: Consultation Hours (medical service magazine)		9:00–9:20 p.m.: Review (news magazine)	Profiles (news magazine)	9:45–10:45 p.m.: Focus Sports (sports magazine)
3sat	7:00–7:20 p.m.: Today (news)	7:20–8:00 p.m.: Culture Time (arts magazine)	Daily Newsreel (news)	8:15–9:45 p.m.: Under Suspicion—A Country Outing (TV-movie/crime)		In the Mangroves (NZ filmlet)	10:00–10:25 p.m.: ZiB 2 (news)
Arte	7:00–7:45 p.m.: The Return of the Narew (documentary)	7:45–8:15 p.m.: Arte Info (news)	8:15–8:40 p.m.: Crackdown on Smokers in NY (reportage)	8:40–9:55 p.m.: Samia (movie/drama [F])			9:55–2:25 a.m.: Route 181—Palestine, Israel (documentary)
RTL		7:10–7:40: Explosive (magazine)	7:40–8:15 p.m.: Good Times, Bad Times (daily soap)	8:15–9:15: Who Wants to Be a Millionaire? (quiz show)		9:15–10:15: Behind Bars—The Women's Prison (crime series)	
RTL II	6:00–8:00 p.m.: **The King of Queens** (U.S. comedy)		RTL II News (news)	8:15–9:15 p.m.: Gay Is Cool—The Fabulous Four (docu soap)		9:15–10:15 p.m.: Wife Exchange (docu soap)	
Super RTL		7:15–7:45 p.m.: **Angela Anaconda** (CDN cartoon)	7:45–8:15: **SpongeBob** (U.S. cartoon)	8:15–9:10 p.m.: **Murder, She Wrote** (U.S. crime series)		9:10–10:10 p.m.: **Murder, She Wrote** (U.S. crime series)	
Vox		7:10–7:40 p.m.: **The Nanny** (U.S. comedy)	7:40–8:15 p.m.: **The Nanny** (U.S. comedy)	8:15–9:05 p.m.: **Fastlane** (U.S. crime series)	9:05–10:00 p.m.: **Third Watch** (U.S. crime series)		10:00–11:00 p.m.: SZ TV (magazine)
Sat 1		7:15–7:45 p.m.: K 11 (crime documentary)	7:45–8:15 p.m.: The Quiz Show (quiz show)	8:15–10:15 p.m.: Pop 2003 (music)			
Pro 7	6:55–7:25 p.m.: **The Simpsons** (U.S. cartoon)	7:25–8:00 p.m.: Galileo (science magazine)	Pro7 News (news)	8:15–9:15 p.m.: No Idea? (comedy series)		9:15–9:50 p.m.: The Office (comedy series)	9:50–10:20 p.m.: Make It Fit (comedy series)
Cable 1		7:15–7:45 p.m.: **Hogan's Heroes** (U.S. comedy)	7:45–8:15 p.m.: **Hogan's Heroes** (U.S. comedy)	8:15–10:30 p.m.: **The Next Karate Kid** (U.S. movie)			

TUESDAY

Channel	7 p.m.	7:30 p.m.	8 p.m.	8:30 p.m.	9 p.m.	9:30 p.m.	10 p.m.
ARD The First	6:50–7:20 p.m.: **Mr. Bean** (U.K. comedy)	7:20–7:50 p.m.: Quiz Show; 7:50–8:00 p.m.: Weather	Daily Newsreel (news)	8:15–9:05 p.m.: Adelheid and Her Murderers (crime series)	9:05–9:55 p.m: In Friendship (drama series)		9:55–10:30: Plusminus (news magazine)

ZDF Second German Television	7:00–7:25 p.m.: Today (news)	7:25–8:15 p.m.: The Little Monk (crime/comedy series)	8:15–9:00 p.m.: Masuria (reportage)	9:00–9:45 p.m.: Frontal 21 (news magazine)		9:45–10:15 p.m.: Today's Journal (news magazine)
BR Third Program Bavarian Television	7:00–7:30 p.m.: Without Warranty (service mag.)	7:30–8:15 p.m.: Pictures of a Landscape: Lithuania (reportage)	8:15–9:00 p.m.: Munich Round (political talkshow)	9:00–9:20 p.m.: Review (news magazine)	Clear as Glass (magazine)	9:45–11:10 p.m.: My Best Enemy (TV movie/comedy)
3sat	7:00–7:20 p.m.: Today (news)	7:20–8:00 p.m.: Culture Time (arts magazine)	Daily Newsreel (news)	8:15–9:40 p.m.: In the Shadow of Power (Part 2) (TV-movie)	Che Lives (reportage)	10:00–10:25 p.m.: ZiB 2 (news)
Arte	7:00–7:45 p.m.: Archimedes (science magazine)	7:45–8:15 p.m.: Arte Info (news)	8:15–8:40 p.m.: Mafia Polska (reportage)	Theme Adolescence in Iran (reportage)	Night: Iran 9:10–10:05 p.m.: Shomal—The Riviera of the Mullahs (reportage)	10:05–11:00 p.m.: **Run Away** (GB) (documentary)
RTL	7:10–7:40 p.m.: Explosive (magazine)	7:40–8:15 p.m.: Good Times, Bad Times (daily soap)	8:15–9:15: Medicopter 117—Every Life Counts (action series)	9:15–10:15: The Clever Ones (crime series)		
RTL II	6:00–8:00 p.m.: **The King of Queens** (U.S. comedy)	RTL II News (news)	8:15–10:30 p.m.: **The Preachers's Wife** (U.S. movie)			
Super RTL	7:15–7:45 p.m.: **Angela Anaconda** (CDN cartoon)	7:45–8:15: **SpongeBob** (U.S. cartoon)	8:15–9:15 p.m.: Stefan Frank, M.D. (drama series)	9:15–10:15 p.m.: Stefan Frank, M.D. (drama series)		
Vox	7:10–7:40 p.m.: **The Nanny** (U.S. comedy)	7:40–8:15 p.m.: **The Nanny** (U.S. comedy)	8:15–9:15 p.m.: Star Search Germany—The Magazine (music show)	9:15–10:15 p.m.: The Star TV Reportage (reportage)		
Sat 1	7:15–7:45 p.m.: K 11 (crime docu.)	7:45–8:15 p.m.: The Quiz Show (quiz show)	8:15–10:15 p.m.: You've Been Sent From Heaven (TV movie/comedy)			
Pro 7	6:30–7:25 p.m.: **The Simpsons** (U.S. cartoon)	7:25–8:00 p.m.: Galileo (science magazine)	Pro7 News (news)	8:15–9:15 p.m.: Anatomy of Crime (crime magazine)	9:15–9:50 p.m.: **Friends** (U.S. comedy series)	9:50–10:20 p.m.: **Scrubs** (U.S. comedy series)
Cable 1	7:15–7:45 p.m.: **Hogan's Heroes** (U.S. comedy)	7:45–8:15 p.m.: **Hogan's Heroes** (U.S. comedy)	8:15–10:20 p.m.: **Curly Sue** (U.S. movie)			

Channel	7 p.m.	7:30 p.m.	8 p.m.	8:30 p.m.	9 p.m.	9:30 p.m.	10 p.m.
ARD The First	6:50–7:20 p.m.: **Mr. Bean** (U.K. comedy)	7:20–7:50 p.m.: Quiz Show / 7:50–8:00 p.m.: Weather	Daily Newsreel (news)	8:15–9:45 p.m.: A Father for the Limpet (TV movie/drama)		9:45–10:30 p.m.: Sex, Scandals, Politics (reportage)	
ZDF Second German Television	7:00–7:25 p.m.: Today (news)	7:25–8:15 p.m.: Coast Guard (crime series)	8:15–9:00 p.m.: The Prince and the Girl (family series)		9:00–9:45 p.m.: ZDF Reporter (news magazine)	9:45–10:15 p.m.: Today's Journal (news magazine)	
BR Third Program Bavarian Television	7:00–7:30 p.m.: Cooking (service magazine)	7:30–8:15 p.m.: The Promised Land (Part 2) (reportage)	8:15–9:00 p.m.: Active Citizen (political magazine)		9:00–9:20 p.m.: Review (news magazine) / Time's Mirror (news magazine)	9:45–11:10 p.m.: **Night Passage** (U.S. movie)	
3sat	7:00–7:20 p.m.: Today (news)	7:20–8:00 p.m.: Culture Time (arts magazine)	Daily Newsreel (news)	8:15–9:50 p.m.: **Heaven and Hell** (Austrian TV-movie/crime)		9:50–10:25 p.m.: Indian Cinema in Austria (reportage)	
Arte	7:00–7:45 p.m.: The Apple—A Declaration of Love (reportage)	7:45–8:15 p.m.: Arte Info (news)	8:15–8:40 p.m.: Child Witches in Kinshasa (reportage)	8:40–10.05 p.m.: Algeria—The Silenced People (Part 1) (documentary)			10:05–0:05 p.m.: Orphée and Eurydice (opera)
RTL		7:10–7:40: Explosive (magazine)	7:40–8:15 p.m.: Good Times, Bad Times (daily soap)	8:15–8:45: Nicola (comedy series)	8:45–9:15: Bernd's Witch (comedy series)	9:15–10:15 p.m.: The Bachelor (dating show)	
RTL II	6:00–8:00 p.m.: **The King of Queens** (U.S. comedy)		RTL II News (news)	8:15–9:15 p.m.: **Stargate** (U.S. sci fi series)		9:15–10:15 p.m.: **Stargate** (U.S. sci fi series)	
Super RTL		7:15–7:45 p.m.: **Angela Anaconda** (CDN cartoon)	7:45–8:15: **SpongeBob** (U.S. cartoon)	8:15–10:20 p.m.: **The Dream Team** (U.S. movie)			
Vox		7:10–7:40 p.m.: **The Nanny** (U.S. comedy)	7:40–8:15 p.m.: **The Nanny** (U.S. comedy)	8:15–9:10 p.m.: **C.S.I.** (U.S. crime series)	9:10–10:10 p.m.: **Medical Detectives** (U.S. documentary/crime)		
Sat 1		7:15–7:45 p.m.: K 11 (crime docu.)	7:45–8:15 p.m.: Soccer, UEFA-Cup (sports)	8:15–11:15 p.m.: Soccer, UEFA-Cup (sports)			
Pro 7	6:30–7:25 p.m.: **The Simpsons** (U.S. cartoon)	7:25–8:00 p.m.: Galileo (science magazine)	Pro7 News (news)	8:15–9:15 p.m.: **Emergency Room** (U.S. hospital/drama series)	9:15–10:15 p.m.: **Without a Trace** (U.S. crime series)		

Cable 1	7:15–7:45 p.m.: **Hogan's Heroes** (U.S. comedy)	7:45–8:15 p.m.: **Hogan's Heroes** (U.S. comedy)	8:15–10:10 p.m.: **Santa Claus** (U.S. movie)				

THURSDAY

Channel	7 p.m.	7:30 p.m.	8 p.m.	8:30 p.m.	9 p.m.	9:30 p.m.	10 p.m.
ARD The First	6:50–7:20 p.m.: **Mr. Bean** (U.K. comedy)	7:20–7:50 p.m.: Quiz Show / 7:50–8:00 p.m.: Weather	Daily News-reel (news)	8:15–10:30 p.m.: German Media Award (awards show)			
ZDF Second German Television	5:50–8:30 p.m.: Soccer, UEFA-Cup (sports)			8:30–10:30 p.m.: Soccer, UEFA-Cup (sports)			
BR Third Program Bavarian Television	7:00–7:30 p.m.: Leisure Time (service magazine)	7:30–8:15 p.m.: Fascination Konwledge (science magazine)	8:15–9:00 p.m.: Cross (youth magazine)	9:00–9:20 p.m.: Review (news magazine)	La Vita (maga-zine)	9:45–10:30 p.m.: The Janitor (family series)	
3sat	7:00–7:20 p.m.: Today (news)	7:20–8:00 p.m.: Culture Time (arts magazine)	Daily News-reel (news)	8:15–9:45 p.m.: At Night When the Day Begins (TV-movie/drama)	9:45–10:00 p.m.: Filmlet / 10:00–10:25 p.m.: ZiB 2 (news)		
Arte	7:00–7:45 p.m.: Voyages, Voyages (travel magazine)	7:45–8:15 p.m.: Arte Info (news)	8:15–8:45 p.m.: The Heritage of the Pope (reportage)	8:45–10:35 p.m.: **The Seventh String** (movie [F])			
RTL	7:10–7:40: Explosive (magazine)	7:40–8:15 p.m.: Good Times, Bad Times (daily soap)	8:15–11:15: Who Wants to Be a Millionaire?—V.I.P. Special (quiz show)				
RTL II	6:00–8:00 p.m.: **The King of Queens** (U.S. comedy)		RTL II News (news)	8:15–9:15 p.m.: The Cleaners—Germany Is Tidying Up (docu soap)	9:15–10:15 p.m.: Do-It-Yourselfer in Heaven (docu soap)		
Super RTL	7:15–7:45 p.m.: **Angela Anaconda** (CDN cartoon)	7:45–8:15: **SpongeBob** (U.S. cartoon)	8:15–9:15 p.m.: Hellish Neighbors (docu soap)	9:15–10:15 p.m.: Good Bye (comedy)			
Vox	7:10–7:40 p.m.: **The Nanny** (U.S. comedy)	7:40–8:15 p.m.: **The Nanny** (U.S. comedy)	8:15–10:10 p.m.: **Anastasia** (U.S. movie)			10:00–10:55 p.m.: Mirror TV (pol. maga-zine)	
Sat 1	7:15–7:45 p.m.: K 11 (crime docu.)	7:45–8:15 p.m.: The Quiz Show (quiz show)	8:15–9:15 p.m.: Inspector Rex (crime series)	9:15–10:15 p.m.: Stefanie In Any Case (hospital/drama series)			

Pro 7	6:30–7:25 p.m.: **The Simpsons** (U.S. cartoon)	7:25–8:00 p.m.: Galileo (science magazine)	Pro7 News (news)	8:15–10:15 p.m.: Berlin Will Die Tomorrow (TV-movie/action)	
Cable 1	7:15–7:45 p.m.: **Hogan's Heroes** (U.S. comedy)	7:45–8:15 p.m.: **Hogan's Heroes** (U.S. comedy)	8:15–9:15 p.m.: What Is My Profession? (quiz show)	9:15–10:15 p.m.: K1 Magazine (magazine)	

FRIDAY

Channel	7 p.m.	7:30 p.m.	8 p.m.	8:30 p.m.	9 p.m.	9:30 p.m.	10 p.m.
ARD The First	6:50–7:20 p.m.: Dating Show 7:50–8:00 p.m.: Weather		Daily Newsreel (news)	8:15–9:45 p.m.: Planned Children and Other Accidents (TV-movie/comedy)		9:45–10:15 p.m.: Brisant Extra (entertainment)	
ZDF Second German Television	7:00–7:25 p.m.: Today (news)	7:25–8:15 p.m.: The Country Doctor (family series)	8:15–9:15 p.m.: A Criminal Case for Two (crime series)		9:15–11:00 p.m.: Our Best—Who Is the Greatest German (show)		
BR Third Program Bavarian Television	7:00–7:45 p.m.: Our Land (magazine)	7:45–9:15 p.m.: Bed and Breakfast (play)			9:15–9:35 p.m.: Review (news magazine)	9:35–10:00 p.m.: Cafe Perjury (court series)	10:00–10:30 p.m.: The Comedians (comedy show)
3sat	7:00–7:20 p.m.: Today (news)	7:20–8:00 p.m.: Culture Time (arts magazine)	Daily Newsreel (news)	8:15–9:50 p.m.: Mysterious Girl Friends (TV-movie/thriller)		Brussels (filmlet [B])	10:10–10:30 p.m.: ZiB 2 (news)
Arte	7:00–7:45 p.m.: Tracks (music)	7:45–8:15 p.m.: Arte Info (news)	8:15–8:40 p.m.: Koreans on the Run (reportage)	8:40–10:30 p.m.: **Adopted** (TV-movie/drama [I])			
RTL	7:10–7:40 p.m.: Explosive (magazine)	7:40–8:15 p.m.: Good Times, Bad Times (daily soap)	8:15–9:15 p.m.: Who Wants to Be a Millionaire? (quiz show)		9:15–9:45 p.m.: My Life and Me (comedy series)	9:45–10:15 p.m.: Rita's World (comedy series)	
RTL II	6:00–8:00 p.m.: **The King of Queens** (U.S. comedy)		RTL II News (news)	8:15–10:00 p.m.: **Space Jam** (U.S. movie)		8:15–10:00 p.m.: **Red Scorpion** (U.S. movie)	
Super RTL	7:15–7:45 p.m.: **Angela Anaconda** (CDN cartoon)	7:45–8:15: SpongeBob (U.S. cartoon)	8:15–9:35 p.m.: **The Story Christmas** (U.S. movie)		9:35–10:10 p.m.: **The Wonder Years** (U.S. comedy series)		
Vox	7:10–7:40 p.m.: **The Nanny** (U.S. comedy)	7:40–8:15 p.m.: **The Nanny** (U.S. comedy)	8:15–10:15 p.m.: **Volcano** (U.S. movie)				

Sat 1	7:15–7:45 p.m.: K 11 (crime docu.)	7:45–8:15 p.m.: The Quiz Show (quiz show)	8:15–9:15 p.m.: **Enterprise** (U.S. sci fi series)		9:15–9:45 p.m.: What Are You Looking At? (comedy show)	9:45–10:15 p.m.: Markus (comedy show)
Pro 7	6:30–7:25 p.m.: **The Simpsons** (U.S. cartoon)	7:25–8:00 p.m.: Galileo (science magazine)	Pro7 News (news)	8:15–10:00 p.m.: **Shriek If You Know What I Did Last Friday the 13th** (U.S. movie)		10:00–0:15 p.m.: **Platoon** (U.S. movie)
Cable 1	7:15–7:45 p.m.: **Hogan's Heroes** (U.S. comedy)	7:45–8:15 p.m.: **Hogan's Heroes** (U.S. comedy)	8:15–10:30 p.m.: **Geronimo: An American Legend** (U.S. movie)			

SATURDAY

Channel	7 p.m.	7:30 p.m.	8 p.m.	8:30 p.m.	9 p.m.	9:30 p.m.	10 p.m.
ARD The First	6:10–7:45 p.m.: Sports 7:45–8:00 p.m.: Weather & Lottery Numbers		Daily News-reel (news)	8:15–10:10 p.m.: **The Mexican** (U.S. movie)			10:10–10:28 p.m.: Topics of the Day (news mag.)
ZDF Second German Television	7:00–7:25 p.m.: Today (news)	7:25–8:15 p.m.: Our Charlie (family series)	8:15–9:45 p.m.: Stubbe—From Case to Case (crime series)		9:45–10:00 p.m.: Today's Journal (news mag.)		10:00–11:15 p.m.: ZDF SPORTSstudio
BR Third Program Bavarian Television	7:00–7:45 p.m.: Our Blue Planet—Ebb and Flood (nature reportage)	7:45–8:15 p.m.: Arts and Carding (arts magazine)	8:15–9:00 p.m.: Somewhere in Bavaria (reportage)	9:00–9:15 p.m.: Review (news mag.)	9:15–9:45 p.m.: Capriccio (culture mag.)	9:45–11:10 p.m.: **Man Without A Star** (U.S. movie/)	
3sat	7:00–7:20 p.m.: Today (news)	7:20–8:00 p.m.: Treasure Island—Taiwan (reportage)	Daily News-reel (news)	8:15–9:45 p.m.: AIDS Gala Concert (charity performance)		9:45–10:30 p.m.: Women in Tailcoats—Female Conductors (reportage)	
Arte	7:00–7:45 p.m.: European Forum (political magazine)	7:45–8:15 p.m.: Arte Info (news)	8:15–8:45 p.m.: Design 2002 (Part 9) (documentary)	8:45–9:35 p.m.: Terra X (science magazine)		9:35–10:30 p.m.: Metropolis (cuture magazine)	
RTL	7:10–8:15: Explosive (magazine)		8:15–9:15: Who Wants to Be a Millionaire? (quiz show)		9:15–10:45: Star Search (music/show)		
RTL II	6:15–8:00 p.m.: **Walker, Texas Ranger** (U.S. crime/action series)		RTL II News (news)	8:15–10:10 p.m.: **Epicenter** (U.S. movie)			
Super RTL	7:10–7:45 p.m.: Super Toy Club (children's show)	7:45–8:15: **Pink Panther** (U.S. cartoon)	8:15–9:35 p.m.: **2 Angels With 4 Fists** (movie/action, comedy [I,F,D])				10:05–11:5 p.m.: Horror Castle (movie/crime)
Vox	7:10–8:15 p.m.: **BBC Exclusive** (U.K. documentary)		8:15–10:15 p.m.: **In the Blue Ground** (CDN TV-movie/crime)				

Sat 1	7:15–8:15 p.m.: The Gong Show (talent/variety)		8:15–11:00 p.m.: **Ghost** (U.S. movie)	
Pro 7	7:00–8:00 p.m.: Talk Talk Talk (best of talk shows)	Pro7 News (news)	8:15–10:00 p.m.: Werner (movie/cartoon, comedy)	10:00–0:20 p.m.: **Lethal Weapon 3** (U.S. movie)
Cable 1	7:15–8:15 p.m.: **The Lost World** (U.S. fantasy series)		8:15–10:30 p.m.: **Patton** (U.S. movie/war, drama)	

SUNDAY

Channel	7 p.m.	7:30 p.m.	8 p.m.	8:30 p.m.	9 p.m.	9:30 p.m.	10 p.m.
ARD The First	7:10–7:50 p.m.: Foreign Policy Magazine / 7:50–8:00 p.m.: Sports		Daily News-reel (news)	8:15–9:45 p.m.: Crime Scene (TV-movie/crime)		9:45–10:40 p.m.: Sabine Christiansen (political talk)	
ZDF Second German Television	7:00–7:10 p.m.: Today (news) / 7:10–7:30: Political Mag.	7:30–8:15 p.m.: Fascinating Universe (documentary/science)	8:15–10:15 p.m.: The Super Hit Parade of German Folk Music (music)				
BR Third Program Bavarian Television	7:00–7:50 p.m.: Advent Singing (music)	7:50–9:15 p.m.: Trouble With Jolante (play/comedy)			9:15–9:45 p.m.: Boulevard Bavaria (magazine)	9:45–10:00 p.m.: Reportage on Sunday / 10:00–10:30: Regional Sports	
3sat	7:00–7:10 p.m.: Today (news) / 7:10–8:00: Political Magazine		Daily News-reel (news)	8:15–9:45 p.m.: Festive Concert (music)		9:45–10:00 p.m.: (reportage) / 10:00–11:30: Documentary	
Arte	7:00–7:45 p.m.: Music Festival (Part 2) (music)	7:45–8:15 p.m.: Arte Info (news)	8:15–8:45 p.m.: Danse en création (music/dance play)	8:45–10:40 p.m.: **Heart Flickering** (movie/drama [F/D/I])			
RTL	7:10–8:15: Emergency Call (reality soap)		8:15–10:35: **What Lies Beneath** (U.S. movie)				
RTL II	6:00–8:00 p.m.: Fame Academy (casting show)		RTL II News (news)	8:15–9:15 p.m.: German Hobby Gardeners (docu soap)		9:15–10:15 p.m.: The Murder Files (documentary/crime)	
Super RTL	7:00–7:25 p.m.: **Recess** (U.S. cartoon)	7:25–7:45 p.m.: **Mr. Bean** (cartoon) / 7:45–8:15 p.m.: Children's Quiz Show	8:15–10:00 p.m.: **Simon & Simon** (U.S. crime series)			10:00–11:40 p.m.: **Crying Child** (U.S. TV-movie/drama)	
Vox	7:15–8:15 p.m.: Fit for Fun TV (health magazine)		8:15–10:35 p.m.: **Ever After—A Cinderella Story** (U.S. movie)				
Sat 1	7:00–8:15 p.m.: Only Love Counts (dating show)		8:15–10:45 p.m.: Stars 2003—The AIDS Gala (charity performance)				
Pro 7	7:00–8:00 p.m.: World of Wonders (science/nature magazine)		Pro7 News (news)	8:15–10:25 p.m.: **Girls United** (U.S. movie)			

Cable 1		7:10–7:40 p.m.: Funny Commercials (clip show)	8:15–10:15 p.m.: **Best Defense** (U.S. movie)	
		7:40–8:15 p.m.: **Laurel & Hardy** (U.S. comedy)		

Note. **Bold** denotes imported program. CDN = Canadian; A = Austrian; NZ = New Zealand; F = French.

Chapter 5

Egypt

Ralph D. Berenger
American University in Cairo

Kamel Labidi
Independent journalist, Cairo

ABOUT EGYPT

Egypt is the second most populous country in Africa and the largest Arab country. Its population, estimated in July 2003 at nearly 75 million, is concentrated on less than 5% of the land (CIA, 2003). Most of the country lies in Africa, but the easternmost portion of Egypt, the Sinai Peninsula, is usually considered part of Asia. The Nile valley and delta are the main centers of habitation. Nearly a fifth of Egypt's 75 million people live in the capital and largest city, Cairo (estimated population of 13 million in 2003). Arabic is the official language of the population, although Western-educated upper middle and upper classes also speak English and French. Coptic Christian church rituals keep alive parts of a language that might have been spoken by the pharaohs.

Egypt's main industries are tourism (which generates the largest amount of foreign revenues), textiles, food processing, chemicals, hydrocarbons, construction, cement, and metals. Estimated GDP for 2003 was $63.3 billion ($45.5 billion in the private sector). Foreign investment in Egypt reached $10.2 billion. GDP growth for 2003 was estimated at 2.74% (CIA, 2003). Illiterates are 45.4% of the population, two thirds of them women (UNDP, 2002). Per capita income in 2003 was estimated at $3,420 (UNDP, 2002).

History

Egypt is an ancient country with a history dating back to 7000 BC. Early settlements thrived in a fertile green strip on each side of the Nile River, a blue ribbon of life-giving water that twists through the brown and barren desert and empties into the Mediterranean. Annual inundations deposited layer upon layer of fertile silt along the river's banks. Around 3000 BC, a developed society emerged along the Nile, long before the two rival kingdoms of Upper Egypt and Lower Egypt merged by 3200 BC.

Egypt's pharaonic legacy was marked by the construction of the Pyramids and other grand structures in Thebes, Memphis, and Luxor. Successive dynasties flourished with international trade and commerce. Beginning in the 1st century BC, a series of hegemonic waves swept over the country—Persian, Greek, Roman, Arab, Turkish, French, and British. Ever since Muslim invaders conquered Christian Egypt in 641 AD, the land has been a part, if not the center, of the Muslim and Arab world, but it retains important aspects of its Christian, Greco-Roman, and ancient indigenous heritage.

The first ruler of Egyptian origin since the pharaohs was Gamal Abdel Nasser, a charismatic Arab nationalist figure, who led the Free Officers' bloodless coup on July 23, 1952, and forced the country's last monarch, King Farouk, into exile. (King Farouk was of Albanian descent.) Nasser restored Egypt's leading political role in the region.

Nasser died in 1970. His successor, Anwar Sadat, who became the first Arab leader to sign a peace treaty with Israel in 1979, slightly loosened the state's grip over society and the media. He was murdered in 1981 by radical Islamicists. The current leader, Hosni Mubarak, became, in 1981, the third in a succession of military officers to become president of Egypt.

BROADCAST BACKGROUND

Communication

Egypt was and is a communications hub between Africa, Europe, Asia, and the Middle East. Writing may have originated there, as did techniques for advertising and propaganda—even the most casual visitor today finds abundant examples of both inscribed on the pharaonic buildings and sites, and in fragments of papyrus in museums around the world. The Greeks established Alexandria as one of the more important cities on the Mediterranean. A great library was established there, and Alexandria was the known world's intellectual center even after the deaths of Cleopatra and Marc Antony.

Napoleon invaded the country at the turn of the 19th century and brought with him the first printing press. Scientists and writers published their studies of the country and created the first great wave of "Egyptomania" to sweep Europe. The Rosetta Stone, discovered by the French, eventually led scholars to decipher Egyptian hieroglyphic writings, which continue to surprise academicians with their richness and insights into normal life of common people.

Egypt's media played a leading cultural role in the Arab world, particularly after the 19th century. The Egyptian Radio Service, the first of its kind in the Middle East, began broadcasting on May 31, 1934. It was established before the country recovered its full political sovereignty from Great Britain.

Following the 1952 revolution, the Egyptian government nationalized all mass media, which were used as propaganda tools for the effective mobilization of the masses and as a catalyst for both social and cultural transformation (Moody, 1999). In 1953, Egypt pioneered radio broadcasting in the Arab World. Radio became an intrinsic part of the Nasserite pan-Arabic era, with several factors combining to help Nasser build the most sophisticated radio system in the Middle East. His desire for Arab unity, campaigns against pro-Western Arab regimes, and Egypt's position as an anti-imperialist base in the Middle East ensured that Nasser had an unsurpassed mass appeal across the Arab world, with millions tuning in to listen to him over the radio (Nasser, 1990). Egyptian radio broadcasts gained an almost mythical quality among Arab listeners as a result—not only for news, but for entertainment as well. Egyptian Arabic, a distinctive linguistic style, became the accent for newscasters and entertainers to emulate in much of the Middle East.

Egyptian radio flourished and had much more impact on Arab masses than Egyptian television. Both Abdallah Schleiffer of the Adham Center for TV Journalism at the American University in Cairo (AUC), and Egyptian writer and former contributor to the *Voice of the Arabs* Mohamed al-Khouly (personal communication, December 2003), suggested that part of the reason radio broadcasting had such an impact on Arabs was because Nasser regularly listened to international radio stations, such as the BBC.

Egypt played a leading role in 1969 in establishing, under the Arab League umbrella, the Arab States Broadcasting Union (ASBU), and in 1976 the Arab Satellite Communications Organization (Arabsat). The daily average radio transmission, which was around 15 hours a day in 1952, rose at the end of the 1990s to 457 hours a day. In the 1950s, the Egyptian Service used to transmit in Arabic, English, and French from two radio broadcasting stations. To date, the following eight radio networks (FM, AM, and short-wave) are broadcasting in 34 languages: Public Program,

Holy Koran, Middle East, Youth and Sports, Voice of the Arabs, Localities, Cultural, and Oriented Radio Stations. Radio and TV buildings are among the most heavily guarded buildings in Arab countries, including Egypt.

Television. On July 1, 1960, Egypt was one of the first countries in Africa and the Middle East to introduce television (Kader, 1986), a date to mark the eighth anniversary of the Young Officers Revolution. From the beginning, the primary source of programming on Egyptian television was films (Amin, 1996). Egypt's film industry dominated—and still dominates—Arab markets and in the process builds a favorable image for Egypt among Arab audiences (Nasser, 1990).

In 1971, the Egyptian Radio and Television Union (ERTU), a government-owned company affiliated with the Ministry of Information, was formed. The union exercised complete control over Egypt's radio and TV broadcasts (Amin, 1996). By the time color broadcasting was introduced in 1977, the majority of Egyptian households had access to television (Kader, 1986). In 1964 Egypt had by far the largest number of TV sets in North Africa, claiming about 1.5 million viewers and about 96,000 TV sets (Kader, 1986). In past years it was easier for researchers to get an accurate number for TV viewership in Egypt, as Egyptian TV owners had to pay a license fee along with their electricity. This is no longer the case, so it is difficult to obtain accurate figures (Moody, 1999). Today, 63% of Egyptians have access to television. The 2000 figure was estimated at 177 televisions per 1,000 inhabitants (World Resource Institute, 2003). More than 80% of Egyptians, according to various sources, seem to rely on radio and television for information in a country where illiteracy remains among the highest in the region.

When VCRs became available in the 1980s, they were not so popular with those who could afford them, inasmuch as Egypt had ample TV programming to keep viewers from watching difficult-to-obtain videotapes—usually purloined copies of copies, mostly in English. Egypt operates on the PAL system, which precluded running many of the popular U.S. videos, which were recorded on NTSC. Dual systems that played both NTSC and PAL, along with the French SECAM, eliminated the compatibility problem. When huge numbers of Egyptians began working in the Gulf region as contracted labor, VCR ownership quickly became a status symbol of the time (Boyd & Straubhaar, 1989).

Satellites. A turning point was marked in 1990 with the introduction of satellite TV into the Arab region shortly before the 1991 Gulf War. Shortly prior to the war, the Egyptian government legalized the import and ownership of dishes (Schleifer, 1998). After the privatization revolution in Europe in the 1980s, Egypt began to rethink its government-controlled broadcasting policies. The move toward privatization resulted in an increase in foreign programming and global, mainly U.S., networks. In doing so, Egypt was also the first Arab country to introduce pay television into the region. The government's privatization plan began with the introduction of the country's first cable system—Cable Network Egypt (CNE), which was the country's first private subscription channel. Initially, its main purpose was to transmit CNN International in Cairo (Napoli & Amin, 1995). Government officials felt the news channel would be important in promoting tourism, and were lured by CNN's promise to provide four free minutes of advertising by the Egyptian Ministry of Tourism.

CNE is no longer simply a carrier of CNN. It currently broadcasts in two systems: wireless cable and satellite direct to homes, which relayed specialized Western channels as well as the Arab Radio and Television (ART) Arabic channels. Globalized media had arrived in Egypt.

When satellite dishes were first introduced in Egypt, they were expensive (about $2,500). Only well-off Egyptians could afford them (Moody, 1999). Many Egyptians living in blocks of flats started to purchase fixed dishes and divide the cost between them (Moody, 1999; Rasheed, 2003). Satellite dish ownership is no longer limited to elites. In 1999 there were 669,000 home satellite dishes (NICI Infrastructure: www.uneca.org), but an estimated 20% of the public are watching satellite television (H.Y. Amin, personal communication, 2003).

Many of the viewers are paying less than $4 a month to entrepreneurs who have set up satellite dishes to pick up "free" stations off various satellites and redirect the signals to private homes, a practice the Egyptian government says is illegal but seems unwilling or unable to stop (Rasheed, 2003). Like the VCR before it, a satellite dish on one's roof is the height of media savvy and fashion in Egypt.

In response to the introduction of satellite broadcasting into the Arab region in 1990, The Egyptian Radio and TV Union (ERTU) launched two satellite channels: Nile TV International in English and French, and the Egyptian Satellite Channel (ESC) in Arabic, broadcasting throughout the Middle East, Africa, and Europe (Forrester, 1998).

In April 1998, Egypt launched its satellite, Nilesat 101, which carried, at that time, 12 satellite TV channels, including 72 radio channels covering the Middle East, Africa, and parts of Asia. It was the first satellite of its kind in the Arab world. In August 2000, a second digital satellite, Nilesat 102, was launched. The number of channels carried by Nilesat rose in 2002 to 160 Arab and international TV channels. Nilesat, which is based on the digital system, also carries 135 radio stations.

Egypt was the first Arab and African country to have its own satellite. Saudi Arabia and Lebanon also have "birds" in the parking lot of space. Israel—a non-Arab Middle Eastern country—has since (in December 2003) launched its second satellite (Agence France Presse, 2003). More than 195 digital channels are now being broadcast over Egyptian satellites, all free other than 105 encrypted channels. There are also 85 digital radio channels. The up-links to Nilesat are from Cairo, England, Italy, Jordan, Lebanon, Iraq, and the Gulf region.

The state, which remains opposed to the establishment of privately owned television and radio, still owns and operates most of Egypt's broadcast media. Egypt has two nationwide terrestrial channels, 1 and

2, and six regional channels: 3 (Cairo, Giza, and Al Qalyoubia), 4 (Suez Canal region), 5 (Alexandria, Al Behira, and part of Marsa Matrouh), 6 (Central Delta region), 7 (Northern Upper Egypt), and 8 (Southern Upper Egypt).

New Directions

The last 3 years, however, have seen the introduction of private TV channels onto the Egyptian television landscape. Al-Mehwar, owned by a group of businessmen, has been operating since late 2001. It is the only private channel to offer news segments, using reports from state-owned television. Dream 1 and Dream 2, owned by Egyptian tycoon Ahmed Bahgat, have been broadcasting since November 2001.

Over the past 3 years, ERTU has also started up a number of new digital channels, focusing on arts and culture, news and current affairs, music, sports, and children's programming. The channels were designed in order to preserve Egyptian identity in the face of competition from foreign programming (Forrester, 2001). ERTU's NileSat DTH package offers channels dedicated individually to drama, children's programs, news, sport, and variety channels from its own studios. It also has 10 channels committed to educational themes, which range from nursery school to university level. In addition, the Ministry of Health operates a channel for the training of medical and nursing staff.

Arab Radio Television (ART), owned by Saudi Arabian Sheik Saleh Kamel, transmits between 12 and 14 hours of television a day from a converted hotel complex. ART has also launched seven pay channels and plans to launch more. Cartoon Network and TNT Classic Movies are on ART, which is carried on both NileSat 101 and ArabSat. NileSat also carries Showtime (Kuwait/Viacom backed) and channels from Libya, occupied Palestine, and Iraq.

In 2000 Egypt unveiled a 3.5 million-square-meter Egyptian Media Production City (EMPC) just outside Cairo. Inaugurated in 1995, the vision was to create the Hollywood of the Middle East. The project, with strong support from the Egyptian government, was designed to attract producers and broadcasters to Egypt, through a variety of tax breaks and other incentives. In conjunction with the NileSat, EMPC is seen as a driving force in keeping Egypt as the Arab world's most prominent film, TV, and radio center. Unrealized have been the hopes that major Western entertainment and film companies would move productions to EMPC state-of-the-art facilities due to Egypt's sunny, warm climate that would accommodate tight shooting schedules, its low production and labor costs, and its varied geographical landscapes ideal for historical period pieces, Westerns, and science fiction productions.

Abdel Rahman Hafez, chairman of ERTU and EMPC, has acknowledged that Egypt's marketing strategy "has failed so far to attract international investors"; he added that the country has still some laws dealing with investment that "deserve to be crushed and put to death because they are obstacles on the road to investment" (El-Guindi, 2003, p. 20). He did not, however, discuss censorship, which many regard as detrimental to the development of EMPC.

The creation of a Free Media Zone in 2000 in the suburbs of Cairo has partially helped EMPC cope with its economic difficulties. Different Arab and international media companies are already using some of the studios of EMPC and technical facilities. But competition is tough, particularly from Dubai Media City and its neighboring Free Media Zone in the United Arab Emirates, where the government seems more open to privatization than its Egyptian counterpart.

"The Egyptian media are not for sale. I am not in favor of privatizing the media, nor for selling the tools that shape the Egyptian mind and protect it against the challenges facing our developing country," former Egyptian Minister of Information Safwat El-Sherif said (personal communication, December 2003). El-Sherif had been in charge of the ministry of information since the early 1980s until 2004 and secretary general of the ruling NDP party (2001–2004). However, his successors apparently view privatization differently, and some movement is now expected in that direction.

BROADCAST REGULATION

Egypt's legal system is based on English common law, Islamic law, and Napoleonic code. The first important regulation organizing the radio service in Egypt was Law No. 98 of 1949. It stipulated that the Egyptian Radio Service "is an independent body of a judicial person and is subordinate to the Egyptian Cabinet" (Egyptian Ministry, 2003). Supervision of the Egyptian Radio Service was entrusted to a new ministerial department established on November 10, 1952, under the name of the Ministry of National Guidance. A following presidential decree (No. 183 of 1958) affiliating the Egyptian Radio Service to the presidency showed to what extent the Egyptian leader himself was involved in running and using radio broadcasting to influence local and regional public opinions.

Television

After the establishment of Egyptian television in 1960, presidential decree No. 1914 of 1961 turned the Egyptian Radio Service into the Egyptian General Authority for Radio and Television (EGART). It was incorporated in 1962 into the Ministry of National Guidance. In 1966, a new department within the same ministry, which later was called the Ministry of Information, was set up under the name of the Radio Service of the United Arab Republic (when Egypt and Syria formed a union from 1956 through 1959).

The establishment of Egyptian television coincided with the adoption of Law 156 of 1960, which nationalized the Egyptian media and granted all licensing prerogatives to the then ruling party, the National Union, later called the Arab Socialist Union. The law also turned all Egyptian journalists into government employees and made membership in the ruling party compulsory.

Egyptian broadcasting is regulated by 33 prohibitions in the "Code of Ethics" observed throughout the ERTU. These prohibitions forbid criticism of state officials, the national system, traditional values, and religious beliefs. Restrictions like this manifest themselves most overtly in limiting live TV broadcasts. Yet live TV broadcasts in Arab countries is what viewers say they want (Sakr, 2000).

In the mounting conflict between censorship imperatives and the demand for live television, the impact of satellite technology is most clearly seen. However, Egypt's Minister of Information and other media power players like to promote the pretense of a liberal media (Forrester, 2001). Indeed, the global nature of satellites, which limits individual governments' ability to control content, has forced Egypt to liberalize its telecommunications sector.

Control Versus Liberalization

In 1989, Law 223 slightly modified Law 13 of 1979. It partly liberalized, for the first time, the subscriber TV market. But all the various amendments to the broadcasting legislation passed during the past 50 years maintain the market for radio and television under the tight control of the Ministry of Information. The existing radio and TV stations fall under the jurisdiction of the Minister of Communications. But the relevant licenses are delivered through ERTU. Radio and TV stations must abide by ERTU's code of conduct. In 2003, for example, ERTU issued a warning to Dream TV. Many thought it was politically motivated.

The Egyptian strict production code, with restrictions as far as religious and sexual issues, does not apply to production within the Free Media Zone, as long it is intended to be consumed outside Egypt.

Egypt's broadcast media have been subject since 1979 (Law No. 13 of 1979) to ERTU, a state-owned body subordinate to the Ministry of Information. A board of directors representing different ministries, including the ministries of information, commerce, and foreign affairs, manages ERTU. ERTU's monopoly on radio broadcasting is still in force. It claims that there are no frequencies available for private stations. Business people eager to see the end of this monopoly retort that there are enough frequencies to support more radio stations. ERTU has been described by a media expert as a "bloated state enterprise" in charge of "entertaining the masses and the regime" (personal communication, December 2003).

With illegal pay-TV piracy gaining ground in Egypt, Cable Network Egypt has formed a joint company with Egyptian Digital Distribution (EDD), which owns and distributes the Saudi-funded ART channels, "to crack down on TV pirates by cutting rates and cooperating closely with the ministry of the interior to strictly enforce regulations against illegal distribution" (El-Hennawy, 2003).

BROADCAST CONTENT

Television in Egypt is a ubiquitous fact of life. All other leisure activities are relegated to the back burner. It is one of the main subjects of conversation at school, in offices, at home, and in the street, as well as being written about in newspapers. Although no rigorous studies have been carried out to analyze the causes behind the overarching influence of the little square box, the combination of economic, political, and cultural factors unique to Egypt are often cited as the reasons for TV primacy.

Television in Egypt both reflects and accelerates the erratic behavior patterns of a rapidly changing society. If, in this context, television sometimes seems like a "rudderless ship, it is because society itself has no driving force capable of steering it in a definite direction or giving it a coherent orientation" (Gharib, 1992, p. 34).

The holy month of Ramadan is the Egyptian equivalent of the American "sweeps week." Stations compete ferociously to air the most popular shows. Besides the normal shows, special serials running from the first to the last day of the month are produced each year and eagerly awaited by millions of viewers. The sunset meal with which citizens break their daily fast is followed by what can only be described as a nightly TV binge. This is partly because people have more time on their hands than during the rest of the year, but also because cinemas and theaters close down and most public activities come to a halt.

Game Shows

Game shows are a relatively new phenomenon to Egyptian television. First introduced in 1998 in response to the flashy Arab and Western counterparts that viewers received through their satellite dishes, they are sponsored by firms that offer substantial prizes to winning contestants. However, their main purpose conspicuously remains that of a small-screen platform for the Egyptian stars of show business.

At first, Egyptians' television was unable to hit on any winning formula for their game shows. The first incarnations featured recognizable actors and actresses as contestants and no real prizes. Later versions sought contestants from every walk of life, but the studio set-ups were always amateurish and naïve. However, the last 2 years have seen a vast improvement, with the ERTU coproducing licensed game shows with foreign teams.

Game shows that have recently made their way into the daily consciousness include the licensed Arabic version of the global hit "Who Wants to Be a Millionaire?" transliterated as *Man Sa Yarbah el Milion*. Fronted by popular and suave Lebanese host Geroge Kirdahy, the show originally aired on the Saudi-owned station Middle East Broadcasting Company (MBC). However, once the Egyptian TV union signed a contract with MBC to coproduce the show from Media City, it began appearing on terrestrial television ensuring a loyal following, as well as generating several low-budget clones. Top prize on "Millionaire" was a million Saudi rials, about $77,000, and questions probed contestants' knowledge of the Koran and Arab esoterica amid the same music, set, flashing lights, and overdramatic pauses as its American cousin. (See chapter 15.)

"Pyramid of Dreams" has also proved highly popular. With the help of an English director and a huge budget, it became one of Egypt's first locally produced hit game shows. It started airing in 2000, with $50,000 given out each month. The weekly show featured popular actor Ezzaat Abou Ouf as host and a bevy of pretty girls dressed in pharaonic garb as helpers.

Game shows in Egypt have been a source of fierce religious controversy and debate, with religious leaders questioning whether such programs are a form of gambling and are contrary to Islamic law. Whereas Egypt's leading religious authority, the Grand Mufti, once deemed "Who Wants to Be a Millionaire?" un-Islamic, the Sheikh of Al Azhar, the religious institution revered by Sunni Muslims all over the world, said there was no objection to such shows because they spread general knowledge.

Religious controversy or not, game shows in Egypt still have low production values. Although Egypt cannot be beaten in the Arab world when it comes to series and films, a little more practice and experience are needed in both game shows and talk shows.

Soap Operas

Daytime serial dramas play a large role in the Egyptian way of life. When it is time for a serial to begin, most family members stop whatever they have been doing and sit transfixed before the screen. Familiar features of every Egyptian's landscape, evening activities are timed around soap scheduling. Most serials deal with social problems. What is involved is not, strictly speaking, social criticism in the sense of analysis of past or present failings suggesting future solutions (Gharib, 1992). Rather, the programs fix viewers' attention on situations with which they can easily identify. In recent years, soaps have also played a role in nudging what is acceptable in conservative Egyptian society as well as challenging accepted stereotypes. In this way, soaps help set agendas for public sphere discourse.

Highly rated series in 2003 included "Aunt Nur." Nabial Ebied plays the role of a psychologist who returns to Egypt after 25 years in the West and discovers problems besetting young wealthy Egyptians who have lost their sense of traditional identity.

Other popular shows included "The Rebellion of the Harem," about a country family where women demand the right to education among other rights, and "A Question of Principle" about a young woman from southern Egypt who runs for elected office instead of her father. Both shows were the most popular of an influx of serials focused on feminist themes, which broke new ground in Egypt's traditional, patriarchal society.

Certain Egyptian serial dramas have become a source of international as well as local debate, most significantly "Horse Without a Horseman." Produced in 2002 by private satellite channel Dream TV, it originally received a cold shoulder by terrestrial TV, but soon after airing, the U.S. Embassy in Cairo called for its ban due to its alleged anti-Semitic message. The series, which starred Mohammed Sobhi, a respected and intelligent comic actor known for his nationalism, made references to the infamous book *The Protocols of the Elders of Zion*. The series' underlying message was that had Arabs read the legendary protocols—discredited as Russian propaganda fiction—they could have prevented establishment of a Zionist state from Palestine.

Another series causing widespread controversy was the 2001 Egyptian comedy about a man and his four wives that drew huge audiences and led to fierce debate about the legal practice of polygamy in Egypt. "The Family of Hagg Mutawall, I," which ran during Ramadan, sparked a spirited discourse in a society where polygamy had rarely been given such a glamorous image (Elbendary, 2001b).

Talk Shows

With the controversial Qatari news station Al Jazeera pioneering Arab political talk TV (PTV), Egyptian television was quick to adopt the format. PTV shows have practically taken over the prime time schedule. On switching on his television, the Egyptian viewer is often greeted with angry faces shouting provocative remarks at each other on screen, under the façade of freedom of expression. Channels now compete over who will deal with the hottest topics and get the best-known guests, who will raise the most controversial issues with more daring, and ultimately who will shout the loudest.

PTV shows in Egypt took off after the second Palestinian *Intifada* (uprising) with shows such as *"Ra'is El-Tahrir"* (Editor in Chief), *"Al-Khatt Al-Ahmar"* (Red line), *"Fi'l Umq"* (In Depth), *"Al-Ra'y Al Thalith"* (The Third Opinion), *"Da'irat Al-Hiwat"* (Roundtable), *"Wara' Al-Ahdath"* (Behind the Scenes), and *"Bidoun Riqbah"* (Without Censorship).

Essentially, this plethora of political programming on prime time television is a direct response to what is perceived as the threat from competing Arab satellite channels. As these channels do not shy away from discussing domestic and foreign policy issues in other countries, including Egypt, then criticism might well start at home on Egyptian channels (Elbendary, 2001a).

In doing so, Egyptian television is now dealing with topics that range from the Arab–Israeli conflict to female genital mutilation, dual citizenship, intermarriage with Israelis, and gender discrimination—issues that were prohibited just a few years ago as "too sensitive" to be discussed on national television. However, it appears that the average Egyptian viewer is shrewdly aware of the hyped dramas that underlie such programming, taking them with a grain of salt (Elbendary, 2001a).

The most popular of these PTV programs in 2003 was *"Ra-is El-Tahrir"* (Editor in Chief), hosted by a respected Egyptian journalist, Hamdi Qandil, one of the few credible sources of news analysis. "Did you hear what Hamdi

Qandil said last night?" was one of the more common morning-after questions. Nevertheless, it remained a vehicle for Qandil to express his opinions, and what he argues is the popular sentiment concerning issues of the day. He has a histrionic style and his commentary is replete with daring questions and remarks. Viewers were fascinated by his apparent lack of inhibition. Qandil's favorite subject is Israeli occupation and aggression, and the United States' "blind support" of Israel (Elbendary, 2001a).

Viewers are skeptical over the sensationalism with which the majority of such programs are presented. Furthermore, the argument is regularly made that the new veneer of liberty such programs have brought to Egyptian television is a safety valve that allows the public to express some of its simmering public anger and irritation with the way Egypt is being managed. They have nonetheless raised the bar of freedom of expression in Egypt.

BROADCAST IMPORTS AND EXPORTS

Egyptian soap operas are exported throughout the Middle East. In 2002 alone, total sales of Egyptian soap operas and radio programs to Arab countries including Saudi Arabia, Kuwait, and the United Arab Emirates were estimated at $20 million. The softness of the Egyptian Pound in 2004 (E£6.20 = U.S.$1.00) will certainly boost TV exports. Egyptian television had produced 13 soap operas that year at a cost of $10 million.

Whereas Egypt has always been the primary exporter of serials and films in the Middle East, import content had been limited to a few programs a week, mainly American serials and films. Although foreign soaps such as "The Bold and the Beautiful" and "The Young and the Restless" proved to be as popular as their Egyptian counterparts, it was the introduction of satellite television in the late 1990s that resulted in an inevitable onslaught of foreign content and English-language programming. Pan-Arab television channels such as MBC have become the primary carriers of popular American programming such as "Friends," "Will & Grace," "Seinfeld," and "Ally McBeal." On Egyptian terrestrial television, foreign programming still remains limited, consisting mainly of recycled English soaps and films.

FILM

Egyptian cinema has always dominated screens within the Arab World, with its production of mass-audience films along the same lines as those of Hollywood. By 1917 there were 80 cinemas in Egypt, and by 1925 an impulse of "national capitalism" led to the Misr Bank's (Egypt's national bank) involvement in financing Egyptian motion pictures. The first Egyptian film is considered to be Leila by Stephen Rosti (1927). It is a story of love, misuse, betrayal, and downfall and was the first in a long line of melodramas. Its star, Aziza Amir, became one of the Arab world's successful women producers.

Egypt's cinema really took off with the introduction of sound during the 1930s. The radio had already made Egyptian singing stars famous throughout the Arab world, and powerful record companies like Odeon and Baidaphone encouraged the singers they had under contract to appear in films, which they coproduced. Unused to Egyptian Arabic, the public in other countries (where often slightly different dialects are spoken) went to the cinema to see their favorite stars. Singers such Umm Kalthoum, Mohamed Abd el Wahab, and Leila Mourad reigned supreme to the end of the 1940s and remain icons of modern-day Egypt.

During the 1930s, the Misr Bank further financed production by sending technicians abroad for training and setting up Misr Studio in 1935. Production increased from 6 films in 1933 to 17 in 1936. Other studios were installed, artists' salaries rose as in Hollywood, and to the musical/comedy genres were added farces and the melodrama, with themes of seduction, implied rape, adultery, murder, and suicide.

The "first lady of the screen" was Faten Hamama, who played orphan/Cinderella type roles and later portrayed the difficult conditions women face in the Middle East. In 1953 Hamama starred with an unknown Syrian-Lebanese Christian, Michel Dimitri Shalhoub, in Egyptian director Youssef Chahine's *Raging Sky*. Converting to Islam, Shalhoub changed his name to Omar Sherif and married Hamama, and they starred together in Chahine's *The Black Waters* (1956), then in *Night Without Sleep* (1958) and *River of Love* (1960). Sharif went on to become Egypt's most recognizable film export, giving memorable performances in *Genghis Khan, Lawrence of Arabia, Dr. Zhivago, Hidalgo,* and in many other films.

The possibility of more realistic films did not emerge until Nasser's Free Officers' Revolt of 1952, on whose leadership the Arab world's frustrations and hopes focused for several years.

Hitherto peaceful coexistence in Palestine between the majority Arab population (Muslim and Christian) and the existing (Sephardic) Jewish inhabitants of the country was severely shattered in 1948. The establishment of the State of Israel wiped Palestine off the map and displaced and dispossessed 780,000 Muslim and Christian Arabs.

The destruction of Palestine was felt throughout the Arab world that was still experiencing European colonialism in many countries. Nasser represented the possibility of a nationalist Arab unity. In 1956 he nationalized the Suez Canal, which provoked an attack by Britain, France, and Israel and led to the second Arab–Israeli war. A plethora of films emerged about the subject, including Ahmed Badrakhan's 1956 *God Is With Us*.

Despite a notable decline in Egypt's film industry during the 1980s and 1990s, in terms of both numbers and quality, Egypt still has one of the most profitable film industries in the world and is in an elite group with the United States and India when it comes to filmmaking without external finance or subsidies. It ranks as the 30th most prolific feature film-producing nation. In 2002 Egyptian films made more that $14.4 million. Between 1989 and 1999, Egypt averaged 45 films a year and remains the mainstay of the Arabic film industry (www.africafilmtv.com). Hit films in recent years have included *Malek Rouhi* (King of My Heart), starring Egyptian superstar Yusra as a businesswoman who falls in love with a younger man, and *Let's Dream of Tomorrow*, starring the "beauty of Egyptian film," Leila Elwi, who plays the role of a businesswoman who falls in love with a married bank president.

As with soap operas and to a lesser extent political talk television, films are pressing the unwritten red lines of Egyptian cultural norms and, in the process, opening discussions on topics previously considered off limits. Egypt media's agenda-setting role in the Middle East cannot be understated.

ACKNOWLEDGMENT

This chapter was prepared with the invaluable assistance and translations of Amy Mowafi, a graduate student at the American University in Cairo.

REFERENCES

Agence France Presse. (2003, December 29). Israel launches second satellite. http://www.news.com.au/common/story_page/0,4057,8277261%255E15306,00.html

Amin, H. Y. (1996) Egypt and the Arab world in the satellite age. In J. Sinclair, E. Jacka, & S. Cunningham (Eds.), *New patterns of global television: A peripheral vision* (pp. 101–124). London: Oxford University Press.

Boyd, D. A., & Straubhaar, J. D. (1989). *Videocassette recorders in the third world*. New York: Longman.

Central Intelligence Agency. (2003). *The world factbook: Egypt*. Washington, DC: Author. Available: http://cia.gov/cia/publications/factbook/geos/eg.html

Elbendary, A. (2001a, June 14). TV meets the madding crowd. *Al Ahram Weekly Online*. Issue No. 538. http://weekly.ahram.org.eg/2001/538/cu2.htm

Elbendary, A. (2001b, December 27). Pride and prejudice. *Al Ahram Weekly Online*. Issue No. 566. http://weekly.ahram.org.eg/2001/566/fe3.htm

El-Guindi, A. (2003, November 7). The head of the Egyptian Media Production City criticizes investment laws. *Al-Hayat*, p. 20.

El-Hennawy, N. (2003, Fall–Winter). Saving Egyptian Pay-TV: CNE fights pirates. *Transnational Broadcasting Studies (TBS) Journal*. Retrieved from http://www.tbsjournal.com

Egyptian Ministry of Information. (2003). *The establishment of the Egyptian Radio Service*. http://www.sis.gov.eg/Calendar/html/cl31598a.htm

Forrester, C. (1998, January). Hollywood on the Nile. *Multi-channel News International*, pp. 25–27.

Forrester, C. (2001, Fall–Winter). High hopes for Egyptian media production city. *Transnational Broadcasting Studies Journal*, 7. http://www.tbsjournal.com

Gharib, S. (1992). Egypt: A national obsession. *The UNESCO Courier*, pp. 33–35.

Goldfarb, Z. A. (2003, July 28). Media imports trigger global culture debates. *The Washington Times*. http://washingtontimes.com/world/ 200300727–104255–2932.htm

Kader, S. A. (1986, May–June). Traditional means of communication and modern mass media in Egypt. *Ektistics*, *318*, 224–230.

Moody, S. (1999). *Pay television in Egypt: Development and impediments*. Unpublished master of arts thesis, The American University in Cairo, Egypt.

Napoli, J., & Amin, H. Y. (1995) Privatization of the Egyptian media. *Journal of South Asian and Middle Eastern Studies*, *18*(4), pp. 39–57.

Nasser, M. K. (1990, December). Egyptian mass media under Nasser and Sadat: Two models of press management and control. *Journalism Monographs*, 24.

Rasheed, D. (2003, August 21–27). Satellite for all? *Al Ahram Weekly Online*, 652. http://weekly,ahram.org.eg/2003/ 652/feat1.htm

Sakr, N. (2000, Fall–Winter) Optical illusions: Television and censorship in the Arab World. *Transnational Broadcasting Studies Journal*, 5. http://www.tbsjournal.com

Schleifer, S. A. (1998, Fall). Media explosion in the Arab world: The pan-Arab satellite broadcasters. *Transnational Broadcasting Studies Journal*, 1. http://www.tbsjournal .com

World Resource Institute (2003, December). *Access to information: Television sets per 1,000 people*. Data Provider: International Telecommunications Union (ITU). http://earthtrends.wri.org/text/POP/variables/558.htm

United Nations Development Program (UNDP). (2002) *Arab human development report 2002: Creating opportunities for future generations*. New York: United Nations.

EGYPT, PRIME TIME, DECEMBER 8–14, 2003

MONDAY							
Channel	7 p.m.	7:30 p.m.	8 p.m.	8:30 p.m.	9 p.m.	9:30 p.m.	10 p.m.
One	Honor Board	Hanady Cartoon	Arabic Series		9 O'clock news	In Depth TV (political talk show)	
Two	Arabic Series		Egyptian Faces	It's All One World (cultural pro-gramming)	Situations and Funnies (hidden camera)	Camellia (English series)	
Three	Events Narrated by History	Local News	Educational Programs		Arabic Series		Your Favorite Songs
Four	The News in English	An Invitation On Air (celebrity interviews)			Voices and Tunes	Behind the Head-lines (politi-cal talk show)	News and Services
Five	Arabic Series		The Other Dimension	The News in French	Good Evening	An English Movie (usually foreign produced)	
Six	A Youth Gath-ering (discus-sion program)	Sun Down	Words from the Quran	Events of the Week	The Channel Six Stadium	Arabic Series	
Seven	An Everyday Story	The Sports Shop	On the Internet		Arabic Movie		News
Eight	News and Opinions	English Series	A South-ern Evening (cultural program)	A Talk with El Shikh el Sharawi (religious program)		Wonders of the World	
TUESDAY							
Channel	7 p.m.	7:30 p.m	8 p.m.	8:30 p.m	9 p.m.	9:30 p.m.	10 p.m.
One	The Egyptian Woman	Hanady Cartoon	Arabic Series		The News	Eye Witness (political talk show)	

Two	Autocross	Cultural Evening	Meditation	Art and Creation	Sports Program	**Camellia** (English series)	
Three	Passport (travel)	Journalism Says (media analyses)	News Report	A Question and a Place	Arabic Series		A Channel Three Report
Four	The News in English	An invitation On Air (celebrity interviews)			Economic Information	Behind the Headlines (political talk show)	News and Services
Five	The News in English	Arabic Series		The News in French	Arabic Movie		
Six	A Meeting with a Man of Authority (interviews)		Words from the Quran		A Look Through the Window of History	Arabic Series	
Seven	The Everyday Story	The Club Table		In the Frame	It's Time	The Light of Civilization	The News
Eight	News and Opinions		Varieties	A World of Secrets	Luck or What? (quiz show)	A Riddle and a Prize (quiz show)	

WEDNESDAY

Channel	7 p.m.	7:30 p.m	8 p.m.	8:30 p.m	9 p.m.	9:30 p.m.	10 p.m.
One	Arabic Movie	Hanady Cartoon	Arabic Series		The News	Discussion Guide (talk show)	
Two	Economical Magazine (current affairs)		Dreams Come True		**Camellia** (English series)		Documents on Air (talk show)
Three	Stars and Cartoons	Local News	The Airport in a Week	Scientist from Egypt	Egyptian Treasures	Arabic Series	
Four	The News in English	An Invitation On Air (celebrity interviews)			Arabic Movie		
Five	Arabic Series		Stars from Alexandria		Good Evening (current affairs)		Remember (historical program)
Six	A Report on the Reading Festival		Words from the Quran		A Religious Gathering		Arabic series
Seven	Southern Creations (cultural program)		Information in a Picture		Tourism and Travel		The News

THURSDAY

Channel	7 p.m.	7:30 p.m	8 p.m.	8:30 p.m	9 p.m.	9:30 p.m.	10 p.m.
One	People's News	Hanady cartoon	The Magic of Darkness	Arabic Series		The News	Win Win (quiz show)
Two	The Sail: Arabic Film					**Camellia** (English series)	Happier Times
Three	Report from the Reading Festival	Local News	Egyptian Honors	Star with the Audience (celebrity interviews)	Arabic Series		Weekend

Channel	7 p.m.	7:30 p.m	8 p.m.	8:30 p.m	9 p.m.	9:30 p.m.	10 p.m.
Four	The News in English	An Invitation On Air (celebrity interviews)			Honestly	Report about the Reading Festival	News and Serials
Five	The News in English	Arabic Series		Sign Language	The News in French	Good Evening	Adventure Clip
Six	Report from the Reading Festival	Thursday Meeting (current affairs)	Words from the Quran		Arabic Series		Facts of Our Lives
Seven	The Everyday Story	Educational Programs		Upper Egypt	Viewer's Opinions (call-in show)	Hope for Tomorrow	The News
Eight	Sports Hour		Luck or What? (quiz show)	Nubian Treasures (cultural program)		Tourism Encyclopedia	News and Opinions

FRIDAY

Channel	7 p.m.	7:30 p.m	8 p.m.	8:30 p.m	9 p.m.	9:30 p.m.	10 p.m.
One	Take Me With You (travel)	Hanady Cartoon	The Days of Civilization : Arabic Series		Nine O'Clock news		
Two	Soccer Game						Camellia (English series)
Three	Arabic Movie	Local News	Resume the Movie		Journalism Says (media analysis)		A Look at the Week's Events
Four	The News in English	An Invitation On Air (celebrity interviews)			On Screen		News and Services
Five	The News in English	Arabic TV series	The Viewer's Guide	Encyclopedia of Alexandria			Remember (historical)
Six	The Everyday Story	My Heart Is With You	The Language of the Past	The Touristic Magazine	The Viewer's Opinions		
Seven	Report about the Reading Festival	Sing Songs	Words from the Queen	The Events of the Week	An Extraordinary Gathering		
Eight	The Friday Encyclopedia	People and Environment	Women's National Council	News and Opinions	The Events of the Week		Monuments of Different Cities

SATURDAY

Channel	7 p.m.	7:30 p.m	8 p.m.	8:30 p.m	9 p.m.	9:30 p.m.	10 p.m.
One	An Appointment with a Star (celebrity interviews)	Hanady Cartoon	Arabic Series		Nine O'clock news		
Two	The Nile's Children		A Musical Opera		Camellia (English series)		Meditation
Three	Computer World	Local News	Egyptians outside Egypt		Arabic Series		The Best Programs
Four	Panorama Port Said	An Invitation On Air (celebrity interviews)			The Miracle of the Quran		News and Services
Five	Arabic Series				Life Is a Moment		Songs

Six	Report about the Reading festival	Honestly	Words from the Quran	The Events of the Week (current affairs)	Agricultural program		Arabic Series
Seven	Educational Program	On Campus (interviews with students)	Requests Granted (music)	Together Let's Understand	Lines (talk show)		Ten o'clock news
Eight	Report about the Reading Festival	The World of Cinema	Arabic Movie				Arabic Series

SUNDAY

Channel	7 p.m.	7:30 p.m	8 p.m.	8:30 p.m	9 p.m.	9:30 p.m.	10 p.m.
One	Zoom	Hanady Cartoon	Arabic Series		Nine O'clock News		
Two	Spot lights	Between Reality and Imagination	A look at the Events (current affairs)				The Red Line (political talk show)
Three	Researchers and Centers	Journalism Says	Jobs and Secrets	Youth and Sports			A Scene from the History of Cinema
Four	The News in English				The Borders of Life		News and Services
Five	Arabic Series				Good Evening		A Whisper Out Loud
Six	A Prize for the Winning Family (quiz show)		Words from the Quran	The Events of the Week	Arabic Movie		
Seven	The Everyday Story	A Legal Opinion	A New Start	Security Valve	Upper Egyptian Literature and Art		Ten O'clock News
Eight	News and Opinions	A Trip in a Question	Between the Past and the Present	Egypt in the Eyes of Others	On Air		Arabic Series

Note. **Bold** denotes imported program.

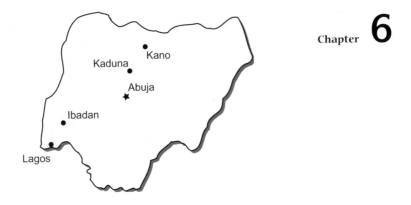

Chapter 6

Nigeria

Anthony A. Olorunnisola
Pennsylvania State University

Tunde M. Akanni
Lagos State University

ABOUT NIGERIA

Nigeria, the most populous Black nation in the world, is located on the south coast of Africa, occupying a land mass of 355,668 square miles. Comparatively, Nigeria's land mass is equivalent to the entire area of Texas, Michigan, South Carolina, and the District of Columbia combined (Nigerian Broadcasting Corp., 2001; Uche, 1989).

Nigeria's population of 126,635,626 (2001 estimates) comprises no fewer than 250 ethnic groups. Each ethnic group is distinguishable by its own language or dialect. The major ethnic and language groups include the Hausa (accounting for 21%), the Yoruba (21%), the Igbo (18%), and the Fulani (11%; NBC, 2001).

Given that Nigerians could not agree on which of the local languages should become the lingua franca, English, introduced by colonial exposure to the British Empire, functions as the language of business, instruction, and broadcasting. In a sizable part of the country, however, the Hausa, Igbo, and Yoruba languages coexist with English as principal languages for all three aforementioned purposes.

Until the agriculture sector was overtaken by crude oil, Nigeria was a leading exporter of a range of produce that included cocoa, peanuts, palm oil, and palm kernel. Nigeria's livestock resources, such as fishery and cattle, were also significant. Since the 1970s and to date, crude oil has replaced agricultural products as the mainstay of Nigeria's economy. Sales of crude oil now account for 98% of the nation's export billings (NBC, 2001).

After independence, Nigeria operated a political structure that revolved around a weak central government and three powerful regions. This structure was reversed in 1975 when Nigeria assumed a 12-state structure at the height of military governance in the country. Nigeria has 36 states altogether.

After more than 25 years of military rule, Nigeria returned to democratic governance in 1999. Nigeria has an executive presidency with a bicameral national assembly and 30 registered political parties. The People's Democratic Party (PDP) is the ruling party, with control over central government, 27 states, and the highest number of seats in the bicameral assembly. Among other international affiliations, Nigeria is a member of the Commonwealth of Nations, the Economic Community of West African States (ECOWAS), and the Organization of Petroleum Exporting Countries (OPEC) and is a leading voice in the newly established Africa Union (AU), formerly the Organization of African Unity (OAU).

BROADCAST BACKGROUND

History

Inception. As is the case in most former colonies, broadcasting was introduced to Nigeria in 1936 as part of the British Overseas Service. The arrangement was such that Lagos, Nigeria, would transmit broadcasts of the British Empire Service from Daventry, England. In due course, the Nigerian Post and Telegraphs Department was mandated to plan for the distribution of radio service (redifussion) to subscribers in three Nigerian cities that included Lagos, Kano, and Ibadan.

A number of scholars (e.g., Uche, 2000) have claimed that a primary goal of colonial broadcasting was to use the service as a major avenue of furthering the distribution of British propaganda. By 1944, however, the clientele of the radio services had grown so much that more distribution centers were set up in Kaduna, Enugu, Calabar, and Port Harcourt. By 1949, no fewer than 4,562 licensed radio sets had been wired to the distribution centers (Obazele, 1996).

Given the upsurge in the number of radio service users, the colonial administration got the signal that Nigerians had a strong appetite for information and that there was the need to do more to address their demand. Subsequently, the government began the move to convert all the existing redifussion stations into fully functional radio stations. In 1952, all the Radio Distribution Services were converted into the nucleus of the Nigeria Broadcasting Service (NBS), headquartered in Lagos. The choice of Lagos was political, largely informed by the city's position as the nation's capital and seat of colonial government. This choice was made in spite of a feasibility report that had earlier advised against coastal Lagos serving as the core of the broadcast service. Jos, in the north, or some other more central location far from the oceanic waves that could interfere with the functioning of the equipment, was recommended.

Not long after its inception, the Nigeria Broadcasting Service was perceived as a government mouthpiece—an outlet completely blind to divergent views and the multicultural composition of the country. To put an end to this perception, members of the Federal House of Parliament worked toward an enactment intended to straighten up the service. They decided to convert the NBS into the Nigerian Broadcasting Corporation (NBC) in 1957 (Uche, 2000). Among others, the enabling act that established the NBC stipulated that the corporation should provide, as a public service, independent and impartial broadcasting services for general reception within and outside Nigeria. The act further stipulated that the corporation should ensure that it reflected the unity of Nigeria and gave adequate expression to the country's diverse cultures. To ensure that the latter mission was implemented, boards of governors at the federal and regional levels were appointed to direct the affairs of the NBC, an initiative that was to confer a reasonable measure of independence in policy making on the boards. A primary duty of the regional boards was to ensure that *regional* programs were consistent with the educational policies of the governments of the respective regions.

In those early years, the Nigerian Broadcasting Corporation ran a three-tier service that included national, regional, and provincial outlets. In addition, an external service called the Voice of Nigeria (VON) was established in 1961 to project the personality, the culture, and the traditions of the peoples of Nigeria to the outside world. The Voice of Nigeria was also mandated to broadcast news of international significance in line with the foreign policy of the federal government. VON broadcasts were disseminated in six languages that included English, French, Arabic, Hausa, Fulfude, and Kiswahili (Uche, 2000).

Clamor for Autonomy. The freedom that regional outlets had to be distinctive in determining program content did not pacify autonomous regions. Their desire for independence soared when some of the regions realized that the creation of independent broadcasting outlets would enable them to establish consistency between their socioeconomic goals and the uniqueness of their citizens. The same action would remove the region from the domineering influence of the federal government via broadcasting.

In 1960, the Western Region became a pioneer when it established a radio station. A television station had begun services a year earlier. The Eastern Region followed suit, and in 1962 the Northern Region government joined its counterparts. Of the three, the Western Region's broadcasting system was the most successful. Endowed with a business plan, the station opened its doors to advertisers from inception. This was a point of departure from the NBC model in which the stations relied on the federal government for budgetary allocations. Soon after the Western Region's broadcasting services operations commenced, management installed a booster station near Lagos to increase reception by listeners in the Lagos area.

The Second Republic. The federal government, under succeeding military regimes, would hold on to all the broadcast stations from 1966 to 1979. However, the broadcasting sector was decentralized in preparation for the democratically elected civilian administration that assumed power in 1979. To make way for an effective decentralization, the military government dissolved the NBC and handed over 20 of its stations to state governments. Stations in Enugu, Ibadan, Kaduna, and Lagos were merged to constitute the Federal Radio Corporation of Nigeria (FRCN). The various states assumed ownership of the stations that had been forcibly taken over from them by the military government. By now, and given the frequent policy vacillations of subsequent years, broadcasting had become one of the most politicized sectors of the Nigerian media. Certainly, military and civilian administrations equally recognized the potency of the sector as a political tool. In 1983 alone, seven stations were commissioned in Abeokuta, Akure, Calabar, Ikeja, Enugu, Jos, and Owerri.

However, the expansionist drive was not to endure as the military struck again in December 1983. Without waiting to be whipped into line, all radio and television stations in the country started hooking up to the federal government-owned FRCN and the Nigerian Television Authority (NTA). Given political realignment of the states with the federal military government and the absence of competitive rancor, the Federal Government opted to prune down the FRCN stations once again. The stations in Akure, Calabar, Ibadan, Ilorin, and Owerri were closed down, leaving no fewer than 2,000 workers unemployed (Uche, 2000).

Television. Unlike the center–periphery spread of radio stations, regions led the growth and development of television in Nigeria. On October 31, 1959, the Western Region installed the first TV mast and broadcast the first TV signal in Africa (Uche, 2000).

While debating the value of the medium, the legislative house in the Western Region concluded that television was going to be of immense benefit to the educational system as there was a dearth of qualified teachers. Members asserted that television's visual advantage would enable the medium to serve as a surrogate teacher. As was done when radio service was established, Western Nigeria Television Service (WNTS) opened its door to commercials from the beginning. Remarkably, the regional government demonstrated a strong commitment to excellence and impartiality from the onset. For example, Section 7 of the Western Nigeria Government Broadcasting Law of 1959 stipulated "that due impartiality (be) preserved in respect of matters of political or industrial controversy or relating to current public policy" (Sotumbi, 1996, p. 173).

Bandwagon Effect.   As was the case when radio service was established, Eastern Nigeria followed the example of the Western Region and on October 1, 1960, used the establishment of its TV service to add more color to the celebrations that accompanied the country's independence. As in the Western Region, education was touted as the prime reason for the establishment of the TV service.

Although more resources were at its disposal, the Federal Government of Nigeria was a late adopter of TV technology. Some federal officials refused to subscribe to the idea, arguing that access to television was sheer luxury and that radio service should instead be expanded. When the federal government finally jumped on the TV bandwagon in April 1962, it did so in partnership with NBC-International of the United States. The collaboration, then known as NBC-TV, provided for a 5-year initial joint ownership during which the station would engage in capacity development to enable Nigerians to take over the management of the station. At the expiration of the 5 years, the foreign partner sold its shares to the federal government and the latter took complete control of the TV service.

As was the case with the radio subsector, the third national development plan (1975–1980) voted $203.6 million for the development of TV projects nationwide. This budgetary allocation enabled the Nigerian Television Authority to convert its monochrome service into a nationwide color service. By the inception of the elected civilian administration in 1979, all TV stations in the country had commenced color transmission to their viewers.

BROADCAST REGULATION

For several years, insiders in and observers of Nigeria's broadcasting sector decried the extent to which succeeding governments' control stagnated creativity, limited the growth and potential of the affiliate industries, and stifled competition. The 1979 Constitution, however, legitimated participation in broadcasting by private owners. Conspicuously missing was constitutional provision for an implementation agency that would handle application processes and enable the entry of independent stakeholders into the sector.

A paradigm shift was witnessed in the broadcasting industry when, by Decree No. 38 of 1992, the Babangida military regime formally established the National Broadcasting Commission. One provision of the decree establishing the commission was that it would advise the federal government on all policy issues pertaining to broadcasting. The commission would also process applications submitted by individuals and/or corporations interested in owning and operating radio and television stations. The commission's terms of reference covered vetting applications for cable, direct satellite broadcasting, and other means of broadcasting. Applicants to the committee include radio and television stations owned by governments at the local, state and federal levels. The commission was also given regulatory control over and an ombudsman role in broadcasting (NBC, 2001).

Public/Private Ownership

Shortly after its creation, the National Broadcasting Commission issued 14 licenses to private investors, mostly for domestic television broadcast via terrestrial transmitters. A number of cable satellite companies were also licensed and empowered to redistribute signals of foreign cable television stations. In 1995, the Commission granted the first direct satellite television broadcast license to DAAR Communications Limited, owners of the Raypower Radio Stations 100 and 106.5 and of African Independent Television (AIT). Minaj Systems, owners of Minaj Broadcast International (MBI), also received a license.

In 2003, 106 TV and 40 radio stations are owned by the federal government. Another 29 TV and 33 radio stations belong to states around the country. Nine TV stations and eight radio stations are owned by private individuals and corporations. Twenty private cable and satellite retransmitting agencies were also licensed by the National Broadcasting Commission (NBC, 2001). On the horizon is the possibility that the commission might license community radio stations.

Prohibitions

Following the deregulation of the broadcasting sector, the National Broadcasting Commission swung into action. It fashioned rules and regulations applicable to the entire gamut of broadcasting, ranging from news and other programs to commercials. The commission is particularly strict with children's fare. According to its code, a program that violates "social values, shows disrespect for law and order, or departs from an honorable lifestyle, is forbidden" (NBC, 2001, p. 47). The code goes further to outlaw X-rated programs and insists that swearing or blasphemous language of any kind must be avoided.

As for news coverage, particularly coverage of crises or conflicts, the commission prohibits presentation of morbid or graphic details of fatalities, injuries, or exaggerated census of casualties. The commission is, however, unclear on how stations should distinguish between graphic details and appropriate visuals. The commission disallows the use of children, women, and sportsmen as models in the advertisement of alcohol or tobacco.

Furthermore, the commission regularly monitors its licensees and when it notices or gets alerted to defiance of its regulations, it employs reminder campaigns via paid advertisements in newspapers and the broadcast media. During political campaigns in the April 2003 national elections, for instance, the Commission published a series of advertisements on the need for the broadcast media to be fair in transmitting messages of politicians representing all political parties.

National Film and Video Censors Board

The National Film and Video Censors Board (NFVCB), a regulatory agency, underscores the interdependence of the film and TV industries in the area of programming. Recently, two midget actors popularly known as Aki and Pawpaw became notorious for appearing in several films in which they commit acts such as smoking, tripping the elderly, running after women, and stealing money. In a recent film and as the scene fades, they were seen smoking, dressed like American rap artists (with jackets, scarves, and boots). In another, they ran rings around an elderly man, who in turn was determined to capture them for an offense they had committed earlier. The young boys decided to punish the adult who had questioned their behavior by tripping him as he rode his bicycle on his way from the farm. In another scene, the same two actors were spying on two adults who were making love (Akpovi-Esade, 2003a).

Many critics, including the National Film and Video Censors Board, saw the slew of films with similar behavior enacted by the actors as a denigration of the African culture and tradition of total respect for elders. Rather than showcase the latter, the board worried that the films would promote and encourage social vices among young people. Subsequently, the executive director of the Censors Board called on producers and marketers of films that featured the midget characters to exercise restraint and be mindful of the negative impact the films could, the censors felt, have on Nigerian children. The executive director also promised that her board would critically review future films in which the notorious midgets appear and append a "not to be broadcast" (NTBB) rating (Akpovi-Esade, 2003b).

Once a film earns the NTBB rating, TV stations can no longer air it. Recently, a local TV station drew the anger of the Censors Board for airing— on a Tuesday morning and, incidentally, a public holiday—a home video in which an actress was seen slashing the throats of and stabbing her victims in cold blood. To curb the reoccurrence of such broadcasts, the Censors Board introduced a new classification policy that would ensure that publicly appropriate films are broadcast to the general public. Codes for promos and trailers on television were also introduced to prevent the use of censored material.

The ratings released by the board include the following:

- G   General Viewing
- C   Children

- NC   Not recommended for Children
                                            below 12
- PG   Parental Guidance
- 18   For mature viewership
- 18 (with symbol of a cutlass)   violent
- 18 (with symbol of a calabash)   film with ritual elements
- RE   Restricted Exhibition
- NTBB   Not to be Broadcast
- SFB   Safe for Broadcast

Note. A "calabash" is a container made from a gourd.

The NFVCB had been particularly emphatic that the foregoing ratings be implemented by TV stations, given that TV stations constitute a major outlet whereby films, censored by the board or not, get to the public (Akpovi-Esade, 2003c).

BROADCAST CONTENT

The entry of private owners following the deregulation of the industry has had a remarkable impact on the broadcasting landscape in Nigeria. As is to be expected, private players, though numerically fewer, have introduced diversity and keen competition to a sector previously dominated by government at the federal and state levels. The expansion of the duration of broadcasting is one significant change brought to the industry by private entrants. In the early years of television, programming began at 4 p.m. on weekdays, as school and the work day generally ended at 3 p.m. Later, African Independent Television (AIT) pioneered early morning telecasts starting at 6 a.m. Today AIT transmits for 24 hours, 7 days a week, the longest ever in the history of television in Nigeria.

In response to the extension of programming by private stations, government-owned TV stations now commence their broadcasts earlier in the day. For instance, the Nigerian Television Authority (NTA) features "A.M. Express" (6:30–9 a.m.) Monday–Friday. The program features interviews with newsmakers and traffic news in such big cities as Abuja, Lagos, and Port Harcourt.

Of the 29 *state*-owned television stations, the Cross Rivers State Broadcasting Corp. (CRSBC) has the longest weekday transmission with 12.5 hours. With 18 hours of continuous broadcasting, Enugu State Broadcasting Service (ESBS) has the longest weekend transmission period. The TV arm of the Broadcasting Corporation of Oyo State (BCOS), which transmits for 8 hours daily, devotes 2 hours to home videos and movies on Mondays, Tuesdays, Thursdays, and Fridays. (See program grid.)

Although the home video and film industries have remained virile in Nigeria, they face pragmatic concerns about distribution, security risks, and costs of producing programs. Over time, producers of home video and films have come to realize that terrestrial broadcasters represent the best outlet for their productions. On the other hand, the video and film industries' need for outlets presents an opportunity for broadcasters (regardless of ownership) whose production budgets are indirectly subsidized when such access is granted to producers who are not on their networks' payroll. As such, viewers craving local content of sorts know to look to terrestrial broadcasters for that aspect of their viewing diet.

Domestic Programs

Prime time domestic programs on terrestrial broadcasting stations are dominated by drama serials—a staple diet on Nigerian television since the inception of the medium in the late 1950s. Some of the domestic series of old continue to elicit nostalgic comments from viewers, and many of them have run for multiple years in their old and new formats.

"The Village Headmaster." This is one of the longest running drama series on the government-owned Nigerian Television Authority (NTA). Started in the 1960s and set within the context of Oja village, several scenes are located at the village school, the King's palace (Oloja of Oja), Bassey Okon's dispensary and store, and Amebo's palm wine joint. Oja is itself a sleepy southwestern Nigerian village with its fair share of domestic problems, complete with rivalry and bickering among its elders. In particular, Balogun (or warlord) is a recalcitrant and stubborn chieftain who, along with other mischievous chieftains, gets a kick out of undermining the authority of the traditional ruler, the Oloja of Oja.

A popular episode features Okoro, a burly character who has slipped into town as if from nowhere. Soon he buys Bassey Okon's dispensary and shop, after the latter declares bankruptcy, and quickly establishes himself as a force in the community. Okoro symbolizes the ubiquitous Igbo trader who has no reservation about settling in just about any Nigerian town or village. He is aggressive and always quick to get into an argument. He enjoys a good joke and, above all, loves the feel of his cutlass in his hands.

Intended to serve as a metaphor for Nigeria, Oja, in spite of its tiny population, has as its greatest attraction the multiethnic composition of its residents. The village was home to a curious sprinkle of stereotypes: the bearded and short-tempered Bassey Okon, who ran the only dispensary in the community as well as an inexhaustible rumor mill; Chief Eleyimi, a loud braggart and the sly Garuba who always nursed the ambition of usurping the position of the headmaster of the village school; Amebo, the rabid talebearer; and, of course, the village headmaster himself—a character whose comparatively higher education placed him in juxtaposition with other villagers. The latter factor frequently represented the coexistence of Western and traditional African values and cultures.

"The Village Headmaster" was well received and appreciated in all parts of Nigeria. While it ran, periodically for 30 years, the drama series provided a rendezvous for Nigerians of all geographic, ethnic, and cultural backgrounds. Several negotiation attempts to bring the serial back to network television as a permanent program have failed, although reruns are often aired.

"Super Story."   A current and highly rated serial, this show airs on the NTA network every Thursday 8–9 p.m., sponsored by Unilever Plc. The serial periodically mirrors and catalogues the various moral ills ravaging the society and proffers a solution to them—typically in a few episodes. There is always a moral at the end of the problems showcased.

A recent episode of "Super Story" titled "Oh Father, Oh Daughter" featured Suara (played by Yemi Adeyemi), a very poor man whose wife's many sacrifices eventually landed the husband a job that practically lifted him out of poverty. Soon after, the family's standard of living appreciated tremendously. Suara's newfound success quickly became a problem as he began to keep bad company and to stay out late. The loss of quality time with his family came to a climax when he became attracted to a "gold-digger" type. For days on end, Suara would not return home as he was engrossed in savoring the attention of his newfound love, Toyin (Shola Shobowale). With the assistance of his extended family, Suara soon sent his wife out of their matrimonial home and brought Toyin home. This marked the beginning of his proverbial end. The moral in the gripping drama included lessons about true love and the pains of betrayal.

Also typical of most drama series of its type, "Super Story" featured an assortment of Nigerian artists drawn from the major ethnic groups. Notable among the actors are Dejumo Lewis, award-winning Jide Kosoko, Ngozi Nwosu, Danjuma Mohammed, and Larry Koldsweat. The drama itself won an excellence award from the International Foundation for Excellence (IFE) in 2002.

"Everyday People."   Broadcast on African Independent Television on Mondays 7–7:30 p.m., this regular serial features a different family each week. The show focuses on encounters of regular people with various life issues, their ongoing successes as well as their failures. Snippets of the lives of about three families are showcased interchangeably as they interact with each other and contend with life in general.

A recent show featured a young, middle-class couple who live in Lagos. The husband's family is steeped in traditional healing methods, while the wife is not so familiar with that aspect of life. A problem arises when her mother-in-law comes by to visit with them after the birth of their first child. Mother-in-law also comes with an amulet prepared especially for the newborn. When the young mother refuses to have the baby wear the amulet, an argument develops between mother- and daughter-in-law. The husband, as educated as the wife and exposed to the idiosyncrasies of each side, chooses to stay out of the fray. Soon after the incident, the child falls sick and the mother is forced by the circumstances to accept the amulet. The foregoing episode is a typical encounter in which each spouse has different social, cultural and, at times, religious baggage to contend with.

Many a time, contentious situations arise in interactions with ever-present members of the extended family.

BROADCAST IMPORTS AND EXPORTS

Nigerian viewers are accustomed to a mixed bag of domestic and foreign programs. Cable and direct satellite broadcasters, who offer exclusively foreign packages of programs, have two problems: absence of domestic programs and high costs (cable and satellite subscriptions are luxuries that most financially strapped Nigerians cannot afford). Thus terrestrial broadcasters can provide a mixed diet of local and foreign TV programming at no additional cost to their viewers.

U.S. Series

TV audiences in Nigeria have had extensive exposure to imported programs dating back to the early years of the medium. In the mid-1960s, "Mission: Impossible," a series that featured a group of extraordinary government spies, was one popular foreign program. Reruns of the series played on government-owned Nigerian Television Authority for many years. Reruns of the series have played on both government and commercial stations in recent years and, in particular, when two successful feature films inspired by the series—*Mission: Impossible* and *Mission: Impossible 2*—starring Tom Cruise, hit the movie channels.

From "The Jeffersons" in the 1970s to "The Cosby Show," African-American comedies are TV perennials. Currently, CBS's "Touched by an Angel" is about the only foreign program run in prime time on government-owned NTA.

The "Young and the Restless" is the only soap opera featured in prime time on the program grid of the current season. Unlike the CBS daytime series, the program runs in prime time, 8–9 p.m. Monday–Friday on Murhi International Television (MITV). The only other difference is that the episodes shown on MITV are frequently not as current as those shown on CBS. For example, the original U.S. airdate of a 2003 episode titled "Deathbed Wedding" was April 6, 1998—5 years earlier.

Reality Shows

There is no reality show in the current season featured on the program schedule posted in this chapter. The previous season, however, witnessed a European reality show that had been localized in other countries. When "Big Brother" came to Africa, its first stop was South Africa (see chapter 7), where M-Net, a South African media company, and a Dutch firm, Endemol, collaborated on the housemate show.

After the first two productions attracted millions of South African viewers, the partners introduced "Big Brother Africa." The latter version included participants from 12 countries: Angola, Botswana, Ghana, Kenya, Malawi, Namibia, Nigeria, South Africa, Uganda, Tanzania, Zambia, and Zimbabwe. Continent-wide viewer participation via direct satellite TV, however, brought 46 nations to the screen for a total of 106 days.

The concept is the same in every country in which it ran prior to the Africa version. Commentators wonder if the notion behind the version is that of a miniature Africa, a microcosmic world that has to grapple with its sociological, ideological, and political differences.

Twelve individuals of mixed genders and nationalities, Nigeria included, are accompanied by 27 cameras, 64 microphones, 4 outdoor microphones, and 12 radio microphones—all of which monitor their activities for continent-wide audiences. Viewers in countries with M-Net affiliate television stations participate by voting (via Web site) and have the final say as to which of the participants gets evicted from the house and who stays.

On one of the episodes, a housemate who was shown taking her bath with her clothes on was evicted for behaving "unnaturally." Cherise Makubale, a 24-year-old Zambian who worked as a procurement officer, walked away with the $100,000 grand prize in September 2003 after she was voted the most loved housemate in Africa by a continent-wide audience.

TV Africa

Competition, whether it is in the area of sports, beauty pageants, or reality shows, has the tendency to draw a lot of viewer attention. Recently, TVAfrica, a free-to-air TV station based in Johannesburg, South Africa, saw an opportunity in negotiating coverage of programs known to appeal to a cross-continental audience. At the height of its operation, TVAfrica had a presence in 40 African countries including Nigeria. Affiliate stations in Nigeria were African Independent Television (AIT), Minaj Broadcast International, and the Nigerian Television Authority (NTA/NTA 2).

At the end of 2002, TVAfrica won the rights to broadcast the Miss World 2002 pageant from Lagos. Muslims protested the immodest displays of the female body; in ensuing riots, 220 people were killed. A journalist who defended the pageant had to flee from Nigeria after clerics issued a *fatwa* (order to kill) against her. The pageant was finally moved to the UK.

Besides a continent-wide military games segment, TVAfrica initiated moves to sign contracts with producers of programs around the world for distribution throughout the continent. The "Young and the Restless," broadcast on MITV and profiled earlier, is distributed by TVAfrica. Plans are in place to do the same with a diet of African-based programs. As recently as July 2003, TVAfrica and Wale Adenuga Productions (WAP) of Nigeria entered such a deal that would enable the pan-African broadcaster to distribute "Odd World," a 30-minute drama serial, to affiliate stations around the continent. "Super Story," one of the shows profiled earlier, came to television from the stable of Wale Adenuga Productions. So did "Papa Ajasco," a comedy aired on the AIT and NTA channels, respectively.

TVAfrica is now bankrupt and off the air. In October 2003, Africa Media Group, major shareholders in TVAfrica, pulled the plug on the continental channel after its debt profile rose $1 million in excess of the value of its assets. Many observers of the channel suggest that TVAfrica would have had better staying power if the owners had opted for ties with more major broadcasters across the continent that are typically government-owned rather than smaller private broadcasters. However, the landmark operations of TVAfrica and its ability to develop an actual footprint of 100 million viewers across the continent have proven to prospective investors that there is potential in continental broadcasting.

External Broadcasting

Voice of Nigeria (VON). With the establishment of the Voice of Nigeria in 1961, Nigeria has for more than 40 years been engaged in international broadcasting by radio. From inception, the Voice of Nigeria was charged with reflecting Nigerian and African perspectives on issues that shape the world. For those many years, VON has been the international radio broadcasting of choice for Nigerians and Africans in other parts of the world who are interested in Nigerian and African culture and political affairs.

"African Monarchy," a weekly series on VON, traces the history of kings and kingdoms in a nostalgic manner. The program looks at the institution from the past to the modifications that have developed over the years. A dimension of the program examines the desire of the institution for relevance in today's society, in particular, within the atmosphere of democratic governance that many African nations now operate. As an external broadcasting organ of Nigeria, the Voice of Nigeria, received worldwide, does not carry commercial advertisements or sponsored announcements.

Global AIT. One of the private TV stations, DAAR Communications Ltd.-owned African Independent Television (AIT), is now on global satellite transmission. The corporation signed an agreement with Comcast Cable Communications, Inc.—the largest national TV cable network operator in the United States—to distribute its signals as a premium channel on the latter's cable network across the United States, its possessions and territories for a 10-year period starting September 1, 2003. The service is a 24-hour-a-day, 7-days-a-week, satellite delivered, English language programming consists of news, sports, variety, and religious programs transmitted via live feed from Nigeria (Aihe, 2003).

Time Warner Cable Network has also agreed to distribute the signals of AIT as well as secure other affiliates for the same purpose. By this development, AIT became the first African channel to be distributed on a 24-hour basis on national cable networks. The channel becomes the second Black television channel (after BET) to be distributed throughout the United States since the inception of TV broadcasting.

AIT also has a presence in the United Kingdom with its location on satellite broadcaster British Sky Broadcasting's (BskyB) digital platform. With its coverage in Central Europe and presence on DSTV, AIT is on the way to becoming capable of initiating uplink and downlink signals from and to any part of the world using its Intelsat platform. AIT operates from Intelsat 901, a global beam that insures that the signals are available in most parts of the world. It also has additional capacity to handle feeds out of Nigeria provided on Intelsat 801, which is scheduled to move to 701. On the strength of this arrangement, DAAR Communications found a major hub on Comcast, which controls 42% of the entire cable penetration in the United States.

REFERENCES

Aihe, O. (2003, September 10). Hi-Tech: AIT takes global stage with Comcast . . . to be launched by President Obasanjo in the US. *Vanguard Online.* http://www.vanguardngr.com

Akpovi-Esade, J. (2003a, May 15). A comedy that is no longer funny. *ThisDay News Online.* http://www.thisdayonline.com

Akpovi-Esade, J. (2003b, May 21). No more dirty dancing, censors board tells artistes. *The Guardian Online.* http://www.guardiannews.com

Akpovi-Esade, J. (2003c, September 11). See Nigeria through Afrisat. *The Guardian Online.* http://www.guardiannews.com

NBC (Nigerian Broadcasting Commission). (2001). *Nigerian radio, television and cable handbook (NIRATCHI).* Abuja: Author.

Obazele, P. (1996). Challenges of radio journalism and management of broadcasting in Nigeria. In O. Dare, O. Uyo, & A. Uyo (Eds.), *Journalism in Nigeria: Issues and perspectives* (pp. 144–156). Lagos: Nigeria Union of Journalists.

Sotumbi, B. (1996). The challenges of television journalism. In O. Dare, O. Uyo, & A. Uyo (Eds.), *Journalism in Nigeria: Issues and perspectives* (pp. 172–182). Lagos: Nigeria Union of Journalists.

Uche, L. (1989). *Mass media people and politics in Nigeria.* New Delhi: Concert Publishing.

NIGERIA, PRIME TIME, MARCH 3-9, 2003

MONDAY							
Channel	7 pm	7:30 pm	8 pm	8:30 pm	9 pm	9:30 pm	10 pm
AIT	Everyday People (serial)	Things We Do for Love	AINET News	AINET News	Passions (U.S. serial)	Passions (U.S. serial)	Taxi Driver
MITV	The Arewa Show	Car Talk	The Young & the Restless (U.S. serial)	The Young & the Restless (U.S. serial)	Music Africana	MITV News	Business News
NTA	African Rythms	NTA News	The Mutanda Show	Economic Matters	Network News	Network News	Crusade
TUESDAY							
Channel	7 pm	7:30 pm	8 pm	8:30 pm	9 pm	9:30 pm	10 pm
AIT	AINET News/ Music	AINET News	EUFA	EUFA	EUFA/Things Fall Apart	EUFA/Things Fall Apart	EUFA/ Kabanana

| MITV | City Business | The Oko Oloyun Show | The Young & the Restless (U.S. serial) | The Young & the Restless (U.S. serial) | Musicals | MITV News | Business News |
| NTA | Infotech Impact | NTA News | Izozo | African Pot | Network News | Network News | Energy Summit |

WEDNESDAY

Channel	7 pm	7:30 pm	8 pm	8:30 pm	9 pm	9:30 pm	10 pm
AIT	Your Choice	Domino	AINET News	AINET News	Passions	Passions	This Life
MITV	Mother and Child	Straight Talk	The Young & the Restless (U.S. serial)	The Young & the Restless (U.S. serial)	Comedy ½ Hour	MITV News	Business News
NTA	Risk and Rescue	NTA News	Maggi Family Menu (cooking show)	Strides	Network News	Network News	Progress Report

THURSDAY

Channel	7 pm	7:30 pm	8 pm	8:30 pm	9 pm	9:30 pm	10 pm
AIT	Papa Ajasco (comedy)	The Taste of Africa	AINET News	AINET News	Passions	Passions	Portrait of Africa
MITV	Insurance World	Towards 2003	The Young & the Restless (U.S. serial)	The Young & the Restless (U.S. serial)	MITV Music Mix	MITV News	Business News
NTA	Twilight Zone	NTA News	The Super Story (serial)	The Super Story (serial)	Network News	Network News	From the Senate

FRIDAY

Channel	7 pm	7:30 pm	8 pm	8:30 pm	9 pm	9:30 pm	10 pm
AIT	Royal Tears	Royal Tears	AINET News	AINET News	Passions	Passions	Primetime Jamz
MITV	The Sports Professionals	The Sports Professionals	The Young & the Restless (U.S. serial)	The Young & the Restless (U.S. serial)	Star Dust	MITV News	Business News
NTA	Going Places	NTA News	Sweet & Sour	Sweet & Sour	Network News	Network News	Society & Style

SATURDAY

Channel	7 pm	7:30 pm	8 pm	8:30 pm	9 pm	9:30 pm	10 pm
AIT	Zenith	Zenith	Livin Next to U	Generations	Search Light	Search Light	Star World Video
MITV	Technology Today	Living for Tomorrow	TV Africa	TV Africa	TV Africa	MITV News	Ayorinde Live
NTA	Health Forum (live)	NTA News	Prime Time Jamz	Prime Time Jamz (musical)	Network News	Network News	Iroko Music

SUNDAY

Channel	7 pm	7:30	8 pm	8:30 pm	9 pm	9:30 pm	10 pm
AIT	Images	Fuji HIS of Commotion (musical)	Genius	Genius	TSM Show	TSM Show	Luventure

MITV	TV Africa	MITV Guest	MITV Guest	MITV News	Under the Heavens	Under the Heavens	TV Africa
NTA	Papa Ajasco (comedy)	NTA News	**Touched by an Angel** (U.S. serial)	**Touched by an Angel** (U.S. serial)	Newsline	Newsline	Christ Embassy

Note. **Bold** denotes an imported program

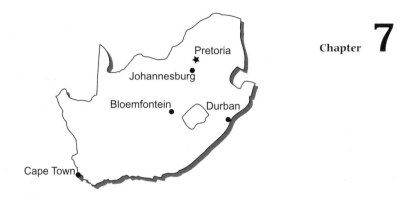

Chapter 7

South Africa

Lesley Cowling
University of the Witwatersrand, Johannesburg

ABOUT SOUTH AFRICA

South Africa, as the name implies, is located at the southernmost point of Africa, where the Indian and Atlantic oceans meet. It is a country that is highly diverse, both geographically and culturally. More than three quarters of its 43 million inhabitants are Black, descended from the indigenous African population, while 11% are White, 9% are "colored," that is, mixed race, and the rest are of Asian descent. There are 11 official languages, mostly indigenous. Although the majority of South Africans speak one of the local languages, English is the dominant language of commerce, government, and the media ("South Africa: The official . . .," 2003).

South Africa is probably best known internationally for the system of apartheid, which entrenched White minority rule over the Black majority and institutionalized racism against the so-called "non-White" population. And South Africa's best-known citizen is Nelson Mandela, one of the leaders of the African National Congress, the liberation movement that led

115

the struggle against apartheid. In the early 1990s, Mandela was released after 27 years in prison and, with other ANC leaders, began negotiations with the White government that eventually led to a new democratic constitution.

The first democratic elections were held in April 1994, and Nelson Mandela became president, followed 5 years later by the election of the current president, Thabo Mbeki. The last decade has thus seen massive change in every area of South African society, from politics and the economy to sport and social life, but the transition is by no means complete, and the legacy of apartheid still influences many aspects of life.

South Africa is the world's leading producer of gold and many other precious metals, and for a long while the performance of the economy was closely tied to the performance of the mining sector. However, the postapartheid government set about liberalizing and deregulating the economy, and diversifying exports. South Africa's GDP in 2001 was $412 billion (World Almanac Education Group, 2003), and the economy has been growing at the rate of about 2.8% a year since 1994.[1] Another government focus has been social development and job creation, but the dramatic gap between the rich and the poor in South Africa remains stark, despite economic growth. It is often said that South Africa is two countries—one that is developed, largely urban, and Westernized; the other mostly rural, Black, and underdeveloped.[2] This duality is reflected in the different living conditions of South Africans, squatter camps or rural huts as compared to suburban houses and townhouse developments. Such social and economic conditions have had implications for broadcasting and media.

BROADCAST BACKGROUND

History

Television was introduced quite late in South Africa because the ruling National Party feared the supposedly corrupting influence of television on the minds of South Africans. For many years, broadcasting was limited to radio, and most radio was controlled by the South African Broadcasting Corp. (SABC), a statutory body modelled on Britain's BBC. When television was finally introduced in 1975, the government made sure it retained control by running the channel as a public broadcaster, under the auspices of the SABC. TV advertising was only permitted in 1978, and the channel's

[1] From a discussion document on the economy published by the South African government in November 2003. See http://www.safrica.info/doing_business/economy/fiscal_policies/tenyeareconomy.htm

[2] In the November 3, 2003, edition of the newspaper This Day, opposition politician Patricia de Lille is quoted as saying: "South Africa and Brazil have had the largest Gini coefficients and inequalities between rich and poor for 30 to 40 years. . . . You can always talk about [South Africa as] a two-nation state, not so much divided between black and white, but between rich and poor, because there are lots of up and coming black middle class people."

major income came from license fees collected from the owners of TV sets (Mersham, 1993).

It was 1982 before TV1 was joined by TV2 and TV3, which broadcast on the same channel until they were separated in 1983. Whereas TV1's programs were broadcast in Afrikaans—the language of the ruling party—and English, TV2 broadcast in Nguni languages such as Xhosa and Zulu and TV3 in Sotho languages. By the late 1980s, TV2 broadcasts drew a daily viewership of 1.75 million people and TV3 had an audience of 1.6 million. A fourth channel, TV4, was introduced in 1985 (Mersham, 1993).

Issues of language and culture dominated program decisions at the SABC throughout the 1980s. Apartheid ideology saw South Africa's population as distinct and separate groups, which needed to be served with different programming in different languages. Although this policy was applied as a way to avoid the integration of South Africans of different races, South African media specialist Gary Mersham (1993) makes the point that it led to the development of indigenous language programming on a scale unprecedented in Africa. The SABC put much of its resources into developing Afrikaans drama and other programming. The dramas made in African languages were less well resourced and generally considered to be of a low standard and either "skop, skiet en donner" (cops 'n' robbers) stories or rural sagas.

The channel also experimented with a number of different ways to deal with imported programs, at one point dubbing French, German, and English programs into Afrikaans and other local languages. Later, the channel ran simulcasts—programs that had been dubbed, but had their original soundtracks broadcast on radio at the same time as they were running on television (SABC, 2003). Questions of language have remained important to the SABC, but the broadcaster no longer dubs programs and tends to use subtitles instead. The bulk of programming now is in English, but there are still a substantial number of vernacular programs on SABC1 and SABC2.

Television's increasing inroads into advertising caused some alarm among South African newspaper groups, whose revenue base began to be seriously eroded. A consortium approached the government in 1984 to propose that it be allowed to own and operate a subscription channel. The government agreed, and M-Net began broadcasting in 1986, using SABC transmitters to deliver a scrambled signal that could only be unscrambled by a special decoder (Mersham, 1993). However, the SABC retained a firm grasp on news programming, and M-Net was confined to entertainment programming and prohibited from broadcasting news or news actuality until the 1990s. M-Net from the first had a different image from the stuffy, uptight SABC, broadcasting mostly international shows from Britain and America. However, its subscription base meant that it reached largely an affluent, White audience.

The transition from the apartheid system caused a series of upheavals in television, especially at the SABC, which led to the repositioning and the renaming of the channels several times. The final relaunch of the new SABC in 1996 saw the channels being somewhat prosaically named SABC1, SABC2, and SABC3. Changing politics was not the only impact on the broadcaster—the new government's economic policy, with its emphasis on deregulation and privatization of previously state-owned corporations, put pressure on the SABC to commercialize.

The launch of a new free-to-air commercial channel, e-tv, and the introduction of DSTV, a satellite service that offered subscribers a range of different channels to choose from, pushed all TV channels into a race for advertising and audiences. The competition was exacerbated by the arrival of electronic media and new commercial radio stations.

Channels

Currently there are four free-to-air channels broadcasting in South Africa—the three SABC channels and e-tv. A fifth channel, M-Net, is still subscription only, but is open to nonsubscribers 5–7 p.m. every evening, a period called M-Net open time. All channels depend on advertising for revenue, although the SABC still receives license fees and M-Net receives subscriber fees, so all operate to a greater or lesser degree as commercial channels. However, all channels have conditions attached to their licenses by the broadcasting regulator, the Independent Communications Authority of South Africa (ICASA), which means they cannot operate in an entirely unrestricted fashion and have to fulfil certain obligations to the South African public (see Broadcast Regulations in the next section).

In general, the character of television in South Africa has changed dramatically in the last 12 years. Programming was previously restricted and limited by the state, which applied the political ideology of apartheid and conservative Calvinist values. Shows were monitored for sex, bad language, certain kinds of violence, and, of course, liberal ideas. Programming is now much more diverse and more inclusive of South Africa's many different communities and minority ideas. About 18 million adults watch television daily (SABC, 2003).

Positioning themselves in the market has been a constant process of trial and error for the various channels, partly because of competition for advertising and partly because South African audiences have been changing and becoming more sophisticated. Although they love local shows, audiences also want to see international shows. Also, the interests of advertisers and audiences do not always coincide, so channels can find they grow their ratings only to lose revenue. However, in the last few years, the channels have settled into more stable "personalities" and established their market niches, as shown in Table 7.1.

Owned by a consortium that includes Black empowerment groups, e-tv, being the new kid on the block, has been inclined to do things differently. It is the one channel that has not tied itself into a particular niche, but draws different audiences for different programming, sometimes a mass audience for frankly trashy programs and sometimes an affluent audi-

TABLE 7.1
Share of Television Audience by Channel: 2001

Channel	Share of Audience	Audience Profile
M-Net	6.3%	Mostly White and affluent
DSTV	1.8%	Mostly White and affluent
SABC1	29.1%	Mostly Black, mass market, strong youth component
SABC2	24.5%	Family-oriented. A strong Afrikaans-speaking representation early evening, because of local language programs, then a Black audience for African language programming after 8:30
SABC3	17.2%	Mostly affluent, 58% Black, rest shared between groups
e-TV	19.2%	Complete mix depending on programming. Going for a mass audience

Note. Nielsen Media Research/Hanka Sonnekus-Roos, Manager: Foreign Acquisitions SABC3 (personal communication, November 2003).

ence for quality dramas. Right from the start, e-tv ran a lot of movies, just like the pay channel, M-Net. An initial deal with Time Warner also meant that e-tv had the pick of Time Warner series, including HBO winners like "The Sopranos." Soon the evening line-up of news at 7 p.m., followed by a movie at 8 p.m., caused problems for SABC3, as e-tv news attracted an audience for news, then held on to it for the 1½ to 2 hours of the movie.

SABC3 eventually fought back by moving its 8 p.m. news to 7. Because this bulletin is only a half-hour, channel managers reasoned, audiences would tend to watch the 7:30–8:30 p.m. show, often a reality show, family drama, or game show. Sonnekus-Roos says that if the viewers stick with the 7:30 show, then they are more likely to stay with prime time programming (personal communication, November 2003). This strategy took some time to have an effect, but now SABC3 has increased audience share in prime time.

By running soft porn or erotica in the late evening, e-tv broke the mold of TV broadcasting in South Africa. The channel screened all the Emmanuelle films, a real revolution for viewers who a few short years ago would have been prosecuted for possessing such material. Also, e-tv scored a huge hit by introducing a number of wrestling shows. "WWE Velocity" and "International Raw" rate in the top 10 of the channel's shows.

Meanwhile, the SABC has been juggling to trade off its public service mandate against its need to make money. In about 1999, the broadcaster was instructed by the government to run one of its channels—SABC3—as a commercial channel and SABC1 and 2 as public service channels, using the commercial channel to subsidize the public service channels (SABC, 2003). However, this strategy has proved difficult, and the SABC now expects all its channels to be more or less self-sufficient. Members of Parliament have recently become uneasy about some of the implications of commercialization, however, and the government may once again reconsider the role of the broadcaster.

BROADCAST REGULATION

A new regulator was created in 1993 to take over broadcasting responsibilities that had fallen to various government departments under apartheid. It was later expanded to oversee telecommunications as well and was renamed the Independent Communications Authority of South Africa (ICASA, 2003). The authority has the responsibility of issuing licenses to TV and radio stations and setting the conditions for the operation of the broadcasters. It is also charged with monitoring the broadcasters, hearing complaints, managing the frequencies, and protecting consumers.

Potential broadcasters have to apply for licenses, and public hearings are held before the licenses are granted. There are three types of licenses: public, private (or commercial), and community for both radio and television. A large number of community licenses have been issued for radio frequencies. However, there is no community television as yet. Community broadcasting is not for profit and must serve the interests of a particular community and have community support and participation.

The regulations also place limits and restrictions on ownership. Foreign ownership is limited to 20% of any broadcasting company. No company may own more than one private TV license, more than two private FM radio licenses, or more than two private AM licenses. The Independent Broadcasting Authority (IBA) Act No. 153 of 1993 also restricts cross-media ownership, with print companies prohibited from owning different media in the same market to prevent the dominance of one big company in a geographical area.

The authority can set conditions for broadcasters on how much local content or South African music (in the case of music radio) they must carry and in what categories. Currently, the SABC is expected to carry at least 55% local content, mandated in Chapter vi of the IBA Act. Broadcasters must commission programming from a wide range of production companies and insure significant Black representation among those companies.

All broadcasters are expected to adhere to a code of conduct, specifically in regard to children. The regulator has specified that the adult "watershed period" begins at 9 p.m., and until that time, broadcasters should be sensitive to violence, sexual explicitness, and bad language. Broadcasters are also expected to avoid shows that glamorize violence, particularly against women and special groups. (However, as the code of conduct also states that violence and sexual explicitness that is integral to drama, education, and other types of programming is acceptable, it would be difficult in the case of a dispute to distinguish between gratuitous and dramatic violence.) The code of conduct also contains provisions relating to news.

The industry monitors itself when it comes to broadcast content, by agreement with ICASA. The National Association of Broadcasters, which represents most broadcasters, set up the Broadcast Complaints Commission of South Africa to hear complaints from the public. The Advertising Standards Authority hears and adjudicates disputes around advertisements. The monitoring section of ICASA specifically monitors how broadcasters are fulfilling their license conditions.

BROADCAST CONTENT

Soap Operas

Soap operas, both local and international, are the most watched programs on all channels, even though most of them are broadcast before prime time. The South African Advertising Research Foundation (2003), the media industry's independent research body, publishes a weekly list of the 10 most watched shows per channel; invariably the soaps dominate the list.

The oldest daily TV soap opera is "*Egoli*," which aired first in 1992, and is still broadcast on M-Net open time at 6 p.m. "*Egoli*," the Zulu name for Johannesburg (literally, "The Place of Gold"), has mostly White characters who speak English or Afrikaans or switch between the two languages, sometimes in one conversation. The habit of sliding between languages has become characteristic of South African soaps, although now languages like Sotho and Zulu are also included.

The most watched soap is "Generations," which is set in the Johannesburg advertising world and deals with the lives of members of the rich Moroka family. "Generations" was the first soap created by a Black producer, Mfundi Vundla, whose brother Peter started one of the first Black advertising agencies. Broadcast at 8 p.m. in prime time, its ratings have grown year after year since the first episode was broadcast in 1993, and it has become something of an institution among Black viewers, who sit down to watch it as a family. The world it depicts is "aspirational"— wealthy, urban, and upmarket—far from the reality of the lives of most of its viewers. It has never been much watched among White viewers as, until recently, the English news was broadcast at the same time on SABC3.

Apart from the fact that the Morokas are Black and South African and are in advertising, not fashion, "Generations" bears a strong resemblance to America's "The Bold and the Beautiful," the next most watched soap in the country. "Bold" is on SABC1 at 6 p.m., following "Days of Our Lives," and it draws big audiences despite its early broadcast slot. All three soaps are repeated the next morning on SABC1.

Another local soap, "*Isidingo*," often tops the audience ratings at SABC3, but still falls way below "Generations." "*Isidingo*" was introduced in mid-1998 in the euphoric period after South Africans had voted for their first democratic government and there was a great spirit of reconciliation, and the early series rode the wave of "one-nation viewing." The fast-moving soap, which its producers prefer to call a "daily drama," was initially set in a mining town and told stories about the residents of the town, including all the various communities—Black miners, retired White miners, shopkeepers, and the mine manager's family. "*Isidingo*" has maintained its fast pace and its racial diversity, but has moved away from the gritty realism.

In the late 1990s, "*Isidingo's*" large "rainbow" audience began to be eroded by new programs aimed at niche markets. The first group to move away were Afrikaans speakers, when an Afrikaans soap was introduced in the same time slot on SABC2. Called "*Sewende Laan*" (Seventh Avenue), the soap revolves around characters who live and work in a neighborhood street. It stays away from violence and sex and so attracts families who like to watch television with their children. With "Backstage," the South African version of "Fame," e-TV joined the battle of the 6:30 soaps. Set in a school of the arts, its young, hip characters attract a Black youth audience, but it does not get the ratings of "*Sewende Laan*," which leads the pack.

South African soaps differ from American soaps in a number of ways. First, they tend to move faster and have more action, without the long monologues and dialogues so beloved of "The Bold and the Beautiful." Secondly, they usually have a much bigger cast of characters at any one time than an American soap. The soaps tend to present society as nonracial, even if the characters are mostly drawn from one racial or cultural group; diversity is shown through the mixing of languages, as mentioned earlier.

Soap audiences in South Africa can be more passionate and less cynical about their programs than international audiences. Actors may be accosted in the streets by viewers, who mistake them for their characters. In an episode about polygamy in "*Isidingo*," where the father of a family insisted on taking a second and younger wife, causing much heartbreak to his wife of many years, many female viewers—one of whom slapped the actor—identified strongly with the wife.

Drama

In the early days, South African television was seen as an opportunity to develop local culture—in particular, the culture of the ruling Afrikaner elite. This view gave rise to a whole industry devoted to telling stories of the Afrikaners, past and present, which followed the conventions set down by the subsidized Afrikaans film industry. Botha (1997, online) argued that such films "seldom attempted to explore a national cultural psyche. As such, they were a closed form, made by Afrikaners for Afrikaners, with little or no attention to their potential to say something important about their society to an international audience."

However, some interesting drama did come out of this era, most notably the work of director Manie van Rensburg. His 1983 four-hour drama, "*Verspeelde Lente*" (Wasted Springtime), has been described as "not only a sombre, pessimistic look at Afrikaner urbanisation and a struggle to retain the land," but also, an "epic of social realism, stylistically characterized by the use of minimal music, long shots of lonely figures against barren Cape landscapes and simply edited" (Botha, 1997, online). Van Rensburg explored the relationship of the Afrikaner to the land in several more dramas, then went on to tell stories about the rise of Afrikaner nationalism—"Heroes" in 1985 and "The Fourth Reich" in 1990. He committed suicide in 1993 at the age of 48.

English-speaking Whites were less well served. The prevailing view of the powers at the SABC was that they were not really South African, but immigrants from the United Kingdom and elsewhere, and therefore would be satisfied with imported English-language programs.

Although not well-funded, some dramas did become popular. One was the weekly series "The Villagers," which told stories about the White inhabitants of a mining town. Some years after the series ended, one of the producers projected the mining town into a postapartheid present and turned it into the soap, "*Isidingo*," this time including stories about the Black residents as well.

An industry also grew up around the making of Black language drama. However, unlike Afrikaans drama, made by Afrikaners for Afrikaners, Black programming was created and produced by Whites. The resulting shows were mostly low-grade cops-and-robbers stories or melodramas, and little effort was made to capture contemporary township life. However, the shows gave experience to Black actors and production teams and thus prepared the way for the development of Black television.

One of the first shows to break the mold of "ethnically pure" programming was a sitcom built around the personal magnetism of the experienced and popular Black actor Joe Mafela. "*S'Gudi, S'Naysi*" (It's Good, It's Nice) attracted a large following for its portrayal of township life, with stories written around a trickster character played by Mafela. The show's chief scriptwriter, Richard Beynon, says the ideas were generated from workshops with the cast and crew, then structured into sitcom episodes (personal communication, November 2003). The show made use of the mingling of languages common in the townships, with a large dollop of English and the use of a colloquial local language called *tsotsi-taal* (thieves' language).

"*S'Gudi, S'Naysi*" was the most watched show among Black viewers in 1990, and also attracted White and Indian viewers to a Black family sitcom for the first time (Mersham, 1993). Words from the show also made it into colloquial language in the townships; Beynon is most proud of "bedbugs," a term he invented for the tenants who live in township yards, which became popular currency (personal communication, November 2003).

Edutainment

As it became clear in the early 1990s that the political dispensation was changing, the SABC had to reinvent itself and all its programming. At the same time, many donor agencies and nongovernmental organizations (NGOs) shifted the focus on antiapartheid movements to transformation initiatives; media were identified as the way in which Black South Africans who had previously been unable to vote could learn about their rights. Also, the increase of HIV/AIDS infection was recognized as a problem that needed urgent attention, particularly in the area of prevention. Two "edutainment" series were developed in the early 1990s to educate viewers through the medium of story-telling.

"Soul City," a weekly drama set in a clinic in a South African township, carried stories that revolved around public health issues—from AIDS to prejudice against the disabled to domestic violence. Although the objective of the series was essentially didactic—teaching viewers about health—the drama succeeded in attracting a large audience because of its adherence to the principles of good drama and is still running today, 10 years after its inception. The series has been funded by the South African government, SABC, leading corporations, the United Nations, and the European Union, and is associated with a radio drama and printed resources for use in print media and schools.

An even more difficult subject was tackled in the series "*Khululeka*" (Be Free)—election rights and procedures. Broadcast in 1994, before the first democratic elections, the series wove its stories around characters like Wonke Wonke, a man who cares about his community; his wife, Mpho; and their daughter Dudu. "*Khululeka*" later broadened its focus to include issues of human rights and community responsibility. According to research conducted by the Community Agency for Social Enquiry (2003), two thirds of a sample of 1,200 African adults in three provinces had watched "*Khululeka*," identified with the characters, and felt they had learned about voting and human rights from the program. The series is still running. Other dramas have built on the edutainment model in the last 10 years, many of them commissioned by the SABC's Education Department and funded by government or other donors. This has meant more resources than usual being available for research and for increased production value. Edutainment has moved further away from the "instructive" mode toward quality drama, breaking new ground in 1999 with the school drama "*Yizo, Yizo.*"

The aim of the series, funded by the Education Department, was "to spur the nation into facing up to the problems in our schools" (Motanya, 1999). Writer and director Teboho Mahlatsi was quoted as saying it was a matter of "combining the elements of the research findings and the many anecdotes collected and weaving these stories into believable characters and events" (Motanya, 1999, online). With its moody visual style, a soundtrack based on local hip-hop music, brilliant characterization, and achingly poignant stories, the series struck a nerve with Black viewers. It attained almost a cult status with young people, who saw a vivid portrayal of their problems and concerns, although more conservative older viewers were concerned that violence and sex were being glamorized by the no-holds-barred program.

This concern erupted into anger in the second series, when an episode showed two young men being raped in prison. South African viewers, who have been able to stomach same-sex rape and violence in the American prison series "Oz" without blinking, found it too much in a local series, and the debate went all the way to Parliament, where one or two elected representatives asked whether this kind of programming should be allowed. But after much public debate, it was largely accepted that "Yizo Yizo," although at times unpalatable, was reflecting an issue in society that needed to be debated. An independent study found that "Yizo Yizo 2," a second series that also achieved huge audiences, had "succeeded in achieving its key objectives: 99% of the learners and 95% of the parents [in the sample] said that the series had positive messages" (Community Agency for Social Enquiry, 2003).

"Yizo Yizo" led the way for more gritty edudrama, such as "Gaz'lam," the story of a rural boy who comes to the urban flatlands of Johannesburg, and "Tsha Tsha," set in a small town in the Eastern Cape, both dealing with social problems and AIDS and often portraying in graphic and specific detail safe and unsafe sexual behavior in order to educate young people.

Other Programming

Although local drama is very popular, it is a small proportion of all TV programming because it is costly to make. Thus a lot of local programming consists of talk shows, game shows, and music videos. South Africa now has its own well-known talk show hosts, from Phat Joe, an in-your-face local guy with an American accent, to the more mature Felicia, who has been savaged by media critics but is liked by audiences.

Comedy has become prominent in recent years, with local stand-up comics being featured on SABC3 and attempts to do comedy shows like "Saturday Night Live." Periodically a local sitcom appears, some in the mold of "S'Gudi, S'Naysi," as well as not-very-successful attempts to follow the American-style sitcom, and some uproariously popular Afrikaans shows.

IMPORTS AND EXPORTS

South Africans love local shows. With a few exceptions, they top the ratings. Often, the quality of the show is no indicator of how well it will be liked—audiences may choose a poor quality local show over a high quality imported one. Despite this, however, local content programming makes up less than half of programming across all five channels. Why is this?

The reasons are purely commercial. It is more expensive for the channels to commission and pay for local programs—especially dramas and documentaries—than to buy foreign imports. These higher costs are not offset by having bigger audiences, as advertisers often do not support local shows. Advertisers often look for affluent audiences, and affluent, more educated, audiences are often the ones who watch international programs. According to SABC3's manager of foreign acquisitions, Hanka Sonnekus-Roos, foreign imports come with a track record when they are aired in South Africa (personal communication, October 2003).

When "Dallas" was first shown on SABC in the late 1970s, it had South Africa's TV audience riveted. Newspaper posters screamed: "Who shot J.R?" at one crucial juncture in the series. The trials and tribulations of rich, dysfunctional families have continued to fascinate South Africans. Advertisers know what audiences and ratings they are likely to get with the third season of "Sex and the City" or "Law and Order," but a new local drama is an unknown quantity.

One strategy is to do local versions of international formats: advertisers and channels know what they getting, but the show can be counted by the regulator as local content, thus fulfilling license conditions. Some popular imported formats have been British quiz shows like "Who Wants to Be a Millionaire?" (see chapter 14) and "The Weakest Link," talent competitions like "Pop Stars" and "Idols," and reality shows like "Big Brother." "Big Brother Africa," which M-Net ran in 2003, was broadcast across the continent through M-Net's satellite service and was wildly popular (see chapter 9). "Idols" regularly makes newspaper headlines and is among the top 10 weekly shows for M-Net.

Imported programs tend to come largely from the United States, followed by Britain and Canada. The most popular programs in recent years have been the sci-fi drama "Dark Angel," Peter Benchley's "Amazon," and sitcoms like "Frasier," "Will and Grace," and "Friends." Reality shows like "Survivor" and "The Amazing Race" are popular, along with shows like "Ripley's Believe It or Not" and "Guinness World Records." Family programming like "Touched by an Angel" and, on the other end of the religious spectrum, "Charmed," also rate high.

British comedy does well in South Africa. Rowan Atkinson as "Mr. Bean" is perennially popular, and so is his show "The Thin Blue Line," as well as the sitcom "My Family" and the British/Indian comedy show "The Kumars at 42." Some of the channels have also experimented with Canadian imports like the cop shows "Cold Squad" and "Da Vinci's Inquest," and these have rated well.

South Africa does not export many shows and formats, as they do not easily translate into other cultures. However, South African soaps and dramas are having an impact in Africa, where many viewers have signed up to South African satellite channels, which include a lot of South African content. The SABC has a news channel called SABC Africa, which broadcasts for a few hours a day, and runs stories from all over the continent. Although not a "good news" channel, it has a strong development and feature focus, and does not do only the usual famine, disaster, and war coverage associated with Africa. It also has interviews and discussion around African issues, and is generally a much more informed look at Africa than most global news channels.

RADIO

Radio in South Africa is the most democratic of all media, reaching the highest number of South Africans—about 27 million—in the greatest number of languages (South African Advertising Research Foundation, 2003). Radio also has a much longer history than television. The first radio broadcast in South Africa was made in December 1923 by the South African Railways, more than 50 years before television arrived.

"Wireless," as it was then called, was transmitted by three different companies in three different regions of South Africa, but the small numbers of listeners and limited revenue from license fees made radio unprofitable. Government established the SABC in August 1936, conceived along similar lines to the BBC (Development of Broadcasting in South Africa, 2003). At first, all broadcasts were in English, but Afrikaans came on stream in 1937 and African languages in 1942.

The first commercial station, Springbok Radio, began broadcasting in 1950, and the SABC introduced news services in the same year. The 1960s saw a huge expansion of radio stations to include a number of African language stations and more commercial stations. A comprehensive FM network was set up to assist in the expansion of services to rural areas (Development of Broadcasting in South Africa, 2003).

In the 1990s, there were few commercial radio stations other than the SABC. However, the new government set out to deregulate the radio environment and in 1996, under orders from the new broadcast regulator, the SABC sold six of its stations to private enterprise (Development of Broadcasting in South Africa, 2003). These became commercial stations, and more commercial stations were licensed, creating a much more competitive environment for radio and for all media.

The SABC now comprises 19 radio stations, consisting of 13 public service stations, two community stations, and four commercial stations. These stations cover 13 languages and more than 19 million people. For commercial reasons, SABC radio has had to attract advertising to the vernacular language stations, which has meant a move away from an entirely public service ethos. However, the top six stations with the greatest listenership are all SABC African language stations, and number seven is a private music station—formerly SABC, which broadcasts in English and also in Afrikaans.

Another new development in radio in the late 1990s was the introduction of the category of community radio. The ideals of development motivated the policy, creating a system by which communities, particularly minority or disadvantaged communities, could apply for licenses to run nonprofit stations. Communities could be geographic or what was dubbed "communities of interest," for example, lovers of classical music or religious groups or older people.

More than 75 community stations have been licensed and are up and running, but many have found it difficult to survive, relying on volunteers with a lack of skills and funding from NGOs and funding agencies. Some community stations have managed to sell advertising because they attract an affluent audience and thus have turned more commercial in orientation. Community broadcasting is small in relation to commercial and public service broadcasting, attracting just over 4 million listeners out of 27 million. However, they serve an important function in fulfilling the needs of small or minority communities that big national stations are, by their nature, unable to focus on.

REFERENCES

Botha, M. (1997). The cinema of Manie van Rensburg: Popular memories of Afrikanerdom. In *Kinema: A Journal for Film and Audiovisual Media*. Available: www.arts.uwaterloo.ca/FINE/juhde/botha972.htm

Community Agency for Social Enquiry. (2003). Available: www.case.org.za.media.html

Development of Broadcasting in South Africa (2003). Available: www.sabc.co.za/oldsite/this_is_the_sabc/devepment.pdf

IBA Act-Independent Communications Authority of South Africa (2003). Available: www.ICASA.org.za

Mersham, G. M. (1993). In A.S. de Beer (Ed.), *Mass media for the nineties: The South African handbook of mass communication* (pp. 173–197). Pretoria: J. L. van Schaik.

Motanya, P. (1999). "Yizo Yizo" on the screen: Show us the way it is. In *The Teacher*. Available: www.teacher.co.za/9902/yizo.html

South African Advertising Research Foundation. (2003). Available: www.saarf.co.za

South African Broadcasting Corporation. (2003). Available: www/sabc.co.za

South Africa: The Official Gateway. (2003). Available: www.safrica.info

World Almanac Education Group. (2003) *The world almanac and book of facts, 2003*. New York: World Almanac Books.

SOUTH AFRICA, PRIME TIME, OCTOBER 2003

MONDAY						
Channel	7 p.m.	7:30 p.m.	8 p.m.	8:30 p.m.	9 p.m.	9:30 p.m.
SABC1	The Parkers (sitcom)	News (Zulu)	Generations (local soap)	Emzini Wezinsizwa (Zulu sitcom)	Soccerzone (local sport)	
SABC2	News (Afrikaans)	The Guardian (U.S. drama)		News	Whammy (game show)	Motswako the Mix (local talk show)
SABC3	News (English)	Charmed (U.S. fantasy)		Just Shoot Me (U.S. sitcom)	Will and Grace (U.S. sitcom)	Keen Eddie (U.S. comedy drama)
e-TV	News (English)		Ed (U.S. drama)		The West Wing (U.S. drama)	
M-Net	E.R. (U.S. drama)		Film: The Man Who Sued God			Sport
TUESDAY						
Channel	7 p.m.	7:30 p.m.	8 p.m.	8:30 p.m.	9:00 p.m.	9:30 p.m.
SABC1	The Tribe (U.S. sci-fi series)	News (Xhosa)	Generations (local soap)	Tsha Tsha (local drama/repeat)	New York Undercover (U.S. drama)	

	News (Afrikaans)	Once and Again (U.S. drama)		News	Muvhango (Venda family drama)	Ashifashabba (comedy)
SABC2	News (Afrikaans)	Once and Again (U.S. drama)		News	Muvhango (Venda family drama)	Ashifashabba (comedy)
SABC3	News (English)	Survivor Amazon (American reality show)		Cold Squad (Canadian crime drama)		Special Assignment (local investigative documentary)
e-TV	News (English)		3rd Degree (local current affairs)	Wanda at Large (sitcom)	Felicia on e (local talk show)	
M-Net	A.U.S.A (drama)	Smallville (U.S. fantasy)		C.S.I. Miami (U.S. drama)		24 (Drama)

WEDNESDAY

Channel	7 p.m.	7:30 p.m.	8 p.m.	8:30 p.m.	9:00 p.m.	9:30 p.m.
SABC1	Half and Half (sitcom)	News (Zulu)	Generations (local soap)	Girlfriends (U.S. sitcom)	True Life	
SABC2	News (Afrikaans)	Gilmore Girls (drama)		News	Muvhango (Venda family drama)	Stokvel (local sitcom)
SABC3	News (English)	The Weakest Link (local version of U.K. quiz show)		Living in Captivity (U.S. sitcom)	My Family (U.K. sitcom)	The Kumars at No 42 (U.K. comedy)
e-TV	News (English)		Red Alert (medical actuality)	British soccer		
M-Net	Still Standing (sitcom)	Friends (U.S. sitcom)	Film: Beautiful Joe			

THURSDAY

Channel	7 p.m.	7:30 p.m.	8 p.m.	8:30 p.m.	9:00 p.m.	9:30 p.m.
SABC1	That's So Raven (sitcom)	News (Xhosa)	Generations (local soap)	Zola 7 (local talk show)	Film: Danger Beneath the Sea (American action)	
SABC2	News (Afrikaans)	8 Simple Rules for Dating My Teenage Daughter (U.S. sitcom)	According to Jim (U.S. sitcom)	News	Meloding (local music show)	Local Sport
SABC3	News (English)	JAG (American action drama)		Ripley's Believe It or Not (U.S. actuality series)		Interface (local talk show)
e-TV	News (English)		The Whole Nine Yards (U.S. movie)			
M-Net	The Guardian (drama)		Head-to-Head (local rugby)		Hornblower (miniseries)	

FRIDAY

Channel	7 p.m.	7:30 p.m.	8 p.m.	8:30 p.m.	9:00 p.m.	9:30 p.m.
SABC1	My Wife and Kids (U.S. sitcom)	News (Zulu)	Generations (local soap)	Gazlam (local drama)	One (local music)	
SABC2	News (Afrikaans)	Hack (U.S. drama)		News (multilingual)	The X-Files (U.S. sci-fi)	
SABC3	News (English)	Top Billing (local magazine program)		Life (U.S. movie)		

e-TV	News (English)	**Good Morning, Miami** (U.S. sitcom)	**Thieves** (drama)		**Seven Days** (U.S. fantasy)	
M-Net	**Without a Trace** (U.S. drama)		**The Patriot** (U.S. movie)			

SATURDAY

Channel	7 p.m.	7:30 p.m.	8 p.m.	8:30 p.m.	9:00 p.m.	9:30 p.m.
SABC1	Friends Like This (local version of BBC game show)	News (Xhosa)	**NYPD Blue** (U.S. crime series)		The Phat Joe Show (local comedy talk show)	
SABC2	News (Afrikaans)	The Res (local drama)		News (multilingual)	Go for It! (local game show)	**Mrs Doubtfire** (U.S. movie)
SABC3	News (English)	**Ned and Stacey** (U.S. sitcom)	**The Siege** (U.S. movie)			
e-TV	News (English)	**Whose Line Is It Anyway?** (U.S. comedy game show)	**Drop Dead Gorgeous** (U.S. movie)			
M-Net	**John Doe** (U.S. fantasy)		**What Women Want** (U.S. movie)			

SUNDAY

Channel	7 p.m.	7:30 p.m.	8 p.m.	8:30 p.m.	9:00 p.m.	9:30 p.m.
SABC1	Asikhulume (local current affairs)	News (Zulu)	**Malcolm X** (U.S. movie)			
SABC2	News (Afrikaans)	Fokus (Afrikaans current affairs)	Glory, Hallelujah	News	**Martin** (U.S. sitcom)	**Jumanji** (U.S. movie)
SABC3	News (English)	**Providence** (U.S. drama)		**My Family** (U.K. sitcom/repeat)	**Sex and the City** (U.S. drama)	Local Golf
e-TV	News (English)	**King of Queens** (U.S. sitcom)	**Enemy of the State** (U.S. movie)			
M-Net	Carte Blanche (local investigative program)		**We Were Soldiers** (U.S. movie)			

Note. **Bold** denotes imported program.

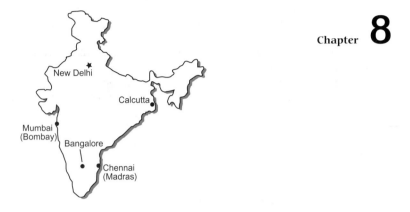

Chapter 8

India

Sandhya Rao
Texas State University

ABOUT INDIA

India is an ancient country whose history dates back to about 2500 BC. Early civilization thrived in the Indus Valley and later near the Ganges River. Many kingdoms flourished in India over the centuries. Having gained independence from Great Britain on August 15, 1947, India is a sovereign, socialist, secular, democratic republic.

Geographically, the Indian subcontinent is located in Southeast Asia and has Tibet (the Xizang Autonomous Region of the People's Republic of China), Bhutan, Nepal, Myanmar, Bangladesh, Sri Lanka, and Pakistan as neighbors. India is the seventh largest country in the world in size (*Britannica Book of the Year*, 2000), occupying 3,287,263 square kilometers (The Europa World Year Book, 1999).

Of India's population of a little over 1 billion, about 65% are literate. The number of females per 1,000 males is 933 (Census of India, 2001). Although the official national languages are Hindi and English, India has about 17 major regional languages and about 600 other languages and dialects. A majority of Indians (about 82%) are Hindus; also, 12% are Muslims, 2% Christians, 2% Sikhs, and the rest belong to other religions (Census of India, 1991).

India has been in the forefront of information technology in recent years. Software and software personnel are exported on a large scale. Liberalization policies especially in the 1990s have resulted in an average growth rate of 6% (*The World Factbook*, 2004). The country's middle-class population of 250 million has attracted many multinational companies to the country. The estimated gross domestic product for 2002 was $515 billion and the gross domestic product per capita for 2002 was $494 (International Telecommunication Union, 2003).

BROADCAST BACKGROUND

History

Radio began as a small private enterprise in the early 1920s. The Indian Broadcasting Company was formed in 1927 when amateur radio clubs, which had mushroomed in several large cities, joined together, but financial problems plagued this company. After the government took over the company, it stopped commercial broadcasts and got revenues from license fees that radio set owners had to pay each year. Initially called the Indian State Broadcasting Service, the radio network's name was later changed to All India Radio. Radio served the interests of the elite and broadcast colonial propaganda until 1947, when India gained her independence from the British (Kumar, 1998). The government subsequently expanded the radio network, which was considered an important tool of information and entertainment. The fact that radio sets were relatively inexpensive enabled them to penetrate even rural areas quickly. In addition, literacy was not a required skill as it was for the print media.

Television came to India in 1959, but remained at an experimental stage until 1965. The first television transmitter established in New Delhi was part of a UNESCO project to explore the potential of television as an educational tool. Even though regular programming was broadcast in New Delhi starting in 1965, television was slow to diffuse around the country. Doordarshan, as the then wholly government-run television is called, broadcast mainly educational and developmental programs. In 1975, the government launched an experimental project covering 2,400 villages in six states. The Satellite Instruction Television Experiment (SITE) aimed to broadcast programs pertaining to topics such as health, adult literacy, and agriculture. Television was considered a "luxury" and radio was used as the main mode of communication.

Doordarshan, which registered rapid growth and diffusion in the 1980s, established an extensive terrestrial network. In 1982, 40 new transmitters were set up to encourage people to watch the ASIAD, a major Asian sporting event that was held in India. This was when color television was introduced. By 1984, 52% of the population was covered by television (Malhan, 1985).

Cable

In 2003, 40 million homes were estimated to have cable and 90 million had terrestrial connections. Cable television entered India during the Gulf War in 1990 and dramatically changed entertainment television. Relatives of the many Indians living in the Gulf area demanded satellite dishes through which people could watch CNN. STAR TV, an Asian satellite TV service, was launched in 1991. Domestic satellite television services included Zee TV launched in 1992 and El TV started in 1994. Soon there were various cable channels, both foreign (such as CNN) and local (such as Jain TV and Sun TV; *Manorama Year Book*, 1995). Sun TV launched channels with regional language programming. There are an estimated 100 channels accessed in different parts of the country.

Doordarshan added several new channels to its network, including cable channels, in order to meet the increasing competition from private networks. There was also a shift in the content to include more entertainment and regional-language programming. By 1998, Doordashan had 17 channels and an 87% audience reach. As a public service broadcaster, Doordarshan has emphasized news and current affairs programs; it has 71 regional news bulletins each day originating from 18 state capitals (Doordarshan, 2003). Doordarshan broadcasts programs that are national, regional, and local to cater to the needs of various types of audiences in different languages. It started a sports-only channel in 1999. It also has a DD India channel that broadcasts Indian programs to various countries around the world. Its interactive educational channel, called Gyandarshan, works with other educational institutions and schools to provide a range of educational programs.

Initially, Doordarshan, which followed the BBC model, got its revenue from license fees. This system changed in 1976 when commercials began to be accepted in order to increase revenue. In the 1980s Doordarshan's income from advertisements rose with popular programs such as *"Hum Log," "Ramayan," "Mahabharat," "Buniyaad,"* and *"Yeh Johai Zindagi."* For the year 2001–2002, Doordarshan's revenue was Rs. 6,152.10 million.[1]

According to a study done by a research firm (Indian Cable, 2003), cable penetration rose rapidly from 412,000 households in January 1992 to 1.2 million in November 1992. It increased to 3.3 million in 1993 and by the end of 1994, it had risen to 11.8 million. Cable and satellite penetration was much higher in urban than in rural areas in 1995. By 1999, of the 70 million television households, 22 million homes were estimated to have cable and satellite connections. In the tilt toward cable, video parlors that rent movies have lost much business.

---

[1]One U.S. Dollar = 45 Rupees (approx.) in late 2004.

Pay TV costs 150–350 rupees to set up (K. Bamzai, personal communication, August 4, 2003). Indians are estimated to spend about three or four times more hours viewing television than reading newspapers. They pay about Rs. 150 a month for a cable connection and about Rs. 30–70 toward subscription to one or two newspapers. Since 1993, print advertising's share of national advertising has come down from over 60% to around 43% (Kohli, 2003).

With the coming of cable television, cable operators mushroomed in the country. In 2003, it was estimated that there were anywhere between 30,000 and 60,000 cable operators. In general, each network has about 2,000 subscribers. In smaller towns and rural areas, however, the average size of the networks is about 200–300 homes (Indian Cable, 2003). Large companies such as InCablenet, Hathway, Siticable, Asianet, and others invested much money in building extensive networks. This competition has led smaller operators to band together and form companies that franchise their cable television to serve even smaller operators. Thus the cable industry has not allowed concentration of power in the hands of large companies. In most instances, large companies operate by franchising through a chain. For example, InCable has a million subscribers in Mumbai, 70,000 of them as direct subscribers and the rest served by franchises.

In July 2004 the Conditional Access System (CAS) continued to be a hotly debated topic (Indian Television, 2004). The CAS is a proposal that allows viewers to watch pay channels via a set-top box. This system is expected to help cable operators compete on a par with the multisystem operators who are partly or wholly owned by broadcasters and get pay channels at lower rates (Bamzai, 2003a). The set-top box could also work as a people meter and measure viewership patterns. Cable channels such as STAR TV prefer to get direct-to-home television. Zee TV, on the other hand, owns an extensive cable network and hopes to benefit by the CAS. Pay channel viewers pay anywhere from Rs. 152 to Rs. 286 for the pay channel packages, depending on how many channels they get. The set-top box costs about Rs. 4000. There is also apparently a shortage of set-top boxes available. As of this writing, the CAS issue was yet to be resolved.

STAR TV

Rupert Murdoch, head of the $15 billion News Corp. and 100% owner of STAR TV, stands as a giant in the Indian TV landscape. STAR TV entered India in 1991 and was initially owned by a Chinese businessman until it was taken over by Rupert Murdoch in 1993. By that year, about 25% of TV households had access to STAR TV (Chan, 1994). STAR India has registered a high growth rate in about a decade's time. Many of its 11 channels, such as STAR Plus are top-rated cable channels. STAR Movies was the first pay channel to be introduced in India in 1994. In 1996, STAR added programming in Hindi. In 1999 STAR and Zee TV split, with Zee becoming a Hindi-only channel, speaking the language of the youth. Peter Mukerjea became the CEO of Zee TV, while James Murdoch, Rupert Murdoch's son, was appointed as chairman and CEO of STAR. In 2000 STAR surged forward, investing money in local programming. Its program *"Kaun Banega Crore-pati"* (Who Wants to Be a Millionnaire?), popularly known as KBC, became a highly successful program and phenomenally increased the revenues of STAR (Kohli, 2003; see chapter 14.)

STAR has the highest revenue, even though Doordarshan has a much wider reach of TV audiences. STAR is estimated to have an audience of 55.9 million, which is a low second, far behind Doordarshan's national channel DD1, which has an estimated audience of 233 million. Sony Entertainment and Eenadu and ETV have 39.9 million and Zee TV has an estimated 33.3 million viewers. Zee has a large revenue size and could become a serious competitor.

It is apparent that the cable industry is surging ahead of the publishing industry. Bennett, Coleman & Co. Ltd. continues to be India's largest media giant, worth Rs. 1,500 crores. It is India's most respected and largest publishing company. Its flagship publication, the *Times of India* newspaper, has editions coming out of 10 cities in India. The company also owns *Femina*, India's leading English-language women's magazine. Bennett, Coleman's businesses include events, music, and radio. Its estimated total readers/audience is 6.1 million (Kohli, 2003). STAR India, worth an estimated 1,200 crore, is a close second to the 160-year-old Bennett, Coleman.

BROADCAST REGULATION

Broadcast reform has been slow to evolve. Considering that broadcast media were government owned for several decades and that the growth of television was slow, this is not surprising. For a long time, the Indian Telegraph Act of 1885 was the only legal instrument. The Chanda Committee report, which revealed dissatisfaction regarding government-controlled information, was the first major public assertion that people were unhappy with government-controlled media (Ninan, 1998). The 1990s saw a tremendous growth in the cable industry in particular and broadcasting in general, necessitating an updated bill pertaining to broadcasting. The Broadcasting Bill of 1997 addressed these needs. The bill allows the Broadcasting Authority of India, an independent authority, to regulate broadcasting services. Major functions of the broadcasting authorities include management of frequencies, granting licenses for broadcasting services, and facilitating a wide range of quality programming (The Broadcasting Bill, 1997). The bill also recognized that opening the TV field for competition from private broadcasters could better cater to the needs of the fragmented audiences in India.

In 1999, a New Telecommunications Policy was introduced. Even though the government had introduced a telecommunication policy in 1994, due to rapid developments in the field in the 1990s, the NTP of 1999 was launched. Some of the main objectives of the policy are to increase access to telecommunications, modernize the telecommunications infrastructure and make it more efficient, protect the defense and security interests of the country, and facilitate Indian telecommunication companies to become international players (New Telecommunications Policy, 1999).

BROADCAST CONTENT AND RATINGS

A dichotomy in Indian television was that television spread primarily in the urban areas, but the programming was mainly educational and rural in bias. Although the entertainment content increased in the 1980s, it was still a low percentage of the overall programming. Besides, Doordarshan had just one or two channels in most cities and regional-language broadcasting was limited. Audiences had few choices and were often frustrated. Some notable programs during the 1980s were a popular prodevelopment soap opera, *"Hum Log"* (We the People), and serials based on the epics *Ramayan* and *Mahabharat*. *"Hum Log"* carried messages of family planning, family harmony, and national integration. *"Ramayan"* can be termed more as a phenomenon as it commanded more audiences and advertising money than had any program in the history of Indian television.

Game Shows

In July 2000, the program *"Kaun Banega Crorepati,"* the Hindi counterpart of "Who Wants to Be a Milllionaire?" (see chapter 14) transformed television. This program, hosted by Amitabh Bacchan, a popular movie star, generated several clones (K. Bamzai, personal communication, August 4, 2003). KBC inspired jokes, theme parties, catchphrases, books, and advertisements. Children played the game at parties, on school buses, and in school. The novelty of this program is said to be the main reason for its success (Bhandare, 2000). Several game shows that enjoy good ratings are film based. For example, shows such as *"Anthakshari"* and *"Padutha Theeyaga"* are contests based on one's knowledge of film songs. Teams compete with one another to sing a snippet from an Indian film starting with the last word of the previous snippet. The team that lasts the longest is declared the winner.

Soap Operas

Soap operas are among the most popular shows on television. Following the resounding success of *"Kyunki Sas Bhi Kabhi Bahu Thi"* (Because Mother-in-Law was a Daughter-in-Law Once), numerous similar family soaps centered on the mother-in-law–daughter-in-law relationship began to be shown. Contrary to the traditional portrayal of the mother-in-law as a negative character, she is depicted as an intelligent, well-dressed, and reasonable person on whom daughters-in-law model themselves. In 2001, *"Kyunki"* overtook the successful *"Kaun Banega Crorepati"* game show in popularity. Others such as *"Kahani Ghar Ghar Ki"* (The Story of Every Household), *"Kahin Kissi Roz"* (Sometime Some Day), *"Kasauti Zindagi Kay"*

(Benchmarks of Life), *"Kundali"* (Horoscope), and *"Shagun"* (Good Omen), all on STAR TV; *"Aan"* (Pride) and *"Koi Apna Sa"* (Someone to Call Your Own) on Zee and *"Heena"* (Henna) and *"Kutumb"* (Family) on Sony soon followed. The mother-in-law has the major role in all these soaps. Many reflect more modern values, such as in *"Kyunki"* where the mother-in-law is willing to get her widowed daughter-in-law remarried and in *"Kahin Kissi Roz,"* where the mother-in-law is supportive of her daughter-in-law when her son errs. For anyone familiar with traditional Indian culture as depicted in Indian movies through the ages, this is a revolutionary change. However, these episodes are not consistently present. On the contrary, by and large these soaps are criticized as showing the same mother-in-law in a new and glamorous garb. The soaps also focus on the dynamics within the house. The mother-in-law is portrayed as a homemaker and as being dependent on her son financially and emotionally. She is also shown as someone who wants to retain her powerful position within the family. The critics argue that in real life, the modern mother-in-law is a blend of tradition and modern values and, in urban areas, also lives in nuclear families. Others argue that the soaps do not have to reflect reality (Vasudev, 2002).

Among the soaps that were popular in 2003 were those starting with the letter K. Strange as this may sound, Ekta Kapoor, movie star Jitendra's daughter, who makes soaps about family dynamics, has given all the soaps titles starting with the letter K, which has been lucky for her. In July 2003, 12 of her soaps were on various channels and were top rated. Although the women characters are strong in these soaps, they are not career women. The most popular of these is *"Kyuki Sas Bhi Kabhi Bahu Thi."* The star of this serial, Smriti Malhotra, has her own daily talk show like the Oprah show (K. Bamzai, personal communication, August 4, 2003).

Mythological Serials

The popularity of the mythological serials of the 1980s, the *Ramayan* and the *Mahabharat*, led to several other serials based on mythology. In a country where more than 80% of the population is Hindu, these serials are watched with reverence. Examples of mythological serials are *"Vishnu Puran"* (The Epic of Vishnu), *"Ma Shakti"* (The Power of a Goddess), *"Shree Brahma, Vishnu, and Mahesh," "Jai Mata Ki"* (Hail Mother Goddess), *"Jai Ganga Maiya"* (Hail Mother Ganges), and *"Shree Krishna."* These serials get very high audience ratings and therefore fetch huge amounts of advertising revenue. Mythological serials are colorful, dramatic, action packed, full of special effects, and more expensive to produce than regular social serials.

Film-Based Programs

India's flourishing film industry has contributed much to TV content. India produces the most films each year in the world. Films are produced in at least 15 languages. Video parlors that were very popular in the 1980s have been put out of business with the coming of cable television. People watch movies on television. Other popular programs, such as *"Chritrahaar,"* are based on film music. Film-song-based programs such as "*Chaaya Geet*" (soothing music), "*Chitrahar*" (A String of Pictures), "*Rangoli*" (Motif), "Lux Hit Parade," "Philips Top Ten," and "*Colgate Top Takkar*" have proliferated on TV channels (Agrawal, 1998). Movie stars have found another channel for their talents. Many act in TV serials or are hosts and hostesses of TV programs. For example, Simi Garewal conducts a successful show on which she interviews celebrities. Their already established popularity helps promote the TV programs in which they appear.

Ratings

Research organizations began to introduce the people meter in 1996, recognizing the need for audience measurement and for rating the programs. Competition for advertising money was increasing due to the increase in the number of cable channels. Prior to this, Doordarshan dominated the scene and all ad revenue went to Doordarshan. A. C. Nielsen and ORG MĀRG's Indian National Television Measurement (INTAM) are among the companies that began measuring audiences. It was estimated that in 1995, the revenue from TV ads was about 2500 crores (Joshi, 1999).

INTAM ratings for the top 10 programs in cable and satellite homes from August 3, 2003, to August 9, 2003, show that all 10 programs were shown on STAR Plus. These were popular serials such as "*Kyunki Sas Bhi Kabhi Bahu Thi,*" "*Kahaani Ghar Ghar Ki,*" "*Kasauthi Zindagi Kay,*" and "*Des Mein Nikla Hoga Chan*" (The Moon Must Have Risen in My Country). The top 10 in all TV homes showed that DD1 (Doordarshan's national channel) had a number of programs rated and STAR Plus had some programs, for example, "*Aap Beeti*" (Retrospection), "*Ankhe*" (Eyes), and "*Shaktimaan*" (Superman). Doordarshan has a wider reach than cable television.

There have been disagreements about the rating system. In 1996, Zee filed suit against Bennett, Coleman and Company Ltd., for publishing an article that said Sony was ahead of Zee based on Nielsen ratings. Ratings for the same period presented by ORG–MĀRG's ratings showed that Zee was leading. Better ratings get more advertising money and hence the battle is over the advertising money (Joshi, 1999).

BROADCAST IMPORTS AND EXPORTS

India exports channels and content to numerous countries around the world through popular channels such as STAR and Zee. The state-owned Doordarshan's international reach extends to about 150 countries around the world (Doordarshon, 2003). DD also provides technical assistance such as up-linking facilities. DD's main international audiences are Indians living abroad. DD India, the international channel, was launched in 1995 (Doordarshon, 2003). Zee Telefilms Limited (Zee) is the world's leading producer of Hindi programming, estimated to have a reach of 225 million viewers in more than 80 countries (http://www.Zee Television.com/html/AboutZee.

asp, accessed on 1-12-04). Numtv.com is a web-based company that offers major TV channels to the Indian diaspora worldwide. This company plans to create an Asian portal by including content from other Asian countries such as China and South Korea (http://www.newindpress.com/newsitems .asp?ID=IE820030925091224&Page=8&Title=NRIs&rLink=0).

Early on, the import content was limited to one or two programs in a week, mainly British or other European serials and films. With the introduction of cable television in the 1990s, foreign content and English language programming increased. In the mid-1990s the programs in local languages, however, were more popular. Initially, it was feared that foreign programming on cable television would have a negative impact on Indian culture. It was soon realized, however, that once the novelty of watching soaps such as "The Bold and the Beautiful" and "Santa Barbara" wore off, audiences went back to watching local language soaps. In a survey carried out in 1996, it was found that Western serials were less frequently watched and provided the least satisfaction to cable subscribers and non-subscribers alike (Rao, 1998). With the increasing popularity of cable television, numerous American programs such as "Friends," "Frasier," "Boston Public," "Dharma and Greg," "X-Files," "Whose Line Is It Anyway?," "Law and Order," and "Ally McBeal" are shown regularly on cable channels (see the grid on pp. 6–7).

Even though there is Western programming on channels such as CNN, most soaps and programs are old ones being recycled. Costs of production, unlike in most other Third World countries, are lower compared with imported, syndicated programs. This could be due to the well established film industry in India (K. Bamzai, personal communication, August 4, 2003).

FILM

The Indian film industry, affectionately nicknamed Bollywood, is a major cultural force in India and many of the neighboring countries. An average of about 800 films are produced each year ("Brief History," 2003) in about 15 languages—primarily in Hindi, Tamil, and Telugu languages. The typical *masala* movie (formula film) has all the ingredients of a blockbuster—heroes, villains, vamps, songs, dances, romance, colorful costumes, attractive locations, drama, emotion, folklore, mythology, and traditions. This formula, with a focus on songs and dances, has provided escapist entertainment, successfully distracting the masses from the daily grind, if only for a few hours. In general, Indian films have social themes.

Mumbai (earlier known as Bombay), the hub of the film industry, is India's Hollywood. The first feature film was produced in 1913. The first film with sound, *Alam Ara*, however, was produced in 1931. In the 1930s the most popular theme for films was to take a stand against social injustice. The first color film, *Kisan Kanya*, was released in 1937 (Mathew, 1996). The more serious films are categorized as "art films" and these explore social problems. In 1952 India participated in the International

Film Festival for the first time. Satyajit Ray put India firmly on the international map with his films like *Pather Panchali*, which won numerous international and national awards. The 1960s produced entertaining films that were blockbusters. This genre of films became the trend in the decades that followed. In recent times, movies such as *Salaam Bombay*, *Elizabeth*, and *Lagaan* (Tax) have either won international awards or have been nominated for these. *Filmfare*, a popular film magazine, sponsors each year the *Filmfare* Awards, India's version of the Academy Awards.

The number of films produced each year has registered a downward trend since the 1990s, mainly due to the coming of satellite television and cable television. Cinema halls have given way to high-rise office buildings. All films that are released to the public have to go through the Central Board of Film Certification.

ACKNOWLEDGMENTS

I wish to thank Raj Chengappa, Managing Editor of *India Today*, for providing me with useful background information on the subject during my visit to New Delhi, India, in August 2003. I also wish to thank Kaveree Bamzai, senior editor, *India Today*, for the valuable information she provided during my interview with her. I wish to thank S. Sudhakar, Jyothi Sudhakar, and Sarita Khanna for their timely assistance in providing the translations and schedule for the prime time grid.

REFERENCES

Agrawal, B. C. (1998). Cultural influence of Indian cinema on Indian television. In S. R. Melkote, P. Shields & B. C. Agrawal (Eds.), *International satellite broadcasting in South Asia* (pp. 123–130). Lanham, MD: University Press of America.
Bamzai, K. (2003, July 14). CAS Trap. *India Today*, pp. 23, 25.
Bhandare, N. (2000, August 28). The Crore-party's on. *India Today*, pp. 68–69.
Brief History of Indian Movie Industry. (2003). http://www.indiaonestop.com/film.htm
Britannica Book of the Year (2000). Chicago: Encyclopaedia Britannica, Inc.
Broadcasting Bill. (1997). http://www.indiancabletv.net/broadcast.htm
Census of India. (1991). [online]. Available: www.censusindia.net (2000, January 30).
Census of India. (2001). http://www.censusindia.net
Chan, J.M. (1994). National responses and accessibility to STAR TV in Asia. *Journal of Communication, 44*(3), 112–131.
Doordarshan. (2003). http://www.ddindia.com/dd_about.html accessed on Aug. 20, 2003.
The Europa World Year Book (Vol 1). (1999). London: Europa Publications.
Indiacabletv.net. http://www.indiancabletv.net accessed on Aug. 20, 2003.
Indiantelevision.com. (2004). Retrieved August 12, 2004, from http://www.indiantelevision.com/special/y2k4/comment/cascommentjul04.htm
International Telecommunication Union. (2003). Basic Indicators. (Online) Available: http://www.itu.int/ITU-D/ict/statistics/ (August 12, 2004).
Joshi, N. (1999, February 8). Row over the TRPs. *India Today*, pp. 70–71.
Kohli, V. (2003, June 2). The making of India's biggest media house. *Businessworld*, pp. 30–38.

Kumar, K. J. (1998). History of television in India: A political economy perspective. In S. R. Melkote, P. Shields, & B. C. Agrawal (Eds.), *International satellite broadcasting in South Asia* (pp. 19–46). Lanham, MD: University Press of America.

Malhan, P. N. (1985). Communication media—yesterday, today and tomorrow. Meerut, India: Link Printers.

Manorama Year Book. (1995). Kottayam, India: Malayala Manorama.

Mathew, J. (1996). Cinema. In *Malayala Manorama* (pp. 607–610), Kottayam, India.

Ninan, S. (1998). History of Indian broadcasting reform. In M.E. Price & S.G. Verhulst (Eds.), *Broadcasting reform in India: Media law from a global perspective* (pp. 1–21). Delhi: Oxford University Press.

New Telecommunications Policy. (1999). http://www.indiancabletv.net/newtelecompolicy.htm

Rao, S. (1998). Viewing of Doordarshan by cable subscribers in Bangalore, India: Is there a difference with non-subscribers? In S. R. Melkote, P. Shields, & B. C. Agrawal (Eds.), *International satellite broadcasting in South Asia* (pp. 181–203). Lanham, MD: University Press of America.

The World Factbook. (2004). http://www.cia.gov/cia/publications/factbook/geos/in.html Econ 11-21-04.

Vasudev, S. (2002, January 21). Witches in Diamante. *India Today*, pp. 72–73.

Zee Television. (2004). http://www.zeetelevision.com/html

PRIME TIME, INDIA, JULY 20–31, 2003 (CONSTRUCTED WEEK)

MONDAY

Channel	7 p.m.	7:30 p.m.	8 p.m.	8:30 p.m.	9 p.m	9:30 p.m.	10 p.m.
Hindi							
Sony	Chart Busters (music-based)	Music Mantra (music-based)	Ab Ayega Mazaa [Now It's Going to Be Fun] (comedy)	Kuch Kehti Hai [She Is Saying Something] (serial)	Kusum (serial)		Achanak-37 Unexpected (suspense)
Zee TV	Ek Nazar [One Glance] (serial)	Piya Ka Ghar [Husband's Home] (family drama)	Pyar Zindagi Hai [Love Is Life] (serial)		Astitva Ek Prem Kahani [A Love Story] (serial)	Milit (serial)	Kitty Party (serial)
Star Plus	Kum Kum Pyara Sa Bandhan [Kum Kum, a Lovely Bond] (serial)	Shaka Laka Boom (music-based)	Krishna Arjun (mythological serial)	Kasauti Zindagi Kay [Touchstone of Life] (serial)	Des Mein Nikla Hoga [Place From Where It Has Risen] (serial)		Kahani Ghar Ghar Ki [Story of Every House] (serial)
Network							
Doordar-shan 1	Regional News	Dance	News	Samachar (news)	Musku-rahat [Smile] (serial)	Serial: CID Officer	
DD Metro	Pal Do Pal (serial)	Your Top Ten (music-based) 7:55: Aan-khon Dekhi [Eye Witness] (fact-based serial)	Ramayan (mythological serial)	Kuntee (serial)	Papa (serial)	Jai Ganga Maiya (Hail Mother Ganges) (serial)	Shantala (serial)

Udaya	Kun-kuma Bhagya [Good Luck of "kun-kuma"] (serial)	Hogli Bidi Sir [It's Okay, Sir] (comedy)	Apartment (suspense)	News	Sahasa Laxmiyaru [Adventurous Women] (serial)	Kavalu Daari [Crossroads] (serial)

TUESDAY

Channel	7 p.m.	7:30 p.m.	8 p.m.	8:30 p.m.	9 p.m	9:30 p.m.	10 p.m.
Hindi							
Sony	Chart Busters	Music Mantra	Biographics	Current Bollywood	Kusum	Naam gum Jayega	Achanak-37
Zee TV	Ek Nazar	Piya Ka Ghar	Pyar Zindagi Hai	Chausath Panne	Astitva Ek Prem Kahani	Milit	Kitty Party
Star Plus	Kum Kum Pyara Sa Bandhan	Shaka Laka Boom	Khichdi	Kasauti Zindagi Kay	Kehta hai dil		Kahani Ghar Ghar Ki
Network							
Doordarshan 1	News 7:15: Music	Dance	News	Samachar	Mera Hum Safar	Ujala	Chatrapati Shivaji
DD Metro	Antarman	Shiv Mahapuram	Hello Inspector	Kuntee	Papa	Jai Ganga Maiya	Kartavya
Kannada*							
Udaya	Kunkuma Bhagya	Hogli Bidi Sir	Apartment	News	Sahasa Lakshmi	Chandrika	Kavalu Daari

WEDNESDAY

Channel	7 p.m.	7:30 p.m.	8 p.m.	8:30 p.m.	9 p.m	9:30 p.m.	10 p.m.
Hindi							
Sony	Chart Busters	Music Mantra	Boogie Woogie	Goonj Ateet Ki	Kusum	Naam gum Jayega	Achanak-37
Zee TV	Ek Nazar	Piya Ka Ghar	Pyar Zindagi Hai	Chousath Panne	Astitva Ek Prem Kahani	Milit	Kitty Party
Star Plus	Kum Kum Pyara Sa Bandhan	Shaka Laka Boom	Son Pari	Kasauti Zindagi Kay	Sanjivini		Kahani Ghar Ghar Ki
Network							
Doordarshan 1	Regional News 7:15: Music	Chitrahaar	News	Samachar	Shayad Tum	Chori Chori Chupke	Galti Kiski
DD Metro	Baar Baar Dekho	Flop Show	Hello Inspector	Kuntee	Papa: Serial	Jai Ganga Maiya: Serial	Shantala
Kannada*							
Udaya	Kunkuma Bhagya	Hogli Bidi Sir	Apartment	News	Sahasa Laxmiyaru	Chandrika	Kavalu Daari

THURSDAY

Channel	7 p.m.	7:30 p.m.	8 p.m.	8:30 p.m.	9 p.m	9:30 p.m.	10 p.m.
Hindi							
Sony	Chart Busters	Music Mantra	Meri Biwi [Wonderful]	Sambhav Asambhav	Kusum	Naam gum Jayega	Achanak-37
Zee TV	Ek Nazar	Piya Ka Ghar	Thursday Premiere: Kehta Hai Dil Baar Baar				
Star Plus	Fox Kids Continued	Shaka Laka	Kyun Hota Hai Pyar	Kasauti Zindagi Kay	Hullja Sim Sim		Kahani Ghar Ghar Ki
Network							
Doordar- shan 1	News 7:15: Music	Pakistan Reporter	News	Samachar	Khushiyan	Aankhen	
DD Metro	Idhar kamala udhar dhamal	Khabrein Bollywood Ki	Hello Inspec- tor	Kuntee	Kinare Milte Nahin	Filmon Ka Guldasta	Kartavya
Kannada*							
Udaya	Kunkuma Bhagya	Hogli Bidi Sir	Apartment	News	Sahasa Laxmiyaru	Chandrika	Kavalu Daari

FRIDAY

Channel	7 p.m.	7:30 p.m.	8 p.m.	8:30 p.m.	9 p.m	9:30 p.m.	10 p.m.
Hindi							
Sony	Chart Busters	Music Mantra	Kya Hadsaa Kya Haqeeqat		Devi	Heena	CID
Zee TV	Ek Nazar	Bollywood Buzz	Anthakshari		Jeena Isi Ka Naam Hai		Sa re ga ma pa
Star Plus	Popstars 2	Karishma Ka Karishma	Kuch Kar Dikhana Hai		Shararat	Unlimited Josh	
Network							
Doordar- shan 1	News	Regional Chitrahaar	News 8:20: Parlia- ment News	Samachar	Shakti	Film	
DD Metro	Yeh Kya Ho Raha Hai 7:55: Aankhon Dekhi	Hello Inspector	Hello Inspector	Kuntee	Kinare Milte Nahin	Telefilm	
Kannada*							
Udaya	Kunkuma Bhagya	Hogli Bidi Sir	Apartment	News	Sumangali	Chandrika	Kavalu Daari

SATURDAY

Channel	7 p.m.	7:30 p.m.	8 p.m.	8:30 p.m.	9 p.m	9:30 p.m.	10 p.m.
Hindi							
Sony	Chart Busters	Music Mantra	Kya Hadsaa Kya Haqeeqat		Devi	Heena	CID
Zee TV	Ek Nazar	Count Down	Non Stop Bollywood Hungama		Jeena Isi Ka Naam Hai		Sa re ga ma pa
Star Plus	Popstars		Kuch Kar Dikhana Hai		Shararat		

Network							
Doordar-shan 1	Regional News 7:15: Health Show	Off the Beaten Path	News	Samachar	Shakti		Aap Beeti
DD Metro	Jo Jeeta Wohi Sikandar	Ekka Begum Badshah 7:55: Aankhon dekhi	Hello Inspector	Musiban bol Ke aayee	Feature Film		Kartavya

Kannada*							
Udaya	Movie			News	Film Continues	Kuhu Kuhu	Namma Sutha

SUNDAY

Channel	7 p.m.	7:30 p.m.	8 p.m.	8:30 p.m.	9 p.m	9:30 p.m.	10 p.m.
Hindi							
Sony	Kapil Dil Se	Meri Biwi Wonderful	Kya Hadsaa Kya Haqeeqat		Film		
Zee TV	Ek Nazar	Piya Ka Ghar	Pyar Zindagi Hai		Chausath Panne	Milit	Kitty Party
Star Plus	Sonpari	Jubilees Plus	Film: Pyar Tune Kya Kiya				

Network							
Doordar-shan 1	News 7:15: Ghazal	Ocean Development	News	Samachar	Jasoos Vijay	Aagaaz: Special Music Concert	
DD Metro	Yeh Kya Ho Raha Hai 7:55: Aankhon Dekhi	Feature Film in Hindi					

Kannada*							
Udaya	Kunkuma Bhagya	Hogli Bidi Sir	Apartment	News	Sumangali	Chandrika	Kavalu Daari

Note. Each state has a regional language. Kannada is the regional language of Karnataka State. The source of information for the program grids is *Deccan Herald,* a leading English newspaper of the state. Due to duplication of weekday programs, only Monday's shows are translated.

Chapter 9

Japan

Tsutomu Kanayama
Sophia University, Tokyo

Tomoko Kanayama
Keio University, Tokyo

ABOUT JAPAN

The Japanese archipelago includes (from largest to smallest) four main islands: Honshu, Hokkaido, Kyushu, and Shikoku. In 2003, the total population was 126.67 million; total households numbered 49.26 million (Ministry of Public Management, Home Affairs, Posts and Telecommunications [MPMHAPT], 2003b). Currently, 30% of Japan's households reside in the Tokyo metropolitan (Kanto) area (MPMHAPT, 2003c).

With a low birth rate of only 1.32 babies per adult female in 2002, the working population may not be able to support the aged population in the near future (MPMHAPT, 2003a). By the year 2025, Japan is expected to rank as the world's first gray nation, with 25% of its citizens being over 65.

145

Japan's Diet (parliament) includes the House of Representatives and House of Councilors. As in England (see chapter 6), the prime minister, as the country's chief executive, is chosen by the majority party's members rather than being elected directly. The Liberal Democratic Party has ruled Japan almost continuously after World War II.

Japan, the world's second largest economic power after the United States, has suffered since the 1990s' bad loan crisis. This aftermath of the go-go economy of the 1980s is referred to as the lost decade of economic growth—a contrast to the rapid growth in much of the global economy (Harada, 1999). At this writing, the national budget is burdened by the issuance of government bonds, so that the national debt has steadily increased. Since the beginning of the 21st century, Japan has set in motion procedures to the remove bad loans that have disturbed economic growth. Also, the government has tried to remove structural impediments in order to stimulate the Japanese economy and reorganize government-supported organizations, encouraging competition through deregulation. For example, it hopes to privatize the Japan Highway Public Corporation monopoly, which builds toll roads and collects whatever toll fees it wishes.

Likewise, the protectionist broadcasting and telecommunications industry is slated to become competitive. Barriers previously excluded new entrepreneurs, but now small-scale organizations can challenge conventional broadcasters thanks to new policies of the Ministry of Public Management, Home Affairs, Posts, and Telecommunications, or MPMHAPT (before 2000, the Ministry of Posts and Telecommunications, or MPT; Kanayama, 1998).

BROADCAST BACKGROUND

History

In 1926, Japan's first moving image—the symbol of () in Japanese, which is pronounced "ee"—was transmitted via the prototype TV system invented by Kenjiro Takayanagi. According to the Broadcast and Culture Research Institute of NHK—Japan Broadcasting Corp. (Nippon Hoso Kyokai, 2003), Japanese broadcasting evolved through seven stages: the commencement and expansion of radio broadcasts (1925–1936); wartime radio broadcasting (1937–1945); democratization and development of broadcasting (1945–1952); perfecting television (1930–1953); initial spread of television (1953–1959); full slate of popular programs (1960 – 1983); and progress in TV technology (1963 to present).

During wartime, from the Sino-Japanese War to the end of the Pacific War, the totalitarian Japanese government restricted free speech and manipulated public opinion, using radio to justify Japan's move to war (Takeyama, 2002). A symbolic shift away from prewar radio propaganda occurred in 1945 when Emperor Hirohito's voice declared the end of the Pacific War.

Subsequently, as Japan democratized, radio entertained the general public with new programs such as *"Nodojiman"* (Proud of good singing) and quiz programs (Cooper-Chen, 1997). Radio enjoyed a Golden Age until the appearance of television in 1953 (Nippon Hoso Kyokai, 2003).

The first programs were aired by both the public broadcaster, NHK, and a commercial entity, the Nippon Television Network Corp. (NTV), presaging the Japanese dual broadcasting structure that exists to this day. Early on, watching television was a group activity because the first black-and-white televisions were too expensive for individual households to buy (Okamura, 2003).

Broadcasters placed sets in public areas such as railway stations, where people, particularly on the way back home after work or school, could stop and watch shows—the most popular genre being professional wrestling. A single event in 1959—the live broadcast of the 50-minute wedding parade when the present emperor married a commoner—dramatically increased TV set sales (*Minkan Hoso*, 2001).

Four technical advances ensued: (a) color television, 1960; (b) UHF television, which added channels beyond the scarce VHF bandwidth, 1968 to 1970; (c) new FM radio channels, late 1960s to the 1970s; and (d) NHK's experimental satellite broadcasting channel, 1984 (*Minkan Hoso*, 2001).

After the "oil-shock" period in the early 1970s, Japan's economic growth indicators rose dramatically through the 1980s. In the 1990s, further developments occurred in Japanese broadcasting: (a) deregulating communication satellites to allow transmissions directly to TV households equipped with special antennas, 1992; (b) introducing low-powered community FM stations in order to provide more community-based information; and (c) beginning full digital transmission by communication satellite TV services (1996), broadcast satellite services (2000), and terrestrial TV services (partially in 2003; *Minpo Binran*, 2003).

Revenue Sources

In 1958, advertising worth 15.7 billion yen went to radio, while 10.5 billion yen went to television. In 1959, for the first time ever, TV advertising revenues exceeded those of the radio industry (*Minkan Hoso*, 2001). TV ad revenues today exceed those of all other media and reached 1.9 trillion yen in 2003.

By contrast, public broadcaster NHK relies almost totally on viewer fees. The fees are collected by automatic bank payments or by NHK fee collectors who personally visit each home. NHK's operating income in 1990 of about 496.4 billion yen increased to 673.8 billion yen in 2003 (Uesugi, 2003). For 2003, NHK had collected viewer fees from about 38 million of Japan's 49 million households for the terrestrial broadcasting service and 11.7 million households for the satellite broadcasting service by July. NHK, the world's largest public broadcaster, with 12,000 employees, has downsized from 16,902 employees in 1979 (Uesugi, 2003).

Terrestrial Broadcasting

Over-the-air broadcasting is still a main distribution route, accounting for 128 commercial stations in addition to the NHK network system (*Minpo Binran*, 2003). Unlike unified NHK, the five commercial networks were built through affiliation agreements between local stations and five "key stations" in Tokyo: Tokyo Broadcasting System (TBS), Fuji Television Network (Fuji TV), Nippon Television Network (NTV), Asahi National Broadcasting (TV Asahi), and Television Tokyo Channel 12 (TV Tokyo).

The commercial TV networks in turn grew to be affiliated with national newspapers: TBS with *Mainichi Shimbun*; NTV with *Yomiuri Shimbun*; Fuji TV with *Sankei Shimbun*; TV Asahi with *Asahi Shimbun*; and TV Tokyo with *Nihon Keizai Shimbun*. Circulations of the five national newspapers (morning editions) in 2002 were: 10.1 million—*Yomiuri Shimbun*; 8.32 million—*Asahi Shimbun*; 3.96 million—*Mainichi Shimbun*; 3.07 million—*Nihon Keizai Shimbun*; and 2.02 million—*Sankei Shimbun*. This structure developed because in the early days of television, when broadcast stations had minimal capital investments, national newspaper companies (as majority stockholders) influenced policy and editorial stance. Today NTV, TV Asahi, and TV Tokyo still somewhat reflect this parent–child relationship; however, TBS and Fuji TV are largely independent.

In the late 1990s, Japan's media landscape changed dramatically; terrestrial, satellite, and cable broadcasting were coexisting with broadband content distribution through the Internet. (The Internet took about 1% of advertising revenues in 2001.)

Satellite Broadcasting

Broadcast satellite (BS) broadcasters use powerful 120 W satellites, whereas communication satellite (CS) broadcasters use 50.1 W satellites. In this age of digital television (DTV), Japanese broadcasters have already set up digital transmitters and in-house facilities to provide terrestrial DTV signals. DTV operations will start first in three areas: Kanto (including Tokyo), Kinki (including Osaka), and the booming Chukyo area, home to the Toyota Motor Corp. (MPMHAPT, 2003b). Started in December 2000, Japan's transition process to full digital operation is expected to be completed in 2011.

CS broadcast service started as an analog service (ACSat) in 1992 and, due to spectrum capacity, the number of channels did not increase rapidly. However, when digital CS service (DCSat) began in 1996, the number of channels available with CS service became larger, reaching a total of 241 channels in 2002.

BROADCAST REGULATION

The guarantee of freedom of speech and expression in Article 21 of the 1946 Constitution is qualified for Japanese broadcasting. According to the

Broadcast Law, Article 1, Section 2, broadcasting is defined as transmitting wireless signals received directly by the public. The basic framework of Japanese broadcasting policies is derived from the 1950 Broadcast Law and, for technical matters, from the 1950 Radio Law.

The Radio Law regulates broadcast stations' frequencies and deals with technical matters. The Broadcast Law's Article 3 forbids censorship of any programs provided that they: do not harm public safety; are in good taste; are politically balanced; report factually; and present varied viewpoints on controversial issues as far as possible (Omori, 1994).

Article 44 of the Broadcast Law outlines the requirements that NHK must meet, including political impartiality, different viewpoints on controversial issues, and nurturing new culture while preserving the culture of Japan's past. Article 32 of the Broadcast Law requires everyone with a radio (until 1968) or television equipped to receive NHK's broadcasts to pay a fee. These receiving fees are paid on an equal basis by all owners of TV sets. The monthly fee is approved by the Diet each fiscal year and can be paid by automatic account transfer or to door-to-door collectors.

After World War II, the Occupation forces created an independent commission modeled on the U.S. Federal Communications Commission, but Prime Minister Shigeru Yoshida revoked its powers in 1952. Thereafter, the Ministry of Posts and Telecommunications (MPT) had authority for policymaking, ordinances, planning, and broadcast frequency allocation (*Minkan Hoso*, 1961). Regarding advertising, a regulation allows a maximum of 6 commercial minutes per 60-minute TV program. However, by airing many short programs, networks can boost TV commercial time.

The MPT uses *ipponka chosei*, a phrase commonly translated as "coordination," when there are a number of applicants for a single broadcasting license; the MPT facilitates the creation of a joint venture representing all influential applicants rather than engaging in a competitive selection process (Weinberg, 1991).

In April 1996, the MPT gave permission to STAR TV, Ted Turner's TNT, and the Cartoon Network to begin satellite broadcasts. Currently, the digital environment means regulations must deal with both broadcasting and telecommunications.

BROADCAST CONTENT AND RATINGS

Nowadays the lines between entertainment and news/educational programs are blurring, but traditionally defined, entertainment programs include dramas, quiz and variety shows (including comedy), cooking/food shows, and animation. In 2000, the time devoted to the "entertainment" category of programs varied between the public and commercial networks during the average broadcast day (Kataoka, 2001):

- NHK general channel: news 43.9%, education 11.3%, culture 29.5%, and entertainment 15.3% (broadcast time—24 hours),

- NHK educational channel: education 75.9%, culture 20.3%, news 3.8% (broadcast time—24 hours)
- Commercial broadcast stations: news 19%, education 12.2%, culture 25.2%, entertainment 39.4%, advertisement 2.9%, and others 1.3% (broadcast time—23 hours 39 minutes).

Dramas

Japanese home drama "is a genre that developed in Japan under the influence of American soap operas and situation comedies"; it mirrors the home life of ordinary people, providing a documentary account of social changes (Sata, 1991, p. 207). In the late 1970s, 2-hour drama specials became popular, particularly among housewives who could not go out to see movies. In the early 1980s, social conflicts among young people were portrayed in home drama series. Excellent dramas were produced during the period, including "*Kita no Kuni kara*" (From the North County), "*Kinyobi no Tsumatachi he*" (For the Housewives on Friday), and "*Fuzoroi no Ringotachi* "(Irregular Apples).

In the late 1980s through the 1990s, as more women joined the work force, home dramas targeted fashion-conscious, conspicuously consuming young females aged 20 to 34. Trendy dramas of this type, with original titles in English, included "Tokyo Love Story," "Long Vacation," and "Beautiful Life," all of which garnered ratings above 30%. Recently, home dramas have trouble even gaining ratings of 20%. NHK's popular "Television Saga" has presented annually a new telenovela every Sunday evening since 1961, depicting historical events and figures in Japan. Similar to home dramas, even this popular series has been struggling to get high ratings in recent years. The main reasons causing lower ratings are poor plan and scripts, lack of popular actors who attract huge audiences, and lifestyle changes (specifically among younger viewers).

Quiz and Variety

The TV variety show remains a perennial favorite in Japan. A typical variety show has several celebrity hosts and many performing entertainers. According to Stronach (1992, p. 62), the variety show "creates the feeling of a group—a group into which the audience is constantly invited." At least two or three variety shows air in prime time every day. In recent years, this format has been adapted to incorporate talk show segments. In "*Takeshi no TV Takkuru*" (Takeshi's TV Tackle), for example, main host Takeshi Kitano, a comedian, actor, and internationally recognized movie director, talks with celebrities and politicians alike. Injecting politics and economics into the lighter fare of variety shows has broadened the appeal of the genre.

Japanese audiences also love quiz programs, the formats of which are usually home grown. In the 1980s, quiz shows became more information oriented, gathering a wide range of information from over the world. "*Naruhodo the World*" (Let's Go—the World), for instance, featured both an in-studio host and a peripatetic on-location host who presented a travelogue from exotic locales before asking the questions that constituted the quiz. In 2003, "*Toribia no Izumi*" (The Spring of Trivia) moved from a midnight slot to prime time because of its popularity. Despite questions based on trivial, even useless, information, the show racked up good ratings (20% or higher) every week. The "Millionaire" show is a rare example of a successful imported quiz format (see chapter 14).

Cooking/Food Shows

In Japan's food culture, cooking and recipes are a common topic in daily conversation. Often quiz and talk shows depict celebrities eating on camera, so not surprisingly, cooking and food shows themselves are a popular entertainment genre. Formats range from how-to demonstrations of recipes to travel shows (wherein celebrities taste dishes and profile gourmet restaurants throughout Japan and overseas) to chefs' competitions. "*Ryouri no Tetsujin*" (Iron Chef), which gained a following overseas, pitted the well-known iron chef against a challenger.

The "*SMAP × SMAP*" food show targets young audiences. Divided into two teams, the pop male vocal quartet SMAP cooks two sumptuous dinners for a guest celebrity judge. Foreign celebrities like Will Smith and politicians like former cabinet minister Makiko Tanaka have appeared on the show.

BROADCAST IMPORTS AND EXPORTS

After World War II, Japan had to rely on imported TV content, but domestic production evolved so dramatically that in 1971 Japan became a net TV exporter, sending out more hours of programming than it brought in (Ito, 1990). However, the monetary value of broadcast imports has exceeded exports; for example, in 1995, imports cost U.S. $248 million, while exports earned only $53 million (see Table 9.1). Recently, the dramatic increase of TV channels available in Japan has forced program providers to rely more on overseas fare, such as Hollywood movies (Tadano, 2002).

TABLE 9.1
Broadcast Imports Versus Exports (in $millions)

	1991	1992	1993	1994	1995
Import	200	318	230	198	248
Export	33	37	41	47	53

Note. Ministry of Posts and Telecommunication (1997).

Imports

U.S. programs have dominated imports since the 1950s. In early imported series, such as "Bonanza" in the 1960s, well-known U.S. actors "spoke" perfect Japanese. Today, properly equipped sets enable a viewer to switch back and forth between the original sound track or a dubbed version. Recent imported series include "Sabrina," "ER," "Friends," "Ally McBeal," "The West Wing," "CSI," and "Alias."

For several new satellite channels, sports fill up air time: soccer games from the United Kingdom, Italy, and Spain as well as major league baseball, National Hockey League, National Football League, and National Collegiate Athletic Association sports programs from the United States. Japanese especially love to watch their baseball superstars Nomo, Ichiro, and Matsui when NHK airs games broadcast on U.S. television.

In 1995, foreign programs filled 5.7% of the total airtime of terrestrial broadcasts, with 86.2% of these programs coming from the United States (Ministry of Posts and Telecommunications, 1997). Considering total airtime of satellite broadcasting, foreign TV programs occupied a much larger share (31%) with the United States still the dominant country (72.4%) supplying such programs.

TV programs from elsewhere are also popular in Japan, especially British police-detective dramas, such as those featuring Agatha Christie's Detective Hercule Poirot and "The Adventures of Sherlock Holmes." Recently, Japanese audiences have had more opportunities to watch TV dramas from Asian countries, particularly South Korea. In the summer of 2003, a popular Korean drama series, *"Fuyu no Sonata"* (Sonata in Winter), did well in ratings against Japanese dramas in prime time.

Exports

Resentment of pre-1945 Japanese colonial rule prompted Taiwan and Korea to ban Japanese TV programs, but Taiwan lifted its ban in 1993. Korea's relaxation occurred in stages: movies and videos in 1998, various other TV shows in 2000, and most animation in 2004. Asia is the primary receiving area of exports (47.3%), followed by North America (25.7%), Europe (12.2%), South America (5.6%), the Middle East (1.8%), and other (7.5%) in 1995. Genres of programs are drama (37.5%), quiz and variety (36.2%), animation (9.1%), documentaries (7.6%), and other (9.6%).

Japanese dramas travel best to other Asian countries, such as Taiwan, China, Thailand, Malaysia, and Indonesia. The boom in exports, carried on STAR TV, started in about 1992. According to a Fuji executive, "Fellow Asians aspire to Japanese fashion and leisure activities, but in Europe, Japanese faces are not well accepted" ("Sekai ni," 1994). Obstacles to entering the U.S. market include local (not universal) themes, slow story development, and U.S. resistance to subtitles (Fujii, Suzuki, Bargreen, & Kawasaki, 2003).

One Japanese drama, "Oshin," a 297-episode telenovela spanning the years 1907–1983, did find enthusiastic audiences in 28 countries (Svenkerud, Rahoi, & Singhal, 1995). In Iran, ratings hit a high of 70% for this story of a woman's perseverance despite adversity; the national TV system deemed Oshin's spirit of self-sacrifice a good example for the Iranian people (Mowlana & Rad, 1992).

Quiz and variety format transfers constitute a special type of export (see chapter 14) whereby the originator licenses, for production overseas, the idea, set design, game rules, and accumulated know-how. For example, Nihon Television Network has sold formats of its popular quiz and variety programs—"*Majikaru Zunou Pawah*" (Magical Brain Power), "*Quiz Sekai ha Show by Shobai!!*" (World Business Show)—to Italy, Spain, Taiwan, Thailand, and other countries.

Japanese animation, aired in most Asian countries without editing, has gained universal acceptance. However, U.S. broadcasters typically edit out violent and sexually explicit content (Kusanagi, 2003). Changes in names of characters and story lines may be made to eliminate some Japanese cultural elements that do not travel well.

TV Anime

Since the first TV animation or "anime" (pronounced "an-ee-may") was broadcast in 1963—the 30-minute anime series "*Tetsuwan Atom*" (Astro Boy)—more than 1,000 anime programs have been produced in Japan ("TV anime," 2003). In order to create TV animation shows at a reasonable cost, the producer must limit the number of cel drawings per minute by controlling motions of the characters. This form, called "limited animation," was pioneered by U.S. producers such as Hanna-Barbera (Kusanagi, 2003).

In the 1950s and 1960s, popular U.S. series using the "limited animation" form—"Crusader Rabbit," "Huckleberry Hound," "Yogi Bear," "The Flintstones," and "Popeye"—were imported into Japan. Before being exposed to these cartoon series, Japanese animators had believed that animation had to mimic live-action dramas. When a trial of the limited animation form in "Astro Boy" met with phenomenal success (a rating of 40.7%), the genre was off and running. The final section of this chapter analyzes why TV anime has attracted Japanese audiences for so many years.

Story Centrality. In Japanese limited-motion, story-centered animation, each character has a "literary" function. Consequently, Japanese TV anime is often compared to a complicated novel (Kusanagi, 2003). Today the story-oriented style encompasses genres such as science fiction, space, adventure, mechanical creatures and robots, sports, school life, home drama, historical events and legends, fairy tales, fantasy, classical literature, romance, cooking, politics, business, *samurai* warriors and battles, and many others.

Varied Audiences. In the early era of anime (1960s), most programs targeted children. In the 1970s through 1980s, TV anime also focused on the teenagers who had grown up with watching early TV anime series, by expanding themes and genres for these viewers. Because of the anime boom at that time, TV anime programs became standard fare in prime time during weekdays and weekends. In addition, a new generation of animators who had grown up with TV anime emerged in the 1980s. These new animators created much more detailed and sophisticated characters, designs, and stories for TV anime series (e.g., speed fighting, romance with pretty young girls, elaborate mechanical creatures), which could satisfy anime fans (e.g., "Robotech") (Misono, 1999).

Family-oriented anime programs also gained a solid following. "*Sazae-san*," which portrays the daily life of a typical Japanese family, has aired nationwide since 1969 and is still popular today (ratings of 20% or higher). Classic literature, masterpieces, and stories from old Japan and around the world ("The Little Princess," "Moomin," "A Dog of Flanders") hold appeal as anime regardless of age and gender.

Adult anime included "Introduction to Japanese Economics," broadcast in the late evening, which explained difficult concepts to business men and women and general audiences in an easy, enjoyable way. Less educational adult love stories and fairy tales can be viewed after midnight. Other themes like mothering, gay and lesbian lifestyles, and cooking attract myriad audience segments.

Character Business. In Japan, the selling of goods that use popular anime characters, such as stationery, toys, clothes, and foods, is a big business. It was started when the sponsor of "Astro Boy," a confectionery company, sold chocolate carrying imprints of Astro Boy characters. Success among children motivated other businesses to use Astro Boy characters for their own products. The character business generates revenues not only for these companies, but also for the anime production that has the character license. The "Astro Boy" production company, in fact, gained more than $1 million dollars in those early days from license fees alone (Misono, 1999).

Although the companies using anime characters also typically sponsor the TV anime, they sometimes participate in designing characters of the anime that they sponsor. For instance, mechanical creatures or robot anime, such as "Tranzor Z," exploded as a toy fad in the 1970s. For sponsors, the TV anime itself served as a 30-minute advertisement of their products. The same licensing phenomenon hit the United States when "Pokemon" went into U.S. syndication in the late 1990s. There were various kinds of Pokemon goods in the U.S. market, including Game Boy software (by Nintendo), comics and videos (by Viz Communications), dolls and figures (by Hasbro), and trading cards (Kusanagi, 2003). Burger King used Pokemon characters as bonus prizes in sales promotions.

Synchronization With Other Media. The anime industry coordinates the release of comic books (called *manga*), movies, videos, TV games, satellite and CATV programs, and anime fan magazines for maximum impact.

A typical Japanese child born after World War II has literally grown up with reading *manga*. For example, one of the most popular *manga*, *Shukan Shonen Jump* (a weekly boys' comic) claims a weekly circulation of 6.2 million copies (Cooper-Chen, 1997). Popular stories and characters in *manga* are conversation topics among children. Like TV anime, printed *manga* have evolved as their readers have matured. As Schodt (1986) observed, Japanese businessmen read comics on their way to work on public transportation. Of hundreds of *manga* stories, the most popular become TV anime series (e.g., "Sailor Moon," "Kinnikuman," "Dragon Ball," "Pokemon," "Yu-Gi-Oh!," and "Yu Yu Hakusho"). The print *manga* and TV versions thus can reinforce each other synergistically. Furthermore, the theme song of a popular TV anime series can achieve hit status, sometimes at the level of a million-seller.

In the 1980s, with the diffusion of home computers, the TV and game industries became closely linked. The game Dragon Quest, for example, was designed by cartoonist Akira Toriyama, who created "Dragon Ball." Pokemon, initially a popular game, later became a *manga* and TV anime.

In sum, the buzzwords "blur" and "convergence" apply aptly to Japanese TV anime. Whereas anime fans form something of a cult following in the West, in Japan the anime game is big business. Boundaries are disappearing among the TV, movie, video, and game sectors, creating a vast mass market in which anime fans are consumers.

REFERENCES

Cooper-Chen, A. (1997). *Mass communication in Japan*. Ames, Iowa: Iowa State University Press.

Fujii, K., Suzuki, Y., Bargreen, S., & Kawasaki, I. (2003). Asia information sending. http://www.hbf.or.jp/grants/pdf/j%20:/11-ji-fujii-pdf

Harada, Y. (1999). *Nihon no ushinawareta jyu-nen* [The lost decade of Japan]. Tokyo, Japan: Nihon Keizai Shimbun-sha.

Ito, Y. (1990). "The trade winds change": Japan's shift from information importer to an information exporter, 1965–1985. In J. A. Anderson (Ed.), *Communication yearbook 13* (pp. 430–465). Newbury Park, CA: Sage.

Kanayama, T. (1998, March). *Japanese television broadcast regulation in transition*. Unpublished doctoral dissertation, Ohio University, Athens.

Kataoka, T. (2001). *Shin noso gairon* [New version for understanding broadcasting]. Tokyo, Japan: NHK Books.

Kusanagi, S. (2003). *America de Nihon no amime ha dou miraretekitaka?* [How has Japanese animation been viewed in the United States?]. Tokyo, Japan: Tokuma Shoten.

Ministry of Posts and Telecommunications (MPT). (1997). *1997 white paper*. http://www.soumu.go.jp/joho_tsusin/policyreports/japanese/papers/97wp3.html

Ministry of Public Management, Home Affairs, Posts and Telecommunications (MPMHAPT). (2003a, July 31). *The Second Period Governance Evaluation and its related plan*. http://www.soumu.go.jp/s-news/2003/030731_5.html

Ministry of Public Management, Home Affairs, Posts and Telecommunications (MPMHAPT). (2003b, April 14). *The Summary Report by the Study Group on the Future Broadcasting Figure in the Age of Broadband*. Tokyo, Japan: SGFBF.

Ministry of Public Management, Home Affairs, Posts and Telecommunications (MPMHAPT). (2003c). *Japan's population status and households as of March 31, 2003*. http://www.soumu.go.jp/c-gyousei/020918.html

Minkan Hoso 10nen Shi [The ten-year-history of commercial broadcasting]. (1961). Tokyo, Japan: The National Association of Commercial Broadcasters in Japan.

Minkan Hoso 50nen Shi [The fifty-year-history of commercial broadcasting]. (2001). Tokyo, Japan: The National Association of Commercial Broadcasters in Japan.

Minpo Binran 2002/2003 [NAB Handbook 2002–2003]. (2002). Tokyo, Japan: The National Association of Commercial Broadcasters in Japan.

Minpo Binran 2003/2004 [NAB Handbook 2003–2004]. (2003). Tokyo, Japan: The National Association of Commercial Broadcasters in Japan.

Misono, M. (1999). *Sore ha Atom kara hajimatta* [It was started by Astro Boy]. In M. Misono (Ed.), *Zusetsu Terebi Anime Zenshu* [Encyclopedia of TV anime] (pp. 7–89). Tokyo, Japan: Hara Shobo.

Mowlana, H., & Rad, M. (1992). International flow of Japanese television programs: The "Oshin" phenomenon. *Keio Communication Review, 14,* 51–68.

Nippon Hoso Kyokai. (2003). *Broadcast Museum permanent exhibits.* Japan Broadcasting Corporation. http://www.nhk.or.jp/bunken/museum-en/h31-e.html

Okamura, R. (2003). *Terebi no 21seiki* [Television's 21st century]. Tokyo, Japan: Iwanami Shinsho.

Omori, Y. (1994). Broadcasting. In Foreign Press Center/Japan (Ed.), *Japan's mass media* (pp. 43–64). Tokyo, Japan: Foreign Press Center.

Sata, M. (1991). Conclusion. In K. Goto, H. Hirahara, K. Oyama, & M. Sata, *A history of Japanese television drama* (ch. 7). Tokyo, Japan: Japan Association of Broadcast Art.

Sekai ni ureru nihon no bangumi [Japanese programs are being sold throughout the world]. (1994, June 29). *Chunichi Shimbun,* p. 8.

Schodt, F. (1986). *Manga! manga! the world of Japanese comics.* Tokyo, Japan: Kodansha.

Stronach, B. (1992). *Popular culture in Japan and America.* Tokyo, Japan: Seibido.

Svenkerud, P., Rahoi, R., & Singhal, A. (1995). Incorporating ambiguity and archetypes in entertainment-education programming: Lessons learned from "Oshin." *Gazette, 55,* 147–168.

Tadano, T. (2002). *Hollywood eiga to Nihon no eiga shijo* [Treatment of Hollywood movies in Japanese video market]. In M. Sugaya & K. Nakamura (Eds.), *Eizo Kontentsu Sangyo-ron* [Video contents industry: An introduction] (pp. 239–259). Tokyo, Japan: Maruzen.

Takeyama, A. (2002). *Rajio no kidai* [The age of radio]. Tokyo, Japan: Sekai Shiso-sha.

TV anime list. (2003, September 14). Available: www.begets.co.jp/tvmanga/db/history/history60.html

Uesugi, T. (2003). *NHK no Don Ebisawa Katsuji* [NHK's tycoon Katuji Ebisawa]. *Bungei Shunju, 81*(12), 94–105.

Weinberg, J. (1991). Broadcasting and the administrative process in Japan and the United States. *Buffalo Law Review, 39*(3), 615–735.

JAPAN, PRIME TIME, NOVEMBER 17–23, 2003

MONDAY							
Channel	7 p.m.	7:30 p.m.	8 p.m.	8:30 p.m.	9 p.m.	9:30 p.m.	10 p.m.
Public NHK-General Ch. 1	News 7 including Weather	Close-up	Wonder of Nature	8:45 p.m.: News	News 9	9:15 p.m.: Yumemiru Budo (drama)	News 10
Public NHK-Educational Ch. 3	8 Simple Rules (series)	7:25 p.m.: Montana (cartoon)	Welfare Network	8:30 p.m.: Health 8:45 p.m.: Sign Language News	Cooking	Home Handicrafts	World of Hobbies

Commercial NTV Ch.4	Meitantei Conan (cartoon special)	TV Programs of the World (variety)	TV Programs of the World	8:54: News & Weather	Super TV: Info Frontier 8:54 p.m.: Topics		Lion Sensei (drama)
Commercial TBS Ch.6	6:55 p.m.: Tokyo Friend Park (game variety)		Mito Komon (samurai drama)	8:54: News	Last Scene (suspense drama)		
Commercial Fuji Ch.8	7:04 p.m.: Men's World Cup Volleyball: Japan vs. China		Men's World Cup Volleyball: Japan vs. China	8:54: News & Weather	Beginner (drama)	9:54: Gourmet	10:00: SMAP x SMAP (variety special)
Commercial TV Asahi Ch.10	Kozure Okami (samurai drama) 7:54 p.m.: Guide		Miracle TV	8:54 p.m.: Topics	TV Tackle	9:54 p.m.: News Station	
Commercial TV Tokyo Ch.12	Disease Prevention (variety)	7:53 p.m.: Kazuo Toku- mitsu's Info Spirits		8:54 p.m.: Guide	Home Economics 9:54 p.m.: Topics		CSI—Crime Scene Inves- tigation (U.S. series)

TUESDAY

Channel	7 p.m.	7:30 p.m.	8 p.m.	8:30 p.m.	9 p.m.	9:30 p.m.	10 p.m.
Public NHK-General Ch. 1	News 7 including Weather	Close-up	NHK Song Concert	8:45 p.m.: News	News 9	9:15 p.m.: Project X	News 10
Public NHK-Educational Ch. 3	Junikoku-ki (cartoon)	7:25 p.m.: Big Wolf on Campus (series) 7:50: Topics	Welfare Network	8:30 p.m.: Health 8:45 p.m.: Sign Language News	Cooking	Home Handicrafts	World of Hobbies
Commercial NTV Ch.4	Ito's Home (family talk variety)		7:58 p.m.: Sanma & Stars (talk variety)	8:54: News & Weather	Nemuranai Denwa (suspense drama)		
Commercial TBS Ch.6	6:55 p.m.: Quiz Variety		7:54 p.m.: Let's Go to School (variety)	8:54: News	K-1 World Max (martial arts)		
Commercial Fuji Ch.8	7:04 p.m.: Men's World Cup Volleyball: Japan vs. Canada		Men's World Cup Volleyball: Japan vs. Canada	8:54: News & Weather	Anata no Tonari ni Dareka Iru (drama)	9:54: Guide	10:00: Hakoiri Musume (drama)
Commercial TV Asahi Ch.10	Amusement of Travel Special			8:48 p.m.: Guide 8:54 p.m.: Topics	London Boots' Love Aid (variety)		9:54 p.m.: News Station
Commercial TV Tokyo Ch.12	Shukan Pokemon Hoso-kyoku (cartoon)	Wagamama Fairy Mirumo de Pon Golden (cartoon)	Info Paradise	8:54 p.m.: Family Treasure Appraisers (variety) 9:54 p.m.: Topics			Dawn of Gaia

WEDNESDAY

Channel	7 p.m.	7:30 p.m.	8 p.m.	8:30 p.m.	9 p.m.	9:30 p.m.	10 p.m.
Public NHK-General Ch. 1	News 7 including Weather	Close-up	Trial & Success (science variety)	8:45 p.m.: News	News 9	9:15 p.m.: Rediscover- ing Japanese History	News 10

Channel	7 p.m.	7:30 p.m.	8 p.m.	8:30 p.m.	9 p.m.	9:30 p.m.	10 p.m.
Public NHK-Educational Ch. 3	Kasumin (cartoon)	7:25 p.m.: State of Grace (series) 7:50: Topics	Welfare Network	8:30 p.m.: Health 8:45 p.m.: Sign Language News	Cooking	Home Handi-crafts	World of Hobbies
Commercial NTV Ch.4	Interview Variety	Music Variety	Music Variety	8:54: News & Weather	World Surprising News	9:54: Topics	Kyohansha (drama)
Commercial TBS Ch.6	Household Secrets		7:54 p.m.: Golden Muscle (variety)	8:54: News	Discover 99 (variety)	9:54: Topics	Koibumi (drama)
Commercial Fuji Ch.8	Stars' Talk Variety		7:54 p.m.: Hexagon (quiz)	8:54: News	Trivialists (variety)	9:54: Guide	Comedy Rock & Roll
Commercial TV Asahi Ch.10	Soccer Preview	7:15 p.m.: A Match Soccer: Japan vs. Cameroon			9:18: Guide 9:24: Topics	9:30 p.m.: Aibo (drama)	
Commercial TV Tokyo Ch.12	Tennis no Oji-sama (cartoon)	Naruto (cartoon)	7:55: Topics / 8:00 p.m.: Dreamy Trips		8:54 p.m.: Tokuso Keiji Toyama Reiko (suspense drama)		

THURSDAY

Channel	7 p.m.	7:30 p.m.	8 p.m.	8:30 p.m.	9 p.m.	9:30 p.m.	10 p.m.
Public NHK-General Ch. 1	News 7 including Weather	Close-up	Edo Period Life	8:45 p.m.: News	News 9	9:15 p.m.: Problem Busters	News 10
Public NHK-Educational Ch. 3	Smallville (U.S. series)	Mujin Wakusei Survive (cartoon)	Welfare Network	8:30 p.m.: Health 8:45 p.m.: Sign Language News	Cooking	Home Handicrafts	World of Hobbies
Commercial NTV Ch. 4	Celebrity Troubleshooters		7:54 p.m.: National Intellectual Ranking (quiz)	8:54: News & Weather	Master of the Best Cooking (variety)	9:54: Topics	Downtown's Talk Variety
Commercial TBS Ch. 6	6:55 p.m.: Ethological Variety		7:54 p.m.: Uta-ban (music)	8:54: News	Et Alors (drama)	9:54: Weather	Manhattan Love Story (drama)
Commercial Fuji Ch. 8	7:04 p.m.: Men's World Cup Volleyball: Japan vs. U.S.A.		Men's World Cup Volleyball: Japan vs. U.S.A.	8:54: News & Weather	Tunnels' Variety	9:54: Guide	10:00: Shiroi Kyoto (drama)
Commercial TV Asahi Ch. 10	Cocorico's Variety: Useless Legend Makers	7:54 p.m.: Guide	Shin Kyoto Meikyu Annai (drama)	8:54: Topics	Trick (drama)	9:54 p.m.: News Station	
Commercial TV Tokyo Ch.12	Pocket Monster AG (cartoon)	TV Champion		8:54: News	U.S. Movie: Thrill Seekers		

FRIDAY

Channel	7 p.m.	7:30 p.m.	8 p.m.	8:30 p.m.	9 p.m.	9:30 p.m.	10 p.m.
Public NHK-General Ch. 1	News 7 including Weather	Metropolitan News	Friday Showtime	8:45 p.m.: News	9 9:15 p.m.: Korogashi Ogin (samurai drama)		News 10
Public NHK-Educational Ch. 3	Teenagers' Internet Debate	Teenagers' Internet Debate	Health	8:45 p.m.: Sign Language News	Living Q & A		Fancy Foods
Commercial NTV Ch. 4	Ninety-Nine's Variety		Mysterious Riddles (variety)	8:54: News & Weather	9:03 p.m.: U.S. Movie: 101 Dalmatians		
Commercial TBS Ch. 6	6:55 p.m.: Super Friday		Super Friday	8:54: News	SMAP Nakai's Variety	9:54: Weather	Yankii Boko ni Kaeru (drama)
Commercial Fuji Ch. 8	7:04 p.m.: Men's World Cup Volley-ball: Japan vs. Serbia and Montenegro	Men's World Cup Volleyball: Japan vs. Serbia and Montenegro		8:54: News & Weather	Jigoku no Hanayome (suspense drama)		
Commercial TV Asahi Ch. 10	Doraemon (cartoon)	Atashin-chi (cartoon)	7:54: Guide / Music Station	8:54 p.m.: Un-Nan Uchimura (self-produced variety special)		9:48: Topics	9:54: News Station
Commercial TV Tokyo Ch. 12	Pochi-Tama (pet animal variety)		7:54: Topics / Dream House	8:54: News	Plumpies (variety)	9:54: Topics	You Can Be Picasso (art variety)

SATURDAY

Channel	7 p.m.	7:30 p.m.	8 p.m.	8:30 p.m.	9 p.m.	9:30 p.m.	10 p.m.
Public NHK-General Ch. 1	News 7 including Weather	Tsurube's Trip Without a Plan		8:45: News & Weather	R.P.G (drama)		
Public NHK-Educational Ch. 3	Ryori Shonen K-taro (drama)	7:25 p.m.: Jr. High Diary 7:55 p.m.: News	NHK Junior Special (drama)	8:45p.m.: Topics	Business School	World Art Museums	ETV Special
Commercial NTV Ch. 4	Super Special			8:54: News & Weather	Ashita Tenki ni Naare (drama)	9:54: Topics	Gods of Entertainment (variety)
Commercial TBS Ch. 6	Amazing People (variety)	8:56: Topics	Mysteries of Mind and Body	8:54: News	World Mysteries (quiz)	9:54: Land-scapes	Broadcaster (news variety)
Commercial Fuji Ch. 8	Victory (drama)			8:54: News & Weather	U.S. Movie: The Green Mile		
Commercial TV Asahi Ch. 10	Crayon Shin-chan (cartoon)	7:28 p.m.: Bobobo-bo, Bo-bobo (cartoon)	Incredible Discoveries	8:54: News & Weather	Yako Ressha no Onna (suspense drama)		

Commercial TV Tokyo Ch.12	Restaurants in Port Towns (Saturday special)	8:54: News	Advertising Paradise (town info variety)	9:54: Topics	Masters of Beauty

SUNDAY

Channel	7 p.m.	7:30 p.m.	8 p.m.	8:30 p.m.	9 p.m.	9:30 p.m.	10 p.m.
Public NHK-General Ch. 1	News 7 including Weather	7:20 p.m.: Seeing Is Believing (quiz)	Musashi (samurai drama)	8:45 p.m.: News & Weather	NHK Special (documentary)	9:50 p.m.: Sunday Sports	
Public NHK-Educational Ch. 3	Thunderbirds (series)	7:25 p.m.: Puppet Play 7:55 p.m.: News	Sunday Art Museum		NHK Symphony Concert: Oratorio No.25, Dutoit (Conductor)		Art Theater
Commercial NTV Ch. 4	6:55 p.m.: TOKIO's Variety: Tetsuwan Dash		7:58 p.m.: Informative Entertainment: Far East Research Co.	8:54: News & Weather	Legal Advice (variety)	9:54: Topics	Oshare Kankei (talk show)
Commercial TBS Ch. 6	Amateur Video Quiz		Wonderful Animals (quiz)	8:54: News	Suekko Chonan Ane San-nin (drama)	9:54: Topics	Experiencing the World (variety)
Commercial Fuji Ch. 8	Kochira Katsushika-ku Kameari Koen-mae Hashutsu-jo (cartoon)	Men's World Cup Volleyball: Japan vs. Venezuela		8:54: News & Weather	Encyclopedia of Living (info variety)	9:54: Topics	Domoto Bros. (talk & music)
Commercial TV Asahi Ch. 10	6:56 p.m.: Best in Japan (variety)		7:58 p.m.: Family Before and After (variety)	8:54: News & Weather	**U.S. Movie: Bad Boys**		
Commercial TV Tokyo Ch. 12	Stay in the Country		7:54 p.m.: Sunday Big Variety			9:48: Music 9:54: News	Perfect Pastimes

Note. **Bold** denotes imported program.

Chapter 10

China

Hong Cheng
Ohio University

ABOUT CHINA

Situated in eastern Asia, the People's Republic of China, home to nearly 1.3 billion people, is the most populous nation on earth today. With an area of 9.6 million square kilometers (about 3.7 million square miles), China is second only to Russia and Canada in size, and is almost as large as the whole of Europe or about the size of the continental United States. China shares borders with 14 countries and has an extremely diverse climate.

People and Government

Administratively, China is divided into 23 provinces, five autonomous regions, and four municipalities—Beijing, Shanghai, Tianjin, and Chongqing, which are directly under the administration of the central government, and two special administrative regions (SARs)—Hong Kong and Macao. The sovereignty of the two SARs was handed over from the United

Kingdom and Portugal, respectively, to China in the late 1990s. China regards Taiwan as its 23rd province ("China," 2003).

The Communist Party of China (CPC) is the political party in power, promoting multiparty cooperation and political consultation. The National People's Congress is the highest legislative body in China. The State Council is the highest executive organ of state power and the highest organ of state administration in the country.

There are 56 ethnic groups in China. The Han people form the largest, numbering 1.1 billion and making up 93.3% of the country's population ("China," 2003). By far the most important Chinese tongue is *Putonghua* (Mandarin), meaning "ordinary or common language." Although unified by their traditions and cultural traits, and the written characters of their language, many of the Han speak some mutually unintelligible dialects such as *Yue* (Cantonese), *Wu* (Shanghaiese), or *Minbei* (Fuzhou), which display marked regional differences.

History

With a recorded history of more than 4,000 years, China is "one of the few existing countries that also flourished economically and culturally in the earliest stages of world civilization" (Encyclopædia Britannica, 2003, p. 2). China's relative isolation in its long history made possible the flowering and refinement of its culture, but it also left the country poorly prepared for the outside world when it was confronted by technologically superior foreign nations in the mid-19th century. There followed a century of decline and decrepitude, as China found itself largely helpless in the face of a foreign onslaught.

In 1949, when the Communist Party of China came to power and the People's Republic was founded, China went through a socialist transformation aiming to institute state ownership. From 1957 to 1966, China consolidated its socialist reconstruction. In the wake of that period came the so-called Cultural Revolution (1966–1976), which threw the country into a decade of social turmoil and enormous economic losses.

A new era in modern Chinese history began in late 1978 when the Third Plenum of the 11th CPC Central Committee decided to shift the focus of the party's work to socialist modernization and set a policy of reform and opening up to the outside world. The radical change in the party's orientation brought to an end the decade-long chaos and cleared the way for more than two decades of prosperity in the nation. Today, a market system has basically taken shape in China. A variety of ownership forms coexist with the public ownership, driving the country's annual growth rate at a brisk pace of up to 9%. China's entry into the World Trade Organization in 2001 is believed to have further spurred China's economic expansion ("CPC," 2003). The rapid economic growth has offered numerous opportunities for foreign investments. Currently, China is the largest recipient of foreign direct investments among developing countries ("About China," 2003).

The current Chinese leadership pays great attention to the importance of culture, seeing it as "a significant indicator of a nation's strength," parallel to economic development, and "the inner power that invigorates a nation" ("Three Represents," 2003, p. 2). Specifically, the emphasis is put on how to "build a socialist morality with Chinese characteristics," how to "retain the advantage of the traditional Chinese culture . . . while learning from other cultures as [China] opens wider to the rest of the world," and how to "find harmony between economic development and morals, individual achievements and the benefits of the whole society, as well as relations between man and nature" ("Three Represents," 2003, p. 2). Given the predominant role the Chinese government plays in the country, this new policy toward the cultural industry, including TV entertainment, deserves our attention.

BROADCAST BACKGROUND

History

Chinese television first went on the air in Beijing on May 1, 1958, broadcast to only about 30 TV sets in the national capital city. Aired by the then Beijing Television (BTV), the programs were broadcast at 7 p.m. only twice a week, with each day's broadcast lasting between 2 and 3 hours (Chang, 2002; Cooper-Chen, 2003; Yan, 2000). Later in 1958, a second TV station was launched in Shanghai, China's largest metropolis and commercial center. Both stations had one channel, carrying a similar 2 to 3 hours of daily programming, broadcast four times a week.

Soon TV stations emerged in other major cities. Within the next 2 years, 16 of the then 29 provinces, municipalities, and autonomous regions had their own TV stations. All programs were transmitted in black and white (Chang, 2002). By 1961, there were 26 TV stations in China. Political interferences and economic setbacks slowed down television's growth in the country during the next 15 years or so (Yan, 2000). In 1976, when the Cultural Revolution was over, 25 provinces, municipalities, and autonomous regions in China could receive BTV's signals. In May 1978, BTV was officially renamed China Central Television (CCTV), "becoming the country's most authoritative TV network and delivering for the first time a truly national broadcast service" (Chang, 2002, p. 9).

Although China began to explore color TV broadcast transmissions as early as the 1960s, it was not until 1973 that color came to TV stations in Beijing, Shanghai, and Tianjin, the three municipalities at that time (Chang, 2002; Yan, 2000). By the early 1980s, all TV stations in China were equipped to broadcast in color on the Phase Alternation Line (PAL) system (Li, 1991). When Beijing Television became CCTV, Beijing also got its own local station, still called BTV (Yan, 2000).

In 1972, the first ground satellite reception station in China was set up in Beijing to facilitate domestic and international program exchanges. By the early 1980s, a complete national TV network was in place, linking provincial stations to transmitting, channel-switching, and relay stations (Yu, 1990).

Since the 1980s, Chinese TV has enjoyed enormous growth. In 1983, there were only 52 TV stations in the country. By 1985, the number totaled 202. This rapid growth of the TV industry was partly due to a new governmental strategy that encouraged the establishment of a four-level (national, provincial, municipal, and county) TV broadcasting system as a replacement for the earlier centralized mechanism (Chang, 2002). In 2001, China had 357 TV stations and 2,194 channels, broadcasting a total of 183,879 hours per week, with 71,734 hours of them, or 39% of the TV programming, for entertainment ("Development," 2002).

During these few decades, cable TV and satellite transmission of programs also developed rapidly in China. The application of cable wiring technology began in China in the 1960s and 1970s when cable systems were only set up in selected major state-run companies and apartment complexes (Yu & Sears, 1996). That situation began to change when China launched and rented several communication satellites in the mid-1980s and wired numerous small communities surrounding big cities in the late 1980s. By 1997, there were about 2,000 cable stations (above the county level) in China, carrying news and entertainment programs. A typical cable TV viewer in the country could have access to 10 to 20 channels then (Chang, 2002). In 2002, China's TV penetration rate was 94% with 100 million cable TV subscribers. This figure represented a viewing population of more than 300 million, making China the world's largest cable TV market ("Huge potential," 2002).

Revenues

A major momentum for the rapid and sustained growth of China's TV industry over the past two decades is the ever-expanding advertising bonanza. From 1949 when CPC came to power until the mid-1960s, advertising was largely discouraged, although it was never officially banned (Cheng, 1996). During the Cultural Revolution, advertising, labeled as a "symbol of capitalism," largely disappeared in the country (Cheng, 2000). In the wake of the reform and opening up in the late 1970s, Chinese advertising came back to life.

In October 1979, Shanghai Television (STV) broadcast the first-ever TV commercial in the Chinese mainland. Since then, television has been the fastest-growing advertising medium in the country. Its billings have risen from about 5% of the nation's overall advertising business volume in the early 1980s to around 25% since the late 1990s. In 2002, TV advertising billings in China reached 23.1 billion *yuan* (Jia, 2003). Advertising has become a major resource for the financial viability and stability of China's TV industry nowadays.

TV Structure

As an important publicity tool, television in China is regarded as a window for the Chinese viewers to know about their own country and the outside world (Chang, 2002; Li, 1991). With its roots in the Central Broadcast Committee, set up in 1940, the governmental regulator that oversees broadcasting in Communist China has changed its name a few times. In 1949, it was called the Central Broadcasting Bureau (CBB). In 1982, its name was changed to the Ministry of Radio and Television (MRT), which was expanded as the Ministry of Radio, Film, and Television (MRFT) in 1986. Two years later, MRFT was changed to its current name, the State Administration of Radio, Film, and Television (SARFT), still directly under the aegis of the State Council ("Chronological list," 2003).

Role of the Party. In the strict Communist system, the Party (in the name of the state) was concurrently the owner, the manager, and the practitioner of TV broadcasting in China. All stations were under the dual jurisdiction of the party's Central Propaganda Department and CBB (now SARFT). The Propaganda Department was under the supervision of the secretariat and the political bureau of the party's Central Committee. Local supervision came from the party's propaganda departments at provincial, municipal, and county levels. The Propaganda Department set media policies, determined programming themes, and issued operational directives (Hong, 1997). Nowadays, SARFT supervises the management of the TV industry all over the country. Local administrations were in charge of the management and construction of the TV industry at the provincial, municipal, and county levels.

For decades, China's TV system was monopolistically structured, apart from being highly hierarchic (Zhao, 1998). Each level of governmental administration had only one "people's TV station." The reform and opening up that began in the late 1970s gave rise to a change in this monopolistic structure. Since 1992, many provinces have created an "economic station" in addition to the "people's station." The former is in fact a general interest commercial station with a higher degree of autonomy than the latter (Yan, 2000). Some provinces and major cities have established more specialized stations for entertainment, education, and children. The trend toward decentralization and specialization is most likely to continue. The new types of stations are believed to have counterbalanced the lopsided political and propagandist orientation of the "official model" and given fuller play to TV's economic, cultural, and entertainment functions (Zhao, 1998). They are also believed to pave the way for fully independent, commercialized broadcasting in China (Yan, 2000).

CCTV. Why single out CCTV in this chapter? Because it holds an undisputedly dominant position in the Chinese TV industry and exerts enormous influence in the nation. A good knowledge of CCTV will deepen one's overall understanding of Chinese TV.

As the sole national TV station of the People's Republic, CCTV currently features 15 channels with a total of more than 200 daily airing hours. Its programs include news, economics, arts, operas, music, sports, movies, military affairs, science and technology, agriculture, and children, which appear in more than 300 time slots. CCTV attracts a domestic audience of more than 1 billion. About 65% of CCTV's programs are original productions ("About us," 2004).

As a comprehensive, flagship channel, CCTV-1 is the earliest and most influential channel for the station. It covers all of China by satellite, with a daily average of 20 hours. While broadcasting news 13 times a day, CCTV-1 airs domestically made TV drama series and documentaries—ranging from China's ancient legends to stories of state leaders—every evening during prime time ("CCTV-1," 2004).

The other 14 channels of CCTV all have their own foci. Among them, CCTV-3 (for arts), CCTV-6 (movie channel), CCTV-8 (TV dramas), CCTV-11 (traditional Chinese operas and music), and CCTV-Music are almost entirely devoted to entertainment programs. Broadcasting an average of 19 hours a day via satellite, CCTV-3 features popular entertainment as its mainstay, which combines music, literature, theater arts, and information services. Targeting a general audience, it highlights ethnic attractions and involves viewers in several programs as guests or contestants ("CCTV-3," 2004).

Launched on January 1, 1996, and reserved for movies, CCTV-6 covers the country via satellite and broadcasts an average of 17 hours a day. Intended to promote movie and TV culture, it broadcasts Chinese and foreign feature films, documentaries, science and educational films, cartoons, operas, and TV dramas. It also participates in the production of movies and documentaries ("CCTV-6," 2004).

CCTV-8 first aired on May 3, 1999. As a drama channel, it also covers the country via satellite and broadcasts an average of 17 hours a day. Among its programs, domestically made drama series account for 48.8% and imported ones 35%, with the rest being a number of entertainment programs featuring show-business information, music, and other art forms ("CCTV-8," 2004).

To promote China's traditional opera arts, CCTV-11 started broadcasting on July 9, 2001. It embodies the rich Chinese culture by presenting more than 200 types of operas from all over the country. Trying to be both interesting and informative, CCTV-11 emphasizes the relation between opera and Chinese culture. The channel also features modern operas ("CCTV-11," 2004). Music Channel was officially launched on March 29, 2004. With its 18-hour daily programs, this youngest channel of CCTV features a wide variety of Chinese and foreign music and songs ("CCTV-Music," 2004).

Other channels include CCTV News Channel, the first 24-hour, Chinese-language news channel that began a trial operation in May 2003; CCTV-2 for economy, lifestyle, and services programs; CCTV-4, which only catered to viewers in Hong Kong, Macao, and Taiwan in the past, but now is accessible to many Chinese living in other countries; CCTV-7 for military affairs, agriculture, and children's programs; CCTV-9, a round-the-clock, all-English channel providing news, entertainment, and Chinese culture to its global audience; CCTV-10 for science and education; and CCTV-12, devoted to China's western region, as a support to the central government's ongoing plan for developing this most underdeveloped area in the country. CCTV-12's motto is to "let the western region learn about the world, and let the world get to know the western region" ("CCTV-12," 2004, p. 1). Most of these channels present some entertainment programs. Officially launched on December 28, 2003, Children's Channel also broadcasts 18 hours a day, featuring a variety of entertainment shows targeted at the 360 million children and teenagers in China ("CCTV-Children," 2004; "Programs," 2003).

To help CCTV grow and insure successful coverage of the upcoming Beijing Olympics (see chapter 13), construction began on a new site for China's only national TV station in March 2003. This U.S. $600 million architectural colossus is to stand as a Beijing landmark when completed in 2008 ("Architectural design," 2003).

BROADCAST REGULATION

Apart from overall regulations for all media, print and broadcast alike, there are numerous regulations focused specifically on television in China. Since the early 1980s, about 200 sets of regulations, provisions, and rules on TV operations and programs have been formulated in the country. In addition to SARFT, a variety of governmental and party agencies have been involved in the formulation and promulgation of these regulations and rules. They include the CPC Central Propaganda Department, State Council, Ministry of Culture, Ministry of Education, Ministry of Public Security, Ministry of State Security, Ministry of Justice, Ministry of Civil Affairs, State Administration for Industry and Commerce, and State Press and Publication Administration. The involvement of educational, commerce, and security agencies in TV regulation clearly indicates the Chinese government's intent, attempt, and authority to lay out parameters for the TV industry and its practitioners in the country.

Although information security-related and propaganda-related items are often important components of TV regulations, provisions, and rules, the focus of those regulations is more managerial and technical in nature than politically and ideologically oriented (Chang, 2002). Covering nearly every aspect of TV production, dissemination, reception, and consumption in China, these regulations vary from being technical to substantive areas, dealing with drama production, security of facilities, advertising, technological innovation, management, foreign satellite television, imports of foreign programs, ground reception devices, network, relay programs, licenses, staff training, secrecy, educational television, overseas Chinese TV productions, and TV programs in foreign relations. Although many regulations were submitted to the State Council for approval and to the Standing Committee of the National People's Congress for examination, others were administrative statutes issued by SARFT or other ministries and commissions under the State Council (Chang, 2002).

According to Chang (2002), television regulations in China are developed both conceptually and technically. Conceptually, the regulations are mainly focused on what television should do with its informational and entertainment content. The overarching message is that television is powerful given the large audience it is capable of reaching. As such, TV content must be carefully produced and scrutinized. Technically, new communication technologies have made it possible for TV practitioners to explore new ways of production, dissemination, presentation, and reception of content that may not fall within the confines of traditional standards. The dominant presumption is still largely that technology should serve the best interests of society.

As far as TV entertainment programs are concerned, they must, according to related TV regulations in China, contain moral and educational elements. In 1994, for example, SARFT issued specific regulations on the use of imported programs, such as cartoons, TV series, videos, and CDs that come from Hong Kong, Macao, and Taiwan, as well as foreign countries, via purchases, exchanges, or as gifts. The regulations stipulate that all such imports must get the approval of the relevant supervising department, and that no TV station is allowed to broadcast imported products for more than 25% of its program time (Yan, 2000).

On June 1, 1986, the Temporary Regulation of TV Drama Production Permits issued by the then MRFT took effect. Three years later, the regulation was finalized as an official administrative stipulation. According to the regulation, institutional applicants for TV drama production must first obtain an MRFT-issued permit. In cases where applicants operated at local levels, provincial or municipal radio, film, and TV bureaus were authorized to grant such permits. Under this regulation, TV drama permits were divided into short-term drama-specific shooting permits and long-term permits for 5 years (in 1989, the provision was changed to 3 years), subject to review and assessment by the granting authority. Determination and issuance of permits follow a set of comprehensive rules (Chang, 2002).

TV CONTENT AND RATINGS

Audience Measurement

Where there are TV programs, there are ratings. But in the past, TV viewership in the Chinese mainland was determined largely between advertisers and TV stations. Advertisers would have to depend on their own rudimentary research and subjective judgment to determine whether individual programs were reaching the viewers they targeted. As the stakes were getting higher and higher, advertisers became less and less willing to make blind bets. Since Nielsen Media Research made a foray into this fast-growing market soon after China reopened its doors to the outside world, the way TV programs are rated has begun to change. Trying to apply the same methodology and discipline in conducting ratings in China as in other markets, Nielsen has established a reputation in this new market for impartiality in its ratings, partly because it is not affiliated with any business or media conglomerate.

Currently, Nielsen provides metered TV ratings in just 11 major cities in the mainland. It has plans, however, for expanding its services to cover 100 cities in the near future. It also intends to measure both urban and rural viewing. When fully implemented, Nielsen's service will cover 75% of China's total TV advertising spending.

Nielsen's ambitious plan in China is largely driven by demand from advertisers. Such demand shows that the TV industry in this new market is maturing rapidly. In the meantime, heated-up competition among TV broadcasters, including some from overseas, also call for a higher standard of program ratings. The media industry's desire for a higher standard is equally supported by the Chinese government, which wants to gain a more accurate understanding of what people are watching (Liang, 2003).

Besides Nielsen, CVSC-TNS Research (CTR), founded in 1995, is the largest media and marketing research company in Mainland China. Headquartered in Beijing, CTR has regional offices in Hong Kong, Shanghai, Guangzhou, and Fuzhou. Since 1997 the company has enjoyed an average growth of 20% per year. With the largest research network in China, CTR employs more than 330 full-time professionals, including researchers, fieldwork supervisors, and industry experts. By 2003, CTR already owned a consecutive 7-year media marketing and advertising research database in China ("Overview," 2003).

At local levels, some provinces and major cities have developed government-sponsored networks that also collect data on TV viewership periodically. For example, the Guangdong TV Viewership Survey Network is sponsored by the Guangzhou Municipal Statistical Bureau and conducts detailed ratings of TV programs in Guangdong Province, including Hong Kong and Macao programs accessible to Guangdong viewers. The network provides Guangdong Television (GTV) with weekly ratings on all TV programs in the province. GTV owns a weekly publication titled *Guangdong TV Reception Rating*, in which the ratings of various TV programs aired in the province are tabulated on a day-to-day basis. Consistently, most of the highest-rated programs are always entertainment programs, especially some TV drama series.

TV as a Mass Entertainment Medium

Television in China is not only a platform for news and information but is now also "the single, most popular source for family entertainment" across the country. As television has become an undoubted leader of China's cultural industry (based on creative and copyrighted assets such as literature, music, TV, and film), TV culture is seen as the basis of the "new culture of the new century" in China ("Pop culture," 2003, p. 2).

As mentioned earlier in the chapter, TV sets became popular in China in the 1980s and spread into most households by the late 1990s. Until the mid-1980s, TV entertainment programs in China were largely dominated by imported TV dramas from Japan and Western countries (Wang & Chang, 1996). Perceived influences of imported TV programs alerted official censors and regulators, who urged domestic TV program producers to "occupy" the prime time slots with their own programs. In 1986, a total of 1,500 TV drama episodes were made in China. The number jumped to more than 15,800 in 1999. In 2000, there were, on average, 25 new drama episodes shown on Chinese television in any given day (Zhu, 2001).

While domestic TV drama production grows at a rapid rate, official concern about those productions has increased at the same time. TV drama production in China is often criticized as showing lifestyles way ahead of the nation's average living standards and adding to many people's wish for excessive material prosperity. The rationale for the criticism is twofold: On one hand, the production of TV dramas as commodities has turned more and more artistic pursuits into a commercial process; on the other, many high-brow artists and scriptwriters are reluctant to commit their efforts to TV dramas, regarding them as part of the popular and even vulgar culture (Chang, 2002).

Dramas on CCTV

Chinese viewers spend an average of 3 hours a day watching television, and about one third of that time is spent watching drama series. In 2002, more than 800 domestic TV drama producers created more than 20,000 hours of TV dramas. The total TV drama airtime of that year exceeded 50,000 hours. More than 90% of TV channels in China air TV dramas, which account for more than one quarter of their airtime. The popularity of TV dramas varies from the north to the south, however, considering China's vast territory and its people's different tastes. In general, drama series set in China's imperial past attract a large audience in the north, whereas modern love stories are more popular in the east and south ("Soap opera," 2003).

TV drama series generate substantial revenue for TV stations, in some cases up to 70% of the total revenue. Prime time television is largely dominated by TV drama series. Advertising during this period accounts for more than half of the stations' revenue. In 2002, China invested about 2 billion *yuan* on TV drama series, returns on which totaled about 20 billion *yuan*. Despite these overall profits, TV drama production is still a high-risk industry on the Chinese mainland. All told, only 15% of the current series make profits, whereas most have difficulty breaking even and even incur losses ("Soap operas," 2003).

New Year's Programming

Apart from CCTV-1's daily or weekly popular dramas and other regular entertainment programs (as listed on the program grid), its annual Spring

Festival Gala (usually in February on the Western calendar) is worthy of mention here. Since 1983, CCTV-1, joined by CCTV-4 in recent years, has been hosting this national entertainment spectacular on Lunar New Year's Eve. Featuring entertainment programs of all kinds, from traditional Chinese folk dancing and singing to various humorous performances, from episodes of popular Chinese operas to famous foreign ballet pieces, the gala is made of dozens of performances usually lasting more than 4 hours, from 8 p.m. to after midnight. Gathering numerous top singers, dancers, comedians, composers, and choreographers, the gala has become an annual cultural and entertaining feast on the Lunar New Year's Eve, watched by the entire nation and many Chinese overseas. Before this annual show was available, the most important activity for a typical Chinese family was the New Year's Eve dinner. In the past 20 years or so, more and more Chinese families rushed through their dinners that evening in order to feast their eyes on this TV spectacular.

Since the Spring Festival Gala became part of the norm for the Lunar New Year celebration, Chinese viewers hold ever-heightened expectations for the show, which becomes increasingly challenging year after year for anyone involved in the gala, especially its directors. To live up to the audience's expectations, preparations usually begin several months before New Year's Eve, and various new ideas are tried each year. Among others, interactivity has become an eye-catching feature of the show, inside the CCTV performance center and via telephone or e-mail. For the 2004 Spring Festival Gala, CCTV.com—CCTV's website, launched in December 1996— became an information and interactivity center. Before, during, and after the gala, audiences could enjoy what was promoted as "zero-distance" interaction with the gala organizers, conveying their requests for the show, expressing New Year wishes to their loved ones, and making immediate comments on the show.

Programming Challenges

The increasing competition and more flexible market mechanism seem to have made China's TV entertainment industry stronger and more agile. Reversing the trend of the past few years when imported TV programs— especially those from Republic of Korea and Singapore—were among the best-loved programs for millions of Chinese viewers, domestic TV productions are seemingly playing a dominant role in the domestic market.

Much more diverse in subject matters and genres than they used to be, current TV entertainment programs range from costume dramas, cartoon series, and police shows to stories about fights against corruption and dramas about legendary figures. Private TV production companies are mushrooming, as still more popular programs are needed to cater to the ever-demanding appetites and tastes of Chinese audiences. For example, the Enlight Media Co., founded in 1998, is well known to Chinese TV viewers for its "Entertainment Live," a TV special covering entertainment, sports, fashion, health care, and TV drama series. Similarly, the Joyful

Media Co., founded in 1999, is best known for its game shows, such as "Fun, Fun, Fun" (Zhu, 2003b).

Nowadays, most Chinese families can receive more than 40 TV channels. The gap between supply and demand has resulted in a serious duplication of programs, especially drama series, giving rise to a situation in which viewers may watch the same show simultaneously on a number of cable channels ("Soap operas," 2003).

The major reason for the lack of variety in programs on Chinese television is the lack of professional TV program producers. Some media scholars in China have called for the setup of more TV program production companies. They warned that if domestic companies do not move quickly and explore the content-providing market soon enough, many viewers will also seek entertainment elsewhere, most likely on the Internet, and more Western companies will make localized programs for Chinese audiences ("New shows," 2002).

IMPORTS AND EXPORTS

Transnational Media

For years, global media giants (see chapter 2) have been attempting to get footholds in the fast-growing TV and cable market in Mainland China. Before 2001, however, only Hong Kong-based Phoenix TV and Sun TV, and Macao-based Five Star TV had successfully realized commercial operations in the mainland (Jia, 2001). Since 2001, the hard-to-access TV market for global giants has begun to change. In October 2001, CCTV and AOL Time Warner reached an accord—the first time a foreign-owned cable network's program would be broadcast in the Chinese mainland. Under the deal, China Entertainment Television Broadcast Ltd. (CETV), a U.S.-based Mandarin channel acquired by AOL in 2000, could offer movies, music, and sports programs to viewers in South China's Guangdong Province. In return, China's national all-English channel CCTV-9 began to broadcast on some of Time Warner's cable channels—the first time a CCTV channel was carried on a 24-hour basis on a U.S. cable system ("AOL," 2001).

In December 2001, an entertainment channel of the STAR Group of Hong Kong (see chapter 2) also got permission from the Chinese government to telecast in Guangdong Province. According to the agreement, the STAR Group could, through a cable network, put out a round-the-clock entertainment channel (including music and films) in the Guangdong area. In exchange, Fox, a sister company of STAR, would telecast CCTV-9 in the United States ("Foreign cable," 2001).

In 2002, News Corp. launched a Chinese-made version of the hit U.S. sitcom "Friends." Called "Joyful Youth," the newly filmed program is among a host of locally produced talk shows, dramas, and game shows that STAR Group offers to 1 million cable TV viewers in Guangdong Province (News Corp., 2002). News Corp. plans to invest more than $100 million in a new channel called *Xingkong Weishi* (Star Satellite TV), during the next 3 to 5 years. In the future, News Corp. wants its programs to go national beyond Guangdong (Ghahremani, 2003).

By early 2003, CETV, the first foreign TV channel granted cable TV landing rights in Mainland China through a reciprocal carriage agreement with CCTV in 2001, had expanded its cable distribution from Guangdong Provincial Cable Network to include Guangzhou Cable and Shenzhen Cable Networks, bringing its total number of cable distribution households to 2.2 million. In July 2003, the TOM Group (a Chinese-language media company of Hutchison Whampoa, Cheung Kong Holdings, and other strategic investors) and Turner Broadcasting System Asia Pacific Inc., a subsidiary of AOL Time Warner, joined hands for a strategic collaboration related to CETV. With TOM assuming the management rights of CETV because of its majority equity interest in this 24-hour Chinese-language TV channel, CETV intends to further extend its reach nationwide in China ("TOM," 2003).

Unwilling to fall behind global media giants in the race for a foothold in the Chinese mainland, Hong Kong producers are enthusiastic about selling their original TV programs to this bigger market in the wake of the implementation of the Closer Economic Partnership Arrangement between the special administrative region and the mainland (Zhu, 2003b).

Imported Dramas

The TV industry's rapid growth at various levels in China has also given rise to increasing needs for imported TV dramas from various countries. In 2000, China imported about 1,300 episodes of foreign TV dramas, taking 14.3% of the total dramas shown in the country that year (Zhu, 2001). The widespread presence of foreign TV dramas in the country has also led to large-scale content discipline over the years. In 1990, for example, SARFT authorized bans on the airing of imported programs determined as advocating Western political, religious, and cultural values to the extent of threatening the value integrity of the socialist system or Chinese culture, romanticizing colonialism, parodying the seamy side of Third World countries, or undermining ethnic harmony or national sovereignty. Programs suggesting pornography or promoting violence are prohibited on Chinese television, too, although after adequate editing these programs are often still broadcast (Chang, 2002). On the other hand, six types of content are especially endorsed and encouraged:

- Programs with serious and positive themes featuring progressive thoughts;
- Entertainment contributing positively to culture and morals;
- Programs aimed at spreading knowledge about science and technology;
- Accurate rendition of history revealing laws of progress;

- Programs edifying to the youth and constructive to their growth; and
- Programs with relatively higher aesthetic values. (Chang, 2002, p. 43)

Intended to guide the imports of foreign TV programs, these general and vague rules apparently still leave much room for different interpretations among TV stations.

Exports

Two of CCTV's channels—channel 4 in Chinese and 9 in English—are exported by satellite to more than 120 countries in the world. A special case of TV exports is content aimed at the many foreign tourists and business people that the economic reform and opening up have brought to the Chinese mainland. To cater to the increasing needs of these foreigners (including those from Hong Kong, Macao, and Taiwan) for information and entertainment, major hotels began to operate closed-circuit television. Regarded as a Chinese window on the world and an important means of promoting China's international image, the program content to be shown exclusively in these hotels has been subject to official control and censorship since the mid-1980s. Applications for permits to run closed-circuit television in hotels must be approved by the National Tourism Administration (Chang, 2002).

TRENDS, CHALLENGES, AND OPPORTUNITIES

With China's further opening up and World Trade Organization (WTO) entry, its TV entertainment industry is facing many new opportunities and challenges. From the coexistence of opportunities and challenges emerge some noticeable trends.

New Government Strategies

Facing those opportunities and challenges, the Chinese government is adopting two new strategies. First, it tries to promote strong domestic entertainment groups by encouraging separation of TV production from broadcasting ("New shows," 2002). In December 2001, the China Radio, Film, and Television Group, the biggest-ever state media group in the country, was launched. It pulled together the nation's dominant CCTV, China Radio International, China National Radio, and leading film production companies. It has a fixed asset of 21.4 billion *yuan* and annual revenue of 11.1 billion *yuan* (Hou, 2001).

In the same month, China Broadcasting Network Co. Ltd (CBN), a domestic communication transmission giant that reaches more than 100 million Chinese households, made its debut. As the transmission branch of the China Radio, Film, and Television Group, CBN carries on duties of construction, operation, and development for the group's transmission network. Besides traditional TV and radio program transmission, CBN provides entertainment services such as video-on-demand and high-speed data broadcasting. It also plans to deliver Internet-related services, such as high-speed Internet access, but for now it is focusing on TV broadcasting (Hou, 2001).

Meanwhile, the Chinese government hopes its domestic media, including entertainment media, will become more competitive by catching the wave of the ongoing, worldwide digital revolution. SARFT has published a detailed plan and timetable for the digitalization of the entire country's radio and TV systems. Started in leading metropolises and the eastern regions, this 15-year plan is divided into four phases and set for completion by 2015 ("Timetable," 2003). In 2003, China had about 350 million TV sets. To digitalize all these TV sets means a market worth at least 70 billion *yuan* (Zhu, 2003a).

Momentum for China to digitalize its radio and TV systems is the 2008 Summer Olympics. Beijing has launched a "digital Olympics" program aimed to enhance telecommunication infrastructure and network systems to improve its information technology (IT) environment. Beijing broadcasters will deliver the 2008 Olympics to more than 3.5 billion people worldwide. Nine out of every 10 households that watch television are expected to tune into part of the Olympics broadcast. It is believed that the wide use of digital high-definition TV (HDTV) will insure top quality production, transmission, and broadcast of the events at the Olympics (Zhu, 2003a).

Culture as Industry

The development of the cultural industry in China, including TV entertainment, moved slowly compared to the dramatic reform in the economic field, but it is now on a fast track. Given the huge population of nearly 1.3 billion and the prosperous economy, the potential of the cultural sector is formidable. The biggest boost to the sector came from the Chinese government's signals about restructuring the management mechanism of the cultural industry. In 2003, for the first time, the "cultural industry" concept appeared to be parallel with "cultural understanding" in CPC's leading document. This concept is unusual because it represents a significant shift in Chinese leadership's understanding of culture. In the past, the government treated the cultural sector as an ideology rather than an industry. Inasmuch as the ideological role of cultural products was the government's overriding concern, whether they could generate economic returns or not was seldom given consideration.

Reform in the cultural industry is also being pressed by great challenges brought by China's WTO entry. Although the protection period still bars any large-scale invasion of foreign cultural products, the fledgling cultural sector in China has already sensed the chill of global competitions. Overall, WTO membership brings China more opportunities than challenges. However, penetration of Western cultural capital and products, accompanied by the transition of Western values, has caused China's cultural industry, including TV entertainment industry, to realize that it cannot afford to lose any more time, but must run on the fast track (Hua, 2003).

REFERENCES

About China. (2003). *OCRA Worldwide* http://www.ocra.com/services/hk_china_business 01.asp

About us. (2004). *CCTV.com*. http://www.cctv.com/english/20030805/101215.shtml

AOL to broadcast in South China. (2001, October 25). *China Daily* http://www1 .chinadaily.com.cn/en/doc/2001–10/25/content_90340.htm

Architectural design for new CCTV site announced. (2003, December 17). CCTV.com http:// www.cctv.com/english/20030730/100214.shtml

CCTV-1. (2004). CCTV.com http://www.cctv.com/english/20030805/101257.shtml

CCTV-3. (2004). CCTV.com http://www.cctv.com/english/20030805/101259.shtml

CCTV-6. (2004). CCTV.com http://www.cctv.com/english/20030805/101265.shtml

CCTV-8. (2004). CCTV.com http://www.cctv.com/english/20030805/101272.shtml

CCTV-11. (2004). CCTV.com http://www.cctv.com/english/20030805/101277.shtml

CCTV-12. (2004). CCTV.com http://www.cctv.com/homepage/profile/12/index.shtml

CCTV-Children. (2004). CCTV.com http://www.cctv.com/homepage/profile/15/index .shtml

CCTV-Music. (2004). CCTV.com http://www.cctv.com/homepage/profile/16/index.shtml

Chang, T. K. (2002). *China's window on the world: TV news, social knowledge and international spectacles.* Cresskill, NJ: Hampton Press.

Cheng, H. (1996). Advertising in China: A socialist experiment. In K. T. Frith (Ed.), *Advertising in Asia: Communication, culture and consumption* (pp. 73–102). Ames, IA: Iowa State University Press.

Cheng, H. (2000). China: Advertising yesterday and today. In J. P. Jones (Ed.), *International advertising: Realities and myths* (pp. 255–284). Thousand Oaks, CA: Sage.

China at a glance. (2003). *People's Daily* http://english.peopledaily.com.cn/china/home .html

A chronological list of leaders of all previous years. (2002). *SARFT* http://www.sarft.gov .cn/manage/publishfile/53/987.html

Cooper-Chen, A. (2003, August). *Entertainment East and West: A comparison of prime time U.S. and Asian TV content using the methodology of the National Television Violence Study.* Paper presented at the annual convention of the Association for Education in Journalism and Mass Communication, Kansas City, MO.

CPC central plenum to focus on reform. (2003, October 15). *CCTV.com* http://www.cctv .com/special/1104/1/1.html

Development of radio and TV in China. (2002). *SARFT* http://www.sarft.gov.cn/manage/ publishfile/51/1095.html

Encyclopædia Britannica. (2003). http://search.eb.com/eb/article?eu=127705&tocid=0 &query=china&ct=

Foreign cable TV entertainment channel permitted to set in motion in Guangdong (2001, December 20). *People's Daily.* http://english.peopledaily.com.cn/200112/20/ eng20011220_87141.shtml

Ghahremani, Y. (2003, January 13–19). Rupe chips away at China. *Variety,* p. 39.

Hong, J. (1997). China. In H. Newcomb (Ed.), *Encyclopedia of television, Vol. 1* (pp. 360– 362). Chicago: Fitzroy Dearborn.

Hou, M. (2001, December 19). Broadcasting giant materializes. *China Daily.* http://www1 .chinadaily.com.cn/en/doc/2001–12/19/content_98584.htm

Hua, H. (2003, August 26). Culture looks to get leading role. *China Daily,* p. 5.

Huge potential in broadcasting market—forum (2002, August 22). *China Daily* http://www1.chinadaily.com.cn/en/doc/2002–08/22/content_133178.htm

Jia, H. P. (2001, October 23). Macao TV service wins nod to beam into mainland. *Business Weekly* http://www1.chinadaily.com.cn/en/doc/2001–10/23/content_90020.htm

Jia, Y. B. (2003). An analysis of 2002 Chinese advertising billings. *Modern Advertising*, (4), 16–18.

Li, X. P. (1991). The Chinese television system and television news. *China Quarterly, 126*, 340–355.

Liang, H. F. (2003, June 20). Highly rated way to channel up profits. *China Daily* http://www1.chinadaily.com.cn/en/doc/2003–06/20/content_240044.htm

New shows would keep eyes on screens. (2002, February 27). *China Daily* http://www1.chinadaily.com.cn/en/doc/2002–02/27/content_108421.htm

News Corp. hopes to make new "friends" in China. (2002, March 4). *People's Daily* http://english.peopledaily.com.cn/200203/04/eng20020304_91350.shtml

Overview. (2003). *CVSC-TNS Research* http://www2.cvsc-tns.com/menu_42/menu_54/menu_68/index.html

Pop culture goes global. (2003, June 10). *China Daily* http://www1.chinadaily.com.cn/en/doc/2003–06/10/content_168477.htm

Programs of CCTV Children's Channel (2003, November 26). *CCTV.com* http://www.cctv.com/news/science/20031126/101461.shtml

Soap operas become Chinese favorite. (2003, March 21). *People's Daily* http://english.peopledaily.com.cn/200303/21/eng20030321_113693.shtml

Three Represents—CPC's new thinking. (2003). *China.org.com* http://www.china.org.cn/english/zhuanti/3represents/68733.htm

Timetable for Chinese TV's analog-to-digital transition. (2003). *SARFT* http://www.sarft.gov.cn/downstage/page_22_1.jsp

TOM, AOL Time Warner's Turner Broadcasting form partnership for CETV (2003, July 3). *People's Daily* http://english.peopledaily.com.cn/200307/03/eng20030703_119342.shtml

Wang, J., & Chang, T. K. (1996). From class ideologue to state manager: TV programming and foreign imports in China, 1970–1990. *Journal of Broadcasting & Electronic Media, 40*, 196–207.

Yan, L. Q. (2000). China. In S. A. Gunaratne (Ed.), *Handbook of the media in Asia* (pp. 597–526). New Delhi: Sage.

Yu, J. (1990). The structure and function of Chinese television, 1979–1989. In C. C. Lee (Ed.), *Voices of China: The interplay of politics and journalism* (pp. 69–87). New York: Guilford Press.

Yu, X. J., & Sears, A. (1996). "Localism" in Chinese media context: An examination of a closed circuit community cable system. *Journal of Broadcasting & Electronic Media, 40*, 208–226.

Zhao, Y. Z. (1998). *Media, market, and democracy in China: Between the party line and the bottom line.* Urbana and Chicago: University of Illinois Press.

Zhu, G. (2001, March 27). Six problems of TV drama production remain urgently to be solved. *World Journal*, p. C6.

Zhu, L. Y. (2003a, October 8). Digital era dawns at Olympics. *China Daily*, p. 9.

Zhu, L. Y. (2003b, September 5). Media fair explores trends. *China Daily*, p. 9.

CHINA, PRIME TIME, NOVEMBER 24-30, 2003
(CCTV programs only)

MONDAY

Channel	7 p.m.	7:30 p.m.	8 p.m.	8:30 p.m.	9 p.m.	9:30 p.m.	10 p.m.
CCTV-1	CCTV News	7:31 p.m.: Weather 7:38 p.m.: Forum	7:55 p.m.: TV Drama: Honor	8:51 p.m.: TV Drama: Honor 9:49 p.m.: Science & Technology			Evening News
CCTV-2	7:10 p.m.: Golden Land	Commercial Bridge 7:40 p.m.: Frontline	Life	Economy & Law	Economic News	Economy 30 Minutes	10:05 p.m.: Biz China
CCTV-3	7:05 p.m.: TV Storytelling: The Yang Family's Marksman	7:32 p.m.: Performance Arena	8:28 p.m.: Theater: Our Beautiful Life				10:06 p.m.: World of Dances
CCTV-4	News in Brief 7:10 p.m.: TV Drama: The Three Kingdoms		News in Brief 8:10 p.m.: Across China 8:40 p.m.: Two Sides of the Straits		China News		Chinese Showbiz
CCTV-5	Light Sports	Soccer World				Sports World	10:05 p.m.: Sports Documentary: Vast Oceans & Deep Seas
CCTV-6	7:16 p.m.: Cartoon: Challenging the Emperor	7:45 p.m.: Classical Chinese Movie: The Last Frenzy			9:33 p.m.: Classical Chinese Movie		9:56 p.m.: **European Movie: My Tutor**
CCTV-7	Farmers' Special: Learning to Sew	Military News	Children in the East	8:45 p.m.: Community Special: So That's How It Is!	9:17 p.m.: Tips on Farming	9:52 p.m.: Farmers' Focus	10:07 p.m.: Tips on Getting Rich
CCTV-8	7:14 p.m.: Sound from Screens	7:33 p.m.: Primetime Show: Into Balibao	8:27 p.m.: Primetime Show: Public Procurator-General		9:19 p.m.: Previews	9:49 p.m. Popular Theater: Thunderbolt Police	
CCTV-9	Worldwide Watch	Dialogue	Culture Express	Documentary	Biz China	Rediscovering China	CCTV News
CCTV-10	Outlook—English Magazine	Science & Technology 7:35 p.m.: Environment	7:50 p.m.: Science ABC	8:20 p.m.: Discovery	9:10 p.m.: Science Stories	9:35 p.m.: Journey of Science	Light of Science & Technology
CCTV-11	Beijing Opera Episodes	7:35 p.m.: Traditional Opera: Zhejiang Opera: He Wenxiu	8:38 p.m.: Traditional Opera: Zhejiang Opera: He Wenxiu				10:14 p.m.: Movie & TV Theater

CCTV-12	Western* Sound & Pix: Laughter on Rivers & Lakes 7:10 p.m.: Happy Everyday	Heaven, Earth, & Man: Mission	8:05 p.m.: 12/12: Biz Stories on Borders	Western* News		Western* Sound & Pix: Laughter on Rivers & Lakes 9:40 p.m.: Classical Encore: Dream of Red Chamber

*"Western" refers to China's western region.
Note. Due to the extensive number of CCTV programs and channels, only Monday is presented as representative of weeknight prime time.

SATURDAY

Channel	7 p.m.	7:30 p.m.	8 p.m.	8:30 p.m.	9 p.m.	9:30 p.m.	10 p.m.
CCTV-1	CCTV News	7:31 p.m.: Weather 7:38 p.m.: Forum	7:55 p.m.: TV Drama: Rings of the Bell in Shaoguotun	8:51 p.m.: TV Drama: Rings of the Bell in Shaoguotun 9:49 p.m.: Science & Technology			Evening News
CCTV-2	Commercial Bridge 7:05 p.m.: Frontline	7:25 p.m.: Life	Economy Special: Absolute Challenges		Economic News	Economy 30 Minutes	10:05 p.m.: Fortune 52
CCTV-3	7:05 p.m.: TV Storytelling: The Yang Family's Marksman	7:32 p.m.: Weekend Rendezvous		8:38 p.m.: Hits of Sounds and Pictures		9:42 p.m.: Performance Arena	10:08 p.m.: Infinite True Feelings
CCTV-4	News in Brief 7:10 p.m.: TV Drama: The Three Kingdoms		News in Brief 8:10 p.m.: Across China 8:40 p.m.: Two Sides of the Straits		China News		Let the World Get to Know You
CCTV-5	Sports News	2003/2004 National Women's Volleyball Tournament				Sports World	2003/2004 German Level A Soccer Tournament (Round 14)
CCTV-6	7:02 p.m.: Cartoon: Challenging the Emperor 7:21 p.m.: Popular Science Movie: Ant Breeding and Utilization	7:45 p.m.: Songhe-sponsored Action Movie: Chivalrous Adventure in Shanghai				9:42 p.m.: Popular Movie Hour	9:56 p.m.: Tianlishi-sponsored Popular Movie Time: Science Eccentric
CCTV-7	6:05 p.m.: Big World of the Countryside	7:30 p.m.: Military News	Children in the East	8:45 p.m.: Community Special: So That's How It Is!	9:17 p.m.: Tips on Farming	9:52 p.m.: Forum on the Countryside	10:42 p.m.: Airtime for National Defense
CCTV-8	7:13 p.m.: Sound from Screens	7:33 p.m.: Primetime Show: Public Procurator-General		8:27 p.m.: Primetime Show: Public Procurator-General	9:19 p.m.: Previews	9:48 p.m.: Popular Theater: Thunderbolt Police	
CCTV-9	Worldwide Watch	Dialogue	Culture Express	Documentary	Financial Review	Travelogue	CCTV News

CCTV-10	Outlook—English Magazine	Science & Technology 7:35 p.m.: Environment	7:50 p.m.: Science ABC	8:20 p.m.: Everybody	9:10 p.m.: Science Stories	Scientific Investigation	Light of Science & Technology
CCTV-11	Beijing Opera Episodes	7:35 p.m.: CCTV Theater in the Air					21:53 p.m.: CCTV Theater in the Air
CCTV-12	Western* Sound & Pix: Smart Teen 7:10 p.m.: Happy Everyday	Heaven, Earth, & Man: White Ghost	8:05 p.m.: 12/12: Biz Stories on Borders	Western* News			Western* Sound & Pix: Smart Teen 9:40 p.m.: Glamour 12: Beautiful Zhuang Village

* "Western" refers to China's western region.

SUNDAY

Channel	7 p.m.	7:30 p.m.	8 p.m.	8:30 p.m.	9 p.m.	9:30 p.m.	10 p.m.
CCTV-1	CCTV News	7:31 p.m.: Weather 7:38 p.m.: Forum	7:55 p.m.: TV Drama: Rings of the Bell in Shaoguotun	8:51 p.m.: TV Drama: Husbands of Three Sisters		9:49 p.m.: Science & Technology	Evening News
CCTV-2	Frontline		7:40 p.m.: Economy Special: Special 6+1		Economic News	Economy 30 Minutes	10:05 p.m.: Dialogue
CCTV-3	7:05 p.m.: TV Storytelling: The Yang Family's Marksman	7:32 p.m.: Grand Performance		8:38 p.m.: Meet with You		9:25 p.m.: Arena of the Divine Land	10:31 p.m.: Song of the Week: Motherland
CCTV-4	News in Brief 7:10 p.m.: Five Continents Happy Together		News in Brief 8:10 p.m.: Across China 8:40 p.m.: Two Sides of the Straits		China News		Interactive Sunday
CCTV-5	6:55 p.m.: Peak Moment	2003/2004 National Women's Volleyball Tournament				Sports World	2003/2004 Italian Level A Soccer Tournament (Round 11)
CCTV-6	6:51 p.m.: Movies of Next Week 7:15 p.m.: Cartoon: Challenging the Emperor	7:45 p.m.: Viewers' Special on Sunday: Search for the Gun			9:23 p.m.: Chinese Movie News (2003 Weekend Edition)	9:45 p.m.: Special-topic Documentary: Tour of World Movies **Dubbed Movie: Peak of the Courage**	
CCTV-7	The Vast Countryside: Green Farms	7:30 p.m. Military News	Children in the East	8:45 p.m.: Community Special: So That's How It Is!	9:17 p.m.: Tips on Farming	9:52 p.m.: Legal Advisers	

CCTV-8	6:57 p.m.: All Over the World: Across the World 7:14 p.m.: Sound from Screens	7:33 p.m.: Primetime Show: Public Procurator-General		8:27 p.m.: Primetime Show: Public Procurator-General	9:19 p.m.: Previews	9:43 p.m.: Popular Theater: Lies Covered Up	
CCTV-9	Worldwide Watch	Dialogue	Culture Express	Documentary	Business Guide	China This Week	CCTV News
CCTV-10	Window of CCTV-10	Science & Technology 7:35 p.m.: Environment	7:55 p.m.: Community Special: UNESCO in Action—Its History	8:55 p.m.: Community Special: World AIDS' Day Special		9:50 p.m.: Weekend Stories	
CCTV-11	Beijing Opera Episodes	7:35 p.m.: Life in Traditional Operas	8:05 p.m.: Drama in Drama	8:50 p.m.: Grand Stage of China			10:19 p.m.: Grand Stage of China
CCTV-12	Western* Sound & Pix: Love Songs 7:10 p.m.: Happy Everyday	Bon Voyage: (2003–42) Into Shenong's Native Place	Western* News		9:40 p.m.: Galaxy of Hits (2003–41): Showcase of Ten Years' Best		10:30 p.m.: Galaxy of Hits: Showcase of Ten Years' Best

*"Western" refers to China's western region.
Note. **Bold** denotes imported program.

Chapter 11

Brazil

Regina Coeli da Silveira e Silva
Universidade Salgado de Oliveira, Rio de Janeiro

ABOUT BRAZIL

The People

Brazilians come from varied places. Their heritage derives from native Indians, Europeans (the Portuguese and other European immigrants), Asians, and Africans (brought in as slaves by the Portuguese during the colonial period, 1500–1822). This ethnic melting pot yields a Brazilian people of tremendously varied skin color and appearance.

But in contrast to these differences, Brazilians share the same language, values, and a love for samba and soccer. This chapter explores the media's role in creating this common culture.

Brazil, a nation about as large (8,514,205 square kilometers) as the United States, covers half of South America and borders 9 of the other 11 South American countries. The population, 175 million people, accounts for more than half of South America's population and of its GDP. The country is divided into five different regions with differing customs and

183

folklore and even different spoken accents—but Portuguese is the spoken language in the entire country. Illiteracy is 10.9%.

Brazil has been called the land of opportunity. It is also called "Belinda"—part Belgium, part India—because of its gross disparity in distribution of income. Brazil is a country "under construction" where social mobility is possible. One example is the current president, Luis Inacio Lula da Silva, popularly known as Lula. Lula migrated from the poor, dry northeastern region to São Paulo, the richest state in Brazil. Another example is Juscelino Kubitschek, who also rose from poverty to become president, 1956–1960. His Czech grandfather had come to Brazil by the end of the 19th century and worked as a carpenter. Kubitschek is widely known for building Brasilia, the new capital, in the middle of the country.

History

Brazil was discovered by Cabral, a great Portuguese navigator, in 1500 and became a colony of Portugal. Brazil gained independence from Portugal in 1822 at the hands of the Portuguese king's son, Don Pedro I. He soon went back to Portugal and left his Brazilian-born son, Don Pedro II, as the Brazilian emperor. In 1889, inspired by the republican government of the United States to the north, Brazilian military forces overthrew the monarchy and established the republican system in Brazil.

In 1964, due to the fear of Communism spreading throughout Latin America, military forces took over President Joao Goulart's progressive government. Only in 1982 would the military leader Joao Batista Figueiredo peacefully return the administration of the country to civilian hands.

Brazil is a federal republic with 26 states and one federal district, the capital, Brasilia. The presidential system mandates direct elections (one person, one vote) for a term of 4 years for the president, state governors, mayors, and congressional representatives.

Brazil is the world's fifth largest exporter of airplanes and the world's largest exporter of beef, chicken, sugar, coffee, soy beans, orange juice, and . . . telenovelas, which has made Brazil a major player in the international media scene.

BROADCAST BACKGROUND

Today, more than 90% of Brazilian households have TV sets. Globo ranks as the world's fourth largest commercial network, after its three U.S. counterparts—ABC, CBS, and NBC (Straubhaar, 1984). Television was first seen in Brazil during the 1939 Rio de Janeiro exposition—an experimental closed system set up with German equipment.

The Pioneer

Nine years later, in 1948, the famous Brazilian entrepreneur Francisco de Assis Chateaubriand Bandeira de Melo, owner of both the main radio chain of broadcast stations, *Emisssoras Associadas*, and of the chain of newspapers called *Diarios Associados*, made the decision to open up a TV station in Brazil.

Like President Lula, Chateaubriand, the father of TV broadcasting in Brazil, also migrated from the northeastern part of the country to the south, seeking a better life. Born in the poor state of Paraiba, Chatô (his nickname) took up law at the public (and free) University of Recife. In addition to studying, he needed to earn money and help his poor family, so he worked as a free-lance reporter. In 1917, following other bright and ambitious northeastern people, Chateaubriand moved to Rio de Janeiro.

He quickly got a job at the prestigious daily newspaper *Jornal do Brasil* and contacted many business people in the course of his law practice. He soon raised money to purchase a small conservative morning newspaper called *O Jornal*, which would turn into a media empire: a conglomerate of newspapers, radio stations, the first TV station, and first TV network in the country.

After he decided to open up a TV channel in Brazil, this entrepreuneur imported equipment from the United States. On its arrival in Brazil in March 1950, the equipment was displayed in a parade in the streets of São Paulo (the largest city of the country) in true Chateaubriand style. In addition, he also imported 200 TV sets and located them throughout the city of São Paulo.

Throughout the year 1950, several experimental transmissions took place, including an interview with Getulio Vargas, president of the country at that time. Finally, on September 18, 1950, Chateaubriand launched Sao Paulo Tupi TV, PRF 3, channel 3. At the last moment, when one of the two cameras failed and the engineers suggested postponing the show, Chateaubriand refused to disappoint those who had been waiting for it for such a long time. Taking a risk, he decided to broadcast using only one camera. He was successful. Regular transmissions occurred from 6 p.m. to 11 p.m. daily, including a news program entitled "*Imagens do Dia*" (Images of the day).

In the first period of TV broadcasting in Brazil, the largest network *Emissoras Associadas* (the Tupi Network) functioned under Assis Chateaubriand's management. Ever since those early days, television in Brazil has been a private enterprise. The first enterprises were Sul America Seguros, Antartica (now AMBEV), Moinho Santista, and Pignatari.

Chateaubriand's *Tupi Cidade Maravilhosa* (Marvelous City Television) started operating in Rio de Janeiro, the second most populous city, on the city's anniversary day, January 20, 1951. In this same year, Brazilian factories began producing TV receivers.

In 1956, the first interstate transmission took place—a soccer game between Brazil and Italy, broadcast live from Maracanã Stadium in Rio de Janeiro to São Paulo. In order to send the signal 300 miles from Rio de Janeiro to São Paulo, clever engineers had to build antennas between the two cities.

By this same year, there were 15 TV stations throughout Brazil, reaching an audience of about 1.5 million Brazilians. Three of these stations were located in São Paulo; 2 in Rio de Janeiro; and 2 in Belo Horizonte. Chateaubriand owned 11, one each in Rio de Janeiro, São Paulo, Curitiba, and Porto Alegre in the south; Fortaleza, Recife, Salvador, São Luis, Campina Grande, and Belém in the northeast; and Goiânia in the west-center of the country.

Later, more interstate programming was produced. *"Paulistas e Cariocas,"* a program about the people born in São Paulo and in Rio de Janeiro, was one of the first interstate productions. Soon the infrastructure improved, and Tupi TV, Chateaubriand's system, sent images and sound to São Paulo, Rio de Janeiro, and Belo Horizonte, a network extending throughout 1,200 kilometers, using several transmission towers and antennas.

Tupi TV became the foundation for TV broadcasting in Brazil, serving as a school for all those who wished to be a part of this technological marvel. Tupi produced the first Brazilian-made news program, as well as the first telenovela. Tupi Network, the undisputed leader in TV broadcasting, was also responsible for the first color transmission, capturing a high percentage of the audience. Tupi set the agenda for contemporary content and formats; the other stations simply followed suit.

In fewer than 10 years, Brazil had turned into a TV nation, with more than 2 million people having access to TV entertainment, soap operas, news, sports, shows, dramas, and comedy programs. Brazil boasted more than 300,000 TV sets, not only in homes but also in clubs, neighborhood associations, and public places.

In September 1959, in an effort to guarantee the continuity of his Tupi TV network empire after his death, Chateaubriand donated 49% of his network to the 22 employees most loyal to him. Three years later, after suffering a stroke, he donated the remaining 51% of his shares to the same people and also his son. As a result, after his death in 1968, his son sued the other owners of the network. This action contributed to the network's failure.

After Chateaubriand's death, his empire resented his son's leadership and the several owners of the largest TV network in the country were unable to keep Tupi in business. Chateaubriand remains an icon in Brazilian media for his pioneering deeds and entrepreuneurship, but the successful Brazilian television of today belongs to Roberto Marinho, the founder of Globo.

Without Chateaubriand's leadership, the Tupi TV empire collapsed and opened the way for newcomers such as *Rede Globo* (the Globo Network) and SBT—*Sistema Brasileiro de Televisão* (the Brazilian Television System) and others.

Networks

Television is, by far, the most pervasive communication medium in Brazil (Kottak, 1990). It carries more than half the publicity and advertising investments in the country, totaling about $3 billion per year (Projeto Intermeios, 2001). As of June 2001, Brazil had 281 nongovernmental, ad-supported TV stations that produced their own programs and 8,740 rebroadcasting stations (*Ministério das Comunicações*, 2004). In addition, the government sponsored the commercial-free Educational TV Network. The following profiles of the six television networks covering most of Brazil are in order of the size of their audience.

Globo Network. On April 26, 1965, at exactly 11 a.m., the newsman Roberto Marinho, owner of a Rio newspaper, launched Globo TV (channel 4) one year after the armed forces had taken over Brazil's government.

Thanks to the Tupi network, Brazilians had already acquired the TV habit. However, as a new channel that offered no major innovations, it took a city flood for Globo to appeal to and be accepted by the audience. Regular programming was interrupted, and journalists went live on location to interview flood victims. Response was generous when Globo launched a campaign for the victims asking for donations, which many people brought directly to Globo headquarters. After Globo delivered the donations, its ratings gradually started to increase (da Silva & Eduardo, 1985).

Soon after the first Globo TV channel was launched in Rio de Janeiro, others were started in São Paulo, then in Belo Horizonte, Brasilia, Recife, and other locales. Globo reinvested 100% of its profits for the first 14 years (Simões, Costa, & Kehl, 1986).

In the 1970s, the decline of the Tupi network and the military government's aim to use communication as a means for uniting and developing the country was exploited by Roberto Marinho, who followed all censorship requests. The cooperation was mutually beneficial.

The armed forces viewed broadcasting as an important tool for development and integration. Therefore, during the military period (1964–1984), telecommunication technology was made available in the country: A terrestrial network using microwave transmission technology was established throughout the whole country; two Brazilian communication satellites were launched; and several earth satellite stations (up-link and down-link) were built. Such technical facilities allowed TV networks to broadcast their programs—shows, sports, game shows, and news—simultaneously to the whole country. Globo Network took the most advantage of such infrastructure.

By using the new microwave network infrastructure established by the government, Globo news programs were instantaneously broadcast to the main cities all over the country, including (via rented INTELSAT channels) the north of the country. Thus Globo's national TV network broadcast the world soccer games in England in 1966; the launching of the space ship Apollo IX in 1968; men walking on the moon in 1969; and the World Cup tournament in 1970, when the Brazilian national soccer team won the cup for the third time.

Today, Globo employs more than 8,000 people. The network has its own authors, directors, actors, journalists, producers, musicians, tailors, engineers, and all kinds of technicians and specialists. Annually, Globo can produce more than 5,000 hours of programs—telenovelas, miniseries, specials, comedies, musicals, event coverage, variety programs, reality shows, game shows (in general with celebrities), and several news programs. It is by far the largest producer of original TV programs in the world (*A História da Rede Globo*, 2004).

Globo has built a studio complex on the outskirts of Rio de Janeiro named PROJAC. This production center takes up an area of 1,300,000 square meters, of which 120,000 square meters are stages, superstudios, production sets, and warehouses. The PROJAC minicity has adjustable buildings, streets, streams, bridges, plazas, and churches, which can be modified from one telenovela to another, as quickly as the following day. The insides of buildings and homes can be totally transformed, according to the specific scenarios needed (personal visit to PROJAC, 2003).

Globo's network of 113 TV stations means programs can be seen in 99.84% of Brazil's 5,043 cities. Roberto Marinho's empire also includes GloboNews (24-hour cable), Globo Radio, *O Globo* (a newspaper), *Extra* (a newspaper); Globo Records, Editora Globo (Globo publishing house for books and magazines), globo.com.br (an Internet provider) and the Roberto Marinho Foundation. Marinho died in 2003 at the age of 98.

SBT Network. Silvio Santos, the entrepreneur who founded SBT, grew up in poverty and, as a young man, worked as a street vendor. Later on, he started a business, through TV ads, where people would make monthly payments and be in the running for prizes. Regardless of winning prizes or not, these people would get their investment back in the form of merchandise. Santos rented TV time and presented a program that was a mix of game shows, variety entertainment, reality shows, and advertisements for his business, products, and prizes.

Business was so good that in August 1981, Silvio Santos launched his own TV network, SBT—*Sistema Brasileiro de Televisão* (Brazilian Television System). He started with four TV stations that he had bought, through deception, from the Assis Chateaubriand empire. Santos aimed his lowest-common-denominator programming at the large, lower income audience. Within 2 years, SBT had increased its audience share to 30%, second only to Globo.

SBT has, since the 1980s, kept its position as the second network in audience share. During the 1980s, it operated totally in the red. Early in the 1990s, Silvio Santos changed SBT's profile, investing more in quality and aiming for more profits. Ratings went down, but the revenues went up.

In 1995, Project SBT 2000 included building a production city in Anhanguera—São Paulo. Now complete, the $120 million SBT Television City, occupying 231,000 square meters, is a start-to-finish production center, from designing to recording to broadcasting. The Anhanguera Television City daily provides facilities such as restaurants, banking, medical services, parking, and transportation for about 3,000 employees.

Ever since the year 2000, SBT has boasted the second largest number of TV stations in Brazil, with more than 100, strategically located to reach

98% of the Brazilian population. Today SBT has 25% of the audience and 21% of commercial revenues (*A História da Rede SBT*, 2004).

Bandeirantes Network. *Rede Bandeirantes de Televisão* (Bandeirantes TV Network) was launched in May 1962, starting with channel 13 in São Paulo. Main TV stations in the following cities are: channel 13 in São Paulo (SP); channel 6 in Taubaté, SP; channel 14 in Campinas, SP; channel 10 in Presidente Prudente, SP; channel 7 in Rio de Janeiro; channel 2 in Curitiba, Parana; channel 7 in Belo Horizonte, Minas Gerais; channel 7 in Salvador, Bajia; and channel 10, in Porto Alegre, Rio Grande do Sul.

On May 13, 1967, Bandeirantes TV was launched with a music show. Very concerned with good quality and having imported new technology equipment, it produced *"Os Miseráveis"* as its first telenovela. Unfortunately, in 1969 a fire destroyed the studios and most of the equipment, so imports replace domestic production (*A História da Rede Bandeirantes*, 2004).

Today, Bandeirantes Network programming covers the state capitals and other main cities in Brazil and the complete area of the rich state of São Paulo. They present a variety of programs such as cartoons, sitcoms, news, movies, humor programs, fashion, music, talk shows, and sports. It is a fine network by Latin American standards, but not in the league of SBT or Globo.

Record Network. On September 27, 1953, the Machado de Carvalho family launched Record TV, channel 7 in São Paulo city, with diversified programming, but concentrating on sports. They later expanded in the state of São Paulo.

In May 1960 a studio caught fire. In July 1966 a fire in the main installation destroyed new equipment and more than 300 million videotapes of movies and programs. In 1969 another fire damaged two of their theaters, Consolação and Paramount (*Rederecord*, 2004).

In 1954, the network launched its first sports program, "Round Table," to accompany live transmissions of soccer games. It also produced its first adventure miniseries, *"Capitão 7"* (Captain 7), in the 1950s. In 1955, it launched the first children's game show in Brazil, *"Grande Gincana Kibon"* (Kibon Big Game), which would last for 16 years.

Record TV Network also produces telenovelas, news, and Brazilian music shows. It has its own broadcasting stations in four of the five Brazilian regions, totaling 12 stations. In addition, broadcasting programs to every region of the country is made possible through agreements with rebroadcasting stations.

Rede TV! This is a fast-growing network. When it started broadcasting in 1999, it had only five broadcasting stations; today, *Rede TV!* has 28. Moreover, it has also invested in six production centers, one in each of these capitals: São Paulo, Rio de Janeiro, Belo Horizonte, Recife, Fortaleza, and Brasilia. Although it covers about 3,500 cities in the country using its own stations and other rebroadcasting stations, it still gets only a small share of the audience.

Rede TV!, which invests in quality and technology, has a large production facility called Alphaville 1 and is now building Alphaville 2 with an investment of $15 million. Both Alphaville 1 and Alphaville 2 take up an area of 20,000 square meters (*Redetv*, 2004).

Educational TV. The Brazilian government supports commercial-free TV stations called *Televisão Educativa* (Educational TV). Lacking centralized planning and launched independently in different states, the first of these TV stations sponsored and managed by the government was at Pernambuco Federal University, launched in 1967.

There are educational TV stations scattered throughout Brazil in nine cities: Amazonas, Ceará, Espírito Santo, Maranhão, Pernambuco, Rio de Janeiro, Rio Grande do Norte, Rio Grande do Sul, and São Paulo. Together they form the Brazilian Center for Education Foundation, which sponsored an educational telenovela entitled *"João da Silva."*

One finds the highest quality programming on Culture TV, the São Paulo station, due to the much higher support it receives from the state of Sao Paulo (Bortoliero, 1982). In 1997, led by Cultura TV, a new institution, *Associação Brasileira de Emissoras Públicas, Educativas e Culturais* (ABEPEC), was established. ABEPEC launched *Rede Publica TV* (Public TV Network) with the objective of designing unique programming to be broadcast by every public TV station.

At the beginning, these TV stations used to broadcast primarily educational programs for elementary and high schools. Today educational TV programming also includes news, culture, and entertainment, all having education as their main objective.

Within schools, a program called *"TV Escola"* (School TV) was launched by the federal government in 1995. It includes all elementary public schools with more than 100 students—50,000 schools, 1 million teachers, and 29 milllion students.

The programs have two parts: the first part helps guide and improve teaching and management; and the second part provides education professionals with tapes on varied class subjects. Each school receives one TV set, one video cassette recorder, and one satellite antenna.

The preceding six TV networks are broadcast free, without any charge to viewers. Different companies provide different kinds of cable or satellite TV systems which charge viewers for receiving their transmission.

According to a survey conducted by Pay TV Surveys, in March 2001 there were 3.54 million subscribers to pay TV in Brazil. Cable systems account for 58% of the subscribers; Direct Broadcast Satellite (DBS) technology, 32%: and Multipoint Multichannel Distribution Systems (MMDS), 10%. DBS technology allows services like pay-per-view and even interactivity.

Several companies provide these systems in Brazil. They are mainly NET Brasil, with 64% of the market, and TVA, with 16% of the market. The remaining 20% is shared among several other independent companies.

The March 2001 comprehensive study conducted by Pay TV Surveys/ Grupo de Midia (*Almanaque ABRIL*, 2003), on pay television also showed that when people face economic difficulties, pay television is the first service that they omit. One of the reasons may be the availability of high-quality free television all over the country.

BROADCASTING REGULATION

In the early TV days, the government was so pleased with the entre-preneurs who had invested their own money in the new medium that it imposed no regulation (Del Bianco, 1993). In October 1959, Armando Falcao, the minister of justice, issued the first telecommunication regula-tion, which limited commercial breaks to under 3 minutes. Because com-mercials brought in TV revenues, the commercials were getting excessive.

In 1962 the government established the *Conselho Nacional de Comuni-cacoes*—CONTEL, a national regulatory council. In that same year, Con-gress also approved the sweeping Law #4.117, the *Código Brasileiro de Telecomunicações* (Brazilian Telecommunication Code). It limited initial channel concessions to 3 years, which could be extended to 15 years, but said that the government would cancel any concession should the TV station broadcast any messages with class, ethnic, religious, or other ste-reotypes. Regarding programming, the stations were supposed to broad-cast an average of at least 25 minutes of Brazilian-made movies per day, and every foreign movie had to be dubbed into the Portuguese language. Technical matters were also regulated.

In 1964, after military forces took over the government, the military heavily invested to improve telecommunication infrastructures, but also imposed severe censorship on every kind of programming. Humor pro-grams could not criticize the government, news could not report the exces-sive force used on suspected Communists or political activists, and even telenovelas could not deal with political or other sensitive matters related to social or economic development (Stepan, 1973).

The military government got the Congress to approve changes to the Brazilian Constitution (Skidmore, 1988). According to the new Brazilian Constitution, non-Brazilians could not own, in whole or in part, mass media enterprises. However, the new Globo TV Network already had an agreement with Time-Life Inc., whereby Time-Life provided Globo with both funding and technical help, in return for a 30% share of Globo's annual profits. In September 1968, when the government required that Globo abrogate the agreement, Globo had to borrow from the Brazilian banks in order to pay about $6 million to Time-Life. Roberto Marinho, the owner of Globo network, had to put up virtually everything he owned as security. In 1969, Time-Life and Globo separated (Page, 1995).

Legislation, which still applies today, guarantees political parties free TV time for campaigns. Stations broadcast such political messages simultane-ously to the whole country at prime time, during the months before elections.

In 1980, media censorship finally ceased after the military government decided that the next president should be a civilian, not an Army officer. In 1984, the entire Brazilian TV system (all the networks) joined a popular political movement to take back from Congress the right to vote and choose the next president of the country. The return to civilian government and more democratic rule had inspired a popular revulsion against media censorship. Thereafter, Brazilian media became generally free of heavy regulation. However, the Brazilian Constitution (Art. 221) states that the government can authorize use of the airwaves under these specific conditions, among others:

- education, cultural and news broadcast should be provided;
- ethical and family values must be respected; and
- only Brazilian-born or citizens naturalized for more than 10 years may own broadcast entities.

Under Jose Sarney, the first civilian president, the first post-military minister of communication was Antonio Carlos Magalhães, a well-known politician. (In the military period, all the ministers of communication were military electrical engineers.) During Sarney's government (1985–1990), concessions for new broadcasting stations were awarded principally to politicians and their friends or relatives.

Nowadays, a new procedure awards radio/TV channels, starting with a bid by the Ministry of Communications. The candidate needs to go through various Congressional committees, two each in the House of Representatives and the Senate: the Board of Science, Technology and Communications and the Law and Constitution Commission. Only after these approvals will the concession be granted. The authorization for broadcasting operations will last for 10 years and can be renewed (Almeida, 1995).

As in most countries, the government allocates the frequencies on the spectrum to avoid electromagnetic waves interference among channels. Governments must report the allocations to the United Nations International Telecommunication Union (ITU).

BROADCAST CONTENT AND RATINGS

Under military censorship, every sentence to be broadcast had to be approved in advance. After 1991, the new political climate brought about a media explosion. New radio and TV stations opened up, ready to take advantage of the technological resources that the military government had established in the 1970s and 1980s. In addition, several communication schools opened in public and private universities to train the personnel demanded by this media explosion.

The *Instituto Brasileiro de Opinião Pública* (Brazilian Public Opinion Institute), or IBOP, is the most prestigious opinion research institute in Brazil. IBOP data on TV ratings are used by stations to set advertising

TABLE 11.1
Program Ratings on Five TV Networks, Brazil

Ratings in February 2000		Ratings in November 2003	
GLOBO		GLOBO	
Terra Nostra 8PM Telenovela	46	Celebrities 8PM Telenovela	48
Jornal Nacional	40	The Big Family	43
Special TV 50th Year	38	Jornal Nacional	40
International Boxe	38	Fantastic Life Show	38
Direct Line	38	RJ TV 2nd Edition	37
SBT		SBT	
Anything for Money	25	Spectacular Movie	18
Nice Sunday	24	Tele-drawing	16
Million Show	20	Nice Sunday	15
Privilege of Love Telenovela	20	All Against One	15
Ratinho's Program	20	Million Show	15
RECORD		RECORD	
Raul Gil Program	18	Big Saturday	07
Raul Gil Program	15	Jornal do Rio Local News	05
Alert City	13	The Truth	05
Raul Gil Program	11	The Game of Life	04
Jornal da Record	10	Jornal da Band News	04
BANDEIRANTES		BANDEIRANTES	
Football (Soccer)	10	GuetoGroup	09
Football (Soccer)	07	Raul Gil program	07
Movie	06	Our Sunday	06
Jornal da Band	04	Special Record Movie	06
Band Cine Premium	04	Big Police Man	06
REDE TV!		REDE TV!	
Choice TV	04	I saw it on Rede TV!	03
Serie TV	03	Fame TV Best Moments	03
Special Magic TV	03	Superpop	03
Jornal da TV	03	Open Channel	03
Ball in the net	03	Fame TV	03

Note. Data compiled by the author, from Instituto Brasileiro de
Opinião Publica Ent. (IBOPE).

charges during programs for commercial insertions. As Table 11.1 shows,
the ratings are extremely uneven, with Globo programs outdistancing all
of the other main TV networks. "Celebrities," a Globo 8 p.m telenovela,
had the highest rating of the week on the program grid, 48 points.

Telenovelas

The Brazilian telenovela, which differs from Western soap operas, is the
centerpiece of Brazilian prime time television; like novels, they have a
beginning and an end. Telenovelas had their origins in the popular *folhetim*
(radio novels). The Brazilian National Radio station aired 116 such novelas
from 1943 to 1945. At first, the texts were adapted from other sources;

later, special writer/producer teams created original novelas (Andrade, 2000).

In 1963, SP Excelsior TV broadcast live "2-5499 Ocupado," the first daily Brazilian telenovela (Fernandes, 1982). From then on, the genre developed into the most popular media product in Brazil. In Brazil, the telenovela acquired specific attributes different from other Latin American forms of the genre.

First, topics tend to involve current issues, such as the gap between rich and poor, the environment, alcohol/drug addiction, or political problems. Ortiz, Borelli, and Ramos (1988) recount that in the 1960s and 1970s, many telenovela authors had Communist affiliations, but because of media censorship, they had no other outlets of expression. Today, telenovela themes, conflicts, and emotions reflect modern points of view (Sodré, 1991).

Second, the audience includes not only housewives, but also husbands and children. Watching is a family affair for families from all walks of society: men and women, young and old, people from different social classes and different cultural levels (Andrade, 2000). Watching telenovelas every night has become a national ritual (Melo, 1988). Faithful viewers seem to need their daily TV fix.

Third, because of its pervasiveness, the genre can shape public opinion as well as influence lifestyles and behavior (Pimentel & Queiroz, 1989). Various studies indicate that telenovelas' varied themes (sociological, political, ecological, ethical) have exerted strong impacts on Brazilians (Melo, 1988), given Brazil's effective TV system that can reach the entire nation.

Specifically, the Globo telenovela has produced measurable effects (Silva, 1993) such as an increase in the number of organ donations ("De Corpo e Alma," August 3, 1992 to March 6, 1993). Telenovelas can create awareness of AIDS ("O Portador," 1991), drugs ("O Clone," 2002), responsible voting ("O Salvador da Pátria," 1989), missing children ("Explode Coração," 1995), racial stereotypes ("De Corpo e Alma," 1992–1993), sexuality ("Mulheres Apaixonadas," 2003), landless peasants ("O Rei do Gado," 1996–1997), urban violence, violence against women, and respect for the elderly ("Mulheres Apaixonadas," 2003), the challenges of technology ("Barriga de Aluguel," 1990; "Explode Coração," 1995; and "O Clone," 2001–2002), and religion ("A Viagem," 1994; "A Padroeira," 2001–2002).

Fourth, the telenovela genre attracts the best writers, producers, directors, song writers, composers, and singers, who relish the chance to participate in the next Globo hit. Each Globo telenovela has its own set of songs, many times written and composed specifically for that story (Fernandes, 1982). Even specific characters have their own musical themes that allow the audience to identify which character is on the screen. Audiences are rewarded with Brazil's best talent every night.

Fifth, Brazilian telenovelas constantly vary the settings of their stories. Stories play out in the rich southern regions or in the poorest inland of the northeast, in cosmopolitan Rio de Janeiro and Sao Paulo, or in the Amazon rain forest. Some Brazilian telenovelas have even been shot on location in Japan, Italy, Portugal, and France. Along with showing these different places in Brazil, Globo telenovelas portray local customs as well as idiomatic linguistic expressions. Globo telenovelas are a travelogue that enhances a sense of national solidarity.

Racial Issues

Media studies have found Afro-Brazilians to be portrayed by and large as service persons or outlaws; even in TV commercials, they are either absent or in stereotyped roles (Subervi-Vélez & Oliveira, 1991). However, some changes are being made, especially by Globo. *"De Corpo e Alma"* (1992 Globo), for example, turns stereotypes on their heads (Silva, 1993). The story includes relationships between a White judge and a Black judge, a White mother and a Black mother, a White boy and a Black boy.

In March 1994, Globo launched *"A Próxima Vitima"* (The Next Victim), the 8 p.m. telenovela, about a rich, intellectual Black family that had a slow-witted White maid. In January 2004, Globo launched a telenovela wherein the main character, a Black woman, falls in love with a White man—whose fiancee, a pretty White woman, has negative characteristics. In addition, the hosts of *"Fantastic Life Show,"* the highly rated, two-hour Globo Sunday night extravaganza, have been, since 1997, White Pedro Bial and Afro-Brazilian Gloria Maria.

Interactivity

Brazilian audiences affect telenovelas, as well as vice versa. Characters' fates depend on audience reactions; authors cannot predict the end when a show begins (Fadul, 1993). Thus telenovelas are semi-interactive.

In 1991, Globo TV developed and launched an entirely interactive weekly program, which by early 1994 has been exported to 28 countries. In "You Decide," a one-hour fiction program, the main character faces a specific decision-making situation (Silva & Barreto, 1999). TV viewers can call a toll-free number to register a "yes" or "no." As the plot develops, the screen shows the number of telephone calls being received. At the end of the program, the "yes" and "no" responses determine which of two pre-taped endings the station will air. The best Brazilian actors and actresses appear in this program. During each episode, 50,000–60,000 viewers participate with their opinions.

Comedies

Most humor in Brazilian television uses a skit format whereby each 50-minute show includes 8 to 10 different segments. One such sketch program, *"A Praça é Nossa,"* has been on air for about 20 years. Brazilian comedy veers toward political satire, skewering mainly state governors, ministries, or the president; it also critiques everyday Brazilian life, recent events, and the Brazilian people themselves (for example, *"Casseta e Planeta,"* Globo TV). Therefore, many foreign humor programs do not succeed with the Brazilian audience.

Globo has produced a few situation comedies (a serial program with continuing characters). "*A Grande Familia*" (The Big Family) portrays six people living in the same house: the father, mother, 19-year-old son, 20-year-old daughter and her 23-year-old husband, and grandpa (the mother's father); it did well in recent ratings (see Table 11.1). "*Os Normais*" (Normal People) tells different stories about the same "normal" couple every Friday night.

Globo TV has popularized three comedians who, by coincidence, all come from Ceara, a northeastern state: Chico Anisio, Renato Aragao, and Tom Cavalcanti. Renato Aragao, who specializes in humor for children, has become the representative of UNICEF in Brazil. His "*Criança Esperança*" (Children and Hope), a weeklong Globo telethon held every August or September, raises $2–$3 million per year for poor children. Even some Brazilian telenovelas have made their audiences laugh. Globo often broadcasts a comic story in its 7 p.m. telenovela slot.

Game Shows and Reality Shows

The SBT network's adaptation, the "Million Show," is the most popular game show in Brazil (see Table 11.1 and chapter 14); Silvio Santos, the network's creator, hosts the program himself. Game shows are very common as segments within Brazilian TV youth and children's programming (featuring school children as live audiences) as well as within variety programs. Players may be young actors and actresses (Cooper-Chen & Silva, 1992).

The phenomenal Xuxa, born Maria da Graça Meneghel, started her career as a children's game show hostess in hot pants. Through endorsements and marketing of products, she became the first Latin American to appear on the Forbes list of wealthiest entertainers. Blue-eyed blonde Xuxa and Afro-Brazilian soccer star Pelé made headlines as an interracial couple after they met in 1980, when she was 17 and he was 40 (Simpson, 1993). Xuxa, who had a daughter in 1998, now appears only for 45 minutes every morning on Globo as hostess of "Xuxa in the World of Imagination."

Globo had an original reality show, rooted in physical endurance, named "*No Limite*" (On the Edge) in 2002. Globo also attracted large audiences for its "Talent Contest" (similar to "Star Search") with two series in 2001 and 2002.

Some reality shows are format transfers from overseas (see chapter 14). Globo launched the first "Big Brother Brasil—BBB1," in 2002. It was a big hit. After that, Globo has had "BBB2" and "BBB3." The fourth round of "Big Brother Brasil" will be launched in January 2004. Meanwhile, SBT launched "Casa dos Artistas" (Artists's House) with the same imported BBB format.

BROADCAST IMPORTS AND EXPORTS

Telenovelas are the main TV export. At Globo studios, production is dubbed into various languages, and the Brazilian culture is exported to more than 130 different countries (*A História da Rede Globo*, 2004).

Globo Enterprises started exporting telenovelas to Portugal in 1975. *"Gabriela"* was the first telenovela to be exported. RTP—*Radio e Televisão Portuguesa*, a government-run TV station—had soon imported around $3.7 million in Brazilian TV products. Angola, Mozambique, and Guinea-Bissau, all former Portuguese colonies, imported Brazilian telenovelas because they required no dubbing. After entering the Portuguese language market, Globo aimed exports at Hispanic Latin America. This task involved translating formats from Brazilian PAL-M to the American NTSC system and competition from Argentine and Mexican telenovelas, which were already in Spanish.

In 1981, Italy was the first non-Iberic European importer of Brazilian telenovelas, soon followed by France, Spain, and Germany, and later by Hungary, Poland, Lebanon, North Africa, and China. In only 7 years, 1981–1987, more than 27 Brazilian telenovelas had been aired in several European countries. *"Escrava Isaura"* (Slave Girl Isaura) was, by far, the most widely exported telenovela—even to mainland China (Melo, 1988).

As for imports of television programs, the severe military censorship of 1964 to 1984 decreased Brazilian-made programming and opened a window for American-made movies and programs such as "Bat Masterson," "Bonanza," "Bewitched," "Lost in Space," "Father Knows Best," and others.

SBT, before becoming the second largest Brazilian TV network, imported several telenovelas from Mexico and a few U.S. sitcoms, but they could not compete with Globo's telenovelas. North American films are now the main imported media product shown on all Brazilian networks, but they are seldom shown in prime time. Only Record TV will show a foreign movie before 10 p.m., due to its financial difficulties.

The commercial value of exports far outdistances imports, due to the so-called *Padrão Globo de Qualidade* (Globo Quality Pattern) of Globo's telenovelas and to its aggressive efforts in the international market.

REFERENCES

A História da Rede Bandeirantes. (2004). http://www.tvmemoria.com.br
A Historia da Rede Globo. (2004) http:// www.tvmemoria.com.br
A História da Rede SBT. (2004). http://www. tvmemoria.com.br
Almanaque ABRIL. (2003). *A enciclopédia da Atualidade—Brasil e Mundo.* São Paulo: Editora ABRIL. (2 volumes)
Almeida, A. M. (1995). *Legislação de TV.* In C. Almeida & M. E. Araújo (Eds.), *As perspectivas da televisão Brasileira* (p. 137). Rio de Janeiro: Imago Editora.
Andrade, R. (2000). *O fim do mundo: Imaginário e teledramaturgia.* São Paulo: Anablume Editora.
Bortoliero, S. (1982). *TV Cultura: A saúde como prioridade da TV Pública. Comunicarte,* 1(1), 133–134.
Cooper-Chen, A., & Silva, R. C. S. (1992, August 16–20). *Television game shows in Brazil and the United States.* Paper presented at the biannual meeting, International Association for Mass Communication Research, Guaruja, Brazil.
da Silva, L., & Eduardo, C. (1985). *Muito além do jardim botânico.* São Paulo: Summus Editorial.

Del Bianco, N. R. (1993). FM no Brasil 1970–79: Crescimento incentivado pelo regime militar. *Comunicação & Sociedade, 12*(20), 139–150.

Fadul, A. (1993). La telenovela Brasilena y la busqueda de las identidades nacionales. In N. Maziotti (Ed.), *El espectaculo de la pasion: las telenovelas Latinoamericanas* (pp. 136–143). Buenos Aires: Ediciones Colihue.

Fernandes, I. (1982). *Memória da telenovela Brasileira.* São Paulo: Editora Brasiliense.

Kottak, C. (1990). *Prime time society: An anthropological analysis of television and culture.* Belmont, CA: Wadsworth.

Melo, J. M. (1988). *As telenovelas da Globo—Produção e exportação.* São Paulo: Summus Editorial.

Ministério das Comunicações (2004). http:www.mc.gov.br

Ortiz, R., Borelli, S. & Ramos, J. (1988). *Telenovela: História e produção.* São Paulo: Editora Brasiliense.

Page, J. (1995). *The Brazilians.* New York: Addison-Wesley.

Pimentel, A., & Queiroz, M. (1989). Uma novela rural: Impacto de Roque Santeiro em duas comunidades rurais Brasileiras. In J. de Melo (Ed.), *Comunicação na América Latina: Desenvolvimento e Crise* (p. 168). Campinas: Papirus Editora.

Projeto Intermeios (2001). *Meio & Mensagem.* Rio de Janeiro: Associacão de Propaganda e Marketing.

Rederecord. (2004). http:www.rederecord.com.br

Redetv. (2004). http:// www.redetv.com.br

Silva, R. C. S. (1993). *Extensão da teoria da formação da agenda para a ficção e sua aplicação à teledramaturgia Brasileira* [An extension of the agenda-setting concept to fiction and its application to the Brazilian teledrama]. Unpublished research report, Universidade Federal Fluminense, Rio de Janeiro.

Silva, R. C. S., & Barreto, M. (1999). Análise do programa nocê decide com base: nos níveis de julgamento moral de Kohlberg. *Nacional de Pós-Graduação e Pesquisa em Educação.* GT: Educação e Comunicação. *22ª Reunião Anual da Anped—Associação.* Caxambu, September 26–30.

Simões, I. F., Costa, A. H., & Kehl, M. R. (1986). *Um país no ar: História da TV Brasileira em três canais.* São Paulo: Editora Brasiliense.

Simpson, A. (1993). *Xuxa: The mega-marketing of gender, race and modernity.* Philadelphia: Temple University Press.

Skidmore, T. (1988). *Politics of military rule in Brazil.* New York: Oxford Unviersity Press.

Sodré, M (1991). *Rede imaginária.* São Paulo: Ed. Companhia das Letras.

Subervi-Vélez, F., & Oliveira, O. (1991). Negros (e outras etnias) em comerciais da televisão Brasileira: Uma investigação exploratória. *Comunicação e Sociedade, 10*(17), 79–101.

Stepan, A. (1973). *Authoritarian Brazil: Origins, policies and future.* New Haven, CT: Yale University Press.

Straubhaar, J. (1984, Spring). Brazilian television: The decline of American influence. *Communication Research, 11*, 221–240.

BRAZIL, PRIME TIME, NOVEMBER 24–30, 2003

MONDAY												
Channel	6 p.m.	6:30 p.m.	7 p.m.	7:30 p.m.	8 p.m.	8:30 p.m.	9 p.m.	9:30 p.m.	10 p.m.	10:30 p.m.	11 p.m.
Educational TV–2	Thinking About You		Brasil Gold	@titude .com	National Geographic		Expedi- tions	About Brazilian movie	News	Round table	
Globo TV–4	06:05 p.m.: Chocolate with Pepper Brazilian (telenovela)		06:55 p.m.: RJ/TV 2nd edition Local news	07:15 p.m.: Kubanacan Brazilian (telenovela)		8:15 p.m.: Jornal Nacional News	8:55 p.m.: Celebrities Brazilian (telenovela)		9:55 p.m.: Cine Movie		

Network TV–6	6:15 p.m.: Open Channel	7:30 p.m.: Fame TV	8:30 p.m.: **Pedro, the Fishy** (Mexican tele-novela)	9:05 p.m.: Jornal da TV News	10:00 p.m.: Superpop
					11:30 p.m.: Dynamic Reading

Bandeirantes TV–7	5:30 p.m.: Urgent Brasil	7:20: Jornal do Rio Local News	7:35 p.m.: Jornal da Band News	8:25 p.m.: Total Sport	8:50 p.m.: Faith Show	9:45 p.m.: g4 Brasil Drops	9:50 p.m.: Good Night Brasil

CNT TV–9	6:00 p.m.: Consume Well	6:30 p.m.: Life Tiny Things	8:30 p.m.: Power game	9:30 p.m.: CNT Jornal News	10:00 p.m.: Thousand and One Nights

SBT TV–11	6:05 p.m.: Passion Limit (telenovela)	7:05 p.m.: Whirl the Whirl	7:40 p.m.: Jornal do SBT - News	8:00 p.m.: **Just a Few Flees** (Mexican tele-novela)	8:30 p.m.: A Bunch of Passions (telenovela)	9:30 p.m.: **Smallville** (U.S. series)	10:15 p.m.: Hebe Program (variety live show)

Record/Rio TV–13	5:35 p.m.: City Alert	7:35 p.m.: Jornal da Record News	8:30 p.m.: Bahia 50 Degrees	10:00 p.m.: Movie

TUESDAY

Channel	6 p.m.	6:30 p.m.	7 p.m.	7:30 p.m.	8 p.m.	8:30 p.m.	9 p.m.	9:30 p.m.	10 p.m.	10:30 p.m.	11 p.m.
Educational TV–2	Thinking About You		Brasil Gold	@titude.com	National Geographic		The Truth	Provoca-tions	News	Observing the Press	
Globo TV–4	6:00 p.m.: Chocolate with Pepper Brazilian (telenovela)	06:50 p.m.: RJ/TV 2nd edition Local news	07:10 p.m.: Kubanacan Brazilian (telenovela)		8:15 p.m.: Jornal Nacional News	8:55 p.m.: Celebrities Brazilian (telenovela)		9:55 p.m.: Casseta e Planeta		10:55 p.m.: Mankind's city	
Rede TV–6	6:15 p.m.: Open Channel			7:30 p.m.: Fame TV		8:30 p.m.: **Pedro, the Fishy** (Mexican tele-novela)	9:05 p.m.: Jornal da TV News		10:00 p.m.: Superpop (variety)		11:30 p.m.: Dynamic Reading
Bandeirantes TV–7	5:30 p.m.: Urgent Brasil		7:20 p.m.: Jornal do Rio Local News	7:35 p.m.: Jornal da Band News	8:25 p.m.: Total Sport	8:50 p.m.: Faith Show		9:45 p.m.: g4 Brasil Drops	9:50 p.m: Good Night Brasil		
CNT TV–9	6:00 p.m.: Doublé Sided	6:30 p.m.: Life Tiny Things				8:30 p.m.: Power Game		9:30 p.m.: CNT Jornal News	10:00 p.m.: Thousand and One Nights		
SBT TV–11	6:05 p.m.: Passion Limit (telenovela)		7:05 p.m.: Whirl the Whirl	7:40 p.m.: Jornal do SBT—News	8:10 p.m.: **Just a Few Flees** (Mexican tele-novela)	8:40 p.m.: A Bunch of Passions (telenovela)		9:30 p.m.: **Smallville** (U.S. series)	10:15: Spectacular Movie		
Record/Rio TV–13	5:35: City Alert			7:35 p.m.: Jornal da Record News		8:30 p.m.: Bahia 50 degrees			10:00 p.m.: Movie		

WEDNESDAY

Channel	6 p.m.	6:30 p.m.	7 p.m.	7:30 p.m.	8 p.m.	8:30 p.m.	9 p.m.	9:30 p.m.	10 p.m.	10:30 p.m.	11 p.m.
Educational TV–2	Thinking About You		Brasil Gold	@titude .com	National Geographic	8:30: National Geographic	Poor Access		News	General Comment	
Globo TV–4	06:00 p.m.: Chocolate with Pepper Brazilian (telenovela)		06:50 p.m.: RJ/TV 2nd edition Local news	7:10 p.m.: Kubanacan Brazilian(telenovela)		8:15 p.m.: Jornal Nacional News	8:50 p.m.: Celebrities Brazilian (telenovela)		9:55 p.m.: Heavy Cargo (serial fiction)		10:55 p.m.: Soccer game
Rede TV–6		6:15 p.m.: Open Channel		7:30 p.m.: Fame TV		8:30 p.m.: Pedro, the Fishy (Mexican tele-novela)	9:05 p.m.: Jornal da TV News		10:00 p.m.: Superpop (variety)		11:30 p.m.: Dynamic Reading
Bandeirantes TV–7	5:30 p.m.: Urgent Brasil			7:20 p.m.: Jornal do Rio Local News	7:35 p.m.: Jornal da Band News	8:25 p.m.: Total Sport	8:50 p.m.: Faith Show	9:45 p.m.: g4 Brasil Drops	9:50 p.m.: Good Night Brasil		
CNT TV–9	6:00 p.m.: Doublé Sided	6:30 p.m.: Life Tiny Things				8:30 p.m.: Power game	9:30 p.m.: CNT Jornal News		10:00 p.m.: Thousand and One Nights		
SBT TV–11	6:00 p.m.: Passion Limit (telenovela)		7:00 p.m.: Just a Few Flees (Mexican tele-novela)	7:30 p.m.: Jornal do SBT—News	8:00 p.m.: Whirl the Whirl	8:30 p.m.: A Bunch of Passions (telenovela)		9:30 p.m.: Smallville (U.S. series)		10:30 p.m.: Cine Espectacular	
Record/Rio TV–13	5:50 p.m.: City Alert			7:35 p.m.: Jornal da Record News		8:30 p.m.: Bahia 50 degrees			10:00 p.m.: Cine movie		

THURSDAY

Channel	6 p.m.	6:30 p.m.	7 p.m.	7:30 p.m.	8 p.m.	8:30 p.m.	9 p.m.	9:30 p.m.	10 p.m.	10:30 p.m.	11 p.m.
Educational TV–2	Thinking About You		Brasil Gold	@titude .com	National Geographic		Debating Law		News	Art with Sérgio Brito	
Globo TV–4	5:55 p.m.: Chocolate with Pepper Brazilian (telenovela)		06:45 p.m.: RJ/TV 2nd edition Local news	07:05 p.m.: Kubanacan Brazilian (telenovela)		8:15 p.m.: Jornal Nacional News	8:55 p.m.: Celebrities Brazilian (telenovela)		10:10 p.m.: The Big Family		10:55 p.m.: Straight Line
Rede TV–6		6:15 p.m.: Open Channel		7:30 p.m.: Fame TV		8:30 p.m.: Pedro, the Fishy (Mexican tele-novela)	9:05 p.m.: Jornal da TV News		10:00 p.m.: Superpop (variety)		11:30 p.m.: Dynamic Reading
Bandeirantes TV–7	5:30 p.m.: Urgent Brasil			7:20 p.m.: Jornal do Rio Local News	7:35 p.m.: Jornal da Band News	8:25 p.m.: Total Sport	8:30 p.m.: Faith Show	9:45 p.m.: g4 Brasil Drops	9:50 p.m: Good Night Brasil		

	6 p.m.	6:30 p.m.	7 p.m.	7:30 p.m.	8 p.m.	8:30 p.m.	9 p.m.	9:30 p.m.	10 p.m.	10:30 p.m.	11 p.m.
CNT TV–9	6:00 p.m. Plastic Surgery	6:15 p.m.: Image Group / 6:30 p.m.: Life Tiny Things				8:30 p.m.: Power (game)		9:30 p.m.: CNT Jornal News	10:00 p.m.: Thousand and One Nights		
SBT TV–11	6:10 p.m.: Passion Limit (telenovela)		7:10 p.m.: Whirl the Whirl	7:40 p.m.: Jornal do SBT—News	8:10 p.m.: **Just a Few Flees** (Mexican tele-novela)	8:30 p.m.: A Bunch of Passions (telenovela)		9:30 p.m.: Ratinho's Program (variety live show)		10:30 p.m.: Movie	
Record/Rio TV–13	5:50 p.m.: City Alert			7:35 p.m.: Jornal da Record News	8:20 p.m.: Lost World		9:00 p.m.: Report Record News		10:00 p.m.: Live Variety Show With Adriana Galisteu		

FRIDAY

Channel	6 p.m.	6:30 p.m.	7 p.m.	7:30 p.m.	8 p.m.	8:30 p.m.	9 p.m.	9:30 p.m.	10 p.m.	10:30 p.m.	11 p.m.
Educational TV–2	6:00 p.m.: Thinking About You		Brasil Gold	@titude .com	8:00 p.m.: **National Geographic**		Red Hot + Rhapsody		News	Margareth Menezes Brazilian Singer	
Globo TV–4	6:05 p.m.: Chocolate with Pepper Brazilian (telenovela)	6:55 p.m.: RJ/TV 2nd edition Local news	7:15 p.m.: Kubanacan Brazilian (telenovela)		8:15 p.m.: Jornal Nacional News	8:55 p.m.: Celebrities Brazilian (telenovela)		9:50 p.m.: Globo Reporter		10:55 p.m.: The Fragile Gender (humor program)	
Rede TV–6	6:15 p.m.: Open Channel			7:30 p.m.: Fame TV		8:30 p.m.: **Peter, the Fishy** (tele-novela)	9:05 p.m.: Jornal da TV News		10:00 p.m.: Superpop (variety)		11:30 p.m.: Dynamic Reading
Bandeirantes TV–7	5:30 p.m.: Urgent Brasil		7:20 p.m.: Jornal do Rio Local News	7:35 p.m.: Jornal da Band News	8:25 p.m.: Total Sport	8:50 p.m.: Faith Show		9:45 p.m.: g4 Brasil Drops / 9:50 p.m.: Good Night Brasil			
CNT TV–9	6:00 p.m.: Consume Well	6:15 p.m.: Life Tiny Things / 6:30 p.m.: Christ the Winner				8:30 p.m.: Vip Room		9:30 p.m.: CNT Jornal News	10:00 p.m.: Thousand and One Nights		
SBT TV–11	6:05 p.m.: Passion Limit (telenovela)		7:05 p.m.: Whirl the Whirl	7:40 p.m.: Jornal do SBT—News	8:10 p.m.: **Just a Few Flees** (Mexican tele-novela)	8:40 p.m.: A Bunch of Passions (telenovela)		9:30 p.m.: Ratinho's Program (variety live show)			
Record/Rio TV–13	5:35 p.m.: City Alert			7:35 p.m.: Jornal da Record News	8:20 p.m.: The World		9:10 p.m.: **Robocop** (U.S. movie)		10:00 p.m.: Movie		11:45 p.m.: News

SATURDAY

Channel	6 p.m.	6:30 p.m.	7 p.m.	7:30 p.m.	8 p.m.	8:30 p.m.	9 p.m.	9:30 p.m.	10 p.m.	10:30 p.m.	11 p.m.
Educational TV–2	The Truth	Review of Brazilian Movies	Super Everything		Observer and the Press		General Comment		Modern Dance / Letters to the Brazilian People		

Globo TV–4	06:05 p.m.: Chocolate with Pepper Brazilian (telenovela)	06:55 p.m.: RJ/TV 2nd edition Local news	07:15 p.m.: Kubanacan Brazilian (telenovela)	8:15 p.m.: Jornal Nacional News	8:55 p.m.: Celebrities Brazilian (telenovela)	10:00 p.m.: Total Mass (humor program)	11:00 p.m.: Super Cine
Network TV–6	5:20 p.m.: Citizen Reporter	6:30 p.m.: Fame TV		8:30 p.m.: **Peter, the Fishy** (Mexican telenovela)	9:10 p.m.: Jornal da TV News	10:00 p.m.: NBA—Before Season	11:30 p.m.: NBA—Live Golden State
Bandeirantes TV–7	6:00 p.m.: Urgent Brasil	7:20 p.m.: Jornal do Rio Local News	7:35 p.m.: Jornal da Band News	8:25 p.m.: Total Sport	8:50 p.m.: Faith Show	9:45 p.m.: g4 Brasil Drops	9:50 p.m.: Incredible videos
CNT TV–9	6:00 p.m.: Mushrooms in the Sun	6:15 p.m.: Image Group	6:30 p.m.: Life Tiny Things	8:30 p.m.: Image Group	9:00 p.m.: Magnavita	9:30 p.m.: CNT Jornal News	10:00 p.m.: Thousand and One Nights
SBT TV–11	6:15 p.m.: Like Mother, Like Daughter (series)	7:10 p.m.: Everwood (series)	8:05 p.m.: Seventh Sky (series)	9:00 p.m.: Smart Move	9:45 p.m.: Travelling		
Record/Rio TV–13	6:00 p.m.: City Alert	7:35 p.m.: Jornal da Record News	8:20 p.m.: The Night Is Ours	10:00 p.m.: Series on the Amazon	11:45 p.m.: News		

SUNDAY

Channel	6 p.m.	6:30 p.m.	7 p.m.	7:30 p.m.	8 p.m.	8:30 p.m.	9 p.m.	9:30 p.m.	10 p.m.	10:30 p.m.	11 p.m.
Educational TV–2	Brazilian Music		By Chance		Roberto D'avila Connection		Sport Vision		Brazil Short Films		
Globo TV–4	5:10 p.m.: Faustão's Sunday (variety program)					8:30 p.m.: Fantastic—Life Show (variety program)				10:55 p.m.: Cine movie	
Rede TV–6	5:00 p.m.: Amaury Junior	6:30 p.m.: Movie Panico			8:00 p.m.: Dynamic Reading	8:15 p.m.: About Soccer			10:00 p.m.: Manual		
Bandeirantes TV–7	5:00 p.m.: Life game		7:00 p.m.: Candid Camera		8:00 p.m.: Total Sport	8:30 p.m.: Sunday at the Theater				10:30 p.m.: Open Channel	
CNT TV–9	6:00 p.m.: Polimport				8:00 p.m.: Check In—Tourism on TV		9:00 p.m.: Round Table		10:00 p.m.: Thousand and One Nights		
SBT TV–11	3:50 p.m.: Nice Sunday					8:30 p.m.: All Against One		9:50 p.m.: Tele-drawing	10:00 p.m.: Movie at Ten		
Record/Rio TV–13	5:00 p.m.: Cine Movie		7:15 p.m.: Cine Movie				9:00 p.m.: Third Time				

Note. **Bold** denotes imported program.

Chapter 12

Mexico

Guillermo Orozco

University of Guadalajara

ABOUT MEXICO

With 100 million inhabitants, located mostly in urban areas, Mexico is the second largest country in Latin America (after Brazil). Alone among Latin American countries, Mexico shares a common border of more than 2,000 kilometers with the United States; the profound inequalities on opposite sides of the border have monumental effects on migration and economics. This historical proximity has also influenced cultural and linguistic exchanges, including bilateral agreements regarding television.

Even though Mexico is a member in good standing of the Organization for Economic Cooperation and Development (OECD), the latest statistics reveal that 60% of Mexicans live at or below poverty level, while the most affluent 15% accumulate greater wealth; the disparity between rich and poor is growing.

Ethnically, Mexico is a racially mixed nation often referred to as *la raza de bronce* (the bronze race). This mixing of Spanish and Indian blood has been a characteristic trait of the growing population since colonial times (16th century on). Today, along with this racially mixed *mestizo* majority, there exist more than 50 ethnic indigenous minorities who speak as many languages and make up approximately 15% of the total population. Ethnic groups live all over Mexico, but are mostly concentrated in the southern part of the country, where in the mid-1990s the well-known and often admired Zapatista liberation movement arose to reclaim native tribal rights.

Culturally, Mexico is a diverse and wealthy nation, renowned as much for its cuisine as for its music, arts, and artisans. Spanish, the official language, with both literary and colloquial forms, represents one of the country's outstanding cultural traits.

Politically, Mexico is a republic comprising 31 states. In theory, its three branches—executive, legislative, and judicial—are balanced and independent. With the conclusion of the Mexican revolution in 1927, ending a 30-year dictatorship, Mexico became a democracy—even though for 71 years (1929–2000) it was ruled by only one political party, the Party Revolutionary Institutional (PRI). It was not until the year 2000 that a much-awaited change took place when Vicente Fox from the opposition National Action Party (PAN) won the presidential elections. This prolonged one-party political history is closely tied to the first 50 years of television in Mexico and continues to influence the integration and coming of age of this Mexican political-media partnership. Television in Mexico represents a cultural, social, and economic phenomenon.

BROADCAST BACKGROUND

Watching television is the most common activity of the Mexicans. In national surveys about media consumption, Mexicans say they prefer watching television as an activity on weekdays as well as on weekends. Only 6 years ago the preferred activity for the weekend was to spend time with the family, but since the year 2000 the favorite pastime is watching television. (One may assume that the family sometimes watches television together, but not always.)

By far the lion's share of advertising monies goes to television—74% in 2000, compared to 10% for newspapers and magazines combined (by 2002, the TV share was down to 71%; Orozco, 2002b). Mexican television at first gives the impression that it has developed along the lines of the competitive U.S. model, because it is an economically successful business enterprise. But in reality, competition has played little or no role in the growth and development of Mexican television.

Dominance of Televisa

Televisa, that mammoth Latin American oligopoly of audiovisual entertainment, has been able to consolidate and establish a stranglehold on the industry. A key source of capital, Televisa is listed on the stock exchange; its owner, Emilio Azcárraga, is one of the wealthiest men, not only in Mexico, but internationally. Televisa productions are exported all over the Spanish-speaking world.

If there is one thing that sets Mexican television apart, it is precisely the permanent eradication of competitiveness between Televisa's empires and the political and economic protection provided by the government in power that has left the country's overall TV market, pay as well as commercial, in the hands of only a few (Hernández, 2000).

In Mexico, the governing PRI party and television have been hand in glove for five decades (Fernandez, 2002; Orozco, 2002b). Even though there have been attempts to manufacture competition (for example, with IMEVISION), this particular historical situation has hampered the development of Mexican television. While other countries in the region have been able to balance healthy economic and political tensions and special interests between one social group and another with a resulting positive impact on quality and creativity in programming, Mexico sadly has not.

As the writer Mario Vargas-Llosa (Orozco, 2002a) said, "The perfect dictatorship exists in Mexico"—referring to the long-standing political power of one party, the PRI. Similarly, a kind of "television dictatorship" by Televisa has been able to sustain expansionist proposals while supporting the government. There is no doubt that Mexicans are Televisa's captive audience; the spectators' lack of demand for quality television results in conformity and a lack of real viewing options.

Today, Mexican television is going through financial, political, and technological changes. Traditional political (PRI) ties must be broken and assets concentrated for the TV industry to compete as a transnational consortium in a contemporary global context (Sinclair, 2001). In order to understand Mexican television today, we have to review some historical incidents and characteristics of Mexico's TV pioneers.

History

Television in Mexico, inaugurated on August 31, 1950, made its initial transmission the following day, September 1, when President Miguel Alemán gave his State of the Union address. The future course of Mexican television lay in the hands of three leaders, who commercially exploited the medium.

The **first** of these "three pioneers" was Rómulo O'Farril, representing the "unbending" business sector of the country; he was the first to obtain a franchise, channel 4. It was managed under the auspices of Television of Mexico, S.A., a company created expressly for this purpose in the 1940s with infrastructure and technology brought in from the United States. The mid-1940s was a high point for the initial expansion of Mexican industry, stimulated as much by the peace following the Mexican revolution as by the boom times after the end of World War II. The vision of this entrepreneur made the conglomerate Televisa (of which channel 4 later became a part) persistently influential and up to date with the most advanced technology.

The **second** leader was Emilio Azcárraga Vidaurreta, a radio magnate. His XEW, nicknamed "doubleu" and transmitting since 1943, called itself "the Voice of Latin America from Mexico." With unique insight into the business of entertainment and accumulated experience in radio broadcasting, this mogul and his son and successor, Emilio Azcárraga Milmo, became the strongmen of Mexican television (Fernandez & Paxman, 2000). The Azcárragas settled for TV channel 2, today known as the "channel of the stars," which emerged as a successful business. Due to this tycoon's past in the world of radio, channel 2's emphasis on content over images and forms set it apart from other Mexican television enterprises.

The **third**, Guillermo González-Camarena, was more of a technician and inventor than a businessman obsessed with profits. An engineer by profession, he had been experimenting with black-and-white as well as color and had managed to patent a Mexican chromatic TV model (Mejía, 1998). Nevertheless, this model was not generally accepted, being less lucrative than other patents that were compatible with existing TV companies. As sociologist Raymond Williams cautioned, technology adoption doesn't depend on scientific accomplishment, but on profitability in the marketplace (Orozco, 1996). Camarena was given a license to run channel 5.

Competition and Monopoly.   Channel 4 (XHTV) televised its first transmission June 27, 1950; channel 2 (XEW), March, 21, 1951; and channel 5 (XHGC), on May 10, 1952 (Hernández, 2000). Thus three Mexican television TV projects were, if only for 5 years, set in motion; true competition seemed possible among the recently established TV conglomerates, but they were aborted by direct presidential intervention. From the ruins of these three channels, on March 25, 1955, a monopoly company was born: Telesistema Mexicano. This company would later give birth to the oligopoly Televisa (Sánchez, 2000a).

By the beginning of the 1970s, another source of competition sprang up in the form of a boom in regional television assisted by local governments. The growing popularity and programming creativity of regional channel 8 from the northern city of Monterrey was spreading all over the nation. In 1973 the possibility of two large, competitive TV companies was extinguished when once again a presidential intervention created Televisa. Former president Miguel Alemán participated as a stockholder, alongside his son of the same name, who was elected governor of the state of Veracruz for a 2000–2006 term.

In 1983 the government created a national TV system, IMEVISION, which became highly politicized (Orozco, 2002a). It ended 10 years later when the Mexican government put up for sale this national system, which had its beginnings in 1968 with channel 13. Channel 13 and channel 7, with national coverage, were purchased by another industrialist, Jorge Salinas-Pliego, with funds coming from the brother of the then president of Mexico; thus was guaranteed an alliance with the new TV company, TV Azteca, and the politicians in power (Orozco, 1996).

In 1997, what came to be known as "the war of the TV stations" was raging. Both networks, Televisa and TV Azteca, tried to dominate Mexican audiovisual air space using their own air time on talk shows and news reports. At this stage, many such segments on daily news shows were features or scandals about one side or the other of these competing broadcast stations. Suddenly, in June 1999, the war ended when both networks were faced with orders to exploit coverage of the assassination of a TV celebrity in order to degrade the recently elected democratic government of the opposition party in Mexico City. This unexpected alliance, that all viewers were a party to, was the beginning of what is known today as the Mexican "television duopoly" (Orozco, 2002b).

Channels 11 and 22, the educational and cultural channels, have, during the history of Mexican television, functioned as escape valves. Channel 11, created in 1959 as part of the public National Polytechnic Institute, had enormous potential (Orozco, 1996), but was never truly public (Fuenzalida, 2001; Rincón, 2001). In 1991, channel 22 emerged from a proposal to the incumbent president by a group of nationally recognized intellectuals, communicators, and artists. To safeguard one of the frequencies of IMEVISION that the government was selling at the time, channel 22 was protected from commercialization. The channels, having limited influence, did not transform Televisa´s formula of cheap shows and telenovelas. Channel 11 reached only the outskirts of Mexico City; channel 22 is hard to see outside of central Mexico.

BROADCAST REGULATION

From its beginnings in 1950 to the year 2000, Mexican television was in theory private, but tacitly allied with the PRI government's interests. Officials seemed to have understood from the beginning that it wasn't politically correct to directly support state television; it was easier and more acceptable to let industry take responsibility for TV performance that meshed with government criteria and objectives. This policy, however, was covert rather than overt. Then in 1969, a regulation obligated the media to give 12.5% of their air time to be used as seen fit by the government in exchange for lower taxes. In October 2002, the president of Mexico abolished that decree, ending the last official state regulatory control over television.

Before the year 2000, an unwritten rule governed television entrepreneurs in Mexico: Never openly criticize or oppose the government. The administration's taut alliance with television was summarized succinctly in *Proceso* magazine in 1997 by "the tiger," Emilio Azcárraga Milmo: "In Televisa we are PRIistas, and he who isn't, should get out" (Fernandez & Paxman, 2000, p. 13).

Since 2000, with a new president, Vicente Fox, and a new political party in power, the traditional alliance between Televisa and the government has been broken. Televisa anchormen even felt free to ridicule the current president. The parties have been unquestionably negotiating under the table, resulting in the elimination in 2002 of the 12.5% of air time, but also allowing competition represented by CNI, channel 40. On the other hand, presidential and other non-PRI party activities are enjoying positive coverage on the TV screen for the first time (Orozco, 2003).

Even though there are fixed rules governing radio and TV licenses, the process of authorizing franchises is murky (Toussaint, 1998). In theory, anybody with certain prerequisites can apply for and obtain a permit, but in reality only certain groups have been successful. The law stipulates the kind of license granted. For network or commercial television, the permit lasts for 30 years; for other TV services, like cable, the time varies (Sosa, 1998).

Certain limitations are stipulated: No violent content, pornography, or, generally speaking, obscene scenes or language frankly offensive to certain viewers. Advertising of certain products is also restricted, for example, alcohol during the afternoon hours when supposedly more youngsters and children are watching. The amount of advertising should not exceed one third of each program's total time (Sosa, 1998). However, as any viewer well knows, in practice one sees more commercials than there should be.

Federal laws for radio and television were promulgated in 1960 and 1973. Since then, small modifications and revisions have been made, but modernization is clearly needed (Fernandez, 2002). These laws guarantee both freedom of expression in the media and the citizen's right to information. Nonetheless, due to the PRI government's alliance with TV executives, media reform has failed several times over the last 20 years; regulation remains a work in progress (Corral-Jurado, 1998).

The last attempt to update federal radio and TV law was promptly characterized by media moguls as "a gag order." In 1998, the national media reform effort by congressmen of the National Action Party (PAN), then the opposition party, fell apart. One positive result of this reform effort, however, was that a code of ethics was written; it was endorsed by a majority of the media allied with the National Chamber of Radio and Television Industries.

TV NETWORKS AND PENETRATION

Since 1993 Mexicans have had available six types of television. The **first** type, broadcast commercial television, is essentially the Televisa and TV Azteca duopoly and their relay stations across the nation. Each network has at least two channels with national coverage: Channels 2 and 5 of Televisa and channels 7 and 13 of TV Azteca. There are also regional channels. Further included in this category are state channels that temporarily survived monopolization and are owned by groups of local businessmen, like channel 6 of Guadalajara. Belonging to this group as well is channel 40, transmitting on UHF, created in 1994; originally and exclusively as a news channel, it has been enlarging its programming and may break free of its partial dependence on TV Azteca.

The **second** type is cultural/educational television, channels 11 and 22, financed primarily with public funds. A pioneer in children's educational television, channel 11 has received important international acclaim for its children's shows, such as "*El Diván de Valentina*" (Valentina's Couch) and "*Bisbirije*," which participated in a Jeunesse Award in Munich, Germany, in 2003 in the best children's program category. UNESCO recognized Channel 22 as the best cultural TV enterprise of the year in 1996. Unfortunately, neither of these channels is seen in the majority of Mexican homes, their ratings not even reaching 12 points.

The **third** type is regional television, which includes state TV systems financed with assorted funding through private and governmental resources, with resulting uneven development, quality, and programming. These TV stations, forming part of a nationwide system, have tried to uncover and transmit diverse regional culture around the country. A regional channel was assigned to almost all of the country's 31 states. Some of them stand out for their creativity and production quality, such as the channel of the state of Michoacán or Quintana Roo. Others, however, fell into the hands of governments that saw, in regional television, a great opportunity for political or party propaganda and exploitation. Still others were left in oblivion, neither converted into political propaganda machines for their governors nor given adequate funding in order to be fully functional as cultural channels, as has been the case with channel 7 in the state of Jalisco.

A **fourth** type is instructional (classroom) television. Transmitted through the EDUSAT satellite of the Ministry of Education, its signal can be seen in many of the country's public schools and in other educational institutions: universities, institutes, museums, and cultural centers. A high school system, Telesecundaria, has been running for more than 20 years. The goal of reliably receiving a satellite signal at each school remains elusive, as infrastructure does not exist in certain regions of the country. At present this service only reaches one third of the schools, located mostly in major cities; thus instructional television, in spite of certain advances, has not met its chief objective: compensating for educational deficiencies in the majority of school-aged children.

This televised instructional programming is produced mainly within the General Office of Educational Television, which boasts a high-quality production center, where video producers have been trained for generations. There are two other governmental agencies that produce instructional television in Mexico: one is TV-UNAM, part of the National Autonomous University of Mexico, which basically follows the university's curricular course material and which is at times transmitted through local Televisa channels. The other, The Latin American Institute for Educational Communications (ILCE), was originally an institution subsidized by the OEA and UNESCO, which was later totally taken over by the Ministry of Mexican Education. This institute produces some programs that are transmitted on the country's commercial television. This educational satellite has transmitted well over 15,000 hours of televised material in 1999 alone.

The **fifth** type is pay television, which includes three subtypes: cable, begun in 1969, by different companies, but mainly run by Televisa; the Multivision Encoded System, which was created in 1989 and functions as a multichannel, multipoint distribution system on a super high frequency air wave; and Direct TV and commercial television by satellite (Sky TV), both created at the end of the 1990s, taking their signal into the homes of those who subscribe to their services. The various types of pay television have not developed as expected and have shown only modest growth, concentrated in Mexico City and a few other important Mexican metropolises.

In sum, the type of television with major coverage continues to be network (commercial) national television, which is transmitted into practically every Mexican home. The following are the preferred channels in Mexico City, Guadalajara, and Monterrey: channel 2 (Televisa), 42% of homes surveyed; channel 13 (TV Azteca), 39%; channel 11 (cultural), 20%; channel 5 (Televisa), 19%; channel 7 (TV Azteca), 18%; channel 9 (TV Azteca), 11%; channel 4 (Televisa- non national), 11%; channel 40 (alternative commercial), 10%; and channel 22 (cultural), 7%. Respondents could give more than one answer in naming a preferred channel (Orozco, 2000).

BROADCAST CONTENT AND RATINGS

By the end of the 1990s, the dominant program type on the four channels with national coverage (2 and 5 of Televisa and 7 and 13 of TV Azteca) was news, broadly defined to include news magazines and talk shows, a total of almost 180 hours of weekly broadcasts. One channel alone, channel 2 of Televisa, transmitted 30 hours of weekly news in 2003 (Orozco & Medina, 2000).

One survey in Mexico City (Orozco, 2000) found that from 1994 to 1998, the audience's preference in viewing changed from 20% choosing telenovelas to 28% choosing the news. This change reflects a change in Mexican TV news itself, which is more entertaining, more dramatic, and contains more "blood and guts" than before. With these ingredients, TV Azteca and, to a lesser extent, Televisa have succeeded in grabbing eyeballs. Another survey found that in 2001, 50% of respondents listed news as their preferred genre.

With respect to other genres, talk shows and reality shows are broadcast 16 hours a week. In 2003 "Big Brother" was in its second season; in the first, it had a rating of 35 points. Regarding cartoons, channel 5 (Televisa) alone transmits 58 hours a week, while channel 7 (TV Azteca) only broadcasts 5.5 hours. Other national channels do not include these type of shows in their programming.

Telenovelas

Gradually, Mexican TV dramas have evolved from depicting powerful verbal exchanges—due to early television's role as an extension of radio and the emphasis on oral expression in Mexican culture—to programs that make better use of image and visual effects. Telenovela changes are similarly noticeable: from small sets and interiors, where the dramatic action proceeded via exaggerated facial gestures and verbal interactions, to the latest productions, where more natural acting and exterior scenes are used.

The classic Mexican telenovelas have become less important over the years. There were times when morning and Sunday programming was flooded with installments of the current programs. Yet by 2003, only 50 hours of telenovelas were being transmitted weekly—30 hours on channel 2 (Televisa) and 20 hours on channel 13 (TV Azteca). Mexican telenovelas are familiar all over the Spanish-speaking world and compete in quality with those of Globo from Brazil (see chapter 11). The Mexican themes continue to be about romantic relationships, but with some exceptions, such as drug dealers or historical events; in general, it still is not customary to talk about controversial social issues the way the Brazilian telenovelas do.

The dominant theme in Mexican telenovelas still is that of impossible love, as in "Los Ricos También Lloran" (The Rich Also Cry) or "Corazón Salvaje" (Savage Heart), where all types of misfortune befall the couple in love, as in the paradigmatic telenovela of the 1970s, "Simplemente María." However, during the last 5 years, both Televisa and Tv Azteca have made changes in the traditional way of producing telenovelas and in the topics included. To some extent, this might be as a result of international competition, especially from Brazilian and Colombian telenovelas, which regularly deal with contemporary social and cultural issues and introduce other technical innovations.

As examples of innovation, two telenovelas specifically addressed to young people were transmitted during 2003: "Two City Boys to Watch Out For" on Channel 13 and "Clap, the Place of Your Dreams" on channel 2. Both dealt with teenage love, but expanded their scopes to include marriage, free love, AIDS, woman´s rights, sexual relations, and gay lifestyles. In the same innovative vein, "Women's Glance" developed a sequel during 2003. Plotwise, it dealt with the relationship that a divorced woman with two daughters and one son, who was 16 years older than her new partner, had with a man who had been previously single. Technically, producers created an unusual atmosphere by using waist-up camera angles as if one were looking in from behind the scenes.

During the time of the so-called TV stations war (1996–1999), TV viewers in Mexico benefited from witnessing real improvements in TV programming. Telenovelas included more controversial issues and other drama series were created, like "Naked City." As already noted, news as presented by Televisa and TV Azteca became more entertaining and violent and has remained so; furthermore, a talk show boom also took place.

Comedy and Reality

One unique personality in Mexican television has been Roberto Gómez-Bolaños, a comic actor who 35 years ago created the *"Chespirito"* series. *Chespirito*, a Spanish nickname meaning "Little Shakespeare," was brought to the screen in a very funny manner. After the great success of this series, Gomez-Bolaños created his most famous character, *El Chavo del Ocho*, who has been a TV fixture for nearly 30 years straight. This series can be watched nowadays in most Latin American countries. In Brazilian television the series is named *"Chaves,"* while in Peru, since 2001, there is a series called *"La Vecindad"* with Peruvian actors in domestic scenes but having the same characters, issues, and style of El Chavo del Ocho. This actor created *"El Chapulín Colorado"* (The Red Cricket), a series that has also run for years on Mexican television. This series of three has also run for years in Mexican television. These series represent the quintessential Mexican entertainment television.

Political humor has been a rare type of program in Mexican television. Nevertheless, one program, "The Polyvoices," caught the attention of a wide national audience in the 1970s. Recently, "Facts About Stuffed Animals" has given an ironic and comic twist on the news of the day.

Differing from other countries, sitcoms in Mexico have aired only sporadically, perhaps only a single program of this format per decade: the classical Michel family sagas in the 1960s; the Gomez stories, in the 1970s; *"La Criada Bien Criada"* (The Educated Servant) over almost 15 years beginning in the 1980s; and *"A Single Father"* in the early 1990s. Drama, as conveyed in telenovelas as well as in televised theater, such as "Women: Real Life-Cases," has been the most successful television format in Mexico.

Reality shows like "Big Brother," "The Academy," or "Success Operation" have attracted a lot of national attention. As noted earlier, a talk show boom occurred in the late 1990s. However, Mexican talk shows became excessively violent; when on-air slugfests among participants started to become the norm, some talk shows were canceled in 2002.

IMPORTS AND EXPORTS

Latin American countries are flooded with Mexican telenovelas. They successfully compete with soap opera productions from Brazil, Colombia, and Venezuela that also circulate on the continent. Two recent Mexican telenovelas—*"Los Ricos También Lloran"* (The Rich Also Cry) and *"Corazón Salvaje"* (Savage Heart)—boasted high ratings when exported to Europe and Russia. By geographical area, Latin America gets 43% of Mexican exports, the United States, another 43%, and Europe and other countries, 14%.

However, the value of imported television programs reaches more than $150 million annually, whereas exports account for 60% of that figure, which means Mexico has an enormous TV deficit (Sánchez, 2000b; Toussaint, 1998). For example, all the cartoons transmitted on network television are foreign, mostly from Japan and the rest from the United States.

Mexican Televisa channels broadcast abundant imported programming. For example, in the movie category, Televisa airs an average of 1,500 foreign movies a year on its different channels, a total of 57% of all movies (only 43% or 1,200 are Mexican) (Sánchez, 2000b). Even more lopsided, TV Azteca's channels air annually an average of 700 foreign pictures (68% of all movies), versus only 350 Mexican ones. If one considers these two components of the Mexican commercial TV duopoly plus pay systems (cable and multivision), the movie category is 85% foreign.

Even though it seems paradoxical, an even greater number of foreign films are shown by Mexican cultural television. On channel 22, 100% of its movies are foreign, and at channel 11, almost 95%. At both, the aim is to offer only the best of international cinema.

RADIO

Radio is very important to the Mexicans in a different way than television is. It was on the radio where radionovelas originating in Cuba were produced and broadcast. XEW, owned by the Azcárraga family, was a broadcasting station pioneer with its signal reaching not only national territory, but throughout Latin America by means of relay stations emitting signals over the southern part of the continent. Many program announcers and commentators, as well as musicians and singers, who would later grace the small screen, began in radio.

The relationship between radio and television, more than historic and evolutionary, has been economic as well. Televisa owns several radio stations, among them XEW.

Unlike what happened with the TV oligopoly, the radio industry has developed along commercially competitive lines, significantly benefiting radio listeners in Mexico. Naturally there are various business groups that own the majority of the commercial stations, AM as well as FM, but not one group or individual has cornered the market as has occurred with television. On the contrary, radio is perhaps the medium that has experimented esthetically, conveyed news, and been of special service to the community. Since the 1930s, various commercial and private radio stations carry out the task of connecting remote and inaccessible communities, allowing radio listeners to call the station and leave messages for family or friends, which the station transmits at no cost.

Radio also serves a very important informative function, as more than one third of Mexicans, 33 million people, get their news from the radio. In addition to commercial radio, there is the university radio, which contributes alternative programming of superior quality. The principal station is Radio UNAM, from the National Autonomous University of Mexico, located in Mexico City, and Radio U de G, the University of Guadalajara in

Guadalajara. There is also Radio Education and other government-owned stations transmitting innovative programs, along with an entire system of regional, community, and indigenous stations broadcasting in Mexico's many ethnic minority languages.

ACKNOWLEDGMENTS

The author thanks Joyce Jackson and Rodrigo González for their collaboration in this chapter.

REFERENCES

Corral-Jurado, J. (1998). Comunicación y derecho: las leyes de los muertos [Communication and law: The laws of death]. In Comisión de Radio Televisión y Cinematografía, Cámara de Diputados (Eds.), *La reforma de medios. Voces en torno a la iniciativa de la ley federal de comunicación social* (pp. 77–82). México City: Comisión de Radio Televisión y Cinematografía, Cámara de Diputados.

Fernández, F. (2002). *La responsabilidad de los medios de comunicación* [The responsibility of communication media]. Mexico City: Paidós.

Fernández, C., & Paxman, A. (2000). *El tigre: Emilio Azcárraga y su imperio Televisa* [The tiger: Emilio Azcárraga and his emporium, Televisa]. Mexico City: Grijalbo Mondadori.

Fuenzalida, V. (2001). *La televisión pública en América Latina. Reforma o privatización* [Public television in Latin America. Reform or privatization]. Santiago de Chile: Fondo de Cultura Económica.

Hernández, F. (2000). *La expansión internacional de la industria mexicana de la televisión* [The international expansion of the Mexican TV industry]. Unpublished doctoral thesis, Universidad Complutense de Madrid.

Mejía, F. (1998). Del canal 4 a Televisa [From channel 4 to Televisa]. In M. Sánchez (Ed.), *Apuntes para una historia de la televisión mexicana* (pp. 17–20). Mexico City: Revista Mexicana de Comunicación.

Orozco, G. (1996). El rescate televisivo, un desafío cultural de la audiencia [Television rescue, a cultural challenge of the audience]. In G. Orozco (Ed.), *Miradas latinoamericanas a la televisión* (pp. 233–249). Mexico City: Universidad Iberoamericana.

Orozco, G. (2000, March 24). Aumenta divertimento político-noticioso [Political-news entertainment increases]. *El norte*, 2-D.

Orozco, G. (2002a). La televisión en México [Television in Mexico]. In G. Orozco (Ed.), *Historias de la televisión en América Latina* (pp. 203–240). Barcelona: Gedisa.

Orozco, G. (2002b). Televisión y televidentes: Cinco décadas que pudieron ser diferentes [Television and viewers: Five decades that could have been different]. *Revista Universidad de Guadalajara, dossier medio siglo de la televisión en México, 20*(3), 20–37.

Orozco, G. (2003). La televisión en México: Un itinerario para develar su presente [Television in Mexico: An itinerary to track its present]. *Revista Takwá, 7*, 62–69.

Orozco, G. & Medina, D. (2000). Supertemas noticiosos en la televisión mexicana. Análisis de la información en los noticieros [News superthemes in Mexican TV: Content analysis of TV news]. *Comunicación y Sociedad, 37*, 53–87.

Rincón, O. (2001). Realización. Hacia una televisión pública experimental y gozosa [Production: Towards a joyful experimental public television]. In O. Rincón (Coord.), *Televisión pública: del consumidor al ciudadano* (pp. 273–293). Bogotá: Convenio Andrés Bello.

Sánchez, E. (2000a). Globalización y convergencia: Retos para las industrias culturales latinoamericanas [Globalization and convergence: Challenges to the Latinoamerican cultural industries]. *Revista Universidad de Guadalajara, 20*(3), 38–54.

Sánchez, E. (2000b). La televisión y el sector audiovisual mexicano. Breve examen de flujos asimétricos [The television and the Mexican audiovisual sector: A brief examination of assymetric fluxes]. *Revista Universidad de Guadalajara, 20*(03), 55–62.

Sinclair, J. (2001). *Televisión: comunicación global y regionalización* [Television: Global communication and regionalization]. Barcelona: Gedisa.

Sosa, G. (1998). El marco legal [The legal frame]. In M. Sánchez (Ed.), *Apuntes para una historia de la televisión mexicana* (pp. 17–20). Mexico City: Revista Mexicana de Comunicación.

Toussaint, F. (1998). *Televisión sin fronteras* [Television without frontiers]. México: Siglo XXI.

PRIME TIME, MEXICO, NOVEMBER 5–11, 2003

MONDAY

Channel	7 p.m.	7:30 p.m.	8 p.m.	8:30 p.m.	9 p.m.	9:30 p.m.	10 p.m.
Channel 2 (Televisa)	Clap, the Place of Your Dreams (telenovela)		Bride's Veil (telenovela)		Mariana of the Night (telenovela)		The Parody (comic sketches)
Channel 5 (Televisa)	Sabrina, the Teenage Witch (U.S. comedy)	Dragon Ball Z (Japanese cartoon)	Chespirito (comedy)		Big Brother VIP (reality show)		Cine Shock (films)
Channel 7 (TV Azteca)	Telenovela Stars (reality show)		The Simpsons		Facts from Channel Seven (news)	Seventh Line (films)	
Channel 13 (TV Azteca)	Two City Boys to Watch Out For (telenovela)		The Gardener's Daughter (telenovela)		Woman's Glance: The Return (telenovela)		Facts in the Night (news)

TUESDAY

Channel	7 p.m.	7:30 p.m.	8 p.m.	8:30 p.m.	9 p.m.	9:30 p.m.	10 p.m.
Channel 2 (Televisa)	Clap, the Place of Your Dreams (telenovela)		Bride's Veil (telenovela)		Mariana of the Night (telenovela)		The House of Laughs (comic sketches)
Channel 5 (Televisa)	Sabrina, the Teenage Witch (U.S. comedy)	Dragon Ball Z (Japanese cartoon)	Chespirito (comedy)		Big Brother VIP (reality show)		Different Talk (music and interview show)
Channel 7 (TV Azteca)	Telenovela Stars (reality show)		The Simpsons		Facts from Channel Seven (news)	Taxi, Are You Free? (reality show)	Films
Channel 13 (TV Azteca)	Two City Boys to Watch Out For (telenovela)		The Gardener's Daughter (telenovela)		Woman's Glance: The Return (telenovela)		Facts in the Night (news)

WEDNESDAY

Channel	7 p.m.	7:30 p.m.	8 p.m.	8:30 p.m.	9 p.m.	9:30 p.m.	10 p.m.
Channel 2 (Televisa)	Clap, the Place of Your Dreams (telenovela)		Bride's Veil (telenovela)		Mariana of the Night (telenovela)		XHBRBZ (comic sketches)

Channel	7 p.m.	7:30 p.m.	8 p.m.	8:30 p.m.	9 p.m.	9:30 p.m.	10 p.m.
Channel 5 (Televisa)	Sabrina, the Teenage Witch (U.S. comedy)	Dragon Ball Z (Japanese cartoon)	Chespirito (comedy)		Big Brother VIP (reality show)		New Mexican Cinema (Mexican films)
Channel 7 (TV Azteca)	Telenovela Stars (reality show)		The Simpsons (U.S. cartoon)		Facts from Channel Seven (news)	Your Time Is Up! (comedy series)	Seventh Line (films)
Channel 13 (TV Azteca)	Two City Boys to Watch Out For (telenovela)		The Gardener's Daughter (telenovela)		Woman's Glance: The Return (telenovela)		Facts in the Night (news)

THURSDAY

Channel	7 p.m.	7:30 p.m.	8 p.m.	8:30 p.m.	9 p.m.	9:30 p.m.	10 p.m.
Channel 2 (Televisa)	Clap, the Place of Your Dreams (telenovela)		Bride's Veil (telenovela)		Mariana of the Night (telenovela)		The Rush Hour (comic sketches)
Channel 5 (Televisa)	Malcolm in the Middle (U.S. comedy)	Dragon Ball Z (Japanese cartoon)	Chespirito (comedy)		Big Brother VIP (reality show)		Film Shock
Channel 7 (TV Azteca)	Telenovela Stars (reality show)		The Simpsons (U.S. cartoon)		Facts from Channel Seven (news)	The Funniest Stories (comedy series)	Films
Channel 13 (TV Azteca)	Two City Boys to Watch Out For (telenovela)		The Gardener's Daughter (telenovela)		Woman's Glance: The Return (telenovela)		Facts in the Night (news)

FRIDAY

Channel	7 p.m.	7:30 p.m.	8 p.m.	8:30 p.m.	9 p.m.	9:30 p.m.	10 p.m.
Channel 2 (Televisa)	Clap, the Place of Your Dreams (telenovela)		Bride's Veil (telenovela)		Mariana of the Night (telenovela)		The Cage (comic sketches)
Channel 5 (Televisa)	Sabrina, the Teenage Witch (U.S. comedy)	Dragon Ball Z	Chespirito (comedy)		Big Brother VIP (reality show)		Film Shock
Channel 7 (TV Azteca)	Telenovela Stars (reality show)		The Simpsons (U.S. cartoon)		Facts from Channel Seven (news)	Seventh Line (films)	
Channel 13 (TV Azteca)	Two City Boys to Watch Out For (telenovela)		The Gardener's Daughter (telenovela)		Woman's Glance: The Return (telenovela)		Facts in the Night (news)

SATURDAY

Channel	7 p.m.	7:30 p.m.	8 p.m.	8:30 p.m.	9 p.m.	9:30 p.m.	10 p.m.
Channel 2 (Televisa)	The Immortal Pedro Infante Presents . . . (Pedro Infante films)		Women: Real-Life Cases (TV drama)		Cine Premiere Presents . . . (Mexican films)		
Channel 5 (Televisa)	Film Trilogy					Special	Programming
Channel 7 (TV Azteca)	Second Exhibition (films)		Third Exhibition (films)			Fourth Exhibition (films)	
Channel 13 (TV Azteca)	Special Programming				In the Eye of the Hurricane (show business dramas)		The Weakest Rival (game)

SUNDAY							
Channel	7 p.m.	7:30 p.m.	8 p.m.	8:30 p.m.	9 p.m.	9:30 p.m.	10 p.m.
Channel 2 (Televisa)	The Stuffed Animals Family (comedy series)		Big Brother VIP (reality show)				The Play (sports)
Channel 5 (Televisa)	Assorted Films						
Channel 7 (TV Azteca)	Estelar Cinema						
Channel 13 (TV Azteca)	The Weakest Rival (contest)		Telenovela Stars (reality show)				Battle of the Sexes (game)

Note. **Bold** indicates imported program.

III

CROSS-NATIONAL
CASE STUDIES

Chapter 13

The Olympics

Anthony Moretti

Texas Tech University

INTRODUCTION

In their most idyllic version, the Olympic Games are designed to be peaceful competitions in which athletes from all over the world gather together in friendship. Unfortunately, this idealistic definition has rarely—if ever—been evident. One reason, although certainly not the only explanation, is that the media have transformed the games into something beyond mere sporting contests.

The modern Olympic Games trace their origin to the late 19th century and the efforts of Pierre de Coubertin, who believed that international sports could contribute to international peace (Lucas, 1992), and that athletics were an excellent means of making young people healthier and stronger both in body and mind (MacAloon, 1981; Muller, 2000). However, throughout his life, Coubertin warned of potential problems if athletics and big business began working together. For example, at the opening ceremonies of the 1920 Antwerp Olympics, Coubertin told the athletes, officials, and judges in attendance to "keep away the opportunities that are advanced [by profit-motivated people] whose only dream is to use someone else's muscles either to build upon his own political fortune or to make his own business prosper" (quoted in Barney, Wenn, & Martin, 2002, p. 26).

In short, Coubertin's vision for the Olympics has not stood the test of time. The political nature of the games, especially evident during the Cold War tensions between the United States and the Soviet Union, contributed to the warping of the Olympic mystique. Blame also can be placed on the doorstep of the International Olympic Committee (IOC), which never

221

was able to adequately address the issue of amateurism. This never-ending debate eventually led to the entry of professional athletes into the games from many sports; Coubertin's vision, shared by many others, was that professional athletes had no place in the modern Olympic movement.

However, it is impossible to ignore that the media—especially television—have transformed the Olympic Games (and all sports) into something beyond just fun and games. This chapter evaluates the role that television has played in the development of the Olympic Games, and how it often has used its power to shape the Olympics to fit its agenda, even when that agenda was incompatible with the larger aims of the IOC.

Television and Sports: A Brief Overview

Parasite or Symbiosis?   One of the more intriguing and important issues about television and sports centers around the relationship they share. On one hand, there are scholars who see television as a kind of parasite: It takes what it wants from sports and offers nothing of substance in return. Rader (1984), among those who accept this notion, wrote one of the more scathing critiques of television and sports. Rader (1984, p. 5) lamented that by "destroying the distance between the fan and the athlete, by displaying competing (i.e. non-sports) images of the athletes, and by encouraging the athletes to assume self-indulgent personas, television reduced the ability of sports to elevate athletes into heroes." In short, says Rader (1984, p. 5), "Television has essentially trivialized the experience of spectator sports."

On the other hand, there are people who suggest that television and sports exist in a kind of symbiotic relationship: Each makes a substantive contribution to the success that both industries have enjoyed as they worked together. It is perhaps not surprising that IOC officials and those people involved in producing Olympic telecasts are among those who advocate such a position. Jack Ruttle, employed by the CTV television network in Canada, one year before the 1988 Winter Games, which were hosted by Calgary, claimed TV producers and the IOC share similar sentiments about the emphasis that should (or should not) be placed on winning Olympic medals:

> During the normal course of our work all during the Olympic Games, television networks as well don't bring to the task at hand a deep concern for who does the winning either. Indeed, the effort is the event and the assumption is built-in that the best effort will produce a victor.
> Only the individual component parts of our audience—the individual viewer, his [*sic*] or herself—concerns himself with who does the winning. Television will bring it all home regardless. (IOC, 1987, pp. 5–4)

Boyle and Haynes (2000) suggested that television needs sports programming for at least two reasons: to attract consumers and advertisers, and to promote its prestige and power. The economic necessity is discussed throughout this chapter. The self-interest necessity essentially requires that the TV networks secure the broadcast rights to as many diverse and meaningful sports events as possible, so that they can assert to their share-holders and the public that they remain among the industry's leaders. Eastman and Meyer (1989, p. 103) called this process of owning selected, high-profile sports events *differentiation,* which the authors defined as the "separation from competing networks and cable services in audiences' and advertisers' minds." Based on this rationale, one can understand why NBC, which in recent years lost its professional baseball, basketball, and football contracts to rival U.S. networks, eagerly sought out a long-term relationship with the IOC; the deal allowed NBC to bill itself as "the" network for the Olympic Games.

Profits and Culture. There is no doubt that TV executives, producers, and announcers, as they prepare a sports program, are influenced by selected, somewhat interconnected, ideologies. The **first**, economic, recognizes that in a capitalist climate the program must be profitable. A profit is possible (although not guaranteed) by ensuring that the correct type of programming is available to the correct audience, which at the same time can be subjected to various advertisers' messages. Jhally (1989) noted that in this effort the athlete, the media, and the advertisers have formed an inseparable relationship: The advertisers provide money to the networks, which use that infusion of cash to bid for more sports programming, which obviously involves athletes who gain not only financial but also social status through their hefty contracts and ubiquitous TV appearances.

Through this framework, one can see how the National Football League became the powerful league it is today; it has worked tirelessly to mold its product so that it is satisfying to both television and the public. The result is a sport that continuously attracts strong TV ratings (especially for its championship games) and strong advertising support and is played by seemingly larger-than-life men. McChesney (1989) is one who does not hold in high regard the relationship between the advertising and sports communities. However, unlike Rader, he does not place the blame for any problems solely at the doorstep of the TV industry.

The **second** factor influencing the men and women of the TV community can be classified as cultural. Chandler (1988, p. 18) reported that "[p]eople in any culture are clearly disposed to care about specific sports because these are part of their national culture. These sports are played formally in school and informally outside it, are discussed constantly at work and in newspapers and magazines, and are a source of local and national pride." Baseball is a U.S. and Japanese national pastime. Football, basketball, and golf (among others) also can be added to the list of U.S. sports, but not cricket, rugby, or soccer, which are immensely popular in many parts of the world. Conversely, U.S. football is rarely seen and frankly not missed by general audiences in many countries.

No matter where or what sport, the sizable number of viewers knowledgeable about the sport they are watching will bring expectations about what they will see. If those demands are not met, the network's executives and personnel will hear about it. Chandler (1988) added that drama, tension, and timing are among those factors that must be addressed by TV producers and announcers, in order to maintain the audience's interest.

Real (1998) wrote one of the most cited works highlighting the power of culture as it relates to sports. He examined a Super Bowl telecast and suggested that the game—especially in its pre-game hype—was a microcosm of America:

> The structural values of the Super Bowl can be summarized succinctly: North American professional football is an aggressive, strictly regulated team game fought between males who use both violence and technology to gain control of property for the economic gain of individuals within a nationalistic entertainment setting. The Super Bowl propagates these values by elevating one game to the level of a spectacle of American ideology collectively celebrated. (p. 5)

Whannel (cited in Cantelon & Gruneau, 1988, p. 187) argued that a TV production ultimately has four aspects. He called the first *hierarchization*, which recognizes that some themes and/or sports will be highlighted more than others. The second was called *personalization*, which recognizes that events often will be presented from an individual perspective. The third aspect was *narrative*, which reflects the telling of events in the form of stories. Finally, there was the placing of events in the context of frames of reference.

Chandler (1988, p. 2) offered a further important distinction about television: It translates "electronically the three-dimensional flesh-and-blood game onto a two-dimensional screen; [television producers] also lift the game out of its cultural setting, the stadium, and set it in a new cultural context, the living room." This process requires making important selections: What the viewer will (and will not) see; which athletes will be accorded more attention; how graphics and other statistical information will be presented to the viewer; which plays warrant replay; and the language that announcers use in analyzing each play are among them.

In sum, it could be argued that TV producers and announcers are forever trying to incorporate a script into something that is unscripted. Their "script" includes those elements already listed (along with others that were omitted); however, that which they are covering, a sports event, is by its very nature unscripted. No TV producer or announcer anywhere in the world can dictate when an athlete chooses to take a shot or swing a bat or throw a ball; instead they are merely reacting to what the athletes do before, during, and after each play.

TELEVISION AND THE OLYMPICS

An Ever-Growing Partnership

One need only consider the explosion in rights fees paid by U.S. TV networks to the IOC in order to understand the powerful relationship between the two. In 1960, the first time an American network agreed to a rights fee, CBS paid $50,000 and obtained exclusive American coverage of the 1960 Winter Games in Squaw Valley, California (DeMoragas Spa et al., 1995). In 2002, NBC owned the U.S. rights to the Salt Lake Winter Games and paid $545 million for them (Real, 1998). Moreover, NBC also owns the American broadcast rights to the 2004 Summer Games ($793 million), the 2006 Winter Games ($613 million), and the 2008 Summer Games ($893 million; Real, 1998).

Considering these figures, it is understandable why Rader (1984, p. 159) suggested that, starting in the 1960s, "television began to radically alter the shape of the Olympics." According to Rader, "Television enormously increased the number of people who could see the games, intensified national rivalries, became a favorite medium for advertisers who wanted to identify with the Olympics, gave athletes additional opportunities to become celebrities and launch successful commercial careers, and eventually became essential to the financial solvency of the games" (1984, p. 159). Perelman (1987) was less critical. He claimed that over time, TV networks have driven up the price of Olympic broadcast rights but have not received equivalent concessions from the IOC. For example, he notes that television did not mandate that extra sports and events be added to the Olympic program, which, among other issues, made the games more complex for the medium to cover. Furthermore, he argues that the world's TV networks in reality have little say in the overall schedule of the games.

Olympic Nationalism and Internationalism

One of the consistent findings about research into television and the Olympics is the inherent tension between the two institutions. Real (1998) directed a UNESCO study in the mid-1980s that reported that the IOC's ideals of universality and internationalism clashed with TV's presentation, which regularly advanced a nationalistic tone.

Gruneau (1987) agreed that there are inherent contradictions within the Olympic movement that make it difficult for anyone to argue that the IOC is somehow able to stand apart from the commercial pressures that eventually enveloped it. Lee (1990, p. 180) added that the "mass media by and large focus only on the fourth objective of the Olympic Movement (the bringing together of the world's athletes in the sports festival called the Olympics), with minimal lip service accorded to the [other] three aims."

Along similar lines, researchers have found that the political hierarchy of a country often has influenced the coverage or representation of the games. In the aftermath of the 1936 Berlin Olympics, filmmaker Leni Riefenstahl prepared a nearly 4-hour film of the games. "Olympia" is a stunning film that includes numerous images of the athletes who competed in those Olympics. It also contains shots of German Chancellor Adolf Hitler, who comes across as a benign, sports-loving figure, the polar opposite of the man who would order the deaths of millions of Jews and become the instigator of World War II. It is impossible to ignore that "Olympia" served as a rich propaganda tool for the Nazis. Graham (1987, pp. 2/5 through 2/6) noted that the Nazis were neither the first nor the only government that tried to use the Olympic Games to showcase what it believed was virtuous about its society. What made the Nazis and "Olympia" different? "The difference is that the 1936 Games turned out to be a sham," Graham wrote. "Germany had no long range interest in peace, or the peaceful competition of nations. It was a hypocritical gesture."

Moretti (2003) found that press nationalism also might have influenced the coverage that two of America's leading newspapers—the *Los Angeles Times* and *New York Times*—offered of the 1948 through 1988 Summer Games. U.S. athletes appeared as subjects and sources in the newspapers at rates that exceeded the number of medals they won, whereas Eastern European and Soviet athletes appeared in numbers that were inferior to their medal counts.

Earlier it was noted that the Olympics are a complex series of events for any TV network to cover. TV producers, as mentioned, are often influenced by what they believe their audiences expect to see. Thus, American networks provide extensive coverage of figure skating and skiing (during the Winter Olympics) and track-and-field, gymnastics, and swimming (during the Summer Olympics). Whereas these sports are the fare offered to American viewers, such a diet would be rejected in large portions of the world. The same statement in reverse is true. Reid (2000) reported that sports that would have American viewers reaching for their remote controls were widely watched throughout the 2000 Sydney Olympics in other parts of the world. For example, badminton (Britain), judo (Japan), and weightlifting (Iran) drew significant amounts of TV time in selected countries. Meanwhile, Reid added that while NBC often was criticized for its nationalistic reporting of the Sydney Games, it should not be forgotten that the nationalism card also was being played in other countries. Reid (2000, p. 8) made special note of the Russian television network, RTR, which "is a steady cheerleader [for Russia], talking endlessly about the medal chances of our team or our girl."

Reid's (2000) anecdotal observations are consistent with earlier research presented in this chapter; viewers from various countries tune into Olympic events that otherwise lack appeal elsewhere in the world. During the Barcelona games, American audiences watched women's gymnastics and men's swimming more than any other sport. By contrast, their Canadian neighbors watched women's synchronized swimming, and their Mexican neighbors witnessed men's basketball and the men's 50-kilometer walk more than any other event. Romanians were the only other people to place women's gymnastics at the top of their "gotta watch" list; citizens in no other country considered women's synchronized swimming to be the most important event of the games; and the Chinese were the only other group eagerly watching the men's basketball competition (DeMoragas Spa et al., 1995).

Opening Ceremonies

De Moragas Spa et al. (1995) authored what might be the most complete and authoritative examination of television and the Olympics. They, along with researchers from 25 countries, reviewed TV coverage of the 1992 Barcelona Games. One of the more interesting segments of their book, *Television and the Olympics*, focused on the language and other descriptive indicators provided during the opening ceremonies of the 172 competing nations by the separate TV networks.

The researchers coded comments made by the TV networks about the host country, the host city, various Olympic rituals, and the cultural performances associated with the more than 3-hour ceremony. The Cuban television network—Tele-Rebelde—directed 88% of its comments toward Spain, the highest percentage of any broadcaster studied. By contrast, the Indonesian network—TVRI—devoted only 41% of its comments about the host nation, the lowest percentage among those networks studied. The American network—NBC—provided commentary about Spain slightly more than 61% of the time, the sixth lowest percentage. This figure might surprise the reader at first; however, remember that the IOC traditionally offers the games to a particular city and not a particular country. Thus, NBC's announcers would be remiss if they concentrated too heavily on Spain and not enough on Barcelona. In fact, NBC's reporters reserved almost 20% of their comments for the host city; only the Indonesian and Greek television networks made more.

Another issue important to the IOC is a thorough presentation and explanation of the rituals connected to the opening ceremonies. Here NBC's commentary was average, when compared to the other national broadcasters. Approximately 15% of the comments delivered by NBC reporters dealt with these topics. Eleven other broadcasters (led by Indonesia's TVRI at 30%) disseminated more comments, while 12 others offered fewer (Cuba's Tele-Rebelde at 4% was lowest).

The opening ceremonies provide the host city with a literal world stage on which to showcase its unique culture. The singing, dancing, and similar portions of the opening program very well might be the way large portions of the world are introduced to the people and culture hosting the Olympics. NBC reserved almost 4% of its commentary to the cultural performances associated with the opening ceremony. Only four national broadcasters made fewer comments. One possible explanation for this low figure is that NBC's producers perhaps assumed that a majority of its viewers already knew enough about Spanish culture; thus, any further commentary ran the risk of boring the audience.

De Moragas Spa et al. (1995) make two relevant points about the opening ceremonies of any Olympic Games. **First,** in the absence of substantive international coverage of the games (a by-product of the aforementioned tendency to focus on the sports and athletes considered important to a domestic audience) by any one TV network, the opening ceremonies become "the only distinct appearance in the broadcast version of the games" for many nations and their athletes (p. 144). **Second,** the opening ceremony is scripted; thus, network producers and announcers know what is happening and when. The ability to prepare specific comments about a country and its athletes (or to completely ignore them) is one effect of this "script" (p. 148).

There is no question that the Olympic Games rank among the preeminent international sporting events. The World Cup soccer tournament is another event that consistently attracts a large international audience. Another of the intriguing elements of *Television in the Olympics* is the attempt to quantify the size of the Olympic audience. The authors note that international media place the viewership of the Olympics in the billions and specifically at 3.5 billion for the Barcelona Games. However, this figure is impractical based on a number of factors. De Moragas Spa and his colleagues (1995) acknowledge that one of the many problems with attempting to determine a realistic audience figure for the games is that close to 70% of the world's population resides in countries in which there are no reliable audience data. Furthermore, the relevance that people place on the games, the timing of the events, competition from other networks, and how well the event is promoted all affect how many people can be watching the Olympics (or any sports event) at any one time.

Based on these and other factors, the authors report that "the highest possible audience for a single event, such as the opening ceremony, must be estimated to be between 700 million and one billion" (DeMoragas Spa et al., 1995, p. 215). In other words, the multibillion figures discussed in various media outlets look and sound amazing, but they in no way measure up to reality.

In sum, the variety of research about the Olympics demonstrates that they are more than just fun and games. They are a multibillion dollar business in which TV networks, international corporations, politicians, private citizens, and athletes (among others) seek involvement and influence. TV networks perhaps are the most scrutinized "player" in the Olympic movement, because their role is available for so many people to see. Moreover, because of travel and cost restrictions, an overwhelming majority of people from any one country cannot afford to see the games in person. Instead they turn to the TV network that has the rights to show the games in their country for the information they need. Covering the Olympics is a difficult task for the networks to undertake, and they sometimes neglect the athletes from other parts of the world and the larger aims of the Olympic movement.

OLYMPIC COMMERCIALIZATION

The modern Olympic Games began in 1896. From that year to today, the IOC has tried, often without success, to keep international political events out of the Olympic Games. Scholars have suggested a variety of reasons for this failure. Espy (1979) argued that the nationalistic fervor of each

Olympics guarantees that a political shadow will hover over them. Barnett (1990) traced the problem to the tremendous increase in money that the American TV networks are paying for the rights to broadcast the games. Nixon (1988) contended that the hefty price the TV networks pay guarantees that they have to play on those aforementioned feelings of patriotism in order to attract a large number of viewers and better their chances for turning a profit.

TV History

The 1936 Winter and Summer Games, both of which were hosted by Germany, marked the first time the Olympics were televised domestically (Barney et al., 2002), but technological limitations prevented the local organizing committees (OCOGs) from selling international broadcast rights. Following World War II (which forced the cancellation of the 1940 and 1944 games), TV technology improved rapidly but not quickly enough to allow for international broadcasts of either the 1948 or 1952 Olympiads. However, in 1956, American TV networks and OCOGs began a now familiar ritual: How much should the former pay the latter in order to be granted rights to a particular games? The problem that Melbourne organizers faced that year was that the American networks refused to pay for something that they still considered to be a public property (Guttmann, 2002). Lengthy discussions could not bridge the divide; in the end, only taped-delayed, 30-minute highlight films of the 1956 Summer Olympics were shown on a limited number of U.S. TV stations.

In 1960, the TV networks finally agreed to purchase rights fees. As mentioned, CBS paid $50,000 for the Winter Games in Squaw Valley, California (DeMoragas Spa et al., 1995), but it chose to show none of the events live. The same network also paid $394,000 for the Summer Games in Rome, and, once again, all the coverage was tape-delayed (DeMoragas Spa et al., 1995). When the games ended, *New York Times* reporter John Shanley commended CBS for its efforts. He also wrote something that would be prophetic: "[T]he Olympic telecasts have been a fascinating departure from the drab pattern of summertime television programming" (Shanley, 1960, p. C-24). In other words, the Olympics were providing television with original and dramatic summertime programming, while the networks were providing the IOC with money and exposure.

Further technological advances made it possible for TV coverage to be delivered live from Tokyo, the site of the 1964 Summer Games. NBC, which paid $1.5 million for the rights (DeMoragas Spa et al., 1995), was able to provide both live and tape-delayed coverage. However, it hesitated to avail itself of live programming because the network's executives believed that the best way to recoup their investment was to provide nightly tape-delayed shows (Barney et al., 2002, p. 90). In fact, the only live programming was from the opening ceremonies (and that was to East Coast viewers only; people on the West Coast saw them on tape; Barney et al., 2002).

The IOC, recognizing that TV's financial commitment to the Olympic Games would continue growing, realized it needed to come up with a more equitable system for dividing that source of income among itself, the OCOGs, the various National Olympic Committees (NOCs), and the International Federations (IFs) that governed individual sports. The first million dollars would be split among the IOC, the IFs, and the NOCs. The OCOG would receive one third of the second million dollars, with the remaining groups sharing the other two thirds. Beginning with the third million, the OCOGs would get two thirds, with the IFs, NOCs, and IOC sharing the remaining one third (Guttmann, 2002). Some of the IFs reacted negatively (IOC, 1966) and demanded more money; the IOC leadership refused to budge (Wenn, 1995, p. 1).

The American TV networks also were making critical decisions about the future of Olympic telecasts. Senn (1999) noted that in 1968 they determined that the games ought to be treated more as entertainment than as news, which, in part, meant that the Olympics were going to appear regularly in the lucrative prime time hours. As mentioned, Nixon (1988) added that the move toward emphasizing the entertainment element mandated that the patriotic sentiments of viewers would be stimulated, but the integrity of the Olympics and the athleticism of the games might be degraded.

An Uneasy Relationship

It perhaps is not surprising that as the financial relationship between television and the Olympics has increased, the scholarly discussion about the positive and negative effects of this relationship has grown. Whannel (1992, pp. 71–72) argued that as the U.S. TV networks increased their financial commitments to the games, they used their clout to influence how the games are run, including determining "the nature of the ceremonies, the choice of events and the timing of events." It was during the 1988 Olympics in Seoul that the question of when events should be held became an international issue. Several events in which gold medals would be won were moved to the morning so that they could be shown in prime time and live in the United States. A leading Seoul Olympic official justified the schedule, noting that because of television, many Olympic sports had enjoyed continuous growth around the world. Therefore, in his opinion, the schedule had to be designed so as to maximize their economic potential (Larson & Park, 1993).

Pablo Rodas, who directed Paraguay's National Olympic Committee in the 1990s, summed up the uneasy relationship between the TV networks and the IOC perhaps better than anyone else: "The marketing of television rights for the games brought considerable financial benefits to Organizing Committees for Olympic Games, but it should not be forgotten that, however profitable, the granting of exclusive rights to a single television company left the games vulnerable to the whims of the company concerned" (IOC, 1994, p. 360). Whannel (1984) added that as the influence of television on the Olympic movement has increased, the ability of the IOC to define the nature of the games has decreased.

The IOC has enjoyed similar financial benefits from its relationships with its corporate sponsors. It also has met with similar frustrations in controlling the messages these companies present to their publics.

Avery Brundage served as IOC president from 1952 through 1972. During this period, he rejected any attempts to link the IOC with multinational corporations. Guttmann (1984, p. 217) summarized Brundage's attitude perhaps better than any other scholar: "Brundage did not want the IOC to enter into the world of commerce in any way, shape, or form. His conversion to the religion of Coubertin had come about when he perceived the realm of Olympism as a shining place apart from the sordid domain of commerce." In fact, throughout his 20-year term, Brundage often appeared almost indifferent to the financial health of the IOC. Nevertheless, it was during the 1950s, according to Gruneau (1984), that the foundation developed for the IOC's involvement with commercial interests. He suggested that, as the Cold War between the United States and the Soviet Union intensified, both sides began to recognize the potential for athletics to enhance their international prestige. This attitude also spread to their allies, and Gruneau noted that various national Olympic committees in the West became obsessed with beating the Russians. Increased media coverage followed, and advertisers realized that the coverage would draw a large audience from which to pitch their products.

The 1960 winter and summer Olympics marked the beginning of corporate sponsorship of the games, as several companies provided goods and services at no cost. Brundage was not pleased. "The games must never be commercialized," he said in 1960 (IOC, 1968, p. 53). In 1964 and 1968, rival companies distributed their wares, with two shoe manufacturers—Adidas and Puma—paying athletes large sums of money in the process (DeMoragas Spa et al., 1995). The 1972 Munich Games marked the first Olympics in which an organizing committee generated more than 10% of its revenues from sponsorship and licensing deals (De Moragas Spa et al., 1995).

Brundage's resistance to anything commercial ensured that the IOC was slow to respond to and tap into the growing financial deals between host cities and multinational corporations. Lord Killanin, who in 1972 succeeded Brundage, said that when he became IOC president the organization had approximately $2 million in assets. He added that when he retired 8 years later, the IOC's assets had swelled to more than $45 million (Killanin, 1983). Not surprisingly, Killanin's promotion to president provided one of the most important reasons why the IOC began seriously examining how it could build income through corporate sponsorship.

The Transnationals

However, it was not until 1984—four years after Killanin had been replaced by Juan Antonio Samaranch—that the marriage of the IOC and transnational corporations (see chapter 2) was cemented. The Los Angeles organizers were forced to pay for the Summer Games primarily through corporate (and TV) dollars because residents of Los Angeles and California refused to allow public money to be spent on them. As early as 1979, the Los Angeles Olympic Organizing Committee (LAOOC) was projecting that $116 million could be raised from corporate contracts (LAOOC, 1984). In order to reach that amount, it pursued a strategy that no other committee had before: it sought out exclusive sponsors. Thirty corporations signed on, and the LAOOC exceeded its expectations by generating more than $123 million (LAOOC, 1984).

Gruneau (1984) noted that American athletes regularly were used as spokespeople for various LAOOC-contracted sponsors in 1984. He concluded that it did not matter to the sponsors whether the athletes actually used the products they pitched; their primary concern was ensuring that the product was associated with the Olympics. American media organizations were not impressed with the increased perception that commercialization had altered the Olympic movement. The *New York Times* noted, "The games are more than ever seen as a lucrative marketing opportunity; for all but the naive, the money is the message. . . . The spiraling commercialism comes from the enormous costs a host city must pay to stage the competitions. To recoup, sponsors turn to American television and to hawking Olympic symbols for corporate dollars" ("The race . . .," 1979).

The philosophical differences among Brundage, Killanin, and Samaranch could not have been more striking. Brundage feared any association between the IOC and corporations. Killanin recognized that the IOC's financial strength could be ensured only through TV and corporate income. Samaranch fully adopted this policy. In the words of Wenn, "[Samaranch] embraced the notion that money, whether in the form of television revenue or corporate sponsorship, facilitates the promotion and independence of the Olympic Movement without jeopardizing its core values" (Wenn, 1988, p. 89). Samaranch made his opinions about selling the Olympic Movement evident, on the eve of his swearing in as president. "Commercialism is a fact of life and we cannot ignore it," he said. "If the Olympic Movement can take advantage of this commercialism, it can represent a great advantage" (Reich, 1980, p. A-4).

Host Sites

Beginning in 1984, potential Olympic host cities began to see that the Olympic Games could be staged without a sizable infusion of government money. Instead, TV networks and multinational corporations could be counted on to help the city host the games and allow it to make a profit. Certainly the multibillion dollar TV and commercial deals signed by the IOC have dramatically affected the presentation of the games. However, without these business relationships, the Olympics would not be the premier international sports events that they are.

TABLE 13.1
Post-World War II
Summer Olympic Games Host Cities

Olympic Year	Summer Host City
1948	London
1952	Helsinki
1956	Melbourne
1960	Rome
1964	Tokyo
1968	Mexico City
1972	Munich
1976	Montreal
1980	Moscow
1984	Los Angeles
1988	Seoul
1992	Barcelona
1996	Atlanta
2000	Sydney
2004	Athens
2008	Beijing

TV Audiences. The selection of the games' host site (see Table 13.1) could conceivably influence the number of viewers who watch them and therefore how many people are exposed to advertising messages. TV networks ensure a particular rating and share, as they set advertising rates with their sponsors. Failure to meet these predetermined figures means the network must offer make-goods (essentially free advertising time) to those sponsors.

The reader might remember that NBC had difficulty maintaining large audiences during the 1988 Summer Olympics, which were hosted by Seoul, and the 2000 Summer Olympics, which were hosted by Sydney. One of the reasons was that the results of many of the most popular events were already known hours before the network delivered its prime time coverage to the United States.

Similar problems could affect the network in subsequent Olympics that are hosted by cities (such as Beijing) with significant time differences to the United States. These problems would require the network to either set lower advertising rates (which could limit the amount of profit they make from their initial investment) or to offer the aforementioned make-goods to those corporations that purchased commercial time during the telecasts.

Beijing 2008. IOC officials gathered in 2001, once again in Moscow, to decide which city would have the honor of hosting the 2008 summer games. To borrow a sports cliché, the favorite going in was Beijing. And indeed the Chinese city was chosen as the site; Beijing received 56 first place votes, three more than the required number (Longman, 2001).

At the end of the 20th century and continuing into the start of the new century, the United States and China also were involved in an unsettled geopolitical relationship. On one hand, the two nations were major trading partners. According to U.S. Bureau of Census (2001) figures, America imported more than $55 million in goods and services from China in the first 7 months of 2001. It exported slightly more than $10 million to the Chinese in the same period. The Chinese also were moving closer to becoming a member of the World Trade Organization (WTO) in 2001. The United States supported China's plans regarding the WTO, to which it was in fact admitted.

But international concerns about China's human rights record nagged at the U.S.–China relationship and at China's international reputation as a whole. An editorial in the *Columbus* (Ohio) *Dispatch* ("Don't play . . .," 2001, p. A-10) cited figures from Amnesty International suggesting that the Chinese government ordered the executions of more than 1,700 people from April to early June 2001.

In the days leading up to the IOC vote, renewed strains were visible in the U.S.–China relationship. Nevertheless, Perlez (2001) indicated that the Bush administration remained adamant that it would not link these and other political differences to China's efforts at hosting the Olympics; it decided not to offer an opinion on the issue, a change from 1993 when Congress opposed Beijing's first bid (and Sydney won by 2 votes; Shi, 2003).

Readers will have already seen the Athens 2004 games, which at this writing had not yet hit the small screen. They are urged to reflect on the TV version of the Athens games and to view the Beijing 2008 games with one eye on the athletes and another on the programming decisions that affect the version of the games seen in readers' individual countries.

REFERENCES

Barnett, S. (1990). *Games and sets*. London: BFI Publishing.

Barney, R. K., Wenn, S. R., & Martyn, S. G. (2002). *Selling the five rings: The International Olympic Committee and the rise of Olympic commercialism*. Salt Lake City, UT: University of Utah Press.

Boyle, R., & Haynes, R. (2000). *Power play: Sport, the media, and popular culture*. London: Longman.

Cantelon, H., & Gruneau, R. S. (1988). The production of sport for television. In J. Harvey & H. Cantelon (Eds.), *Not just a game: Essays in Canadian sport sociology* (pp. 177–193). Ottawa: University of Ottawa Press.

Chandler, J. M. (1988). *Television and national sport*. Urbana, IL: University of Illinois Press.

DeMoragas Spa, M., Rivenburgh, N. K., & Larson, J. F. (1995). *Television in the Olympics*. London: John Libbey.

Don't play games: Beijing doesn't deserve 2008 Olympics. (2001, July 11). *Columbus Dispatch*, p. A-10.

Eastman S. T., & Meyer, T. P. (1989). Sports programming: Scheduling, costs, and competition. In L. Wenner (Ed.), *Media, sports and society*. Newbury Park, CA: Sage.

Espy, R. (1979). *The politics of the Olympic Games*. Berkeley, CA: University of California Press.

Graham, C. (1987). Leni Riefenstahl's Film Coverage of the 1936 Olympics. In International Olympic Committee (Ed.), *Olympic movement and mass media conference, Calgary, February 1987* (pp. 2/3–2/6). Lausanne, Switzerland: International Olympic Committee.

Gruneau, R. (1984). Commercialism and the modern Olympics. In A. Tomlinson & G. Whannel (Eds.), *Five ring circus: Money, power and politics at the Olympic Games* (pp. 1–15). London: Pluto Press.

Greneau, R. (1987). Television, the Olympics, and the question of ideology. In International Olympic Committee (Ed.), *Olympic movement and mass media conference, Calgary, February 1987* (pp. 7/23–7/34). Lausanne, Switzerland: International Olympic Committee.

Guttmann, A. (1984). *The games must go on: Avery Brundage and the Olympic movement.* New York: Columbia University Press.

Guttmann, A. (2002). *The Olympics: A history of the modern games.* Urbana, IL: University of Illinois Press.

International Olympic Committee. (1966). Minutes from the 64th IOC Session, April 25–28, 1966. Rome, Italy: International Olympic Committee.

International Olympic Committee. (1968). *The speeches of Avery Brundage.* Lausanne, Switzerland: International Olympic Committee.

International Olympic Committee. (1987). *Olympic movement and mass media conference, Calgary, February 1987.* Lausanne, Switzerland: International Olympic Committee.

International Olympic Committee. (1994). *Centennial Olympic Congress report.* Lausanne, Switzerland: International Olympic Committee.

Jhally, S. (1989). Cultural studies and the sports/media complex. In L. Wenner (Ed.), *Media, sports and society.* Newbury Park, CA: Sage.

Killanin, Lord. (1983). *My Olympic years.* New York: William Morrow and Company.

Larson, J. F., & Park, H. (1993). *Global television and the politics of the Seoul Olympics.* Boulder, CO: Westview Press.

Lee, J-W. (1990). The symbiosis of modern Olympics and mass media: Policy concerns for Olympism. In Seoul Olympic Sports Promotion Foundation (Ed.), *Toward one world beyond barriers: The Seoul Olympiad anniversary conference* (pp. 179–185). Seoul: Poong Nam Publishing Company.

Longman, J. (2001, July 14). Delegates hope choice spurs openness. *New York Times,* p. A-1.

Los Angeles Olympic Organizing Committee. (1984). *Official report of the XXIIIrd Olympiad Los Angeles.* Los Angeles: Author.

Lucas, J. (1992). *The future of the Olympic Games.* Champaign, IL: Human Kinetics Books.

MacAloon, J. J. (1981). *This great symbol: Pierre de Coubertin and the origins of the modern Olympic Games.* Chicago: University of Chicago Press.

McChesney, R. W. (1989). Media made sport: A history of sports coverage in the United States. In L. Wenner (Ed.), *Media, sports and society.* Newbury Park, CA: Sage.

Moretti, A. (2003). The cold war and the Olympics: Coverage in the *New York Times* and *Los Angeles Times* of the United States' and Soviet Union's pursuit of athletic supremacy, 1948–1988. Unpublished doctoral dissertation, Ohio University.

Muller, N. (Ed.). (2000). *Pierre de Coubertin: Olympism—Selected writings.* Lausanne, Switzerland: International Olympic Committee.

Nixon, H. L. (1988). The background, nature and implications of the organization of the capitalist Olympics. In J. O. Segrave & D. Chu (Eds.), *The Olympic games in transition.* Champaign, IL: Human Kinetics Books.

Perelman, R. B. (1987). Olympic broadcasters: Dragons or saints? In International Olympic Committee (Ed.), *Olympic movement and mass media conference, Calgary, February 1987* (pp. 5/27–5/30). Lausanne, Switzerland: International Olympic Committee.

Perlez, J. (2001, July 11). U.S. won't stand in way of China bid. *New York Times,* p. A-6.

The race for Olympic gold. (1979, October 1). *New York Times,* p. A-16.

Rader, B. (1984). *In its own image: How television has transformed sports.* New York: The Free Press.

Real, M. (1998). MediaSport: The technology and commodification of postmodern sport. In L. Wenner (Ed.), *MediaSport* (pp. 14–26). New York: Routledge.

Reich, K. (1980, August 3). New Olympic chief sees 1984 challenge to L.A. *Los Angeles Times,* p. A-4.

Reid, T. R. (2000, September 28). What in the world are they watching? *International Herald Tribune,* pp. 1, 8.

Senn, A. (1999). *Power, politics and the Olympic games*. Champaign, IL: Human Kinetics Books.

Shanley, J. (1960, September 4). TV Notebook: Omnibus and other projects being prepared by Saudek—Olympics. *New York Times*, p. C-24.

Shi, L. (2003). *U.S. newspaper coverage of China's two bids for the Summer Olympics, 2000 and 2008*. Unpublished master's thesis, Ohio University.

Tomlinson, A., & Whannel, G. (Eds.). (1984). *Five ring circus: Money, power and the politics of the Olympic games*. London: Pluto Press.

U.S. Bureau of Census. (2001). Available: www.census.gov/foreign-trade/balance/c5700 .html.

Wenn, S. R. (1988). A turning point for IOC television policy: U.S. television rights negotiations and the 1980 Lake Placid and Moscow Olympic festivals. *Journal of Sport History, 25*(1), 87–118.

Wenn, S. R. (1995). Growing pains: The Olympic movement and television 1966–1972. *Olympika: The International Journal of Olympic Studies, 4*, 1–22.

Whannel, G. (1992). *Fields in vision: Television, sport and cultural transformation*. London: Routledge.

Whannel, G. (1984). The television spectacular. In A. Tomlinson & G. Whannel (Eds.), *Five ring circus: Money, power and politics at the Olympic Games*. London: Pluto Press.

Chapter 14

A World of "Millionaires": Global, Local, and "Glocal" TV Game Shows

Anne Cooper-Chen
Ohio University

The former president of Yale, who was later commissioner of baseball, stated, "We can learn far more about the conditions and values of a society by contemplating how it chooses to play, to use its free time, to take its leisure, than by examining how it goes about its work" (Giamatti, 1989, p. 13). TV game shows serve especially well for telling us about the "conditions and values of a society" because the genre is so malleable, so cheap to produce locally, and so ubiquitous.

But what does the global success of "Who Wants to Be a Millionaire?" tell us about the many societies that have embraced it? Nothing like the "Millionaire"'s popularity, week after week, has ever occurred in TV history. Millions watch World Cup soccer, and 700 million to 1 billion people view the opening ceremony of the Olympics (see chapter 13), but these events occur only once every 4 years for a limited run.

On October 13, 2002, Kenya became the 100th country to air the "Millionaire" show. As of December 2003, "Who Wants to Be a Millionaire?" had been licensed or optioned in 107 countries as diverse as Colombia, China, Venezuela, Malaysia, Russia, Singapore, the Philippines, Kazakhstan, Greece, and Poland. In the Czech Republic, 83% of viewers tuned into the show in its first series. "Millionaire," which airs on the commercial Fuji network (see chapter 9), is the only Western game show to be bought by Japan (Celador, 2003).

Created in England (see chapter 3) in 1998, "Millionaire" was brought to the United States in 1999, the first regular prime time U.S. game show since the scandals of the 1950s (Cooper-Chen, 1994). By late 2000, "in a wave of high ratings" (Carter, 2000, p. 14), it was being produced in 35 countries. Then late in 2001, after U.S. ratings dipped, the decision to cancel was made; the farewell show was taped on January 10, 2002. A syndicated daytime version debuted in fall 2002 with Meredith Vieira replacing Regis Philbin as host. The show returned to ABC February 22, 2004, as a special event, hosted again by Regis Philbin, but renamed "Super Millionaire"; the top prize increased to $10 million. On that debut date, it was the highest-rated show on any network, but on the subsequent four nights, it "faded as the competition stiffened" (Carter, 2004, p. C6). In a return engagement in May 2004, "Super Millionaire" likewise enjoyed decent ratings.

Despite some ups and downs in ratings in some countries, "Millionaire" has struck a global chord (Wentz, 2001). What explains this phenomenon?

GLOBAL FACTORS

In theory, "Millionaire" can satisfy all of an individual's mass media needs, as cited by Katz, Gurevitch, and Haas (1973) in their seminal article on uses and gratifications:

1. **cognitive:** acquisition of information from the content of the questions and answers (see Table 14.1);
2. **affective:** the pleasurable fun of interactively playing a game;

TABLE 14.1
The "Millionaire" Quiz: Questions, Show Titles, Prizes, Host Background

Britain

TITLE   Who Wants to Be a Millionaire?
TOP PRIZE   £1 million ($1.5 million)
HOST   Chris Tarrant, radio personality

1. Starting with the earliest, put these four Archbishops of Canterbury in order.
   A. George Carey
   B. Thomas à Becket
   C. Robert Runcie
   D. Saint Augustine

2. In Victorian times, what was a "penny-farthing"?
   A. Stamp
   B. Sweet
   C. Bicycle
   D. Newspaper

(Continued)

TABLE 14.1 *(continued)*

3. Where were Chaucer's pilgrims going when they took turns telling stories?
   A. Ely
   B. Salisbury
   C. Warwick
   D. Canterbury
4. What kind of animal is Rikki-Tikki-Tavi in the Rudyard Kipling story?
   A. Cobra
   B. Tiger
   C. Mongoose
   D. Bear

   1. DBCA; 2. C; 3. D; 4. C.

India

TITLE *Kaun Banega Crorepati* (Who Wants to Be a Crorepati?)
TOP PRIZE 1 crore, or 10 million rupees (about $218,000)
HOST Amitabh Bacchan, film star

1. Start from the oldest, arrange these sons of Kunti, a female character in the Indian epic "Maharabata" in order.
   A. Bhima
   B. Yudhishtra
   C. Arjuna
   D. Karna
2. In the film "Aradhana Prayer," which vehicle is Rajesh Khanna traveling in while singing the song "Mere sapno ki rani kab (Queen of my dreams, when will you come to me?)"?
   A. Autorickshaw
   B. Jeep
   C. Cycle
   D. Motorbike
3. Which of these has served as the Chief Election Commissioner of India?
   A. P. N. Haskar
   B. Montek Singh Ahluwalia
   C. T. N. Seshan
   D. R. K. Dhawan

   1. DBAC; 2. B; 3. C.

Hungary

TITLE *Legyen on is Milliomos* (You Can Be a Millionaire)
TOP PRIZE 25 million forint ($87,750)
HOST Ishtvan Vagao, veteran quiz show host

1. Which literary hero makes a contract with Mephisto?
   A. Phaedra
   B. Faust
   C. Rastignac
   D. Raskolnikov
2. Who is the mother of Romulus and Remus according to mythology?
   A. A wolf
   B. Juno
   C. Minerva
   D. Rhea Silvia

(Continued)

TABLE 14.1 *(continued)*

3. What is the name of Sherlock Holmes's partner?
   A. Dr. Doolittle
   B. Dr. Watson
   C. Dr. Frankenstein
   D. Dr. Alban

   1. B; 2. D; 3. B.

Finland

TITLE   *Haluatko Miljonaariksi* (Do You Want to Be a Millionaire?)
TOP PRIZE   1 million markka (about $153,000)
HOST   Lasse Lehtinen, ex-parliament member

1. Starting with the smallest, put these bra sizes in order:
   A. D
   B. C
   C. B
   D. A

2. If it is noon in Johannesburg, what time is it in Turku, Finland?
   A. 11:00
   B. 12:00
   C. 13:00
   D. 14:00

3. How many stars are on the European Union flag?
   A. 8
   B. 10
   C. 12
   D. 20

4. What Finnish town has a Mika Hakkinen, a Finnish Formula One race car driver, Square?
   A. Porvoo
   B. Vantaa
   C. Turku
   D. Tampere

   1. ABCD; 2. B; 3. C; 4. B.

Israel

TITLE   *Mi Rotza Leihot Millionaire* (Who Wants to Be a Millionaire?)
TOP PRIZE   1 million new shekels ($247,800)
HOST   Yoram Arbell, sportscaster

1. Who from the following in the Bible was swallowed by the earth?
   A. Pharaoh
   B. Bilam
   C. Korach
   D. Yona

2. Which Prime Minister was the youngest, the day he started his position?
   A. Benjamin Netanyahu
   B. Ehud Barak
   C. Yitzhak Rabin
   D. Levi Eshkol

(Continued)

TABLE 14.1 *(continued)*

3. What was the birthplace of Ra'shi, the Bible and Talmud commentator?
   A. Russia
   B. Spain
   C. France
   D. Morocco
4. Soldiers from which brigade conquered the Eastern Wall in 1967?
   A. Golani
   B. Harel
   C. Na'hal
   D. Parachutists

   1. C; 2. A; 3. C; 4. D.

Australia

TITLE Who Wants to Be a Millionaire?
TOP PRIZE 1 million Australian dollars ($595,000)
HOST Eddie McGuire, sportscaster

1. What is Australia's largest bird of prey?
   A. Barn owl
   B. Peregrine falcon
   C. Wedge-tailed eagle
   D. Goshawk
2. "Solid Rock" was a hit song in the early 1980s for which Australian band?
   A. Redgum
   B. The Dingoes
   C. Goanna
   D. Midnight Oil
3. Which Australian cricketer recently admitted making dirty phone calls to a British nurse?
   A. Shane Warne
   B. Steve Waugh
   C. Mark Waugh
   D. Austin Powers

   1. C; 2. C; 3. A.

South Africa

TITLE Who Wants to Be a Millionaire?
TOP PRIZE 1 million rand ($144,600)
HOST Jeremy Maggs, news anchor and morning show host

1. Which word do fans commonly use when a South African soccer team scores a goal?
   A. Ayta!
   B. Ahyay!
   C. Laduma!
   D. Eish!
2. Whose first novel was "The Lying Days"?
   A. J. M. Coetzee
   B. Nadine Gordimer
   C. Andre Brink
   D. Breyten Breytenbach

   1. C; 2. B.

Note. From Kannapell (2000). Copyright © 2004 by the New York Times Co. Reprinted with permission.

241

3. **personal integrative:** strengthening of confidence by getting some of the answers right—highly probable, given the 1 in 4 chance of the multiple choice format—and perhaps even "beating" the in-studio players;

4. **social integrative:** the contact with family or friends through playing the game together or talking about it later; and

5. **tension release:** engagement in the show to a degree that enables one to relax and forget the problems of the day.

To better understand how real people "use" the show, this author devised some questions addressed to "Millionaire" viewers in the United States. In fall of 2001, the Ohio University Survey Research Center carried out a statewide random sample phone survey that included these questions. Given the state's demographic mix that mirrors the nation at large, Ohio is an excellent locale in which to sample U.S. opinion.

The questions were worded as follows: "Now I'd like to ask you some questions about entertainment. There's a game show on TV called 'Who Wants to Be a Millionaire?' that is the first prime time game show since the 1950s. Have you ever watched this show? When you watch this show, do you ever try to answer the questions yourself? Have you ever talked about the show with someone else? Have you ever tried to become a contestant by phoning in answers to the qualifying questions? Have you ever thought about phoning in to answer the qualifying questions?"

The results revealed that the show's appeal cuts across gender, race, and age demographics. Regarding demographic information of those watching the show, 86.5% were Caucasian, 7.1% were African American, 1.2% were Asian, 0.2% were Hispanic, 3% were other, and the rest refused to give racial information. A chi square test revealed no significant difference in demographics and any of the questions about the show: education, religion, income, marital status, children or political disposition. In other words, the show has wide appeal. Of a total of 409 respondents, 346 (84.6%) said they had watched the show. (Indeed, some had their viewing interrupted by the survey pollster.)

The survey results also revealed the effective manner in which the show gratified various needs. An astoundingly high 96.5% of the 346 respondents who watched had tried to answer some of the questions; while choosing A, B, C, or D represents a low level of interactivity, a small percentage (4.9%, or 17 of the respondents) said they had taken the supremely active step of calling the special pay number to try to answer the qualifying questions. The social integrative level—talking to someone about the show—was engaged in by 257 (74.3%) of those who watched. (The poll did not specifically address cognition, personal integration, or tension release.) While acknowledging the show's universal appeal, we have seen in the pages of this book that one TV diet does not satisfy all global citizens. A glance at the program grids in chapters 3 through 12 reveals an amazing variety of TV offerings.

LOCAL FACTORS

By showing that vast differences in national values and preferences exist, Hofstede's (2001) research can help explain why these local TV preferences exist (see chapter 1). He showed that nations can diverge on five dimensions of cultural variability: power distance, individualism, masculinity, uncertainty avoidance, and long-term orientation.

By examining TV game shows in 50 nations, Cooper-Chen (1994) found that local TV tastes converge enough so that one can identify four groups of countries or "Cultural Continents": the Western, East Asian, Latin and Equatorial. These continents are not geographical, but are based on programming preferences. The Western, for example, includes not only Europe and North America, but also Turkey, Australia, and Israel.

The Western game show has these traits: interactivity, civilian players, one male host, emphasis on expensive prizes, five-days-a-week scheduling; and low budgets. The East Asian game show has these traits: celebrity players, male and female cohosts, deemphasis on expensive prizes, once-a-week scheduling, and high production values. Audiences in both the East Asian and Western zones like to mentally participate in TV games by answering questions along with the contestants in the TV studio—a sort of athletics for the mind. This interactivity does not in general characterize locally originated Latin or Equatorial games.

Most Latin game shows, featuring players who perform physical feats, are meant to be watched. In addition, they feature male and female cohosts, emphasize expensive prizes, and have once-a-week scheduling, long time frames, and high production values. The Equatorial model showcases talented students or civilians with intelligence above that of the average viewer, who cannot play along because of the difficult questions requiring rapid-fire answers.

Before "Millionaire," few shows had crossed into another cultural continent. (In the late 1980s, as a rare example, "Family Feud" aired in both the East Asian and Western cultural continents.) More often a show's format moves within one of the cultural continents, such as the success of "Wheel of Fortune" in the West (see the next section). Because it answers universal needs (Katz et al., 1973), the global, cross-Continent success of "Who Wants to Be a Millionaire?" is nearly unique.

GLOCAL FACTORS

The term for changes that occur when a program moves into a new local market is *glocalization* (Chang, 2000). Basic elements of the show are constant because local producers are bound contractually or choose to reproduce the set, the format, and even the catch phrase, "Is that your final answer?" As Hetsroni (2001) points out, controlling for program means that any differences stem from culture. Thus "Millionaire" represents a global laboratory for studying these differences. There are at least six dimensions whereby the power of culture asserts itself, acting on the established format of the show.

Content

Categories of Questions.   Hetsroni (2001), who compared the questions asked in the Russian, U.S., and Saudi versions of "Millionaire," found that the Saudi questions overemphasized national identity, compared to Russia and the United States; the U.S. version emphasized high and low culture/politics, and the economy. Russia was distinct from both and in the middle. Hetsroni (2001) also compared the questions asked in the Polish, U.S., and Israeli versions of "Millionaire" and found only minor differences. Both these studies support Cooper-Chen's (1994) thesis of similarity within but differences between cultural continents. (Israel belongs to the Western zone.)

Difficulty of Questions.   The multiple-choice format insures that the average person (who can usually omit some of the wrong choices) can feel smart. In Singapore, a national uproar occurred over easy questions that young people could not answer, such as arranging the names of four countries in alphabetical order (Youngblood, 2001). However, the examples in Table 14.1 (Kannapell, 2000) seem to point to at least moderate levels of difficulty.

Name of Show—Exact Versus Free Translation.   Saudi Arabia, where *sharia* law forbids gambling, uses the name "Who Will Earn a Million?" Russia uses the name "Oh, Lucky—You Are a Millionaire."

Personnel

Players: Gender, Age, Ethnicity/Nationality.   A dearth of females characterized both the U.S. and U.K. prime time versions ("The rich get . . .," 2000). The Cairo-produced, pan-Arabic version does have female players, veiled and not. The show is a hit largely because it brings in players from all the Arab world (Abou el-Magd, 2002). Singapore players tend to be young (Youngblood, 2001).

Hosts: Gender, Age, Demeanor (Controlling Versus Facilitating).   Regis Philbin is typical of the Western host—an older, White male. At a gathering of hosts, only one was quite young (from the country of Georgia, aged 27) and only two of 23 (from Canada and Portugal) were female (Carter, 2000). When the U.S. version debuted in fall 2002 in syndication, away from network prime time, the show had a female host (Meredith Vieira).

Audience reaction to hosts varies. The adulation accorded top Bolly-wood actor Amitabh Bacchan, who hosts the program in India, has given him a godlike status; viewers even write letters to him in blood (Celador, 2003).

Japan's Monta Mino has tried his best to stretch the role of host; one critic (Penn, 2001b, p. 10) has noticed the "tortuous pauses he inserts between questions. . . . Regis Philbin does not play such tricks on the viewer. He moves things right along." Mino knows that Japanese hosts usually have more power than just asking questions. The Lebanese host of the pan-Arab version likewise exerts control by long pauses before con-firming a right or wrong answer (Abou el-Magd, 2002).

Celebrities as Players. Some say the show's U.S. cancellation resulted from pulling in celebrities—a loss of the "I could do that—that could be me up there" appeal of the show. But not all Western cultures eschew celebrities. "Our celebrity week was huge," said Eddie McGuire, the host from Australia (Carter, 2000). "We haven't done celebrities," said Alain Simons, a host from Belgium (Carter, 2000). In Russia, presidential candi-dates appeared on the show (Scott, 2000).

Audiences in China as well as Japan prefer a game show that has the added attraction of "tarento" (talent) who can joke and talk in a relaxed way on camera. After a comedian's appearance on Fuji's "Millionaire," Penn (2001a, p. 10) commented that "it seems contestants from the general public are being pushed aside in favor of celebrity guests." Subsequently, whenever Fuji added a celebrity, the ratings rose.

Risk Tolerance of Players (Number of Millionaires). U.K. audiences had to wait 2 years (until Nov. 20, 2000) for the first millionaire—who turned out to be independently wealthy and had little riding on the deci-sion. Perhaps "the British temperament" does not have that "willingness to gamble large sums of money—in contrast to the entrepreneurial Ameri-cans" ("The rich get . . .," 2000).

That risk taking yielded 11 millionaires in the U.S. show's episodes, the most in the world (Celador, 2003). In the Arab world version, produced by the Saudi-owned MBC satellite station, two men had won the top prize as of May 2002: a United Arab Emirates doctor and a Palestinian (Abou el-Magd, 2002). Austria has had only one top winner (Celador, 2003).

Production/Scheduling

Prime Time Versus Daytime. A mark of the fall of the U.S. version was its fall 2002 switch into nonprime time slots (via syndication).

Once Versus Multiple Times/Week. The overexposure of the show—airing, at one point, seven nights a week—may have killed the U.S. show. Most countries air the show once or twice a week in prime time.

Audience

Ratings. The phenomenon of the show's climbing to the top in the ratings occurred in many countries. In the United States, success happened quickly; during its second week on the air, August 16–22, 1999, four "Millionaire" episodes were ranked in the top 10 prime time (8–11 p.m.) shows, according to Nielsen Media Research. After the new 1999–2000 season started in the fall, the show did even better. During one week (January 17–23, 2000), its three episodes ranked 1, 2, and 3 among all prime time TV programs (Celador, 2003).

In Hong Kong, at its peak, the show attracted more than one in three residents (Youngblood, 2001). The MBC Arabic version was the most watched show in the region, surpassing (in spring 2002) shows on Al Jazeera; one statistic said that 80% of Arab viewers watched the show ("Top game . . .," 2002).

The ratings picture looked quite different in Japan. "Quiz $ Millionaire" debuted in Japan in April 2000 on Fuji, airing at 7 p.m. on Thursdays. From April to early August, with its civilian players, ratings ranged from 8.0 to 11.3. Then on August 17, the producers tried something different: *Konya wa geinojin ga gala o kakete honki de josen shimasu* (Tonight celebrities will be really challenged to bet for payment); as a result, the ratings doubled, getting more than 20 points for the first time (M. Konaka, personal communication, May 15, 2001).

Ratings are harder to come by in China and other less-developed nations. Clearly, though, in India the show gained the highest ratings in history, attracting about 100 million viewers (Flagg, 2001; Marquand, 2000). Ratings in France regularly achieved a 45% audience share (Celador, 2003).

Run (Startup-to-Cancellation Time Frame). The U.S. flame burned for nearly 3 years, until its May 2002 90-minute farewell, which was taped on January 10; the decision was made in late 2001 to cancel the prime time version. In Hong Kong, the rags-to-riches-to-rags process took just 7 months (Youngblood, 2001).

Critical Reaction

Cultural Commentary. Although game shows themselves have been the target of critics' opprobrium, "Millionaire" has not had such a bad press. The U.S. celebrity versions, which began on May 1, 2000, elicited some negative comments—such that the show had fallen down "to the burlesque level of 'Hollywood Squares'" (Bark, 2002). Pashak (1999) saw, with wistful nostalgia, the show as "the kind of true mass-audience hit that network television used to manufacture regularly, but now seldom does." But any erudition is "very much a byproduct" inasmuch as the sole purpose is "to make money" (Swain, 2002).

Religious Commentary. In Egypt, one cleric condemned the show for its sinful gambling, but a higher cleric, head of the Al-Azhar mosque and university, endorsed it as educational and beneficial (Abou el-Magd, 2002).

Social Commentary. The show can highlight weaknesses in a society. In Singapore, the poor performance of players led to questions about education levels in the nation (Youngblood, 2001). In Russia, where the public lacks trust in institutions, skeptical players wanted to see the cash before they began (privileged personal communication, July 12, 2002).

An analysis of the show's popularity in India attributes its success to "an emphasis on memory and math . . . Brahminical learning stresses memorization"; moreover, the "rigid exam system" gives Indians "an almost maniacal urge to pick up whatever facts" (Marquand, 2000, p. 1).

In the United Kingdom, the show was seen as undemocratic because only the wealthy could risk going all the way ("The rich get . . .," 2000). By contrast, in Canada, Pashak (1999) praised the show as democratic and participatory; not only could anyone theoretically get on the show, but the audience poll and the multiple choice nature reinforce the questions' accessibility; in any case, the show does not hurt anyone (Pashak 1999).

Convergence With New Technologies

The exact nature of the use of technology presumably varies in degree from nation to nation, influenced not only by culture but by availability. A nation with lower telephone penetration, like China, would not be expected to have a rate as high as 5% of its 1 billion people calling in to try out for the show, as was the case in the random sample in Ohio. Indeed, available technology dictates the tryout procedure; French and U.K. would-be contestants can enter the show by either using the premium line phone number, or via SMS. According to a fact sheet (Celador, 2003), the show has exploited spinoffs in developed but not developing nations. These include the following:

- The **"Millionaire" PC game:** The fastest selling PC game, in its first 8 weeks it sold the same number of games that "Tomb Raider" sold in total; 1.3 million were sold in its first year.
- **"Millionaire" Internet sites:** These have been launched or are about to launch in almost 20 countries. There are four versions of the game—a training game, tournament games, multiplayer, and simultaneous (with the TV program) games.
- The **U.K. Internet game:** It increased traffic to the ITV website by over 800% when it launched in April 2000. Germany's RTL site became the country's largest entertainment site due to the launch of the game.
- A **"Millionaire" mobile phone game:** Launched in more than 30 countries with over 250 million subscribers, since its launch, it has generated more than 200 million messages.

• **A mobile text game:** In June 2003, "Millionaire" made history by launching the world's first real-time mobile text game. Viewers on U.K. ITV1 can play along with the TV program by texting their answers to a number. The viewer who texts the most correct answers in the quickest time can win a daily cash prize of £1,000.

• **Interactive game:** One that can be played simultaneously with the TV program on digital television has been launched in several countries.

• **Gaming portal:** Fans can play an interactive game 24 hours a day, 7 days a week through the U.K. Sky's Gamestar. A number of themed games, such as Showbiz, Sport, and Football, have been launched.

• **Air travel:** Passengers on Swiss Air can play as they fly on an in-flight entertainment application that allows people to play alone or with their travelling companions.

• **Telephone:** Spanish fans can now play the game interactively on their telephones using voice response technology. Carlos Sobero, the Spanish host, asks up to 10 questions, and callers answer using keypads 1–4 on their phones. Lifelines are available, and daily prizes awarded to the fastest player. "Millionaire" is also available on Teletext in Italy and Mintel in France.

• **PDA:** In January 2002, "Millionaire" was launched on all personal digital application (PDA) platforms in three languages—English, Swedish, and German.

Other

Size of Prize.   To determine size of prize relative to GDP/capita would entail research related to more than 100 countries, so a few examples must suffice to illustrate national differences. "Millionaire" on British television has a prize of 1 million pounds, or U.S. $1.4 million; even the lower U.S. prize of $1 million is 40 times the average U.S. yearly salary of about $25,000. In Japan, the prize of 1 oku yen, or $1 million when the exchange rate is 1 yen = 1 penny, represents about 20 times the average person's salary of ¥5 million. However, as the ratings remain quite low for civilian shows, in Japan big money does not attract viewers; moreover, winning that amount means little to the celebrities who attract viewers to the show.

In Anhui, China, the prize of 10,000 yuan ($1,200) represents about half the average urban worker's yearly salary—a nice sum, but not the astronomical figures of the Western versions. In India, where the annual per capita income in only $464, the prize of $220,000 is truly a fortune (Marquand, 2000).

Divergence of Unlicensed Versions.   In China in Anhui Province's version, renamed "*Chaoji da yingjia*" (Super Big Winner), after the civilian players have been in the hot seat, celebrities try their hand at questions; they also perform songs or skits and chat with the hosts. Consider also the hosts. In Anhui, two young females and one male host "Super

Big Winner," in accord with the East Asian penchant for male and (young) female game show cohosts (Cooper-Chen, 1994).

"WHEEL OF FORTUNE"

Before the "Millionaire" phenomenon, with all its high-tech accoutrements, there was (and is) "Wheel," which in November 2003 marked its 4,000th U.S. episode by broadcasting from New York's Radio City Music Hall. As of 2000, "Wheel of Fortune" was still running in 54 international TV markets, according to the Nielsen Rating Report (cited in Tunc, 2002). It ranks as the top U.S. syndicated show ("Wheel . . .," 2003).

Its glocalization occurred primarily within the Western cultural continent—as it moved, for example, from the United States to Germany, where "Wheel of Fortune" was produced locally under the name "Glucksrad," and to France, where the show was called "La Roue de la Fortune." "Wheel" had great success in Europe in the late 1980s and early 1990s; in 1991, it became France's top-rated show in prime time, with a 22% rating. In Australia, another country in the Western cultural continent, it earned a rating of 20.6% (Hardy, 1992).

Changes occurred in each "Wheel" market, presaging the glocalization that "Millionaire" experienced. Cooper-Chen (1994), in a wide sample of countries, found various cross-cultural differences, such as size of prizes and gender of hosts.

Skovmand (1992) examined the pace and structure of "Wheel" 1989–1990 in Germany, Denmark, pan-Scandinavia, and the United States. The U.S. show was the most game-oriented, putting the smallest emphasis on talk (rules explanation or question clarification). Of the four hostesses, America's Vanna White and the German "Vanna" remained mute, whereas the Swedish and Danish hostesses engaged in banter. According to Skovmand (1992, p. 96), "A mute hostess would probably, in a Scandinavian context, be taken as a controversial sexist feature, particularly in combination with a male host." Moreover, the four set decors differed markedly—steely grey in Germany; blue and pink pastels in Scandinavia; and "gaudy, glittery vulgarity" in the U.S. "Wheel," Skovmand (1992, p. 97) found.

Turkey, which belongs to the Western cultural continent (Cooper-Chen, 1994), altered the original even more radically. The Turkish version of "Wheel," introduced in 1995, generated publicity from a real-life romantic affair between the letter turner and the host. The host of "Çarkifelek" (the Turkish name for the show), Mehmet Ali Erbil, a well-known comedian, took over the show in the late 1990s on Kanal D. "Çarkifelek" changed the standard taped 30-minute time frame, airing live 8–11 p.m. daily. The show, which featured a bevy of belly dancers, earned phenomenal ratings. Tunc (2002, p. 248) writes that "a Western-imported genre can be an arena of resistance to the culture of the powerful. ["Wheel"] is an obvious return to the Ottoman values in entertainment."

Again local culture asserts itself, as chapter authors from India to Brazil have noted in this volume. As Chang (2001) found with news—"the power of the local is manifest in the current program regionalization and localization" (p. 20)—this study has found likewise true of entertainment. Chang concludes, "Rather than regarding globalization as a process that uniformly subverts local imperatives, it is a process in which the local exercises influences in constituting the global" (p. 20). Glocalization represents a middle ground that will likely characterize the global TV scene for years to come.

ACKNOWLEDGMENTS

Portions of this chapter were originally published in A. Cooper-Chen, 2003, Glocalization of television's "Millionaire" quiz. In D. Demers (Ed.), *Terrorism, globalization, and mass communication* (pp. 117–127). Spokane, WA: Marquette Books, as Cooper-Chen (2003). Used by permission.

REFERENCES

Abou el-Magd, N. (2002, May 30). *Arab World's "Who Wants to Be a Millionaire" adds politics to formula.* Associated Press. Available: www.lexis.nexis.com

Bark, E. (2002, June 27). "Millionaire" goes bust: Game show that became a prime-time phenomenon wraps up tonight. *Dallas Morning News,* p. D8.

Carter, B. (2000, October 9). At TV bazaar, U.S. companies look to buy. *New York Times,* p. C1.

Carter, B. (2004, March 1). "Super Millionaire" helps ABC but doesn't provide mega-payoff. *New York Times,* p. C6.

Celador. (2003, December). *International facts and figures on Who Wants to Be a Millionaire? format.* Retrieved from www.celador.co.uk\news_article.php?id=30

Chang, Y. (2000). Pathway to "glocalization": STAR-TV in Asia, 1991–95. *International Communication Bulletin, 35,* 14–21.

Chang, Y. (2001). From globalization to localization: The world's leading television news broadcasters in Asia. *Asian Journal of Communication, 111,* 1–24.

Cooper-Chen, A. (1994). *Games in the global village.* Bowling Green, OH: The Popular Press.

Cooper-Chen, A. (2003). Glocalization of television's "Millionaire" quiz. In D. Demers (Ed.), *Terrorism, globalization and mass communication* (pp. 117–127). Spokane, WA: Marquette Books.

Flagg, M. (2001, November 9). Broadcasters discover India is receptive to western-style TV. *Wall Street Journal,* p. A4.

Giamatti, A. B. (1989). *Take time for paradise: Americans and their games.* New York: Summit Books.

Hardy, P. (1992, January 27). They're hot and priced right. *Variety,* p. 37.

Hetsroni, A. (2001). Millionaires around the world: Analysis of quiz shows in Poland, Israel and America. *Communications: European Journal of Communication Research, 26*(3), 247–266.

Hofstede, G. (2001). *Culture's consequences, 2nd ed.* Newbury Park, CA: Sage.

Kannapell, A. (2000, August 20). Around the world, what it takes to be a millionaire. *New York Times,* p. D7.

Katz, E., Gurevitch, M., & Haas, J. (1973). On the use of the mass media for important things. *American Sociological Review, 38,* 164–181.

Marquand, R. (2000, September 18). Quizzical India: Where trivia itself can be a lifeline. *Christian Science Monitor,* p. 1.

Pashak, B. (1999, December 6). Show's success lies in careful design. *Report/Newsmagazine,* p. 34.

Penn, W. (2001a, April 26). Televiews. *Yomiuri Shimbun,* p. 10.

Penn, W. (2001b, May 4). Televiews. *Yomiuri Shimbun,* p. 10.

Scott, D. (2000, March 22). Russian campaign lifeline. *Christian Science Monitor,* p. 6.

Skovmand, M. (1992). Barbarous TV international: Syndicated wheels of fortune. In M. Skovmand & K. L. Schroeder (Eds.), *Media cultures: Reappraising transnational media* (pp. 84–103). London: Routledge.

Swain, H. (2002, May 10). When can a game show be an academic study? *Times Higher Education Supplement,* p. 18.

The rich get richer. (2000, November 25). *Economist,* p. 66.

Top game show, suave presenter unite Arabs. (2002, March 12). Africa News Service. Available at web.lexis.nexis.com

Tunc, A. (2002). A genre a la Turque: Redefining game shows and the Turkish version of Wheel of Fortune. *Journal of American & Comparative Cultures, 25*(3/4), 246–248.

Wheel keeps on spinning. (2003, November 10). *The Vancouver Province,* p. B8.

Youngblood, R. (2001, April 27). *Singapore's "Who Wants to Be a Millionaire" reveals gaping education gaps.* Deutsche Presse-Agentur. Available at web.lexis.nexis.com

About the Contributors

Editor

Anne Cooper-Chen, professor of journalism and director of graduate studies at the E.W. Scripps School of Journalism, Ohio University, earned her PhD from the University of North Carolina–Chapel Hill. She worked full time as a journalist for 10 years in Virginia, Pennsylvania, and Tokyo, Japan. Her publications include *Games in the Global Village: A 50-Nation Study of Entertainment TV* (1994), *Mass Communication in Japan* (1997), and 10 book chapters. She was head of the Association for Education in Journalism and Mass Communication (AEJMC)'s International Communication Division, founding head of AEJMC's Entertainment Studies Interest Group, and founding director of the Scripps Institute for International Journalism. She has lectured at universities in China, Japan, Korea, Australia, Malaysia, the Philippines, Taiwan, and Germany.

The Transnationals

Richard Gershon, a professor in the Department of Communication at Western Michigan University, teaches and consults in the areas of law/policy, management, and communication technology. He received his PhD from Ohio University in 1986. Writing extensively on global entertainment conglomerates, he serves on the board of the Center for Global Media Studies. He is the author of *Telecommunications Management: Industry Structures and Planning Strategies* (Lawrence Erlbaum Associates, 2002).

United Kingdom

Jeffrey Griffin, associate professor at the University of Dayton, received both his BA and PhD (1990) from the University of North Carolina–Chapel Hill. He received his MA in journalism from the University of Texas. Dr. Griffin worked as a wire editor at the *Austin American-Statesman* and for the Associated Press in Rome, Italy. Each summer he leads a group of students to London, where he teaches a course in U.K. media.

253

Germany

Thomas Knieper teaches at the Department of Communication Studies at the University of Munich, where he received all his academic degrees. He worked for 4 years as a newspaper cartoonist and 3 years as a travel writer. Dr. Knieper was a visiting professor at the University of Leipzig in 2000. He does research on cartoons and on popular media in Germany and frequently presents his research in the United States.

Klaus Forster also teaches at the Department of Communication Studies at the University of Munich, where he received his MA. He worked as a market research and software consultant and as a freelance computer trainer. His areas of study include quality in journalism, multimedia issues, computer-aided learning, and visual communication. He is currently writing his dissertation about public journalism.

Egypt

Kamel Labidi, a native of Tunisia, currently resides in Cairo. Labidi received undergraduate degrees from the University of Tunis and the Press Institute of Tunis and a graduate degree from the French Press Institute of Paris. In 1989, he was awarded a scholarship for advanced nondegree study at Stanford University. Labidi worked for the national news agency, Tunis Afrique Presse, from 1975 to 1994. His byline has appeared in the *New York Times, Christian Science Monitor, Le Monde Diplomatique,* and the Beirut-based *Daily Star.* He is a specialist in protection of Middle Eastern journalists' free speech.

Ralph Berenger, an assistant professor of journalism and mass communication at the American University in Cairo, Egypt, holds advanced degrees in international mass communication, public administration, and political science. He has published dozens of scholarly articles, has edited *Global Media Go to War: Role of News and Entertainment Media During the 2003 Iraq War* (2004), and is book review editor for *Transnational Broadcasting Studies Journal.* A native of North Dakota, he has more than 30 years of media experience, primarily in Idaho. He has also lived and worked in Bolivia, St. Lucia, Kenya, and Zambia.

Nigeria

Anthony Olorunnisola is an associate professor of media studies at the Pennsylvania State University, where he teaches Media and Society and World Media Systems. His major areas of research include political and development communication in Africa. His work has been published in *Journal of International Communication, Gazette, Equid Novi: Journal for Journalism in Southern Africa,* and other publications. He directs a summer study tour of media in Africa.

Tunde Akanni is a lecturer in and founding member of the School of Journalism, Lagos State University, Surulere, Nigeria, and a founding director of Nigeria's Centre For Free Speech. Akanni has worked as a journalist, human rights campaigner, and media researcher. He was educated at Ilorin (Nigeria), Columbia (New York), and Leicester (England) Universities and the Institute of Social Studies (Netherlands). Akanni is coeditor of *Nigeria: Mass Media and Democracy* and *Ogoni Trials and Travails.*

South Africa

Lesley Cowling, who teaches in the Journalism and Media Studies Program at Witwatersrand University, Johannesburg, received her BA (honors) from Witwatersrand and her MA from Ohio University. She has more than 20 years of experience in print and broadcast media in South Africa, including various posts at the *Mail and Guardian.* She is currently a scriptwriter for *Tsidingo,* a daily TV soap opera in South Africa. Her research focuses on South African media.

India

Sandhya (Sandy) Rao, a professor in the Department of Mass Communication at Texas State University, received her BS and MS in communication from Bangalore University in India and her PhD from Bowling Green State University in Ohio. She has worked professionally as a feature writer in India. A former head of the International Division of AEJMC, Dr. Rao is the coeditor of *Cyberpath to Development in Asia* (2002) and numerous academic papers.

Japan

Tsutomu Kanayama, who teaches journalism and mass communication at Sophia University in Tokyo, received his PhD from Ohio University and his MA from Western Michigan. Prior to coming to the United States, he worked for TBS, a commercial network in Japan, as a sportscaster, news anchor, and game show host. Dr. Kanayama has presented numerous papers and has had studies published in the *Keio Communication Review* and other journals. He is a Fulbright researcher in 2004–2005 in Washington, DC.

Tomoko Kanayama, an assistant professor at Keio University in Tokyo, received her PhD in 2003 from Ohio University. A graduate of Keio University, she has worked in the recording industry and for social service organizations involved with senior citizens. Her research interests include the technological digital divide as related to age and economic status. She has presented numerous papers at conferences in Japan and the United States.

China

Hong Cheng, an associate professor at Ohio University, received his PhD from Pennsylvania State University. A former head of AEJMC's International Division, he spent the 2002–2003 year as a visiting professor at Nanyang Technological University in Singapore. His research focuses on cultural values in Chinese media, especially in advertising. Dr. Cheng, who is originally from Shanghai, China, has had 5 years of professional media experience, including work as a reporter at the *China Daily*.

Mexico

Guillermo Orozco, professor of communication at the University of Guadalajara, also teaches graduate-level courses at Iberoamerican University, Leon, and at institutions outside of Mexico. (He taught in Santiago, Chile, in November 2002.) He has done extensive consulting regarding children's educational TV for the Mexican Ministry of Education. Dr. Orozco has written several books on TV, children, and families. He edited and wrote the chapter on Mexican television for a recent book, *Histories of Television in Latin America*.

Brazil

Regina Silveira e Silva is a professor of communication and education at undergraduate and graduate levels at the Universidade Salgado de Oliveira in Rio de Janeiro, Brazil. She earned both her MA in International Affairs and her PhD in Telecommunication from Ohio University. Dr. Silveira e Silva has done research for the College of the Americas, the Interamerican University Organization, and UNESCO. Her work has also been supported by grants from the Organization of American States and from the Brazilian government. Having written on both info- and edutainment, and on long distance learning, she has coauthored a book on Quality in Research. Prof. Silveira e Silva is the editor of *Caderno de Estudos e Pesquisas*.

The Olympics

Anthony Moretti, an assistant professor at Texas Tech University, wrote his dissertation and various refereed papers at national conferences on the Olympic Games. He worked for nearly 10 years as a news and sports broadcaster in his native California and in Columbus, Ohio. He received his PhD from Ohio University in March 2004.

Author Index

Subject Index